UNDERSTANDING ISLAM AND ITS PRACTICES

Professor Abu Muhammad Abdul Huq, Ph.D.

New York
2001

Published by:
Begum Akhtar Jahan Hoque
and Afroza Huq
2866 Frankel Blvd.
Merrick, NY 11566-5432
USA

Copyright © Prof. Abu Muhammad Abdul Huq

All right reserved. No part of this publication may be reproduced, stored in retrieval system or transmitted in any form or by any means, electronic, mechanical, photocopying, recording, or otherwise without written permission of the author / publisher.

Cataloguing in publication data

Abdul Huq, Abu Muhammad
Understanding Islam and its practices / Professor Abu Muhammad Abdul Huq, Ph.D.

p.; cm.

1. Islam I. Title

Printed in the United States by:
Morris Publishing
3212 East Highway 30
Kearney, NE 68847
1-800-650-7888

To

My Parents for their guidance

My Wife Afroza

For her Encouragement and Support

And for
My son Arefin and My Daughter Afrin

So that they can appreciate their heritage
And be steadfast in it.

May Allah guide them on the right path.

Part I

INTRODUCTORY MATERIALS

TABLE OF CONTENTS

PART I : INTRODUCTORY MATERIALS

List of Illustrations	xiii
Abbreviations	xiv
Introduction	xv
Acknowledgements	xx
Notes	xxi
Books of Ahadith and Their Abbreviations	xxiii

PART II : UNDERSTANDING ISLAM — 1

1. Islam — 3
2. Allah — 7
3. Qur'an — 15
4. Muhammad (s) — 25
5. Shari'ah (Islamic Law) and Sunnah (Traditions) — 39
6. Iman (Faith) — 53
7. Tawhid, Shirk and Kufr (Unity of God, Attributing Partners and Disbelief in Allah) — 63
8. Jihad — 75
9. Islam, Muslims and Their Images — 81

PART III : ISLAMIC PRACTICES ('IBADAT) — 89

10. 'Ibadah : Salat — 91

    Section 1 : General — 91
    Definition — 91
    Salat, Du'a and Dhikr : Relationship — 93

Section 2 : Value, Kinds and Times of Prayer — 94

- Meaning of Salat (Prayer) — 94
- Why Do We Pray — 96
- Significance of Prayer — 96
- Kinds of Prayer — 97
- Fard Salat (Obligatory Prayer) — 98
- Nawafil Salat (Supererogattory Prayer) — 98
- Sunnah Type — 98
- Special Nawafil — 99
- General Nawafil — 99
- Times of (Salat) Prayer — 100
- Forbidden Times of (Salat) Prayer — 101
- Obligations and Prerequisites — 101
- Facing the Direction of Kaaba — 102

Section 3 : Purification — 102

- How to Perform Wudu (Ablution) — 103
- Nullification of Wudu — 105
- Special Consideration in Wudu or Masah — 106
- How to Wipe Over the Socks — 107
- Time Limits for Wiping — 107
- Tayammum (Dry Ablution) — 108
- Physical Purity — 109
- Mindset for Prayer — 110

Section 4 : Call to Prayer : Adhan and Iqamah — 111

- Adhan — 111
- Conditions when Adhan should not be responded to — 113
- Iqamah : The Performance Call — 114

Section 5 : Form and Parts of Prayer — 115

- Synopsis — 115
- Details of Prayer — 117

Recitation of Thana Before Surah al-Fatihah	120
Reciting Behind an Imam	121
Conditions for the Validity of Salat	126
Basic Elements (Arkan) of Salat	127
Invalidation of Prayers	127
Prostration of Forgetfulness (Sajdah Sahw)	128
Salat al-Jama'ah : Congregational Prayers	129
Concentration in Prayer	131
From Whom Prayer will be Accepted	132
Details of Rakahs (Units) in Each Salat - Table	134
Performance of Prayer : Obligatory and Voluntary Acts - Table	135

Section 6 : Fard, Wajib and Witr, Qada and Qasr Prayers — 136

Fard (Obligatory) Prayers	136
Salat al-Witr (The Odd prayer)	136
Friday (Jumu'a) Prayer	140
Eid Prayers	144
Janazah (Funeral Prayer)	148
Qasar (Shortening Prayer in Journey)	154
Qada (Making up for Missed Prayers)	156

Section 7 : Nawafil (Additional) Prayers : Sunnah — 159

Sunnah Mu'akkadah	159
Sunnah Ghair Mu'akkadah	160

Section 8 : Nawafil : Special — 160

Salat at-Tarawih (Special Prayer at Night in Ramadan)	160
Lailat al-Qadr (Night of Power)	163
Tahajjud (Night Vigil Prayer)	164
Ishraq and Duha (Chast) (After Sunrise Prayers)	166

Salat al-Kasuf (Prayer of the Solar and Lunar Eclipse)	167
Salat al-'Istisqa (Prayer for Rain)	168

Section 9 : Nawafil : General — 169

Dakhlil Masjid (Salutation for Mosque)	169
Tahyat al-Wudu (Post Ablution Prayer)	169
Salat at-Tasbih (Prayer of the Divine Glorification)	170
Salat al-Istikhara (Prayer for Guidanc)	171
Salat at-Tawbah wa al-Istighfar (Prayer for Repentance and Seeking Forgiveness)	173

Section 10 : After Finishing Prayer — 176

After Prayer Supplication	176
Invocation After Salat (Prayer)	178
Conclusion	179

Section 11 : Du'a and Dhikr (Supplication and Remembrance) — 180

11. Zakah (Alms Tax) — 185

12. Fasting (Sawm) — 189

13. Hajj and 'Umrah (Pilgrimage) — 197

Hajj	197
'Umrah	205
Fundamentals of Hajj	207
Other Hajj Rituals	207
Fundamentals of 'Umrah	207
Obligations During Ihram	208

14. Five Pillars — 209

PART IV : BEYOND PRAYER — 213

15. Islam : A Way of Life — 215

16.	Righteousness	221
17.	**Halal and Haram (Permitted and Forbidden)**	225
	Principles Pertaining to Halal and Haram	226
	Food and Drink	231
	Condemned Professions and Trade	232
18.	**Manners, Morals and Symbolic Expressions of Islam**	237
	Manners	237
	Morals	244
	Symbolic Expressions of Islam	254
19.	**Muslim Life Cycle**	263
	Section 1 : Birth and Childhood	263
	Section 2 : Marriage	264
	Permanence of Marriage	
	Polygamy	266
	Divorce	267
	Section 3 : Living and the Dead	
	Concept of Life	269
	Twilight Years	269
	Last Wish	270
	Burial Ceremony	270
	Funeral Service	271

PART V : LIFE AFTER DEATH   273

20. **Yaum al-Din wa al-Akhirah (Judgment Day and Life after Death)**   275

PART VI : MISCELLANEOUS   283

21.	Holy Places	285
	Kaaba	285
	Makkah	286
	Madinah	287
	Al-Aqsa	288
22.	**Feasts and Festivals**	291
23.	**Islamic Calendar**	299

PART VII : APPENDICES — 303

A.	Some Short Surahs or Passages for Prayer	305
B.	Selected Du'as and Durud	319
	Selected Qur'anic Du'as	319
	Selected Du'as from Sahih Hadith	328
	Selected Durud	330
	Du'as for Various Situations	335
	Miscellaneous	340
C.	Lord's (Jesus) Prayer	343
D.	Ibn Sina on Prayer	345
E.	Qur'anic Description of a Pious Muslim	347
F.	Overcoming Satan's Force	359
G.	Allah's Most Beautiful Names	363
H.	Prophets of Allah	371
I.	Biographical Notes	373
J.	Short Historical Chronology of Islam	381

GLOSSARY — 383

BIBLIOGRAPHY — 397

INDEX OF THE QUR'ANIC VERSES — 403

GENERAL INDEX — 413

List of Illustration Pages

Bismillah Calligraphy	14
Mount of Light, Makkah, Saudi Arabia	38
Cogregational Prayer at Makkah	52
Kaaba Door	62
Prophet's Mosque and his tomb, Madinah, Saudi Arabia	74
Grand Mosque, Damascus, Syria	80
Bangladeshi and Egyptian mosques	196
Articles of Faith	212
Taj Mahal, India	220
Symbols of Islam	236
Sultanahmet Mosque, Turkey	262
Supplication at Makkah	272
Suleymaniye Mosque, Turkey	282
Masjid Al-Aqsa	290
Qutb Minar, Delhi, India	298
Mosques in the Far East	302
Chinese Mosques	344
The Alhambra, Spain	346
Mosques in Iran and Pakistan	362

Abbreviations

A	Arabic
As	alayhi wa sallam (peace be upon him)
ca.	approximate dates
cf.	compare
cont.	continued
d.	died
do.	ditto, i.e., the same as above
e.g.	exampli gratia, for example
etc.	et cetera, and so on
ibid.	in the same place
i.e.	id est, that is
lit.	literally
No.	number, pl. Nos.
n.b.	nota bene, note well
P.	Persian
p.	page, pl. pp.
q.v.	quod vide, which see
s	sallalahu alayhi wa sallam (peace be unto him)
swt	subhanahu wa taala (glory be to Allah)
vide	see
viz.	Videlicet; namely

INTRODUCTION

$$\text{وَتَعَاوَنُواْ عَلَى ٱلْبِرِّ وَٱلتَّقْوَىٰ}$$

"... And help one another in righteousness and piety ..." (5:2)

The book explains what Islam is as well as the practice of Islam. Having belief is predicated on having principles, and Islam puts a specific set of principles into practice. All Islamic practices are Ibadah, which is worship or service to God. Devotional life among Muslims is fostered by daily prayers. Because of the importance of prayers in Islam, which is the highest form of Ibadah, they are highlighted throughout the book. There is also a section of the book specifically devoted to it. However, Islam rises far above the rituals and dogmas. It is both universal and cosmopolitan. It is because of the universal and cosmopolitan nature of Islam that great emphasis is placed on its concepts, its principles and its rules, which give an overview of Islam. Islam is a practical religion, which makes it possible to live in harmony with all things. Throughout this book, every effort has been made to cite or refer to Qur'anic verses wherever possible. This book attempts to fill a need that both explains Islam and also includes what is practiced in Islam. Great emphasis has been placed on making the book well organized, cohesive and concise by providing necessary details and avoiding controversies.

There are many books of prayers; however, each has its own shortcomings. Some books are incomplete because they do not cover all prayers. Others give prayer formula; however, they do not always give all the three ingredients: formula in Arabic, its transliteration, and translation. Some of the classical prayer books are in Arabic and are not available in translation. Some of the books are so full of minor details that ordinary practicing Muslims are likely to be turned off. Finally, there are hardly any prayer books that explain the fundamentals of Islam as a way of life.

Over the past several decades, Islam has become a significant American religion alongside Christianity and Judaism. Being distinctive in its approach to life, Islam is a unique community of faith. It is because of Islam's characteristics as a unique community of faith and Muslim identity, along with its richness and diversity, that the book focuses on these aspects rather than presenting the breadth of depth of Islam or giving its history.

The book is aimed at a wide audience to include non-Muslims as well. Because Islam incorporates the precepts of both Judaism and Christianity and has much in common with these religions, it is hoped that this book will be useful to members of those faiths in better understanding Islam. Even a cursory glance at the opening chapter of the Qur'an, Surah al-Fatihah (see Appendix for details), shows how much it resounds the Lord's Prayer (Prayer offered by Jesus). Both the content and nature of how it has been presented in this book may be helpful to nonpracticing Muslims in a better comprehension and even appreciation of the Islamic faith.

Another additional audience that this book seeks to serve is the new converts to Islam who are hungry for all kinds of information about their new religion. All those who are beginning to learn to pray will find it especially necessary and important for their practices. For practicing Muslims, it will help to enhance and refresh what they already know. Since a total comprehension of Islam is not a prerequisite for most practicing Muslims, the book is intended to deepen their understanding of

Introduction

it. For those who are well versed in Islam, this can be a book of reference. Islamic schools should also find this to be a useful text. In schools and colleges where Islam is taught as an academic subject, it can be very good support material in those courses.

This book is especially meant for the Muslim youngsters living in North America and Europe. Life is difficult in being a Muslim, and living like a Muslim in the Western world can be especially difficult because of the different social setting and often unfavorable circumstances. Living in a totally different religious, social and cultural background, as well as enormous peer pressure, can make it especially hard for youngsters to follow Islamic practices. Unless a child is born and brought up in a family with a strong religious bent where Islam is practiced with devotion and regularity, the temptations are many to be away from the Islamic path. To flow with the tide of the dominant culture is fashionable, acceptable, and easy. And the young are particularly swayed by this. However, if they have knowledge of Islam and appreciate what Islam means, there is a reasonable chance that they may want to live by it. They need to be told not just what Islam is, does, and stands for, but also the underlying reasons for its precepts and practices. If Islam is comprehended as a way of life and the young adhere to it, it will make them responsible citizens of their respective countries and respectable members of the communities in which they live. It is hoped that this book will help in all these respects.

There are great texts on Islam. I have drawn heavily from them, citing texts even though not all of them are listed in the Bibliography. I have consulted hundreds of books in preparation for this book and have taken the liberty of quoting them extensively. In those instances where the excerpts appear to be lengthy, I sought permission to reprint as recorded under Acknowledgements in the front of the book.

In this book the samples of Islamic calligraphy and architecture are random representations of the vast array of Islamic art. Islamic art is one of great character and beauty, and is the way in which a whole repertory of motifs, and a distinct system, made its mark with an idea and **faith**.

Qur'anic influence made calligraphy the most important art form of its culture. It is found in every area of the Muslim world, throughout Islamic history, and in every type of artistic expression imaginable. Of all the catagories of Islamic art, calligraphy is most prevalent, significant and widely appreciated by Muslims.

St. John's University granted me sabbatical leave to undertake research for a book. This book is the result of research I began during the sabbatical and completed after my retirement.

In summary, the goal of this volume is to enable readers to understand Islam, appreciate what Muslims believe and practice, and help practitioners in their practice. Additionally, it also elucidates how one can live morally and behaviorally, bring about spiritual uplifting, and provide overall enlightenment in all aspects of Islam. I hope, God willing, that this endeavor will in some way be useful. I also seek Allah's forgiveness for any shortcomings and /or unintentional mistakes. May Allah accept this humble effort.

This book would not have been possible without the help and encouragement of friends and family members. Because of their special services, the assistance received from Dr. Mofakhkhar Hussain Khan and Dr. Mujibur Rahman is mentioned separately in the Acknowledgments. I am permanently indebted to Professor Dr. Qazi Din Muhammad, Pro-Vice Chancellor, Asian University of Bangladesh, for reviewing the entire manuscript and giving me valuable suggestions and words of encouragement despite his extremely busy schedule.

Introduction

Many thanks are due my wife, Afroza, for her assistance, support, and inspiring confidence in me. My daughter, Afrin, and son, Arefin, did a lot of typing of my many different drafts in addition to offering many suggestions. I am indeed grateful to them. I am obliged to my late uncle Mohammed Nazrul Hoque for his support and may Allah reward him for it.

Lucrecia Manoogian typed several chapters, for which I am indebted to her. Bernice Linder did a superb job in typing the final draft of most of the chapters and in offering grammatical suggestions. My grateful thanks to her.

Mr. Nurul Islam, United Sugar, Jeddah, took up the responsibility of complicated bi-lingual typesetting. His expertise has given the book its present shape. May Allah reward him for this noble task.

Dr. Earl Blecher has been my constant companion in writing and researching this book. He has given me a hand throughout and he was always available with editorial assistance. Earl has been my support for most of my endeavors and for over thirty years has been my partner in all the anguish I had to endure. May Allah give him guidance and blessing.

My hearty thanks to Tom Geraghty of Geraghty Media Consulting who has been instrumental in doing the cover design and the illustrations, and also to everyone at Morris Publishing for doing a good job of printing the book.

While I have received help from all those mentioned here and also from many others not mentioned by name, I alone am responsible for any and all mistakes and inadequacies in this book, for which I seek Allah's forgiveness. I pray to Allah for His blessings for all those who were involved in the preparation and publication of this book. May Allah give the readers of this book proper guidance. May Allah be pleased with this contribution to Islam. Amin.

ACKNOWLEDGMENTS

Dr. Mofakhkhar Hussain Khan, Deanship of Library Affairs, King Abdulaziz University, Jeddah, Saudi Arabia, provided invaluable assistance in reading, commenting and editing on this book. He also provided invaluable materials, which were not available to me. I am gratefully indebted to him for his scholarly insights, guidance, encouragement, and brotherly love.

Dr. Muhammad Mujibur Rahman, former Professor and Chairman, Department of Arabic and Islamic Studies, Rajshahi University, Bangladesh provided extensive assistance in the Ibadah section of the book. As a religious scholar, he helped me stay focused on the Islamic principles and practices, for which I am grateful.

I am grateful to the following for permission to reproduce copyrighted material:

Islamic Publications (Pvt.) Limited, Lahore, Pakistan, for an extract on permissibility of wiping over socks, from *Everyday Fiqh* by Yusuf Islahi, English version, Abdul Aziz Kamal, p. 74.

Islamic Foundation, Markfield, Leicestershire, U.K., for an extract from *Let Us Be Muslims* by Sayyid Abul A'la Mawdudi.

North American Islamic Trust Inc. for permission to reprint a couple of extracts from *Fiqh us Sunnah*, an extract from *The Life of Muhammad* by Muhammad Husayn Haykal.

Westminster John / Knox Press for permission to reprint the Lord's Prayer from *The Book of Common Worship*, Westminster / John Knox Press, 1993.

NOTES

Qur'anic references are usually given between parentheses. The first figure is the number of the Surah, or Chapter. The numbering following the separating colon indicates the Ayah, or Verse. The verse number may vary by 1, rarely by 2, either way from Qur'an to Qur'an due mainly to joining up or splitting up of those verses or the edition of the Qur'an. Any time the verse quoted is a portion rather than the full verse, an effort has been made to indicate it by using ellipses. Unless the Qur'anic quotation is part of a quotation in the text, it has generally been taken from *The Holy Qur'an: English Translation of the Meanings and Commentary*, King Fahd Holy Qur'an Printing Complex (1411 A.H.) Al-Madinah Al-Munawarah (referred to in this text as the King Fahd edition). This is essentially the translation by Abdullah Yusuf Ali. Occasionally, other translations have been used as listed in the Bibliography.

The Words "Allah" and "God"

In the King Fahd copy of the Qur'an (referred to above), p. viii, Allah is defined this way: "Allah: the proper name of God in Arabic." Allah is Qur'anic but historically it has been pre-Islamic. God with a capital "G," not to be confused with 'god," has been used in the text interchangeably with Allah. Muhammad Asad, in *Message of the Qur'an: Translated and Explained*, uses the word "God" fairly frequently.

Man, Woman

In accordance with Islamic perspective, the word "man" in English has been used as corresponding to *insan*, or human, and possesses no sexist connotation.

Words Not Italicized

The following Arabic words in the text have not been italicized: Allah, Hadith (pl. Ahadith), Qur'an, Muslim, Ramadan, Shariah, Sunnah.

Transliteration

It is generally said that specialists do not need exact transliteration and non-specialists cannot use it. It is for this reason that diacritical marks have generally been avoided in the text except for transliteration of Qur'anic verses. The author is of the opinion that diacritical marks often distract rather than help the reader who is not familiar with letters in languages other than English.

Books of Ahadith and Their Abbreviations

Primary sources consulted are listed here; names of collections of Ahadith that were consulted through secondary sources appear in the text. Biographical information about the prominent Hadith scholars will be found in the Appendix.

Abu Dawud: Abu Dawud Sulayman ibn al-Ash'ath al-Sijistani. Sunan Abu Dawd. 3 vols. Trans. By Ahmad Hassan. New Delhi: Kitab Bhavan, 1990.

Bukhari: Bukhari, Muhammad ibn Ismail al. The Translation of the Meanings of Sahih al-Bukhari. 9 vols. 4th ed. Trans. By Muhammad Muhsin Khan. New Delhi: Kitab Bhavan, 1984.

Muwatta: Malik ibn Anas Al-Muwatta. Trans. By Aisha Abdarrahman at-Tarjumana and Yaqub Johnson. Norwich, U.K.: Diwan Press, 1982.

Sahih Mulsim: Muslim ibn Hajjaj al-Qushayri, Sahih Muslim: Being Traditions of the Sayings and Doings of the Prophet Muhammad as Narrated by His Companions and compiled under Tile Al-Jami-us-Sahih by Imam Muslim. 4 vols. Trans. By Abdul Hamid Siddiqi. New Delhi: Kitab Bhavan, 1977.

Riyadus Saleheen: Nawawi, Imam Abu Zakariya Yahya bin Sharaf An. Riyadus Saleheen. (Arabic-English) Trans. By S.M. Madni Abbasi. New Delhi: Kitab Bhavan, 1984. 940 pp.

***Mishkat*:** Tabrizi, Shaikh Waliuddin Mohammad bin Abdullah al-Khatib al Umari al. Mishkat al-Masabih. 3 vols. 3rd ed. Trans. by Abdul Hamid Siddiqi. New Delhi: Kitab Bhavan, 1990.

***Fiqh*:** Sabiq, As-Sayyid. *Fiqh us-Sunnah*. Indianapolis, Ind.: American Trust Publications, 1991-1992. 5 vols. Various translators.

***Fiqh 2*:** Islahi, Muhammad Yusuf. *Everyday Fiqh*. Trans. By Abdul Aziz Kamal. 2 vols. Lahore, Pakistan: Islamic Publications (Pvt.) Limited, 1989.

***Ihya*:** Al-Ghazzali, Abu Hamid bin Muhammad bin Muhammad. *Worship in Islam: being a translation, with commentary and introduction of al-Ghazzali's book of the Ihya on the worship*. By the Rev. Edwin Elliot Calverley. Westport, Conn.: Hyperion Press, 1981. 242 pp.

***Ihya II*:** Al-Ghazzali, Abu Hamid bin Muhammad bin Muhammad. *Inner Dimensions of Worship*. Trans. From the *Ihya* by Muhtar Holland. London: Islamic Foundation, 1983. 142 pp.

Part II

UNDERSTANDING ISLAM

1

ISLAM

إِنَّ ٱلدِّينَ عِندَ ٱللَّهِ ٱلْإِسْلَٰمُ

The Religion before God is Islam ... (3: 19)

Islam is a simple faith. Its core is the supremacy of One God whose last Messenger is Muhammad (s) sent to all mankind. It rests on the exclusive and emphatic insistence that Islam is the submission to the Divine will of Allah. Judaism, the first monotheistic religion with a transcendent God, and later Christianity, were several centuries old when Muhammad (s) preached Islam in the early seventh century. These three religions are interlinked because in reality they all are worshipping the same One God. These religions believe that God spoke through prophets but each holds different perspectives. Islam regards both Jesus and Moses as prophets. The great difference between Christianity and Islam is the person of Jesus. Although Muslims believe in the virgin birth of Jesus, the Christian concept of Trinity (the union of God, Jesus Christ and Holy Ghost in one godhead) is unacceptable. One of the most striking characteristics of Islam is that it requires its followers to believe that all the revealed religions of the world that preceded it have been revealed by God (cf. 2: 4).

The word Islam has the double meaning of "submission" and "peace." Muhammad Ali explains it best *(The religion of*

Islam: a comprehensive discussion of the sources, principles and practices of Islam. (1990, p. 4):

> The root meaning of the word Islam is to enter into peace and a Muslim is one who makes his peace with God and man. Peace with God implies complete submission to His will, and peace with man is not only to refrain from evil or injury to another but also to do good to him; and both these ideas find expression in the Qur'an as the true essence of the religion of Islam: "Nay whoever submits (aslama) himself entirely to Allah and he is the doer of good to others, he has his reward from his Lord, and there is no fear for such, nor shall they grieve" (2:112). Islam is thus, in its very inception, the religion of peace, and its two basic doctrines, the Unity of God and the unity of brotherhood of the human race, afford positve proof of its being true to its name.
>
> Islam, as stated in the Qur'an, is the true religion of all the prophets of God. Every prophet of God is spoken of in the Qur'an as being a Muslim, i.e., follower of Islam. This demonstrates that the various prophets have, in fact, been preachers of Islam and prophet Muahmmad (s) is its last and most perfect exponent. Muhammad's (s) message is a call for all people to worship God alone, to whom belongs all power and authority, in whose hands lies the power to reward and punish, to grant and withhold, and in whose kingdom all people are equal. Islam raised men from the lowest rung of the social ladder to the highest positions of life; it made of slaves not only leaders, but actual kings. Islam came also as the friend of the poor and the destitute.
>
> Islam does not demand unreasoned belief. Qur'an is replete with verses inviting man to use his intellect, to ponder, to think and to know, for the goal of human life is to discover the truth. The nature of Islam is such that it has a great deal of flexibility and practicability and can cope with changing circumstances.

Islam

Islam is a set of beliefs, a set of rituals (*'Ibadah*), a code of conduct and a way of life.

Belief

The fundamental Islamic beliefs are: belief in Allah, His Angels, Messengers, revealed Books, Day of Resurrection and Fate (i. e., whatever Allah has ordained must come to pass) (Bukhari, v. 1, p. li).

Rituals ('Ibadah)

There are four principal rituals: *Salah* (prayer), *Zakah* (almsgiving), *Sawm* (fasting), and *Hajj* (pilgrimage). All are explained later.

Code of Conduct

Islam lays down a code of conduct for man's life. Qur'an contains those prescriptions dealing with various spheres of human life: social, political, economic, legal and moral.

Way of Life (Tradition)

The prescriptions laid down in the Qur'an are exemplified by the actions and words of Prophet Muhammad (s). He is the living example for Muslims to follow.

In order to understand Islam, it is necessary to understand Allah. Allah can be understood through His words, i. e., Qur'an. The living example of Qur'an is Prophet Muhammad (s). Hence we must understand the Prophet and his traditions (*sunnah*) in order to understand Qur'an and, for that matter, Islam. Islam is a religious belief and faith ordained by God and practiced by Muhammad (s). All of these will be taken up one by one. The religious practices ('*Ibadah*) is central to this book and it will form part III.

إن الدين عند الله الإسلام

Innad dina Indallahil Islam
The Religion before God is Islam (3: 19)

2

ALLAH

أَللَّهُ نُورُ ٱلسَّمَٰوَٰتِ وَٱلْأَرْضِۚ مَثَلُ نُورِهِۦ كَمِشْكَوٰةٍ فِيهَا مِصْبَاحٌ ٱلْمِصْبَاحُ فِى زُجَاجَةٍۖ ٱلزُّجَاجَةُ كَأَنَّهَا كَوْكَبٌ دُرِّىٌّ يُوقَدُ مِن شَجَرَةٍ مُّبَٰرَكَةٍ زَيْتُونَةٍ لَّا شَرْقِيَّةٍ وَلَا غَرْبِيَّةٍ يَكَادُ زَيْتُهَا يُضِىٓءُ وَلَوْ لَمْ تَمْسَسْهُ نَارٌۚ نُّورٌ عَلَىٰ نُورٍۗ يَهْدِى ٱللَّهُ لِنُورِهِۦ مَن يَشَآءُۚ وَيَضْرِبُ ٱللَّهُ ٱلْأَمْثَٰلَ لِلنَّاسِۗ وَٱللَّهُ بِكُلِّ شَىْءٍ عَلِيمٌ ۝

Allah is the Light of the heavens and the earth; the parable of His Light is as if there were a Niche and within it a Lamp: the lamp enclosed in glass; the glass as it were a brilliant star: lit from a blessed tree, an Olive, neither of the East nor of the West, whose oil is well-nigh luminous, though fire scarce touched it: Light upon Light! Allah doth guide whom He will to His Light: Allah doth set forth parables for men: and Allah doth know all things. (24: 35)

The main theme of Islam is Allah. He is at the center and foundation of this major world religion. Muslim conception of Allah realizes the greatness and grandeur of His power and beneficence, and His mercy which has no bounds. The thought of all the goodness and perfection in Him makes one want to praise Him, submit to Him -- that submission is Islam. The word Islam means submission, surrender, obedience and peace. This obedience cannot be practiced unless one firmly believes in the existence of Allah. If a person realizes that Allah hears and knows everything (21: 4; 44: 6) we do in public or private (6: 3, 13; 16: 23), even our inner thoughts (2: 284; 3: 29, and 64: 4), one cannot but be obedient to Him.

Knowledge of Allah and belief in Him constitute the foundation of Islam. There are various ways to know Allah. The great wonders and impressive marvels of the world, in fact all the creations around us are like open books in which we can read about Allah. Another way, an excellent way, is to know and understand Him through His Words, i. e., the Qur'an. In Qur'an there are many pointers, signs (ayats) of Allah (2: 164; 3: 190; 10: 6; 36: 37-40). It is indeed through divine revelation that we can understand Him. Some of the Qur'anic verses will be studied for this purpose.

Allah describes Himself in the Qur'an as follows: The Merciful is established on the Throne: to Him belongs all that is in Heaven and Earth and all that is between them, and all that is beneath the surface (20: 4-6). Allah is eternal (2: 255), precedes all existence (57: 3; 92: 13) and is the cause of all existence (3: 156; 6: 95; 15: 23) which is contingent upon Him. He is all-Powerful (2: 284), all-Knowing, (4: 26) Creator (2: 28), Omnipresent (2: 115), Wisest of Judges (95: 8), and Most High and Great (4: 34).

Qur'an does not say much about the essence of Allah, for it is considered beyond human comprehension (6: 103). However, Allah is described in phrases such as "Nothing is like Him" (42: 11), and "Eyes cannot perceive Him" (6: 103). He is a being who exists by Himself and comprises all the attributes of perfection. While Allah as a Being is incomprehensible, His attributes or qualities (especially those indicated by His most beautiful names, called *al-asma al-husna*) are used to describe Allah and are meant to understand Him in terms of the human experience. But, in essence, Allah's attributes are ineffable. As a basic principle regarding the Divine attributes, Imam Abu Hanifah states (Muhammad Ali, *The Religion of Islam*, p. 116) that Allah does not resemble His creatures in anything, nor do any of His creatures resemble Him.

Among the attributive names of Allah, four stand out prominently and are exactly the names mentioned in the opening chapter of the Qur'an: *Rabb, Rahman, Rahim* and *Malik*. Rabb is considered the chief attribute of Allah. Abul Kalam Azad, in *The Tarjumān al-Qur'ān* (trans. by Syed Abdul Latif), offers the most splendid explanation of this term. Rabb is in a sense the Nourisher and also the Providence, overseeing the care and guardianship of His creatures. The God spoken of here is not the God of any particular race or group of people, but He is God of all mankind and of all forms of creation, the visible and the invisible, and One who provides sustenance appropriate to each object and regulates with every tenderness its growth and development.

Next in importance to *Rabb* are the names *Al-Rahman* (the Compassionate), *Al-Rahim* (the Merciful) and *Malik* (the Master of the Day of Recompense). The terms *Al-Rahman* and *Al-Rahim* are derived from *rhm* (رحم : pronounced as *Rahm*). The Arabic term *Rahm* denotes the kind of tenderness which stimulates in one the urge to show kindness to others. Its connotation is wide enough to cover the qualities of love, compassion, benevolence and generosity. The Prophet (s) is reported to have said: "*Al-Rahman* is the Beneficent God Whose love and mercy are manifested in the creation of this world, and *al-Rahim* is the Merciful God Whose love and mercy are manifested in the state that comes after."

Malik, or specifically *Maliki Yawmiddin* (Master of the Day of Recompense), refers to *'Adalat*, or Justice. Qur'an points out that requital or justice is the inevitable result of one's own action and not arbitrarily imposed. However, Allah also says (39: 53): "Allah forgives all sins." He is *Ghafur* (Forgiving). This term appears 230 times (in noun and verb form) in the Qur'an, whereas *Rahman* and *Rahim*, along with cognate verb forms, occur 560 times (as separate words, *Rahman* appears 57 times and *Rahim* 95 times). This shows that the qualities of love, mercy and forgiveness in Allah are emphasized in the Qur'an more than in any other sacred book. Not only is He the Lord (*al-Rabb*) of the universe, but He is also the Living (*al-Hayy*) and the Giver of Life (*al-Muhyi*), without Whom there would be no life in the world. He is the Knower of all things (*al-'Alim*) (21: 4) without Whom there would be no knowledge.

Allah is the most comprehensive term that encompasses all the divine attributes in addition to the ninety-nine beautiful names each of which evoke a distinct characteristic, some of which are already mentioned. Allah is not only the God of Muhammad (s), but also of Moses and Jesus, and is therefore identical to the divine being of Jewish and Christian sacred history.

Qur'an lays great emphasis on the unity of God. The creed "there is no god but God" contains the negation of false gods and the affirmation of the unity of one true God. Qur'an affirms (21: 26) "Had there been therein (in the heavens and the earth) gods besides Allah, then verily both would have been ruined." The stability of the laws of nature are a proof that the same God rules the earth and the rest of the universe (cf. 43: 84-5). Qur'an advances numerous arguments to prove the existence of a Supreme Being who is the Creator and Controller of this universe.

God is a caring God, a loving one (5: 54). He provides for all (15: 20). That He is the Lord of all creation (*Rabbul 'Alamin* 1: 1) makes it natural for Him to show divine concern for every individual, group, community, country and every form of

Allah

existence. God is Most Merciful (2: 163; 6: 19; 7: 151; 16: 22; 23: 91-2; 37: 1-5; 38: 65-8; 112: 1-4) and not one of wrath. It is a mistake to regard God not of love but of terror because He is "quick in retribution but oft-forgiving and Merciful" (7: 167). He is a fair and a just God (4: 40; 21: 47).

The first article of faith in Islam is Allah. The faith in one God and the virtues attending it purify the soul from evil and wickedness and elevate the human mind. Allah asks of man that he recognize the Almighty as the only sovereign and live his entire life in compliance with His Commandments. He says:

Verily, I am Allah. There is no god but I: So thou serve Me (only) and establish regular prayer for My remembrance." (20: 14)

Understood properly, it must be clear that total submission to Allah is not enough; it has to be followed by complete obedience to Qur'an and Prophet Muhammad (s). Allah says:

Say [O Muhammad (s) to mankind]: "If ye do love Allah, Follow me: Allah will love you and forgive you your sins: For Allah is Oft-Forgiving Most Merciful." (3: 31)

Although Qur'an does not speak often of the love of God, Qur'an explains that God's love is granted only to those who accomplish noble deeds for the good of man and the human society. God denies love to wicked people who are involved in sins that lead to harm and corruption. There are Qur'anic verses that affirm God's love for His worshippers. For example, (2: 222) "For Allah loves those Who turn to Him constantly And He loves those Who keep themselves pure and clean." And also:

Nay, those that keep their plighted faith and act aright, - verily Allah loves those who act aright. (3: 76).

But they never lost heart if they met with disaster in Allah's way, nor did they weaken (in will) nor give in. And Allah loves those who are firm and steadfast. (3: 146)

When thou hast taken decision, put thy trust in Allah for Allah loves those who put their trust (in Him). (3: 159)

Forgive them, and overlook (their misdeeds), for Allah loveth those who are kind. (5: 13)

If thou judge, judge in equity between them. For Allah loveth those who judge in equity. (5: 42)

These are just some examples. This should suffice for anyone who says that the God of Qur'an is without love.

Allah is not just the Creator; He is the Master of orderly creativity. He is the giver of guidance for man and He who judges man, individually and collectively, and metes out merciful justice. He is all-powerful, but with all His might and glory He is essentially the all-merciful God. The power and majesty of God is beautifully captured in the following passages:

He is the God, other than Whom there is none; He is the knower of the unseen and the seen, the Merciful, the Compassionate. He is the God other than Whom there is none, the Sovereign, the Holy, the One with peace and integrity, the Keeper of the Faith, the Protector, the Mighty, the One Whose Will is Power, the Most Supreme! Glory be to Him beyond what they [the pagans] associate with Him. He is the God, the Creator, the Maker, the Fashioner, to Whom belong beautiful names; whatever is in the heavens and the earth sings His glories, He is the Mighty One, the Wise One. (59: 22-24)

And once again:

And who other than Him created the heavens and the earth and sent down for you water from the sky, whereby We cause to grow lush orchards—for it is not up to you to cause their trees to grow! Is there, then, a god beside God? Yet these are the people who ascribe partners to Him! (27:60)

And who other than Him made the earth a firm abode [for you], and set rivers traversing through it, and put firm mountains therein and sealed off one sea from the other? Is

Allah

there, then, a god beside God? Indeed, most of them do not know! (27:61)

And who other than Him responds to the distressed one when he calls Him and He relieves him of the distress and Who has made you [mankind] His viceregents on earth? Is there, then a god beside God! ?little do you reflect! (27:62)

And who other than Him guides you in the darknesses of the land and the sea? And who sends forth winds heralding His mercy [rain]? Is there, then, a god beside God! Far exalted be He above what they associate with him! (27: 60-63)

Further:

To Him belongs whatever is in the heavens and in the earth—He is the High, the Great. The heavens above them are apt to be rent asunder [because of the worship of others than God], while angels glorify the praises of their Lord. (42: 4-5)

Allah is the Supreme Being—all-powerful and omnipresent. All goodness and perfection exist only in Him and proceed from Him. When we refer to Him by His attributes, we confine our vision within the limits of the attributes concerned. But when we refer to Him as Allah, our mind clenches the sum total of all the qualities attributed to Him. Allah is the greatest name of God.

Islamic calligraphy
On a gold plated leaf, Arabic reads:
God the One.

Islamic Calligraphy:
Bismillah in various scripts: *"In the name of Allah, the Most Gracious, the Most Merciful."*

3

QUR'AN

$$\text{ذَٰلِكَ ٱلْكِتَٰبُ لَا رَيْبَ ۛ فِيهِ ۛ هُدًى لِّلْمُتَّقِينَ ﴿٢﴾}$$

This is the Book; In its guidance sure, without doubt to those who fear Allah. (2: 2)

(39: 41) Surely we have sent down upon thee the Book for mankind with the truth. Whosoever is guided is only guided to his own gain, and whosoever goes astray, it is only to his own loss; thou art not a guardian over them.
(Also verses: 5: 15; 18: 27)

Qur'an is the center of Islam. This is the most sacred book for Muslims. It is the compilation of the Divine messages which were, at irregular intervals, revealed to Muhammad (s) by the archangel Jibril from the Tablet (*umm al-kitab*, the Mother of the Book) created by Allah before the creation of the world, together with the Pen which upon His command wrote down His will. Thus, Qur'an is a record of the exact words revealed by Allah through the Angel Jibril to Prophet Muhammad (s). The revelation remained so indelibly imprinted on his mind that he would never forget or falter in reciting the Devine message. Immediately after receipt of a revelation the Prophet (s) would recite it to those companions who were present, and get it written by scribes, who cross-checked it during his life time. He would also ask his companions to memorize it. Practice of memorization of the whole Qur'an still continues among the Muslims and there are innumerable *Huffaz* all over the world. It has thus been preserved both in hearts and plates with such care that there is no way one can get away with mistaken recitation or writing. If one does, others will make instant and spontaneous correction. Thus, not even a letter of its 114 Chapters, *Surahs*, has been changed over the centuries, so that Qur'an remains an eternal book untouched by change and susceptible to no alteration.

The message of the Qur'an is a continuation of that contained in the earlier revelations made " ... unto Abraham, and Ishmael, and Isaac, and Jacob, and the tribes and that which was given to Moses, and Jesus ... " (2: 136). It has a wealth of information, both worldly wisdom and intellectual conceptions, which provide the code of life for mankind (hudal-linnas 2: 185). Qur'an speaks to humanity as a whole, to nations, communities, families, and individuals individually and collectively. Allah says (5: 15-16)

"O people of the book! There has come to you Our Messenger, revealing to you much that you used to hide in the Scripture and passing over much. Indeed there has come to you from Allah a light (Prophet Muhammad (s)) and a plain Book (Qur'an), wherewith Allah guides all those who seek His good pleasure to ways of peace, and He brings them out of darkness by His Will unto light and guides them to the straight way (Islamic monotheism).

The purpose of Qur'an is to furnish guidance to mankind so that they may be led along the path that would bring them to their Creator in a state of complete submission to Him. For that purpose it draws attention to every type of phenomena and reveals vast treasures of profound truths. For instance, Qur'an makes numerous statements based on historical facts to emphasize different aspects of the guidance it sets forth. Moral

Qur'an

values are intertwined with history, and details of daily life are put into a continuum with life hereafter. The Qur'an is strewn with such picturesque representation of facts and ideas, relating to the everyday experiences of the reader so that they appeal not only to his intellect but also to his deeper sensibilities. Qur'an uses metaphors, allegories and parables in order to make verses easily intelligible and create vivid and lifelike impressions on the reader. Qur'an was revealed piecemeal under Divine design (17: 106; 25: 32) to provide for the needs of each situation as it arose, and yet to prove adequate in all unforeseen contingencies.

Qur'an is not like conventional books in that it is not arranged in the order of themes or topics. The order of its chapters, and of its verses in the chapters, is not meant to give the Qur'an a topical structure. Subjects are repeated in different ways and one topic follows another without any apparent connection. It is composed of series of clusters of verses, each cluster treating a different topic, but constituting a complete unit even if it is only one or two lines. Qur'an looks like a book without a beginning or end and serves the purpose of recitation very well because it can be read or recited by beginning at any verse and stopping at any one. Abul A'la Mawdudi in *An Introduction to the Qur'an*, 1982 (pp. 5-7) explains the Qur'an as a unique book this way:

> The reader must bear in mind before he begins the study that this is a unique Book. It is quite different from the books one usually reads. It is unlike conventional books in that it does not contain information, ideas, and arguments about specific themes arranged in a particular literary order. A stranger to the Qur'an is baffled in the beginning because he does not find the enunciation of its themes, its division into chapters and sections, a separate treatment of varied topics, or separate instructions for different aspects of life arranged in serial order:

As Mawdudi points out, the Qur'an "presents creeds, gives moral instructions, acts, laws, draws lessons from historical events, administers warnings, gives good tidings, admonishes the disbelievers, and invites people to Islam." However, a nonbeliever may find the Qur'an confusing because "subjects are repeated in different ways, and one topic follows another without any apparent connection. Intermittently, a new topic emerges in the middle of another following no obvious structure. The speaker, the receiver and the direction of the address may change without any prior notice. There are no signs of chapters or divisions, and historical events are presented unlike those in ordinary history books." In addition, "philosophical problems and metaphysical concepts are uncharacteristic of text books on the same subjects. The language concerning man and the universe is unusual from that of the natural sciences."

The Qur'an is not a book of "religion" in the sense that the word is generally used. It follows its own method of solving cultural, social and economic problems. It also handles the principles and practice of law in a manner quite distinct from sociologists, lawyers and jurists. It is a religious book with its own unique characteristics. Morality is taught in a way that has no parallel on the subject in the whole realm of literature.

In Qur'an, all subjects are blended together in an exceptionally beautiful manner despite the fact that the unwary reader begins to imagine that the Qur'an is a book without any order or interconnection between its verses and the continuity of its subjects. The reader should not approach the Qur'an with common literary notions, Mawdudi warns, for he may be puzzled by its style and presentation and be unable to benefit fully from the treasures contained in it. Only then will the reader succeed in discovering its gems.

In Arabic, Qur'an is a masterpiece of immense literary value fusing the style of presentation with the substance being presented in a blend of unique proportions. This book serves as far more than a source of religious inspiration; prescriptions and proscriptions within it address the whole range of human personal and social behavior. Therein Allah has made clear the "straight path" and given explicit expression to the manner in which humans must live in accordance with His will. All things in the Qur'anic universe begin, continue and end in Allah. Qur'an can be interpreted in many ways, but on the whole it maintains an unparalleled balance. Allah's power knows no bounds but human beings both enjoy a wide array of options and must shoulder responsibility for their actions.

According to Shah Waliullah, the most prominent eighteenth century Muslim intellectual in India, the subject matter of Qur'an as mentioned in *Teachings of Shah Waliullah of Delhi*, by G. N. Jalbani falls into four categories:

1. injunctions that pertain to what is obligatory, approved, disapproved and the forbidden whether they be in connection with worship or dealings of man with man, the household administration and state politics;
2. disputations which relate to misguided groups, namely, Jews, Christians Polytheists and Hypocrites;.
3. divine wonders, wherein the attention of the people is drawn to the wondrous signs of the Almighty in nature;
4. death, its horrors and the effect on man of the events which are to follow it.

According to Al-Ghazzali, as mentioned in *Essential Koran*, (Cleary: 1993, xvi-xvii) Qur'an has six aims. The first aim is knowledge of God, including the essence, attributes and works of God. The second aim is definition of the path to God, by which the "rust" is removed from the "mirror" of the soul so that the light of God may be reflected clearly in the purified soul. The third aim is definition of human conditions at the time of attaining God, i. e., the condition of spiritual fulfillment. The fourth aim is definition of the conditions of people who traveled the path to God, such as the prophets of the past, and the conditions of those who deviated from the path to God, such as the tyrants and oppressors of the past. The fifth aim is definition of arguments of those who reject truth, proofs against these arguments, and exposure of the inherent falsehood and self-deceit underlying these arguments. The sixth aim is definition of the fulfillment of what is required at each stage of the Path to God, including the manner of preparation for the journey. These verses demonstrate the connection between life in human society and the life of the spirit, how the self and the world may be made into vehicles for the journey to enlightenment (here and the hereafter).

The Qur'an postdates the Bible and, in fact all the major scriptures. There is an aura of finality in it. Indeed Muslims understand the Qur'an to be historically final. The Qur'an is revelation's climax.

Man's responsive duty of gratitude and wonder are constant theme of the Qur'an. Allah says, "He has taught (mankind) the Qur'an. He created man. He taught him eloquent speech" (55: 2-4). And later in that *surah*, He says: "Then which of the bounties of your lord will you deny?" (55: 28) The focus of the Qur'an is man. It discusses those aspects of life that lead either to success or failure. Qur'an's interest is in the betterment of man, as indicated in verse 39: 41 cited at the top of this section.

The word Qur'an means Reading, Recitation. It is also called the Criterion (Furqan) a Reminder (dhikr) and also a clarification (Bayan). Its function as a criterion is to distinguish between truth and falsehood. It is the best discourse (39: 23), it gives good tidings to those who believe in it (17: 9). As a matter of fact, Qur'an is known by fifty-five special titles, these may be looked upon as subtitles that explain what the Qur'an is about.

Qur'an is concise, multifaceted and makes a constant demand for the intelligent reflection (4: 82, 38: 29). Qur'an does indeed expect understanding from one who seeks to derive benefit from it (47: 24). It respects intelligence and knowledge

(29: 43) of the reader and assumes that he will exercise it. It draws attention repeatedly to natural phenomena and argues from the physical and material to the moral and spiritual. Repeated attention is drawn to this feature of the Qur'an (e. g. 30: 58). Also it affirms expounding all things necessary for mankind (17: 89).

Qur'an being the word of Allah is purity. It is, therefore, only natural that those who seek to penetrate to its deeper meaning must have purity of thought, action and motive (cf. 91: 9). Qur'an is the Arabic Qur'an. When it is translated into another language, no matter how well done, the words are no longer spoken words of Allah, and therefore no more than the meaning of the Qur'an. Every sentence (in Arabic) has a hold on the pious, thanks to its rhythm, its fascination, and especially because he hears in it the very word of God (imagine being relayed by the Prophet). It enables one to have personal contact with Allah.

Qur'an is a source of divine blessing, tranquillity and guidance. Muslims find great blessings in recitation, memorizing, hand-copying, or even possessing a copy in their homes. It is believed that on the Day of Judgment, the status of a man or woman will be determined by the number of verses of the Qur'an memorized in this life. An even greater source of merit in blessing is found in studying and understanding the principles and precepts of the Qur'an. It sanctifies the heart and home of the Muslim. With the words of the Qur'an, a Muslim expresses his gratitude to Allah by pronouncing "Al-hamdu lillah" (praise be to Allah). Qur'an is a source of blessing in itself through its sounds and letters. It must be remembered that the soul of a Muslim is composed of Qur'anic verses which the faithful recites, viz., "Bismillahir Rahmanir Rahim" (In the name of Allah, the Beneficent the Merciful) to begin every action and "Al-hamdu lillah" (Praise be to Allah) to end.

Qur'an's blessings are limitless and our taking from it depends on the capacity and suitability of our manner and approach to it. Scholars point out whoever reads the Qur'an rightly will find new impulse and initiative and unfailing treasure. Qur'an is meant to be recited, to be listened to, and to be experienced. Allah says: "And recite what has been revealed to you (O Muhammad (s) of the Book (the Qur'an) of your Lord ... " (18: 27). The obligations to Qur'an are threefold: To read it, to comprehend it and to follow it. Qur'an is to be recited calmly and distinctly with mind attuned to its meaning (73: 4, Asad tr. ; Yusuf Ali tr. - in slow, measured rhythmic tones).

Qur'an is divided into114 chapters of varying lengths. According to *Cultural Atlas of Islam* (Ismail R and Lois Faruqi, p. 100), it contains 6, 616 verses, 77, 934 words, and 323, 671 letters. In order to facilitate its reading, the Qur'an is divided into 30 convenient sections, 540 Ruku (subsections). There are 14 places (according to some, 15) in the Qur'an where the words used are so commanding that the reciter bows down in awe to glorify Allah; the reader is indeed required to prostrate at these places.

Anyone who seeks to discover the true meaning and purport of the guidance contained in the Qur'an can afford not to supplicate the Most Beneficent and Most Merciful, for Allah says: " ... Call on Me; I will respond to you [prayer] ... " (40: 60). Reading the Qur'an is the best way to remember Him and there is no time during the day or night that is unsuitable for reading the Qur'an. Every sentence of the Qur'an conveys a lesson that the believer must put into practice.

Qur'an is not God but it is inseparable from Him. All things in Qur'an are seen as deriving from, and returning to "Rabb al-Alamin" (Lord of all beings). All beings incorporate the breadth of the entire universe. Events in the cycle of nature, day and night, winds, rain, oases, harvests, sun, moon and stars in their

Qur'an

courses (cf 36: 40, 3: 190) are all among the ayat or sign of Allah. Allah says: (51: 20-21)

"And on earth there are signs [of God's existence, visible] to all who are endowed with inner certainty, (21) just as [there are signs thereof] within your own selves: can you not, then see?"

The believers, the thoughtful, the sensitive ponder over all these innumerable signs of Allah and are moved to gratitude. How satisfying is it to know (16: 18) "For, should you try to count God's blessings, you could never compute them! Behold God is indeed much-forgiving, a dispenser of grace."

Qur'an is the greatest gift from Allah to mankind. About its magnificence and extraordinary value, Lois and Ismail al-Faruqi in their book, The *Cultural Atlas of Islam* (p. 342) write:

No book ever commanded as wide or as deep a reverence as did the Qur'an; none has been copied and recopied, passed from generation to generation memorized in part or in toto, recited in solemn worship as well as in salons, marketplaces, and schoolrooms as much as the Qur'an. Above all, no book has ever been the cause of such deep religious intellectual, cultural, moral, social, economic, and political change in the lives of millions, or of peoples as ethnically diverse, as has the Qur'an.

Finally, a couple of Qur'anic verses are quoted below that tell about the Qur'an itself:

54: 32 And We have indeed made the Qur'an easy to understand and remember.

16: 89 ... To thee Book explaining all things, a guide, a mercy and glad tidings to Muslims.

11: 1 (This is) is a Book, with verses fundamental (of established meaning), further explained in detail, - from One Who is Wise And Well-Acquainted (with all things)

29: 43 And such are the parables We set forth for mankind, but only those understand them who have knowledge.

47: 24 Will they not, then ponder over The Qur'an? or, are their hearts locked up (from understanding it)?

41: 44 ... It is a guide and a healing to those who believe; and for those who do not believe, there is deafness in their ears and blindness in their eyes ...

Islamic calligraphy
Arabic reads:
Muhammad is the Messenger Of God – may God bless him And give him peace!
By the Turkish calligrapher Nasih Efendi, 1852

4

MUHAMMAD (s)

$$\text{لَقَدْ جَآءَكُمْ رَسُولٌ مِّنْ أَنفُسِكُمْ عَزِيزٌ عَلَيْهِ مَا عَنِتُّمْ حَرِيصٌ عَلَيْكُم بِالْمُؤْمِنِينَ رَءُوفٌ رَّحِيمٌ ۝}$$

"Now has come unto you a Messenger from amongst yourselves: it grieves him that you should suffer, ardently anxious is he over you: to the Believers is he most kind and merciful". (9: 128)

Muhammad (s) was born in about 570 C. E. into a noble Quraish family in the city of Makkah in Arabia. His father died before he was born, and his mother died when he was six years old. He was first raised by his grandfather and at the latter's death he was taken care of by his uncle. Muhammad (s) developed into a sober and responsible young man. In his younger days he was a shepherd. He took care of his family's and neighbors' herds. Later, he used to recall these early days with joy and say that Allah sent no prophet who was not a herdsman. Since his youth his conduct was so perfect, manly and truthful that the people of Makkah agreed to call him, "Al-Amin" or the "truthful or trustworthy." At the age of twenty-five, he married a rich widow fifteen years his senior. She was a relative who, had him under her employment, having justly appreciated his noble qualities, proposed to him despite their age difference. Muhammad (s) was a devoted, loving father and was kind to children. In his 25 years of life with his wife Khadijah, he was the ideal husband.

In about 610, when he was about 40 years old, during one of his periodic meditative retreats in the caves of Hira, near Makkah, the archangel Jibril appeared to him, told him that Allah had chosen him as His messenger, and revealed to him five verses (96: 1-5) of the Qur'an. Muhammad (s) was fearful and shaken up and rushed home to his wife and told her what had happened. Reminding him of his well-known virtues, she assured him that he was too stable to have lost his mental balance. She took him to a relative, Warqa, a Christian, who listened to the revelation and declared it to be the same Truth as that brought by Moses and Jesus. Members of his family immediately declared faith in him. Besides his wife, there were the freed slave Zayid and his young cousin and future son-in-law Ali. Shortly thereafter, Abu Bakr, a long-time friend, also declared his faith. This was the party which made the silent resolve to spread the word of Islam all over the world.

Tradition claims that there was a *fatra* (pause) of three years between the time Muhammad (s) received the first revelations and the time he began to preach publicly to the Quraish. At first, the powers that be in Makkah simply thought that Muhammad had gone mad. But gradually, as their own friends and relatives started joining his small group, they took notice, and before too long they felt threatened. They did what they could to make life difficult for the converts, and Muhammad (s) and his followers went through persecutions and trials. A group of Muslims, the new converts, emigrated to Abyssinia, assured by the Prophet (s) that the King of that land was Christian and would protect them.

By the year 619, when Muhammad (s) was about 50, the situation had become precarious. His wife Khadijah and his uncle Abu Talib were dead; the support of his clan greatly diminished. He finally decided to go to a nearby oasis, al-Taif,

Muhammad (s)

and call on the people there to accept him as Prophet. They repudiated his call and driven him out of the city. In that sad year of recurring calamities and gloom, when tragedy seemed about to engulf Prophet's mission, a gleam of hope came to sustain him. During the pilgrimage season and the sacred months, when the traditional laws forbade violence, the Prophet (s) had by happy chance converted a few people from Yathrib (which became Madinah, i. e., the City of the Prophet) who swore allegiance to him. They returned next year with the good news that his faith was being accepted by many in Yathrib. They asked him to join them and solve some of their problems that were caused by friction among the different groups of people living in that city. In 622 C. E., a delegation of seventy-three men and two women paved the way for his going there by taking pledge to defend Muhammad (s).

Makkah was no longer a safe place for the Muslims to reside in. The Prophet (s) then directed those who had returned from Abyssinia and other converts to emigrate and head for Yathrib. Quietly they started to move out. In a few months, more than a hundred families left their homes and migrated to Yathrib. The Quraishis were on their guard. The migration of the Prophet to a rival city was harmful to them, and they were determined to prevent it at all cost. They decided to kill him. Fearful of the escape of the Prophet, his assassins posted themselves round the Prophet (s)'s dwelling. However, he was able to escape to the house of Abu Bakr and they fled together. They lay hid for several days in a cave hill near Makkah.

The fury of the Quraish was now unbounded. Horsemen scoured the country. Once or twice the danger approached so near that Abu Bakr (r) said in panic, "We are but two," the Prophet said (9: 40) "Have no fear, for Allah is with us." And He was with him. As is well-known, a spider spun its web and pigeons hurriedly built their nests over the cave so that the

Makkans in their pursuit did not imagine that anyone could be hiding in that place (cf. 9: 40).

Muhammad (s) reached Madinah in September, 622 and that year begins the mark of the Muslim era, Hijra (separation, migration). For the Muslims, the word hijra came to mean not only a change of place but the adoption of Islam and entry into the community of Muslims; a new civilization was born with this historic migration.

Prophet Muhammad (s)'s first concern in Yathrib was to build (which he did) his simple place of worship, the masjid, where the faithful could also meet to discuss the affairs of the world. There he organized the community – ummah - as an independent entity. Within a few months of his arrival, he drew up a covenant (some describe it as a constitution and the first one at that in human civilization) spelling out the rights and obligations of every citizen. The Jews were granted religious and cultural autonomy and were recognized as a community along with Muslims. Although in charge, he did not claim the status of a ruler, he was only Allah's Messenger.

The Prophet (s) needed a constitution and a system of defense. The covenant laid down that all groups were to defend Yathrib in case of external attack. Guided by revelations, the Prophet was able to implement the political and social structure of the Ummah, despite exposure to a war of annihilation. His next task was an alliance with the neighboring Jews and pagan Arabs for a common defense and for security and peace in Yathrib. This was accomplished through treaty. This was famous Covenant of Yathrib, resembling in certain aspects that of the League of Nations or of the United Nations, which aimed at the maintenance of peace and security among the various tribes and the creation of a common system of security as a consequence of a common responsibility.

In the third year of the hijra there was the famous Battle of Badr. His enemy, the Quaraish had a larger army but he was still

Muhammad (s)

able to defeat them. The causes of the victory lay in his superior discipline and leadership and the high morale which resulted from his faith in God.

The Battle of Badr was a great victory, especially because it established the Muslim community as a separate political and social as well as a religious entity and confirmed the power of the Prophet (s) but it was not decisive. It was in the year 630 when Makkah fell to Islam. It was prophet Muhammad (s)'s policy to take that city for Islam because aside from its commercial and political importance, it was the religious capital of the Arabs. The way he celebrated the victory is unparalleled in history as narrated by historians. Syed Ameer Ali in his *The Spirit of the Islam* (1922, pp. 95-96 writes:

> The city which had treated him so cruelly, driven him and his faithful band for refuge amongst stranger, which had sworn his life and the lives of his devoted disciples, lay at his feet. His old persecutors, relentless and ruthless who had disgraced humanity by inflicting cruel outrages upon inoffensive men and women and even upon the lifeless dead, were now completely at his mercy. But in the hour of triumph every evil suffered was forgotten, every injury inflicted was forgiven, and a general amnesty was extended to the population of Mecca.
>
> The army followed his example and entered gently and peaceably; no house was robbed, no woman was insulted. Most truly has it been said that through all the annals of conquest, there has been no triumphant entry like unto this one.

Stanley Lane-Poole describes it this way (*Studies in a Mosque*, Beirut, Khayats, 1966, p. 73):

> The day of Mohammed's greatest triumph over his enemies was also the day of his grandest victory over himself. He freely forgave Quarysh all the years of sorrow and cruel scorn with which they had inflicted him, and gave an amnesty to the whole population of Makkah... The army

followed his example, and entered quietly and peaceably; no house was robbed, no woman insulted. One thing alone suffered destruction. Going to the Kaaba Muhammad stood before each of the three hundred and sixty idols, and pointed to them with his staff saying, "Truth is come, and falsehood I fled away!", and at these words his attendants hewed them down and all the idols and household gods of Makkah and round about were destroyed."

Muhammad Husayn Haykal's comment on this general amnesty is superb. Here is a part of what he writes (*The Life of Muhammad*, p. 408):

Oh, the beauty of pardon and forgiveness on the part of the mighty and the powerful! How great is the soul of Muhammad which rose above hatred and above revenge, which denied every human feeling and ascended to the heights of nobility man had never reached before.

Upon returning to Madinah, Muhammad (s) received delegations sent by tribes and settled peoples of Arabia. They came to pay homage to him and to profess faith of Islam. At this time he began to send emissaries to Arabia's neighboring empires.

In the tenth year of the hijra, Prophet Muhammad (s) made his last pilgrimage to Makkah and delivered his historic Farewell speech which was the culmination of twenty-three years of hard work in the fulfillment of his mission. Here is the excerpt from Haykal (pp. 486-7):

O Men, Listen well to my words, for I do not know whether I shall meet you again on such an occasion in the future. O Men, your lives and your property shall be inviolate until you meet your Lord. The safety of your lives and of your property shall be as inviolate that as this holy day and holy month. Remember that you will indeed meet your Lord, and that He will indeed reckon your deeds. Thus do I warn you, whoever of you is keeping a trust of someone else shall return that trust to its rightful owner. All interest obligation shall henceforth be waived. Your capital, however, is yours to keep. You will neither inflict nor suffer inequity. God has judged that there shall be no interest and that all the interest due to 'Abbas ibn 'Abd al-Muttalib shall henceforth be waived. Every right arising out of homicide in pre-Islamic days is henceforth waived. And the first such right that I waive is that arising from the murder of Rabi'ah ibn al Harith ibn 'Abd al-Muttalib. O Men, the devil has lost all hope of ever being worshipped in this land of yours. Nevertheless, he still is anxious to determine the lesser of your deeds. Beware of him, therefore, for the safety of your religion. O Men, intercalation or tampering with the calendar is evidence of great unbelief and confirms the unbelievers in their misguidance. They indulge in it one year and forbid it the next in order to make permissible that which God forbade, and to forbid that which God has made permissible. The pattern according to which the time is reckoned is always the same. With God, the months are twelve in number. Four of them are holy. Three of these are successive and one occurs singly between the months of Jumada and Sha'ban. O Men, to you a right belongs with respect to your women and to your women a right with respect to you. It is your right that they not fraternize with any one of whom you do not approve, as well as never to commit adultery. But if they do, then God has permitted you to isolate them within their homes and to chastise them without cruelty. But if they abide by your right, then to them belongs the right to be fed and clothed in kindness. Do treat your women well and be kind to them, for they are your partners and committed helpers. Remember that you have taken them as your wives and enjoyed their flesh only under God's trust and with His permission. Reason well, therefore, O Men, and ponder my words which I now convey to you. I am leaving you with the Book of God and the Sunnah of His Prophet. If you follow them, you will never go astray. O Men, hearken well to my words. Learn that every Muslim is a brother to every Muslim and that the Muslims constitute one brotherhood. Nothing shall be legitimate to a Muslim which belongs to a fellow Muslim unless it was given freely and willingly. Do not, therefore, do injustice to your own selves. O God, have I conveyed Your message?"

At the end of the sermon, the last verse of the Qur'an (5: 3) was revealed:

This day I perfected your religion for you, completed My favour upon you, have chosen for you Islam as your religion.

Two months after his return from the pilgrimage, the Prophet (s) passed away. The Qur'an stresses mortality even of Prophet. Allah says (3: 144):

Muhammad is no more than a Messenger: many were the Messengers that passed away before him. If he died or were slain, will you then turn back on your heels? If any did turn back on his heels (as disbelievers), not the least harm will he do to Allah; but Allah will (on the other hand) swiftly reward those who serve Him with gratitude.

Muhammad Asad in a footnote to this verse in his translation of the Qur'an captures the dilemma upon Muhammad (s) death in these words (p. 89):

In its wider implication, the above verse restates the fundamental Islamic doctrine that adoration is due to God alone, and that no human being--not even a prophet--may have any share in it. It was this very passage of the Qur'an which Abu Bakr, the first Caliph, recited immediately after the prophet's death, when many faint-hearted Muslims thought that Islam itself had come to an end; but as soon as Abu Bakr added, "Behold, whoever has worshipped Muhammad (s) may know

Muhammad (s)

that Muhammad has died; but whoever worships God may know that God is ever-living, and never dies" (Bukhari), all confusion was stilled.

Muhammad (s) was the only Prophet who fulfilled his mission in his lifetime. His character, his statesmanship, his spiritual accomplishments and his mundane reforms are unparalleled in the history of mankind. His main reforms were as follows:

* Unified the Arabs from the scattered tribes they were
* Rooted out idolatry and replaced it with Islam
* Elevated women's position in relation to men
* Established equality among all members of the society
* Created a society based not on blood ties, but on faith.

In the book *The 100: A Ranking of the Most Influential Person in History* by Michael H. Hart (1991, p. xxix), Prophet Muhammad (s) is ranked first of the one hundred most influential people in history because Muhammad had a much greater singular personal influence on the formulation and establishment of Islam than other prophets had in the formulation and establishment of other religions.

Allah Himself had elevated the dignity of His Prophet (s) by giving him high praise, for He says (94: 4): "And raised high the esteem (in which) though (art held)?"

In a footnote to this Allama Yusuf Ali writes (p. 1974):

The Prophet's virtues, the magnanimity of his character, and his love for mankind were fully recognized even in his lifetime, and his name stands highest among the heroic leaders of mankind. The phrase used here is more comprehensive in meaning than that used for various prophets..."

Allah also says about the Prophet (s) (68: 4): "And surely thou hast sublime morals."

Allah further says (33: 21): "You have indeed in the Messenger of Allah an excellent exemplar."

Here are some examples from the mortals. Shaikh Saadi, Persian sage, said: "In short, after Allah you are the greatest." Major Arthur Glyn Leonard says (*Islam: Her Moral and Spiritual Values*): "Not only great; but of the greatest, i. e., truest man that humanity has ever produced." Thomas Carlyle is of the opinion (in *The Hero as Prophet: Mahomet: Islam*) that in the history of the world there will not again be any man, never so great.

What is it that makes him so great? What made him so rare a figure in history was his ability to convey his vision to people around him so that concepts long known to everyone took on the power to transform other people's lives as they had transformed his. This was accomplished by direct preaching about God, but also changing family life and institutions, and by introducing ritual practices and social morals. His greatest accomplishment was in his teachings and the manner in which he gave them a practical shape by his conduct and behavior in everyday life. One of the Islamic scholars identifies three gifts in Prophet Muhammad (s):

First, there is what may be called his gift as a seer- insight into the fundamental causes of the social malaise of the time, and the genius to express the insight in a form which would stir the hearer. Second, there is Muhammad (s)'s wisdom as a statesman. The conceptual structure found in Qur'an was a framework. The framework had to support building of concrete policies and concrete institutions. Third, there is his skill and tact as an administrator and his wisdom in the choice of men to whom to delegate administrative details.

The more one reflects on the history of Muhammad (s) and of early Islam, the more one is amazed at the vastness of his achievement. The French poet, historian and statesman Alphonse Marie Louis de Lamartine has put it so eloquently:

> If greatness of purpose, smallness of means and astounding results are the three criteria of human genius who could

Muhammad (s)

dare to compare any great man in modern history with Muhammad? Philosopher, Orator, Apostle, Legislator, Warrior, Conqueror of Ideas, Restorer of Rational beliefs of a cult without images: The founder of twenty terrestrial empires that is Muhammad. As regards all standards by which human greatness may be measured, we may well ask is there any man greater than he?

The sign of a great man is when he is the same under all circumstances. He was the same in victory as in defeat; in power as in adversity; in affluence as in indigence. His life in Makkah had been a life of adversity, of trial and danger; in Madinah it was a life of success and prosperity. But in the former as in the latter he remained the same man, and at times gave evidence of that magnanimity of soul, the equal of which the history of the world cannot produce.

In spite of his exalted position the holy Prophet (s) was above all things humble. He did all his work with his own hands, and never allowed anything to be done for him that he could do himself. Daily he milked his own goats, washed and mended his own clothes, repaired his own shoes, and cleaned and swept his own house. His humility is also manifest when he says:

> I too, am only a man. When I give a command in something relating to your din, then accept it and when I tell you something as my personal opinion, then, no doubt, I am also [only] a human being [like you].

Some, when they came before him, felt awed, but the Prophet always put them at their ease by saying, "Be not afraid of me; I am not a king, but a son of a simple woman."

In spite of the nearness of God, in spite of being the greatest of all prophets, Muhammad (s) used to say his prayers with as much zeal as though he was a lost soul seeking God. He would spend his nights standing in prayer regardless of physical pain.

Prophetic mission was not just his hobby or profession but his entire life as is evident from the following verse (6: 162):

"Say, [O, Muhammad!] my prayers and my devotions, my life and my death are all for God, the Lord of the world."

Love of the Prophet, respect for him, devotion to him, are unparalleled. A visit to his shrine in Madinah, a glance through the poetry (naat or rubay) for celebration of the Prophet's Maulid or birthday in any culture will be an indication. (For inadvisability of celebrating Maulid, see under this heading in the chapter Feasts and Festivals.) Naat poetry is related to the spiritual, moral and social values. By and large, these are examples of submission to Allah's will. Here is a popular one attributed to Shaikh Sa'adi:

$$\text{بَلَغَ الْعُلٰى بِكَمَالِه}$$
$$\text{كَشَفَ الدُّجٰى بِجَمَالِه}$$
$$\text{حَسُنَتْ جَمِيعُ خِصَالِه}$$
$$\text{صَلُّو عَلَيْهِ وَآلِه}$$

1. He attained the height eminence by his perfection;
2. He dispelled the darkness [of the world] by his grace;
3. Excellent were all his qualities;
4. Pray for blessings on him and his descendants.

(Translated by Ahmed Deedat, The Choice: Islam and Christianity, Vol 1, 7th printing. Vernlam: Islamic Propagation Center International (IPIC), 1993. P. 158.)

Abdul Hamid Siddiqui, a distinguished Islamic scholar writes (Prophethood in Islam, pp. 46-47) "Muhammad's life is an embodiment of all the attributes, virtues, and qualities found individually in all the prophets. In him the religious zeal of a believer, love for God and humanity, steadfastness and perseverance in the path of righteousness, dauntless courage in the face of hostility, resignation, and submission to the Will of the Creator, together with the qualities of a statesman and social reformer have been so beautifully blended that his personality appears to be an ideal one in all respects, with all the virtues and qualities harmoniously conceived to compliment and support each other: nothing superfluous and nothing lacking- a balance and composure which gives one the feeling of a perfect model for humanity."

Muhammad (s) is a prophet whose message is both universal and transcends the ages. His life and essence are examples of man's better nature and pious yearnings for every generation that seeks salvation.

Allah is beautiful – the Prophet (s) says the truth

The Mountain of Light
This is where Jibril(as) came to Muhammad(s)
Mount An-Nur (top) and Cave Hira (below)

5

SHARI'AH (ISLAMIC LAW) AND SUNNAH (TRADITIONS)

ثُمَّ جَعَلْنَٰكَ عَلَىٰ شَرِيعَةٍ مِّنَ ٱلْأَمْرِ فَٱتَّبِعْهَا وَلَا تَتَّبِعْ أَهْوَآءَ ٱلَّذِينَ لَا يَعْلَمُونَ ۝

"And now have We set thee [O Muhammad] on a clear road of [Our] commandment (shari'atin min al-amr); so follow it, and follow not the whims of those who know not." (45: 18)

Shari'ah refers to rules and regulations that govern the lives of Muslims, derived in principle from the Qur'an and Sunnah. It covers every aspect of daily, individual and societal living. Shari'ah is an all-embracing concept; it covers the basic principles of religion (*din*) as well as law (*fiqh*). Shari'ah is often translated as Islamic law. It covers not just religious law, but also secular aspects of law regulating human acts. The first category is called Ibadah (ritual) that deals purely with religious matters, and the second category is called *Mu'amalat* (transactions) that deals with subjects which form the substance of legal systems such as the civil and criminal law.

Shari'ah covers a great deal of ground that belongs outside of a legal system. Shari'ah tells people what they must do and must not do, but also what they should or should not do. This leads to five categories:

(1) things which are compulsory and must be done (*fard and wajib*);

(2) things which are forbidden and should never be done (*haram*);

(3) actions which are recommended but not compulsory (*mandub or mustahab*);

(4) actions which are not actullay forbidden but are disliked or disapproved (*makruh*);

(5) actions which have to be decided by conscience because there is no clear guidance (*mubaha*).

These come up in different ways at different times in this book, and they are dealt with as appropriate. *Halal* and *haram* form a separate chapter in the book. In short, Shari'ah is the code of conduct that details the manner of worship, ways of life, standards of morals, laws that prescribe and judge between right and wrong.

The basic purpose of Shari'ah is to help in lead an Islamic way of life. The underlying reason behind Shari'ah is to protect the basic human rights of each individual, including the right to life and religion, to earn and own property, to personal honor and dignity, and safeguard the rights of women, children, and minorities. The principles behind Shari'ah deter any pressure groups from imposing burdens or duties on people which go beyond the requirement of Islam.

The sources of Shari'ah are Qur'an, Sunnah, *Ijma* (consensus), *qiyas* (analytical reasoning) and Ijtihad (lit. Exertion) . The authority of the Qur'an is binding on all Muslims.

Shari'ah (Islamic Law) and Sunnah (Traditions)

Shari'ah, however, does not consist simply of the Qur'anic laws. Qur'an is not a comprehensive legal code containing all aspect of human life. However, Qur'an does provide broad outlines and framework for everything, and, of course, in some instances there are detailed guidelines. Next to Qur'an is the authority of the Prophet (s). Shari'ah is primarily divine law, exemplified by Prophet Muhammad (s), explained and elaborated by the interpretative activity of the scholars, masters of *fiqh*. Because of this last element, to the extent it is the interpretation that is the basis in a given situation, to that extent Shari'ah is man-made. However, it must be clearly understood that Qur'an is the religious source of the law, but not a law book. *Fiqh* is the detailed law derived from Qur'an and Hadith covering the innumerable problems that arise in normal everyday life. In other words, *fiqh* is the technique for working out Shari'ah law; it governs the carrying out of Commands of Allah and practices of the Prophet (s) in the minutest detail.

In addition to Qur'an and Sunnah, three other sources of Shari'ah are considered. If a question is not fully answered by consulting Qur'an and Hadith, the consensus of the great Muslims (*Ijma*) is considered by many as the third source. A fourth source is *Qiyas*, which means analogical reasoning, using past incidents with their decisions as precedents in each new situation. Similar to *Qiyas* is *Ijtihad*. It is also a logical deduction on a legal or theological question by a learned scholar or *Mujtahid*. Like a Qur'anic command, neither *Ijma* nor *Qiyas* nor *Ijtihad* is binding. There is a difference of opinion among the different *Madhhabs* and 'ulamas about the validity of accepting *Ijma, Qiyas* and *Ijtihad* as sources for Shari'ah. For example, the Hanbalis, chiefly found in the Arabian Peninsula, and most prominent in Saudi Arabia, have a suspicion about use of reason in religious matters.

Sunnah

The word Sunnah literally means "a well-trodden path." The phrase *sunnaht al-nabi* (the Sunnah of the Prophet) gradually took the place of Sunnah. A report that conveys a Sunnah is called a Hadith. The terms Sunnah and Hadith have come to be used interchangeably. In short, the life and example of the Prophet, his words or deeds, are known as the Sunnah. Muslims believe, and Qur'an confirms (33: 21), that the rules of a right pattern of behavior will be found in the practical example of the Prophet (s). The importance of Sunnah is rooted in such verses as "obey God and obey the Messenger" (4: 59). Muslims have revered the Sunnah as second to the Qur'an as a source of divine guidance and have esteemed Hadith literature as sacred scripture that provides indispensable insight into the revelations of the Qur'an. Qur'an is the sourcebook of Islamic principles and values. The Qur'an deals with broad principles and essentials of religion, often going into details. Allah gave us not only the Qur'an, but also the prophet. Allah says (16: 64):

And upon thee [too] have We bestowed from on high this divine writ for no other reason than that thou might make clear unto them all [questions of faith] on which they have come to hold divergent views, and [thus offer] guidance and grace unto people who will believe.

The Prophet himself supplied the details. He did it in two ways: by giving an explanation in words or by showing in his practice how a Qur'an's injunction was to be carried out. In other words, the Sunnah expounds the principles of the Qur'an by detailing the general, and being specific when and where necessary. To illustrate this point, it may be [pointed out that the total; number of verses in the Qur'an amounts to 6,666, of which 200 are believed to relate to legal regulations, whereas the Hadith concerning such regulations are about 4,000. The two

Shari'ah (Islamic Law) and Sunnah (Traditions)

most important religious aspects of Islam are Prayer and Zakah. When Qur'anic verses concerning these were revealed, no details were supplied. Prophet (s), by his own actions and words, supplied the details under divine guidance.

A Hadith has two parts: a text and a chain of transmitters attesting to the validity of the information. Hadith began to be put into writing about one hundred years after the death of the Prophet (s). Their composition was not completed for another hundred years. In.86 A.H., the Caliph Walid appointed Umar b. Abdul Aziz as the governor of Madinah, who gathered the scholars and entrusted them with the task of writing these down. The sources of what Prophet Muhammad (s) said and did were oral testimonies and reports handed down from one generation to another. Islamic scholars faced the formidable task of verification and compilation. The two most famous compilations are by Imam Bukhari and Muslim. Four other highly revered compilations are Abu Dawud, Tirmidhi, Ibn Majah and Al-Nasai. Shah Waliullah has classified Hadith collections in two categories. In the first class are included *Muwatta* of Imam Malik (94-179 A. H.), *Sahih* of Bukhari (194-256 A. H.) and Sahih of Muslim (d. 261 A. H.). The second class consists of *Jami* of Tirmidhi (d. 279 A. H.), *Sunan* of Abu Dawud (d. 275 A. H.) and Sunan of Nasai (d. 303 A. H.). There is also a third class according to him, but no care was taken to determine their standard.

In regard to the authenticity of Hadith collections, Al-Hafiz Ibn Hajar Al-Asqalani, in his *Bulug Al-Maram* (Riyadh, Saudi Arabia: Dar-us-Salam Publications, 1996, p. 9), puts it this way:

> Most reliable hadith is that one which has been narrated by Bukhari and Muslim. Second reliable Hadith is that one which has been narrated only by Bukhari. Third reliable Hadith is that one which has been narrated by Muslim alone. Ahadith narrated by An-Nasa'i, At-Tirmidhi, Abu Dawd, Ibn

Majah and Muwatta of Imam Malik are graded thereafter in the line of reliability, and then comes the place of Ahadith mentioned in other books. This established order of reliability should be followed where there is a contention.

A list of Hadith compilations appears in the front in Part I. And then, of course, there is Hadith Qudsi. This is the name given to a tradition which records Allah's utterances through the Prophet. No piece of Islamic literature has been so thoroughly examined to prove its reliability as hadith has been. As can be seen from the above, none of these were compiled until the third century A. H. and consequently the authenticity and complete reliability on hadith have been questioned.

The content of Hadith may be summarized under four categories:

1. Ritualistic materials: This is the source for guidance in worshipping with special attention to salat in all its essential aspects.
2. Prophet (s)'s role as a missionary. He was commanded to warn people against polytheism and call people to Islam. Hadith encompasses his missionary work to Muslims as well as to non-Muslims.
3. Muhammad (s) as a human being. Here one learns about the Prophet (s) as a husband, father and friend, and about other personal relationships.
4. Muhammad (s) as a leader. In this category, Hadith covers him as a businessman, statesman, warrior and leader of the community.

The Hadith or Sunnah of the Prophet (s) became the teacher for millions of Muslims in all walks of life throughout the ages.

This discussion can be summarized as follows: Qur'an tells us we should pray; hadith shows us how. Qur'an ordains regular prayer, but it does not specify in a single passage the number of daily prayers or the number of bows and prostrations in each;

Qur'an appoints the times of these daily prayers only in a general way. It is the Sunnah which specifies these by word and deed. Qur'an tells us to fast; hadith gives us details of Ramadan. Qur'an points to the obligations of paying zakah but does not make specifications nor does it fix the amount of money to be paid; Sunnah does. Qur'an is the Truth and the Word of Allah. Hadith is the wisdom and example of Prophet Muhammad (s). Hadith has become a standard of conduct alongside Qur'an. Hadith perpetuates Muhammad (s)'s mission so that he remains a living example for each generation of Muslims.

Islamic Schools of Law (Mahdhab)

Islamic community falls into two major groups: Sunni and Shia. The Shiite element began as a political dispute over leadership of Islam after Prophet (s)'s death but later took religious dimension. Sunnis emphasize the teachings of the Qur'an and follow the prophetic practices. Sunnis represent about 85 percent of the Muslim population.

Sunnis are organized under the four schools on jurisprudence or *Madhhabs*, all of equal standing. Together, these four schools comprise the Sunni understanding of Shari'ah. A *Madhhab* is not a "sect" or "denomination"; it represents something of a group distinction. The four schools are the Hanafite system, which goes back to the work of Abu Hanifah (d. 767 A. D.); the Malikite, which derives from Malik b. Anas (d. 795); the Shafi'ite, coming from the teaching of ash-Shafi'i (d. 819); and the Hanbalite, which was taught by Ahmad b. Hanbal (d. 855).

The Hanafi is quite prominent in most of the Middle East, except in the Arabian Peninsula. It also is predominant in Turkey, Pakistan, Bangladesh, Afghanistan, and among most Muslims in India. Developed in Iraq, the Hanafi school places considerable emphasis on the role of reason and independent legal opinion in the development of Islamic doctrine and law. It is considered the most liberal and adaptable of the four schools and has the most followers. Abu Hanifah was very strict in his acceptance of Hadith. He took meticulous care in investigating the authority of traditions and accepted only a few, the genuineness of which was established beyond doubt.

Abu Hanifah was his title name, his real name being Numan ibn Thabit. He studied under the greatest masters of hadith and jurisprudence, who welcomed him to their company because of his superior intellect and dedication to the juristic discipline. Twice in his life he was invited, then asked, and finally punished for refusing to assume the position of supreme justice, first by the Umawis and second by the Abbasis. He was known and admired for his freedom to speak authoritatively on all matters. He was known as the Great Imam.

Malik ibn Anas, founder of the school known by his name, lived in Madinah. When Khalifah Harun al-Rashid wrote asking him to come to Baghdad so that the Khalifa's son might learn from him, Imam Malik answered, "Knowledge does not travel but is traveled to." Imam Malik became an authority on traditions and jurisprudence. Of his many works, only his famous collection of hadith, al-Muwatta, already mentioned, survives. It is the first written compendium of law produced in Islam containing seventeen hundred judicial traditions of the Prophet (s). Maliki school emphasized the Hadith-Sunnah and the opinions of the Islamic scholars of Madinah. Today, it is followed pervasively in North and West Africa, Sudan and Upper Egypt.

Considered the most legally rigorous of the four schools, the Shafi'i originated from an attempt to reconcile the Maliki and Hanafi schools, but instead became a third school. He is the only Imam who belongs to the Quraishi clan of the Prophet (s). He grew up in Makkah but lived most of his life in Egypt. He visited

Shari'ah (Islamic Law) and Sunnah (Traditions)

many lands including the Hijaz where he was a pupil of Imam Malik ibn Anas, and Iraq where he studied with Muhammad al-Shaybani, the companion of Abu Hanifah. He was intimately acquainted with the Hanafi and Maliki schools of thought, but that which he himself founded was based largely on Tradition, as distinguished from the Hanafi system which was founded on the Qur'an and made very little use of Tradition. Over the Maliki system, which is also based on Traditions, it had this advantage that the Tradition made use by Imam Shafi'i was more extensive, and was collected from different centers while Imam Malik contented himself with what he found at Madinah.

For Imam Shafi'i the Sunnah assumed a primary importance. The Qur'an was to be interpreted in the light of the Sunnah. In his famous treatise al-Risalah (*Shafi'i, al--Kitab ar-Risalah*, edited by Ahmad Muhammad Shakir (Cairo: 1358 A. H.); *Al-Risala fi usul al-Fiqh*, translated by Majid Khadduri (Cambridge, Eng., 1987), composed in Cairo during his last years, he expounded for the first time in a systematic way the origins of Islamic jurisprudence. He was considered to be one of the most learned persons among this Muslim *Ummah*.

One of the many students of law on whom he had a deep impression was Ahmad ibn Hanbal (d. 241/855), who was studying in Makkah at that time. Shafi'i school remains influential in Lower Egypt, the Republic of Yemen, East Africa, and Indonesia and other parts of Southeast Asia. About the Hanbali school, Abu Bakr Fakir writes as follows in his *Manual* (p. 23):

> The least widespread of all the Sunni Schools, the Hanbali School, had its beginnings in Baghdad. The School was rejuvenated by Ibn Taymiyah and his pupil Ibn al-Qayyim al-Jawziyah and their followers during the seventh and eighth century A. H. This rejuvenation process in turn received new impetus during the twelfth century A.H. (18th century C.E.)

at the hands of the Imam Muhammad ibn Abdul Wahhab reform movement in the Nejd [Saudi Arabia].

Today it is the official School of the Kingdom of Saudi Arabia, and has followers numbering about five million in the Arabian Peninsula, Palestine, Syria, Iraq, and other countries.

As a rejuvenator of this school, Abdul Wahhab [d. 1206A.H.] was second only to Ibn Taymiyah and Ibn al-Qayyim. He advocated a return to the religious spirit of the forefathers who, for the basic principles of their religion, referred to the Qur'an and the authentic Sunnah of the Prophet ... he opposed all religious deviations such as the sanctification of domed buildings, the worship of tombs, the performances of the drummers, flute players and dervish dancers.

Besides the above-mentioned scholars there were many others who worked in the field of Shari'ah and made significant contributions. But the above-named personalities made the most mark. These scholars did their best to teach (they were, in fact, teachers and researchers) the people their religion and offer them proper guidance, but they entreated the people from following them blindly because they knew they were not perfect. Unfortunately, however, as it developed, every group thought it sufficient just to follow what was found in their school of thought and to strictly adhere to it. One does not have to belong to any one of these schools. Islamic jurisprudence has become such a technical process that many people prefer not to be identified with any one and simply call themselves Muslims or Sunni Muslims.

The four *Madhhabs* (or Schools) may be shown as follows:

Shari'ah (Islamic Law) and Sunnah (Traditions)

The Masters of Fiqh

Malik b. Anas (713-795
Maliki school

Abu-Hanifah (699-767)
Hanifi school

al-Shafi'I (767-820) Shafi'i school
Rigorous care to verify
Hadiths, especially of
Prophet's Sunnah; use of analogy

al-Shaybani (d. 805)

Ibn-Hanbal (780-855)
Hanbali school Emphasis upon using carefully chosen hadiths; preference for a "weak hadith over a strong analogy"

To understand the process of Shari'ah, the following chart may be helpful:

Shari'ah Process

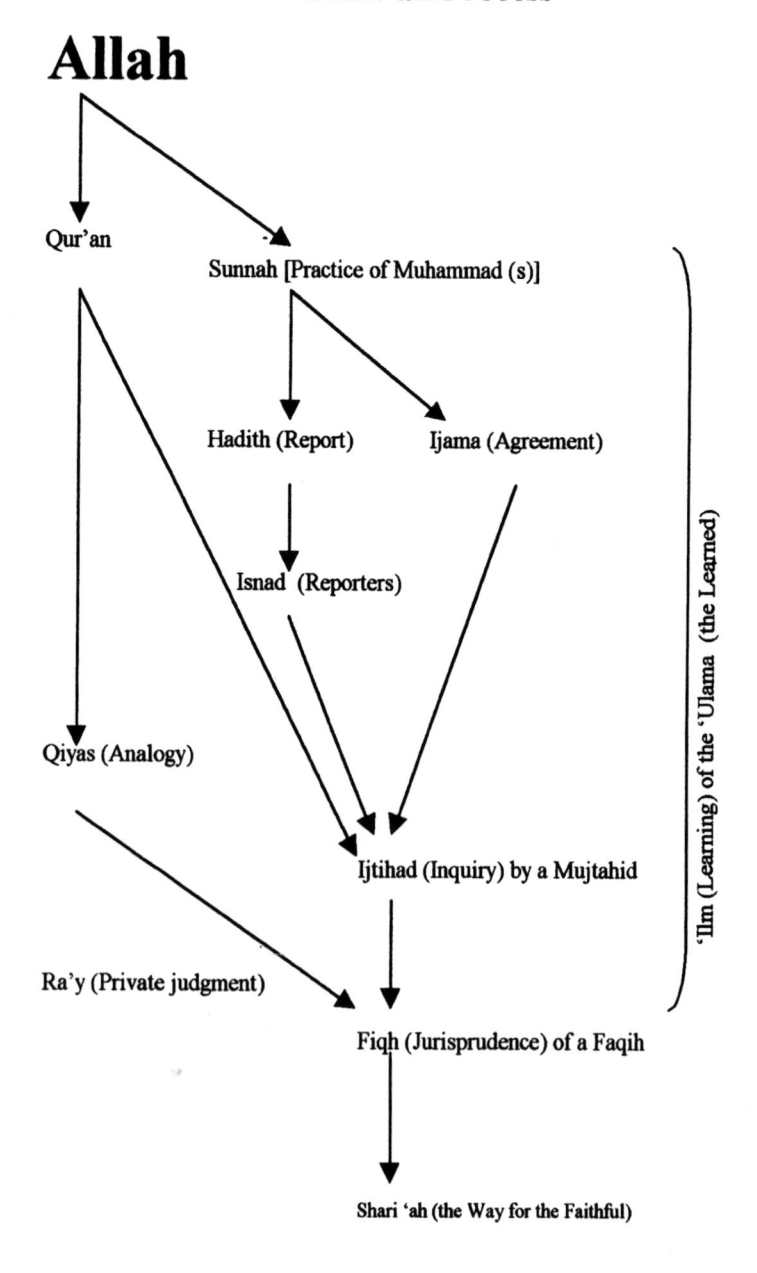

```
Allah
 │
 ├──────────────► Qur'an
 │
 └──────────────► Sunnah [Practice of Muhammad (s)]
                    │
                    ├──► Hadith (Report)
                    │       │
                    │       └──► Isnad (Reporters)
                    │
                    └──► Ijama (Agreement)
```

- Qur'an → Qiyas (Analogy)
- Qiyas (Analogy) → Ijtihad (Inquiry) by a Mujtahid
- Ra'y (Private judgment) → Ijtihad (Inquiry) by a Mujtahid
- Hadith / Isnad / Ijama → Ijtihad (Inquiry) by a Mujtahid
- Ijtihad → Fiqh (Jurisprudence) of a Faqih
- Fiqh → Shari'ah (the Way for the Faithful)

'Ilm (Learning) of the 'Ulama (the Learned)

Sharia : Sunnah (Traditions) and Islamic Law

Example: Muhammad (s) used a toothpick after meals (Sunnah); there is a report to that effect (hadith) transmitted through a chain of reporters (isnad); the mujtahid studies this report (ijtihad) and decides that the use is recommended not only for the Prophet but for the ordinary believer (*fiqh*); it is therefore to be included in the Shariah, the established way of life. (Adapted from Hodgson, Marshall A., *Venture of Islam*, p. 338.

For more biographical information about the Imams, see Appendix.

Shahādah

Declaration of faith

Congregational Prayer at Makkah

Kaaba is the focal point of Islamic Prayer worldwide. According to the Qur'an, it was first built by Ibrahim (as) and his son Ismail(as) as a place for worship of the One God.

During Ramadan, the month of fasting, prayers called *Tarawih* are performed each evening. Towards the end of the month as many as three million worshippers attend these prayers in Makkah alone. This exceeds even the numbers attending the Hajj (the annual pilgrimage).

6

IMAN (FAITH)

أَلَمْ تَرَ كَيْفَ ضَرَبَ ٱللَّهُ مَثَلًا كَلِمَةً طَيِّبَةً كَشَجَرَةٍ طَيِّبَةٍ أَصْلُهَا ثَابِتٌ وَفَرْعُهَا فِى ٱلسَّمَآءِ ﴿٢٤﴾

Don't you see how Allah coins a similitude: Kalimah Tayyibah is like a goodly tree, its roots set firm, its branches reaching into heaven (14: 24).

Iman is the fountainhead of all religious practices. This is an Arabic term for "belief" or "faith." It appears 45 times in the Qur'an. Belief consists of accepting the principles, rules and creed of Islam. If belief is strong, our faith in Allah remains strong. If belief is weak, faith in Allah becomes weak and shaky.

Generally speaking, Islam may be divided into two broad categories: the theoretical or its articles of faith, and the practical that includes all that a Muslim is required to do. In the Qur'an, these two broad divisions are referred to as *Iman* (faith or belief) and *'Amal* (deed or action). The Qur'an establishes a close connection between faith and action: true Iman manifests itself in the right conduct. Qur'an requires the believers to conduct themselves in certain ways. For example, the believers are commanded to obey Allah, the Prophet (4: 59; 8: 1, 20, 24 and

47: 33), perform ritual prayer (2: 43, 83, 110, 177, 239; 4: 77, 103, etc.), spend their wealth in the way of Allah (2: 110, 177, 195, 215, etc.), fight in the way of Allah (4: 76), refrain from making transactions involving interest (2: 275, 276, 278; 3: 130), etc. The relation of faith with deeds must be constantly borne in mind in order to understand the true meaning of Islam.

Qur'an and the traditions of Muhammad (s) define the required measures and establish standards which build up a meaningful faith. It is Iman that distinguishes a Muslim from a non-Muslim. As a summary statement, Iman represents the following: belief in Allah (2: 285; 4: 136); belief in the angels (2: 285); belief in His books (2: 285; 4: 136); belief in prophets (2: 285; 4: 136, 150-151); belief in the Day of Judgment (4: 136), and belief in the Divine Decree of good and evil (Qadr).

Belief in Allah

To believe in Allah is to believe in His Existence, His Oneness in His Attributes, His deserving to be worshipped and supplicated. Belief in Allah is the basic tenet of Islam and, for that matter, of all religions worth the name. Faith or Iman, however, is not synonymous with what in common parlance one understands by the word belief. It is belief impregnated with the feelings of awe and reverence, coupled with the attitude of absolute submission and inviolable surrender, and inestimable sense of value attached to the object of the belief.

Belief in the Angels

His angels are beings created from light. In the Qur'an, angels are spoken of as "messengers flying on wings" (35: 1) and are ordained to obey Allah's words. Qur'an teaches the existence

Iman (Faith)

of angels. It was the angel Jibril who addressed Muhammad (s) on the Night of Power and Glory and on other occasions, but Jibril is only one of the heavenly court of angels. While angels are superhuman, they are creatures whose function, like that of other creatures, is to serve and praise the One God. They also serve such functions as recording human actions, witnessing for or against men at Judgment Day and guarding the gates of hell. There are a host of angels in Allah's kingdom. The prominent ones are Jibril, who brought the revelation from Allah to Prophet Muhammad (s); Israil, called the angel of death; Israfil, who will blow the trumpet at the time of the end of the world.

In addition to angels, according to the Qur'an, there are also jinn. The jinn and angels are two different classes of beings. The jinn are created from fire, and some jinn are believers and some are infidels. The latter are called shaytan, and their leader is called "the Shaytan," Allah's adversary and the tempter of humankind. Muslim teaching is that until the last day, he has authority over all the souls, which he can seduce. For a detailed description of jinn, see Muhammad Asad, *The Message of the Qur'an*, Appendix II.

Belief in His Books

According to the Qur'an, Muslims believe in all the revealed books. They are Tawrat (Torah) of Musa (Moses), Zabur (Psalms) of Dawud (David), Injil (Gospel) of Isa (Jesus) and, of course, Qur'an is the final and the best of them.

Belief in the Prophets

Muslims believe in all the prophets beginning with Adam (as), the last of them being Muhammad (s), the seal of the prophets. The correctness of belief includes the testimony that Muhammad (s) is the Messenger of Allah. There is no Islam without the belief in and obedience to the Messenger of Allah. (For a list of the prophets in the Qur'an, see Appendix.)

Belief in the Day of Judgment

Muslims believe in the Last day, the day of resurrection after death for the reckoning of the people according to their deeds and their appropriate compensation, that is, reward or punishment.

Qadr

Qadr means measure. Allah has measured out everything in His creation and has given it laws by which to govern. Allah is recognized by the Qur'an as the first and ultimate cause of all things. This, however, does not mean that He is Creator of the deeds of man. Allah has given human beings free will. This means that they can choose right or wrong, but they are responsible for their choice.

Kalimah Tayyibah and Shahadah

A man is said to have believed when he simply declares his faith in the Unity of Allah and the Prophethood of Muhammad (s). This is known as *Shahadah* (witness). The essence of Islam is briefly summed up in Shahadah: *La ilaha illa-Allah*, i.e., there is no god but Allah. The utterance of Shahadah is in fact just a start, as will be explained later.

Shahadah is the first and main article of faith. It affirms the acceptance of the absolute unity of God (*Tawhid*). *Tawhid* is

Iman (Faith)

discussed in detail in the next chapter. The complete phrase for Shahadah is:

$$\text{لَا إِلٰهَ إِلَّا الله مُحَمَّدٌ رَّسُولُ الله}$$

La ilaha illa-Allah Muhammad-ur-Rasulullah

There is no god but Allah and Muhammad is Allah's Messenger.

It is composed of two passages occurring in Qur'an, 47: 19 and 48: 29. No statement in Islam is more fundamental than this declaration. It links God, the Prophet and the believers. It has already been mentioned that men become Muslim when this phrase is uttered. But it is not a mere formality; the mere utterance of this phrase does not necessarily make one a Muslim. Understanding it, believing in it, and acting on it are the prerequisites. As a matter of fact, six conditions must be observed before it can effectively make one a Muslim. These are:
(1) it must be repeated aloud;
(2) it must be perfectly understood;
(3) it must be believed in heart;
(4) it must be professed until death;
(5) it must be recited correctly;
(6) it must be professed and declared without hesitation.

This declaration of faith makes one conscious of the Unity and Sovereignty of Allah and man's relationship to Him. It frees man from servitude to other human beings and to his own desires, makes him conscious of the presence of the Almighty God and of his responsibilities towards Him. This Kalimah (word) resounds in every Muslim town five times a day in the call to prayer. It is whispered into the ear of the newborn and is the farewell to the dying. Its continuous litany-like repetition is an essential part in dhikr. This Kalimah is known as Kalimah

Tayyibah. When the words "I testify" are added to it, along with a few more words, it becomes Kalimah Ash-Shahadah:

أَشْهَدُ أَن لاَ اله إلا الله وَحْدَهُ لاَ شَرِيكَ لَهُ واشــــهدُ أَن مُحَمَّــداً عَبْــدُه وَرَسُولُه

Ash hadu al la ilaha illa-Allahu wahdahu la sharikalahu wa ash hadu anna Muhammadan 'abduhu wa rasululu.

I testify that there is no god but Allah and He is one and has no partner and I also testify that Muhammad is His servant and messenger.

There are other invocations as well which express important parts of a Muslim's belief:

Al-Iman al-Mujmal

آمَنْتُ بِاللهِ كَمَا هُوَ بِأَسْمَائِه وصِفَاتِه وقَبِلْتُ جَمِيعَ أَحْكَامِه

Amantu billahi kama huwa biasma ihi wa sifatihi wa qabiltu jamia' ahkamihi.
I believe in Allah (as He is) with all His names and attributes and I accept all His Commands.
There are 99 attributes and names of Allah (for a complete list see Appendix). A Muslim believes in all His attributes.

Al-Iman al-Muffassal

آمَنْتُ بِاللهِ وَمَلَائِكَتِه وَكُتُبِه وَرُسُولِه وَالْيَوْمِ الأخر وَالْقَدَرُ خَيْره وشَره مِنَ اللهِ تَعَالَى وَالْبَعْثُ بَعْدَ الْمَوْتِ

Iman (Faith)

Amantu billahi wa malaikatihi wa kutubihi wa rusulihi wal yawmil akhiri wal qadri Khairihi wa Sharrihi minal lahi ta'ala wal bathi b'adal mawt.

I believe in Allah, in His angels, in His books, in His messengers, in the last day and in the fact that everything good or bad is decided by Allah, the Almighty, and in the life after death.

Kalimah Tamjid

سُبْحَانَ اللهِ وَ الْحَمْدُ للهِ وَ لاَ اِلٰهَ اِلاَّ اللهُ وَاللهُ اَكْبَرُ وَلاَ حَوْلَ
وَلاَ قُوَّةَ اِلاَّ بِاللهِ الْعَلِيُّ الْعَظِيْمُ

Subhan-Allahi wal-hamdullillahi wa la-ilaha illa-Allahu wa Allahu Akbar wa la hawla wa la quwwata illa billahil 'aliyil 'Azim.

All glory and praise be to Allah; there is no god except Allah; Allah is Great; there is no power and no strength except in Allah, the Most Exalted, the Most Sublime.

This Kalimah tells more about Allah and His quality of being All-Powerful.

Raddil Kufr

اَللّٰهُمَّ اِنِّيْ اَعُوْذُ بِكَ مِنْ اَنْ اُشْرِكَ بِكَ شَيْئاً وَّ اَنَا اَعْلَمُ وَ اَسْتَغْفِرُكَ لِمَا لاَ اَعْلَمُ
اِنَّكَ اَنْتَ عَلاَّمُ الْغُيُوْبِ تُبْتُ عَنه وتَبَرَّأْتُ عَنْ كُلِّ دِيْنٍ سِوى دِيْنِ الْاِسْلاَمِ
الْاِسْلاَمِ وَاَسْلَمْتُ وَاَقُوْلُ لاَ اِلٰهَ اِلاَّ اللهُ مُحَمَّدٌ رَسُوْلُ اللهِ

Allahumma inni 'awudhubika min an ushrika bika shaiyan wa ana 'alamu wastaghfiruka lima la 'alamu innaka anta 'allamul ghuyubi tubtu 'anhu wa tabarratu 'an kulli dinin siwa dinil islami wa aslamtu wa aqulu la ilaha illa-Allahu Muhammadur rasulullah.

O Allah, surely I do seek refuge in you from making any parnter with you knowingly, I beg your forgiveness for the sins which I am not aware of; surely, you are the knower of all secrets. I repent for all the sins and make myself proof against all religions except Islam and I accepted it and I declare that there is no god but Allah. Muhammad is the messenger of Allah.

Conclusion

Qur'an frequently mentions iman and good actions together, saying that the two are necessary for salvation. There is a hadith which says that God does not accept belief if it is not expressed in deed and does not accept any deed if it does not conform to a belief. Islam makes a dinstinction between a person who submits to God's guidance by obeying His laws (a muslim) and one who has the deep inner certainty of faith (a mu'min: one who possesses iman), and indeed the difference is very significant. A *muslim* (submitter) may obey God's laws without real depth of faith, while a *mu'min* both possesses this faith and acts on it. Allah says in Qur'an: the Bedouin say, "We have attained to faith." Say [unto them, O Muhammad]: "You have not [yet] attained to faith, you should [rather] say, 'We have [outwardly] surrendered'—for [true] faith has not yet entered your hearts" (49: 14). Iman is thus both believing and practicing. The declaration of faith in the messengership of Muhammad (s) obliges us to follow the teaching and example of the Prophet (s) in all spheres of life.

According to Allama Yusuf Ali (*The Holy Qur'an*, p. 978, footnote 2870), there are seven jewels of our faith: (1) humility

Iman (Faith)

(2) avoidance of vanity, (3) charity, (4) sex purity, (5) fidelity to trusts, (6) fidelity to covenants, and (7) an earnest desire to get closer to Allah.

Iman is an act of personal faith. True faith means putting one's trust in Allah, for He says (65: 3): And everyone who places his trust in Allah, He [alone] is enough." The inner structure of the concept of Iman contains Taqwa (fear of Allah). Allah says (8: 2): "For believers are those who, when Allah is mentioned, felt a tremor in their hearts, and when they hear His revelations rehearsed, find their faith strengthened, and put [all] their trust in their Lord."

In the Qur'an, the words "belief" and "fear" are sometimes juxtaposed (cf. 13: 35). The word Iman signifies the conviction of the heart. The relationship between iman and amal is very well illustrated in the prayer for the deceased (for details about this prayer, see Chapter 10, Section 6):

> Those of us whom you [Allah] would keep alive, keep them alive on Islam; and those of us whom you would cause to die, cause them to die on iman.

This distinction or relationship mentioned above makes it clear that iman is the inner state of mind in which one should be at the time of death and, of course, at any given moment of one's life.

The Kaaba Door

7

TAWHID, SHIRK AND KUFR
(UNITY OF GOD, ATTRIBUTING PARTNERS AND DISBELIEF IN ALLAH)

قُلْ هُوَ ٱللَّهُ أَحَدٌ ۝ ٱللَّهُ ٱلصَّمَدُ ۝ لَمْ يَلِدْ وَلَمْ يُولَدْ ۝ وَلَمْ يَكُن لَّهُۥ كُفُوًا أَحَدٌۢ ۝

Say: He, Allah, is One, the Ultimate Source, He does not give birth, nor was He born [of anyone] and there is nothing comparable to Him (Surah 112).

Tawhid is the belief in the Oneness of Allah. The best known expression of it is that contained in the declaration *la ilaha illa-Allah* (there is no god but Allah). These words convey the significance that there is nothing that deserves to be worshipped except Allah. It is this confession (known as *Shahadah*) which, when combined with the confession of the prophethood of Muhammad (s)—Muhammadur Rasulullah—admits a man into the fold of Islam.

Belief in *tawhid* (the Oneness of Allah) is the first principle of faith in Islam. All the other principles of Islam rest on it. All these are fully dealt with in the Qur'an. Tawhid is the central concept around which all Qur'anic teachings revolve. The Oneness of Allah implies that He is alone and without partners.

This concept emphasizes a rigorous monotheism, stating Allah to be a unique absolute reality. It is best expressed in the Qur'anic chapter cited at the beginning of this chapter and is said to have been revealed in response to questions asked of Muhammad (s) concerning the nature of God. The unity of God is emphasized repeatedly in the Qur'an and echoed in other verses such as the following (2: 163) :

And your God is One God. There is no God but Him, The most Gracious, the most Merciful.

There is only one God, complete, eternal, and undivided. The underlying essence of life is eternal unity rather than the apparent separateness of things in the physical world. Allah is not only the Deity worthy of worship and deserving prayer for seeking help, a guidance and refuge; He is also the Master, Ruler and Sovereign. Belief in the sovereignty of Allah is an intrinsic and inseparable part of *Tawhid*.

God stands alone and supreme. He existed before any other being or thing, is self-subsistent, omniscient and omnipotent. In denying plurality, the Qur'an rejects all forms of idolatry, disallows any association of other divinities with God, and specifically denies all other definitions of God that might compromise unity such as the Christian dogma of the Trinity where "God is the third of the three."

Tawhid produces in a person the conviction that there is no other way to achieve success and salvation except through purity of soul and righteousness of conduct. Such a person has a perfect faith in Allah Who is above all need, related to no one, is absolutely Just, and no one has any hand or influence in the exercise of His Divine powers. After acquiring this belief, he does not regard anything in this world as foreign or strange to him. He looks upon everything in the universe as belonging to the same Lord to Whom he himself belongs. The whole of the cosmos, nature as well as humanity, is created and sustained by

God. The notion of God's sovereignty is expressed in the well-known "Verse of the Throne" mentioned later in the book.

It has been estimated that over 90 percent of Muslim theology deals with the implications of Unity. God, while One, is called by 99 names in the Qur'an. Each one of these is considered attributes of the One Being. Allah is the name of the God which encompasses all the attributes. Believing in the Oneness of Allah and His atrributes is Tawhid.

Abu Ameenah Bilal Philips categorizes Tawhid into three (*The Fundamentals of Tawhid (Islamic Monotheism)*, 1994, p. 2):
1. the Unity of His Lordship or Dominion and His Actions (*Tawhid ar-Rububiyah*);
2. the Unity of Allah's Names and Attributes (*Tawhid al-Asma was Sifat*);
3. the Unity of Allah's Worship (*Tawhid al-'Ibadah*).

The foundations of these categorizations, according to the author cited above, are all implied in the Qur'an, in the explanatory statements of the Prophert (s) and his companions).

Tawhid al-Rububiyah

This is based on the concept that Allah alone caused all things to exist. No one can do that which God has done or that God may do. He sustains and maintains all creation without any need from these. He is Rabbul Alamin, the Lord of all creation or of all forms of life. The basis for the Rububiyah concept is inherent in Qur'anic verses. First, of course, is Surah al-Fatihah where there is "Rabbul Alamin." Then there are others such as the following:

> Allah is the creator of all things, and He alone has the power to determine the fate of all things (39: 62).
> It is Allah who has created you and all your handiwork! (37: 96)

Allah's Oneness is also asserted in His actions as the Qur'anic verses below indicate (10: 31):

> Say: "Who is it that provides you with sustenance out of heaven and earth, or who is it that has full power over [your] hearing and sight? And who is it that brings forth the living out of that which is dead, and brings forth the dead out of that which is alive? And who is it that governs all that exists?"
> And they will [surely] answer: "[It is] God."
> Say, then: "Will you not, then, become [fully] conscious of Him—(32) seeing that He is God, your Sustainer, the Ultimate Truth? . . ."

This confirms what has already been said, i. e., Allah caused all things to exist. There are many other verses on this subject.

Tawhid al-Asma wa as-Sifat

It means affirmation of Oneness of Allah's self and His names and Attributes. His Oneness in atttributes implies that no other being possesses one or more of the Divine attributes of perfection. The quality of His Being is beyond the range of human comprehension or imagination. His names and attributes cannot be explained away. For example, the attributes of hearing and seeing ("He alone is all-hearing, all-seeing" (42: 11)) are also among human attributes but they cannot reach the perfection of Allah's level. Man cannot be given the attributes of Allah. In doing so, one will only set up rivals who share Allah's unique attributes. Allah cannot be given new names or attributes.

Tawhid al-'Ibadah

The other two categories of *Tawhid* mentioned above must be accompanied by this one in order for *Tawhid* to be complete. All worship, in whatever form, must be directed to Allah alone because He is the only One Who deserves to be worshipped, and it is He alone who can grant benefit to the worshipper.

In *Surah al-Ikhlas* mentioned at the beginning of this section, absolute Unity of the Divine Being is proclaimed. God is One and unique in every way without beginning or end. Everything existing or conceivable goes back to Him as its source and is therefore dependent on Him for it, beginning as well as for its continued existence.

All the Prophets of Allah called people towards the fundamental theme of Islam, i.e., *Tawhid*, which is Monotheism. In *Surah al-A'raf*, the seventh chapter of Qur'an, there is a magnificent account of the messages of five prophets, namely Nuh (Noah), Hud, Salih, Shuaib, and Musa (Moses). The call of each of them consists of the same single statement: "O my people! Worship Allah. You have no other God but Him" (7: 85).

Tawhid is the source of all that is good, graceful and benevolent in human life. It brings a high level of discipline in the believer's heart. The very thought that God is with us can be comforting and can create confidence in us. In disobedience and ignorance, people have taken the sun, moon, trees, stones, fire, kings, prophets, priests, saints and other men to be gods. Worshipping any of these is the most atrocious act.

Shirk (Polytheism)

Shirk means partnership, sharing or associating. In Islam it means assigning partners to Allah in whatever form it may take.

Shirk implies that the source of power, harm and blessings comes from another besides Allah. A divided allegiance denies the perfect divine Oneness. The avoidance of *Shirk* is so vital that the Qur'an mentions the word in seventy-five verses. The opposite of *Shirk* is *Tawhid*, which is the rejection of all sorts of association with Allah. It is a tremendous sin, as Qur'an says (4: 48): "Allah forgiveth not that partners should be set up with Him; but He forgiveth anything else, to whom He pleaseth; to set up partners with Allah is to devise a sin most heinous indeed."

According to the Qur'an, man is Allah's vice-regent (*Khalifah*) on earth (2: 30), and this shows that he is in a position of controlling the rest of the earthly creation, as is evident from the following verse: "And He has made subservient to you whatsoever is in the heavens and whatsoever is in the earth, all from Himself; surely there are signs in this for a people who reflect" (45: 13; also see 30: 22).

Obviously, if man was created to rule the world and is endowed to turn everything to his use, he simply degrades himself by taking other things for gods, by bowing before the very things which he has been created to conquer and rule. Hence, *Shirk* is the most heinous of all sins. In accordance with Qur'anic verse (31: 13), *Shirk* is tremendous injustice or wrongdoing: "False worship is indeed the highest wrong-doing." It is definitely a great downfall, as Qur'an says (22: 31): "Being true in faith to Allah. And never assigning partners to Him: if anyone assigns partner to Allah, he is as if he had fallen from heaven and been snatched up by birds, or the wind had swooped (like a bird on its prey) and thrown him into a far-distant place."

The various forms of *Shirk* are summed up in the following verse (3: 64): "That we worship none but Allah; that we associate no partners with Him; and that we do not take human beings for our lords beside Allah."

Tawhid, Shirk and Kufr

Of all the different forms of *Shirk*, idolatry is cited in Qur'an more often than all the others. Idolatry is the most heinous form of *Shirk* and is condemned because it is taken for granted that an idol can cause benefit or do harm. Allah says (34: 22):

> Say: Call upon those [beings] whom you imagine [to be endowed with divine powers] beside God: they have not an atom's weight of power either in the heavens or on earth, nor have they any share in [governing] either, nor does He [choose] any helper from among them.

Allah makes it clear that false gods do not enjoy any power. To suppose that they have some share or that they can give some help to Allah, even though Allah is Supreme, is both false and blasphemous. Obviously, the false gods cannot hurt or benefit anyone.

Shirk implies not only worshipping other gods, but also following one's own desires or anything less than guidance of Allah. According to Imam Fakhr al-Din al-Razi, as quoted in *The Qur'an and al-Shirk* (Polytheism) By Muhammad Ibrahim H. I. Surty (2nd rev. ed., 1990, p. 77), "Shirk is not only the worship of idols but also following the lusts of your carnal self, it is to choose for this world or the Hereafter anything save Allah Almighty." Thus their own urges and fancies become their gods, and they are like slaves to their wishes and desires. Of these, Allah has said:

> Hast thou ever considered [the kind of man] who makes his own desires his deity? Couldst thou, then, [O Prophet,] be held responsible for him? Or dost thou think that most of them listen [to thy message] and use their reason? Nay, they are but like cattle—nay, they are even less conscious of the right way! (25: 43-44). ... And obey not him whose heart we have made heedless of our remembrance, who follows his own desires and lusts, and whose case has gone beyond all bounds (18: 28).

It is obvious from the above that Shirk is the underlying cause of all ill motives that lead to error and misguidance.

It is terrifying to think of the consequences of Shirk, as the following verse reveals (3: 151):

> Soon shall We cast terror into the hearts of the Unbelievers, for that they joined partners with Allah, for which He had sent no authority: their abode will be the fire: and evil is the home of wrongdoers!

Naturally, Paradise will be forbidden to those who commit Shirk, as confirmed in Qur'an: "Whoever joins other gods with Allah, Allah will forbid him the Garden, and the Fire will be his abode." (5: 72). The real prayer is to Allah, and any prayer to anybody or anything else is unacceptable (13: 14):

> To Him is due the true prayer. Any others that they call upon besides Him hear them no more than if they were to stretch forth their hands for water to reach their mouths. But it reaches them not ...

According to Muhammed bin Sulaiman al-Tamimi in *Religious fundamentals that every Muslim should know about* (Jeddah, Darussalam, 1996, pp. 21-25), there are three types of Shirk (polytheism):

1. *Ash-Shirk Al-Akbar* (Major Polytheism).

The major polytheism is to devote any form of worship to anyone or anything other than Allah. This includes belief in the plurality of gods already discussed. This is an unforgivable sin.

2. *Ash-Shirk Al-Asghar* (Minor Polytheism).

The minor polytheism Riyaa (show-off). Riyaa is the practice of performing any of the various forms of worship in order to be seen and praised by people. This sin destroys all the benefits that lie in righteous deeds and calls for a serious punishment.

3. *Ash-Shirk Al-Khafi* (Invisible Polytheism)

The invisible polytheism was explained by the Prophet (s) this way: "The invisible polytheism in this Ummah is more hidden than the track of a black ant on a black stone in a dark night" This type of *Shirk* implies being inwardly dissatisfied with the inevitable condition that has been ordained by Allah.

Kufr

Kufr begins when one ignores or rejects the way laid down by Allah and conducts his life some other way. Just as *Iman* is the acceptance of self-evident truths and commitments to them, *Kufr* is the rejection of the same truths and refusal to abide by them. *Kufr* is basically disbelief in the articles of Faith in Islam. According to the Appendix "*Al-Kufr*: Disbelief and its Manifestations" in *the Qur'an Interpretations of the meanings of the Noble Qur'an in the English language* by Muhammad Taqi-ud-Din al Hilali and Muhammad Muhsin Khan (pp, 1021-1022), there are two aspects of Kufr. Qur'an devotes a considerable number of verses describing the state of mind of a *Kafir* (disbeliever, who has committed a *Kufr*, e. g., "your hearts were hardened: they became like a rock and even worse in hardness (2: 74); ... their hearts grow hard" (5: 13). In contrast, "those who believe, and whose hearts find satisfaction in remembrance of Allah: for without doubt in the remembrance of Allah do hearts find satisfaction" (13: 28).

While *Kufr* is disbelief, it is also thanklessness. Qur'an emphasizes strongly that Almighty God is a God of mercy, grace and goodness. Man owes everything, his existence, sustenance, to Allah. A *Kafir* is one who, having received Allah's benevolence, shows no sign of gratitude but, on the contrary, even acts rebelliously against his Benefactor. *Kufr* is the exact opposite of humbleness and clashes directly with taqwa (fear of Allah) which is the central element of Islam in comprehending its concept. There are different categories of Kufr, as described below:

1. The Major Disbelief (Al-Kufr-al-Akbar*)*

This aspect excludes one completely from the fold of Islam. In other words, he is a *Kafir*. There are five types of this major disblief: (a) *Kufr-al-Takdhib* (Kafir of denial). This implies disbelieving the divine truth or denying any articles of faith. (b) *Kufr-al-Iba wat-takabbur ma'at-Tasdiq* (Kufr of arrogance). This implies rejection and pride to submit to Allah's Commandments after conviction of their truth. (c) *Kufr ash-Shak wa Az-Zan* (*Kufr* of doubt). This implies doubting or lacking of conviction in the articles of Faith. (d) Kufr-al-I'rad (Kufr of disregard). This implies turning away from the truth knowingly or deviating from the obvious signs which Allah has revealed. (e) *Kufr an-Nifaq* (*Kufr* of hypocrisy). This implies hypocritical disbelief. Hypocrisy in deeds is of three types, as the Prophert (s) said: "The signs of a hypocrite are three: when he speaks, he tells a lie; when he promises, he breaks it; and when he is entrusted, he proves to be dishonest."

2. The Minor Disbelief (Al-Kufr al-Ashghar*)*

This aspect of disbelief does not exclude one from the fold of Islam. It is also termed *Kufr al-Ni'mah*. This implies disblief manifesting itself in ungratefulness for Allah's Blessings of Favors.

Tawhid, Shirk and Kufr

The contrast between *Iman* and *Kufr* has been clearly described in Qur'an: "If any do fail to judge by what Allah has revealed, they are all unbelievers" (5: 44). Among the nullifiers of Belief is displeasure with Allah's legislation. To dislike the order which is revealed, Allah has said (47:8): "But those who reject (Allah), for them is destruction." According to Imam An-Nawawi (*Book of Eman*, by Naim Ya-Sin, 1997, pp. 246-7) those who die and meet Allah as disbelievers will never enter paradise even if they did good deeds.

Calligraphic design of Qur'anic Verse 55:13 by Sadiqayn, Dhaka, Bangladesh

Prophet(s)'s Mosque *(above)*

and his tomb *(right)*

8

JIHAD

$$\text{وَجَٰهِدُوا۟ فِى ٱللَّهِ حَقَّ جِهَادِهِۦ}$$

And strive in His cause as ye ought to strive ... (22: 78)

Jihad, "to strive, to struggle" in the way of Allah, is sometimes referred to as the sixth pillar of Islam. The concept of jihad as it is found in the Qur'an and in the writings of the Sunni jurists is defined generally as already noted, as effort or striving in the path of God. The word "jihad" and its derivations with this meaning, appears thirty-six times in the Qur'an. A familiar point is that in the Qur'an the fundamental meaning of jihad is not war but internal effort or striving "in the path of God" (e.g., Qur'an 22:78). In one tradition from the hadith, the Prophet Muhammed(sm) tells his followers on return from battle, they have now returned from the "lesser jihad" (battle) and must turn to the "greater jihad", (the inner struggle for true submission to God). The struggle of the individual man or woman of faith against his or her own ego and the soul towards righteousness and obedience to Allah is jihad.

Jihad, as already alluded to, may be divided into two broad categories: Jihad al-Akbar (Greater jihad) and Jihad al-Asghar (Lesser jihad)

The spiritual struggle of the soul is the former and fighting external forces is the latter. In its most outward sense, jihad came to mean the defense of Dar al-Islam; that is, the Islamic world from invasion and intrusion by non-Islamic forces. When the Qur'an provides a direct injunction to Muslims to fight, the word used is not jihad but qital ("fighting"), or another word built from the same root (e.g., Qur'an 2:190: "Fight [*qatilu*] in the cause of Allah."

Jihad al-Akbar (Greater Jihad)

The Greater jihad is the struggle against oneself, *jihad al-nafs*. Jihad is connected with prayers, Alms-tax (zakah), Fasting and Hajj, and of course Faith (Iman). All five are ordained by Allah for the believers. The daily prayers when performed with regularity and with due concentration according to Sharia, are never ending jihad against the unending battle of forgetfulness, laziness and dissipation. For the devoted to perform ablution (often with cold water) and go out in the chilly night to the mosque, on a wintry night or early morning giving up sleep is indeed a heroic task. Zakah is a form of Jihad because it is not easy to part with one's hard-earned wealth and it is nonetheless fighting with greed. In addition, the fast in Ramadan requires internal and external (physical) discipline to stay away from temptations and passions. Hajj itself is the most excellent of Jihad because of sacrifice (financial and animal), suffering, endurance in hardship, constant vigil, wakefulness and supplication. From the religious point of view, all of the pillars of Islam are indeed inner, and in some instances outer, Jihads. Implicit in all of these are also the struggle against the devil, jihad *didd al-Shaytan*.

According to Imam Ghazzali, the real jihad is the warfare against the passions. This particular endeavor is a personal struggle for the attainment of true Islam, i.e., submission and obedience to Allah. In a broad sense, any struggle done in day to day life to please God can be considered jihad.

Another notion of Jihad is the struggle for the good of the Muslim society and against corruption and deterioration. This implies the realization of Islamic values for which education is critical. Educational Jihad, Jihad *al-tarbiyah*, is related to spreading of Islamic values which is in fact Jihad *al-da'wa* or Jihad for spreading Islam. This can go too far when radical Islamic groups call for the use of violence to spread their "brand of Islam" or to defeat established governments.

Jihad al-Asghar (Lesser Jihad)

The idea of Jihad in a military context is to wage war in the name of Allah against those who perpetrate oppression as enemies of Islam. Allah says:

(2:216) Fighting is ordained for you, even though it be hateful to you; but it may well be that you hate a thing while it is good for you, and it may well be that you love a thing the while it is bad for you: and God knows, whereas you do not know.

What makes external Jihad a binding institution in Islam is the fact that it is a communal and not an individual obligation. In other words, if a section of the Muslims offer themselves for participating in Jihad, the whole community is absolved of its responsibility. But if none come forward, everyone is held guilty. In order to prevent the greater evil, Allah has commanded us to sacrifice our lives and property for His pleasure. Yet, He has forbidden unnecessary bloodshed. Women, children, the crippled, the old, and the sick and the wounded, should under no circumstances be harmed. His order is to fight only those who rise to fight. Allah tells us not to cause unnecessary destruction of even the enemies' lands.

Warfare in the name of Allah is sacred. Anyone killed in the battlefield is a martyr (shahid), and his reward is Paradise (3:157-158,172;47:4). War is not the objective of Islam. It is only the last resort and is used under the most extraordinary circumstances when all other measures fail. Qur'an declares: "God loveth not aggressors." Even in the propagation of Islam a Muslim is not only forbidden to use force but is also commanded to use the most peaceful means. Allah says to Muhammad (s):

(16:125) Invite (all) to the Way Of thy Lord with wisdom and beautiful preaching; and argue with them in ways that are best and most gracious.

Allama Abdullah Yusuf Ali, in a note to his popular translation of the Holy Qur'an (in reference to verse 9:20, footnote 1270, p.503), sums up Jihad this way:

1270. Here is a good description of Jihad. It may require fighting in Allah's cause, as a form of self-sacrifice. But its essence consists in (1) a true and sincere Faith, which so fixes its gaze on Allah, that all selfish or worldly motives seem paltry and fade away, and (2) an earnest and ceaseless activity, involving the sacrifice (if need be) of life, person, or property, in the service of Allah. Mere brutal fighting is opposed to the whole spirit of Jihad, while the sincere scholar's pen or preacher's voice or wealthy man's contributions may be the most valuable forms of Jihad.

In its most general meaning, Jihad refers to the obligation of Muslims individually and collectively, to exert themselves to realize Allah's will, to lead a virtuous life, and to extend the Islamic community by peaceful means such as preaching, education, dialog, etc. A related meaning of Jihad is also to struggle for or defense of Islam. All the external forms of Jihad would remain incomplete if they were not complemented by the

Jihad

greater or inner Jihad which every Muslim must carry out continuously within himself. The Islamic path towards perfection can be conceived and achieved in the light of the greater Jihad.

48:1 Inna Fatahna laka Fatham Mubina.
"Verily We have granted thee a manifest victory."

Qur'anic Calligraphy in Tuluth script.

Grand Mosque, Damascus, Syria (circa 715)
The beauty of this mosque is a legend throughout the Moslem world. The mosaic decorations are the greatest glories of Islamic art. *[Two views; Front entrance. and the interior of the dome (below).]*

9

ISLAM, MUSLIMS AND THEIR IMAGES

إِنَّ ٱلْمُسْلِمِينَ وَٱلْمُسْلِمَٰتِ وَٱلْمُؤْمِنِينَ وَٱلْمُؤْمِنَٰتِ وَٱلْقَٰنِتِينَ وَٱلْقَٰنِتَٰتِ وَٱلصَّٰدِقِينَ وَٱلصَّٰدِقَٰتِ وَٱلصَّٰبِرِينَ وَٱلصَّٰبِرَٰتِ وَٱلْخَٰشِعِينَ وَٱلْخَٰشِعَٰتِ وَٱلْمُتَصَدِّقِينَ وَٱلْمُتَصَدِّقَٰتِ وَٱلصَّٰٓئِمِينَ وَٱلصَّٰٓئِمَٰتِ وَٱلْحَٰفِظِينَ فُرُوجَهُمْ وَٱلْحَٰفِظَٰتِ وَٱلذَّٰكِرِينَ ٱللَّهَ كَثِيرًا وَٱلذَّٰكِرَٰتِ أَعَدَّ ٱللَّهُ لَهُم مَّغْفِرَةً وَأَجْرًا عَظِيمًا ۝

Indeed the Muslim men and the Muslim women, the believing men and the believing women, the devout men and the devout women, the truthful men and the truthful women, the patient men and the patient women, the humble men and the humble women, the charitable men and the charitable women, the fasting men and the fasting women, the men who guard their private parts and the women who do so, and the men and the women who engage much in Allah's remembrance – for them Allah has prepared forgiveness and great reward. (33: 35)

In the Western World, it has become customary to speak of Islam to denote the whole body of Muslim peoples, countries, and states in their socio-cultural or political as well as their religious sphere. As a matter of fact, one definition of Islam given in the prestigious *Random House Dictionary* is: "the whole body of Muslim believers, their civilization, and the countries in which theirs is the dominant religion". The word "Islam" is not synonymous with "Muslim". Islam means submission to the will of Allah and those who follow Islam are called Muslims. To speak of societies or countries as Islamic is to say that the way of life in these countries is Islamic, and this may not necessarily be the case.

Some scholars state that most of what the common people call Islam, is not Islam at all. In fact, the lives of many present day Muslims have become a manifestation which is contrary to Islam. However, there are also many who preserve the prayer and fasting and may even perform Hajj but that does not necessarily make them a complete Muslim. All that Muslims are blamed for has really nothing to do with Islam. Muhammad Iqbal, the spiritual founder of Pakistan gave a general answer to this question when he said, "Nothing is wrong with Islam. All the wrong there is, is in our way of being Muslims." Islam itself cannot be responsible for what goes on under its name.

Islam is a universal religion in which all Muslims are brothers. The term "brotherhood" has a special meaning in Islamic concept. It is not simply that they are brothers; they are equal. Equality is a legal concept while brotherhood proclaims that all men originate from the same source. In the same sense, men and women were created by the same Creator.

Thus Muslims are brothers no matter what culture they reside in whether Arabic, Bangaladeshi, Chinese, Indonesian, etc. Thus Islam has retained its unity. In the interplay between Islam and the various cultures of the world, Muslims may often lack conformity with other Muslims. If this is just cultural, it is alright. There is a problem, however, if the diversity is religious. For example, since there are Turkish Muslims, or Indonesian Muslims, there can not be Turkish or Indonesian Islam. There can not be Islams, there is only one Islam.

As Mohammad Rasjidi in *Islam – the Straight Path* (1958) (p.413) observes:

> There are minor differences ... in the manner of praying, differences of no importance which have grown up through varying interpretations in the schools of jurisprudence. Some people emphasize the performance of optional prayers after the Friday prayers, while others do not. There are slight differences in posture; for example, while standing some people put their hands one upon the other in front of the lower part of the chest, while others bend their hands down. Such differences are of no importance, and the unity is shown by the complete harmony among Muslims as to the times of prayer, the ablutions which must be performed before prayer, and the facing toward the Kaaba in Makkah.

The worldwide geographic spread of Islam naturally contains people of many races and cultures thus creating diversity. They are, however, unified by common faith, Islam. The basic unity of Islam lies in the general agreement in the Muslim world concerning the sources of Islam, the fundamentals of the faith, and the particular requirements which are the obligations of all Muslims. From the beginning, the basic sources of Islam have been Qur'an and Sunnah. Muslims have always looked to Qur'an as their guide and have prayed and fasted and made pilgramages as Prophet (s) did. For details governing their lives, Muslims have relied upon the explication and elaboration of the principles of Qur'an and Sunnah, and this is why we have different schools of law [See discussion under Shariah : Sunnah and Islamic Law]. There is no difference among Muslims concerning the fundamental beliefs in Islam. There is difference though in interpretation and in applications. For example, the degree to which men and women's lives are separated, and women's lives restricted, varies considerably in Muslim societies and is determined by custom and the way in which Islamic law is locally applied. Islamic society has been influenced, and the spread of Islam has been aided by the educational opportunities offered through the mosques, madrasahs and religious leaders. Such education leave a lot to be desired. Sufis also played a great part in disseminating Islamic knowledge and practice quite often resulting in controversies, if not confusion. Those who receive only simple religious instruction have only superficial knowledge of Islam and that can stand in the way of better understanding among Muslims.

In Islam there is no central authority or a center of organized religious activity or an ecclesiastical or religious organization to control, direct or monitor religious activities or behavior patterns. In early Islam it was the Caliphate that was the custodians of Shariah (Islamic way of life). Later the Turkish Ottomans and the Indian Mughals dominated all aspects of Muslim life. In the absence of a central authority, theology was of interest to the 'ulama. The 'ulama are, however, generally incapable of taking any positive steps to reconstruct Muslim society. And yet, it is only the 'ulama who are the 'leaders' in most Muslim countries and weild authority with the masses.

Is Islam the religion of killers engaged in a war against the rest of the world? Even in Muslim countries armed men call for a holy war against everyone who disagrees with them and go on mass killings. How does Islam of intolerance and violence fit with the Islam of tolerance and brotherhood? How does it fit with the religion that inspire the billion people around the globe to pray, to fast, to give to the poor, to make pilgrimage to Makkah in utter submission to Allah?

Today the extremists lure adherents to return to "true religious values of former times". Are they not deceiving their followers as well as the non-Muslim world? Is this a cover for political power and not a religious revival? Qur'an says: "Do not allow your hatred for other men to turn you away from justice. Deal justly; that is nearer to true piety."

In the past the image of Islam in the West as well as in the Orient (for example, India) tended to be foreign, almost sinister. Many writers attribute the most disgraceful stains to Islam and claim that it is void of morality. A careful reading of this book will show that the principles of morality in the Qur'an are at the very least, as sublime as they are in other religions. The virtues imparted by the Qur'an are the same humanitarian virtues that the philosophers and reformers have agreed on and called on people to follow. There is need to refute false notions attributed to it. Islam's various virtues and features need to be expounded to the world. Islam is a universal religion and there is nothing aggressively oriental or anti-Western or anti-other religion or culture about it. Non-Muslims would not know how to accept this when they see what is going on in the Muslim world.

Does Islam condone or even promote war? Does Islam propagate taking of hostages and terrorists? Is Islam inherently an expansionist, missionary movement? Do Muslims intend to take over the world, converting everyone to their way of thinking? A close look at the following verses from the Qur'an may dispell all these notions. Qur'an says (5:32):

...that if anyone slew a person – unless it be for murder or for spreading mischief in the land – it would be as if he slew the whole people: And if one saved a life, it would be as if he saved the life of the whole people." Qur'an also says (2:256): "There is no compulsion in religion...".

About compassion in Islam, the following incident is very well known and cited often. Once in battle, some Muslims killed some children of the enemy who had come in between the fighting soldiers. When the Prophet heard this, he was very angry. He said, "What has happened to the people that they have transgressed the limits and killed even the children"? Someone said, "They were children of the unbelievers". The Prophet said, "Even the best of your people are not better than the children of the non-believers". (Musnad, Ahmad and Nasai).

According to Abul A'la Mawdudi, (*Let us be Muslims* p.112), there are two types of Islam: legal and true. Under legal Islam, the verbal affirmation is taken into account irrespective of what lies in one's heart. This definition provides the legal or cultural basis on which Muslim society is organized. However, in the Hereafter what will count is the faith in heart and that is true Islam. By the same token, there are two kinds of Muslims according to the said scholar: Partial and True Muslim. The Muslims who completely merge their personalities and existences into Islam are the True Muslims. Whatever they do is for the sake of Islam; their behavior is governed by the precepts of Islam. All the others are partial Muslims according to him.

In the Western world it is also quite common to refer to a Muslim as Mohammedan which is totally wrong and unacceptable. Mohammedan or Mohammedanism implies that Muhammad (s) is the originator of the religion which is not the case. The very name Islam goes back to the time of Ibrahim (as), because God had referred this to him (cf. 2:131; 22:78) during his life time. But the original founder of Islam is no one other than God Himself and the date of founding goes back to the age of Adam (as). Islam has existed in one form or another all along from the beginning and it was perfected at the time of Prophet Muhammad (s) as mentioned in Qur'anic verse 5:3. The name of the religion was given to it as already mentioned, by Allah (3:19;

Islam, Muslims and their Images

5:3) and Muhammad (s) was commanded by Him to convey the Message. The word "Mohammedanism" also implies that Islam is no more than another "ism" although one Muslim scholar makes the point that from Islamic perspective, if need be, one could call it "Allahism".

Given the state of Muslim orientation to and practice of Islam in general, it is no wonder that non-Muslims shun Islam. The average person in the West who learns about Islam through the media, may very well be excused if he has misconceptions about Islam or think wrongly and poorly of Muslims.

In the western mind, generally speaking, Islam is seen as a religion of the sword and by and large the Western attitude towards Islam and Muslims remain offensive. The news and the print media often give a distorted picture of Islam. However, lately the situation is getting better in the West. Muslims in the West are slowly and gradually making their presence felt in the society. Muslims must live out their faith in their respective communities. In socialising and in making friends caution must be used so as not to be influenced away from Islam. Allah says (25:27) [on the Day of Judgment the wrong-doer will say] "Ah! Woe to me! Would that I had never taken so-and-so as a friend!"

While Islam means submission, it is possible to be outwardly surrendered without inwardly believing. Belief in essence is more inclusive than submission. Mere utterance of the Shahada (There is no god but God) does not make one a true Muslim; neither does being born into a Muslim family. A Muslim is characterized by eight terms: devout, truthful, patient, humble, compassionate, self-restraining, chaste and ever aware of Allah (3:17; 33:35). For a true Muslim, these moral obligations or characteristics must be met in addition to the requirements of the five pillars (discussed in the chapter named as such).

It must be understood that not a word has changed in Qur'an since its inception; change occurs in Muslims themselves.

Understanding Islam and its Practices

God has promised the reward of greatness and glory and honor for true Muslims, not to those who bear the designation Muslims without performing the duties of a Muslim. A true Muslim is one who acts righteously at all times in obedience to God's commands as found in Qur'an and the Traditions (Sunnah) of the Prophet.

35:43

"...But the evil plot encompasses only him who makes it."

Part III

ISLAMIC PRACTICE ('IBADAT)

10

'IBADAH : SALAT

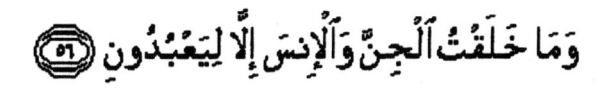

$$\text{وَمَا خَلَقْتُ ٱلْجِنَّ وَٱلْإِنسَ إِلَّا لِيَعْبُدُونِ}$$

And I have not created the Jinn and Mankind but to serve Me. (51: 56)

Section 1 : General

Definition

'Ibadah is the general name for all the individual acts of worship (pl., 'Ibadat), such as the *Shahadah* (testimony of faith), *Salat* (prayer), *Zakah* (alms tax), *Sawm* (fasting), *Hajj* (pilgrimage) and whatever the servant of God (*'Abd-Allah*) does in obedience to and for the pleasure of his Master, the Creator. It is by such acts that the 'Abd expresses his *'ubudiyyah*, his servanthood. It is this wide sense of *'Ibadah* on which the edifice of Islam rests. In other words, *'Ibadah* is Muslims' relationship and their attitudes to Allah. This relationship finds expression in acts of obedience, worship and devotion. Some of these acts are commanded by Allah; others are recommended; while still others are voluntary. Chief among those that are commanded are the five *arkans* (essentials) of Islam, as mentioned above. These are also known as the pillars of Islam. The best form of *'Ibadah* is *Salat*. The Qur'an, however, extends

the concept of *'Ibadah*, as already alluded to, to cover every good deed performed to seek the pleasure of Allah. Abul A'la Mawdudi gives a most brilliant exposition of this concept in *Let us be Muslims*, pp. 139-140:

> You must follow at every step in your lives the law of God and refuse to obey all laws which conflict with His law. Everything you do must accord with the guidance given by God. Only then will your entire lives turn into lives of worship.
>
> In such a life, everything is *'Ibadah*: whether you sleep or are awake, whether you eat or drink, whether you work or rest, whether you are silent or talk, are all acts of worship. So much so that in going to your wives and kissing your children, too, you serve God. All these actions which are usually considered secular and worldly become religious, provided that during their performance you observe the limits laid down by God and remain conscious every moment and that every step of what is approved by God (*Halal*) and what is forbidden by Him (*Haram*), what is a duty and what must be avoided, which actions please God and which displease Him.
>
> You may now ask: "What then is the position of prescribed worship rituals like the Prayer (*Salah*), Almsgiving (*Zakah*), Fasting (*Sawm*), Pilgrimage (*Hajj*) and so on?"
>
> These acts of worship, which Allah has enjoined upon us, in reality prepare us for that greater overall *'Ibadah* that we have to perform throughout our lives. They are the means which turn our lives into lives of worship. Prayer reminds you five times a day that you are slaves of Allah and that Him alone you must serve. Fasting prepares you, for an entire month once every year, for this very service. Almsgiving repeatedly brings home to you the truth that the money you have earned is a gift of God. Do not just spend it on physical pleasures or even solely on material needs; you

must render what is due to your Master. Pilgrimage engraves on your hearts such a love and awareness of the majesty of God that once they take root, they remain with you all your lives.

Salat, Du'a and Dhikr : Relationship

These three practices articulate the Qur'anic concept of worship. *Salat* is the heart or foundation of Islam, and Qur'an instructs Muslims to establish and protect it. As a matter of fact, Qur'an emphasizes at more than eighty places about establishment of *Salat*. *Salat* is our link or bridge to Allah. It is the obligatory prayer a Muslim offers five times a day. Prayer is not only an obligation to be fulfilled, but also a discipline, a means to nurture the soul.

Du'a is a prayer request. It is a prayer of supplication, a way of bringing one's needs, problems and wishes before Allah; it is all kinds of extempore prayer, intercession, spontaneous outpouring of the soul to the Almighty. They include private thanksgiving for some blessings received such as childbirth, passing examinations, recovery from sickness, requests for help, pleas for forgiveness or guidance.

Dhikr is a remembrance, mindfulness of Allah; it is also commonly used to a *sufi* gathering for this purpose. (For a detailed discussion of *Dhikr*, see Section 11, *Du'a and Dhikr*.)

To sum up, there are three types of prayers: *Salat, Du'a* and *Dhikr*. *Salat* is the canonical prayers which has been detailed and exemplified by the Prophet (s). This is the most comprehensive type of prayer, the most well-known aspect of Muslim worship. *Du'a* and *Dhikr* can be a part of it as well. *Du'a* is without any prescribed form, whereas *Salat* is structured. *Du'a* is essentially the prayer of each one of us to Allah by oneself. This type of prayer can be said in any language; *Salat* is essentially in Arabic. *Dhikr*, or the remembrance of Allah, is the very essence of all Muslim prayer; the overall object of prayer is to remember Allah. Again and again, the Qur'an enjoins Muslims to remember Him.

Section 2 : Value, Kinds and Times of Salat (Prayer)

Meaning of Salat (Prayer)

$$\text{اتْلُ مَآ أُوحِىَ إِلَيْكَ مِنَ ٱلْكِتَٰبِ وَأَقِمِ ٱلصَّلَوٰةَ إِنَّ ٱلصَّلَوٰةَ تَنْهَىٰ عَنِ ٱلْفَحْشَآءِ وَٱلْمُنكَرِ وَلَذِكْرُ ٱللَّهِ أَكْبَرُ وَٱللَّهُ يَعْلَمُ مَا تَصْنَعُونَ ۝}$$

Recite what is sent of the Book by inspiration to thee, and establish regular Prayer: for prayer restrains from shameful and evil deeds; and remembrance of Allah is the greatest (thing in life) without doubt. And Allah knows the (deeds) that ye do. (29: 45)
 Also 20: 14, 132; 30: 31; 87: 15; 108: 2 and many others.

Salat or *salah*, the greatest form of remembrance of Allah (*Dhikr Allah Akbar*), is the Arabic name for a Muslim's prayers. The word *Namaz*, a Persian word, is used synonymously with *Salat* in Iran, Afghanistan, Central Asia, South Asia and Turkey. In either case when these words are translated into the English word Prayer without further definition, it is not wholly accurate. Since by usage the word "Prayer" has been used to mean *Salat*, for the purpose of this book the word "Prayer" has also been used for *Salat* or *Salah*.

'Ibadah : Salat

Salat is entering into a state of humble audience with Allah. It is a formal ritual prayer performed five times a day. It also denotes further special types, as will be explained later in this chapter. It is a spiritual communion with Allah; it is adoring reverence and homage to Him. It is an outward expression of a believer's faith in God; it is a sign of obedience to the command of Allah. (For more on this aspect of prayer, see Appendix, Ibn Sina on Prayer.)

Salat is emphasized time and again in the Qur'an. According to a hadith, the first thing that a person would be called to account for on the Day of Judgment is the *Salat*. If it is performed properly, all his deeds become in order, and if it is improper then all his deeds are in vain.

Salat (Prayer) is so important in Islam that it cannot be neglected even when facing the enemy. The institution of prayer is one of the basic and most important pillars of Islam. According to Qur'an (4: 142), laziness and sluggishness in its performance is a sign of hypocrisy. Because of the importance Allah places on *Salat*, He spoke directly to Prophet Muhammad (s) on his ascension to the seven heavens (known as M'rāj), and He spoke without an intermediary.

Salat is a discipline ordained upon all Muslims. Islam is not just a religion; it is also a way of life. By observing these prayers, the Muslim marks the whole day with a spiritual stamp early in the day, at the end of the day, and throughout. So he combines religion with life. Regular performance of *Salat* serves as a repeated reminder during the day and the night of his relationship with his Creator and to keep him from forgetting that he or she belongs to Him. The fundamental point about prayer is that it purifies the soul, refines the character, and keeps one who performs it properly from falsehood and all forbidden acts. Sincere prayer is indeed the remedy for the ills which beset the heart and corrupt the soul.

Why Do We Pray

Genuine prayer, based on humility and submission, illuminates the heart, purifies the soul and teaches man's obligations to the Creator. It is through prayer that the glory and majesty of Allah may be implanted in the believer's heart. Prayer enables man to gain such excellent virtues of character as truthfulness, honesty, fairness and generosity. It raises in him fear and dread of the All-Powerful and directs him to the One God. In this way, his moral standards are raised and his soul is purified. Consequently, he leaves aside lying, falsehood, deception, meanness and disobedience. This goes to prove what Allah has said, as quoted at the top of this section, (29: 45), that prayer restrains from shameful and evil deeds. Prayer is religion in action. Religion is a relation and devotion to the Invisible Power whose existence man feels and acknowledges. When man is faced with hardships and misfortunes, the only hope and the means of contentment is for him to pray. Prayer allows one to release his innermost feelings; it creates an urge within to seek help from the All-Powerful.

We pray to show our gratitude for everything. Prayer is a reminder of our allegiance to God. It is one of the five pillars of Islam and is the supreme act of worship. It leads to success in this world as well as in the hereafter, for Allah says (23: 1; 70: 34-35): "Successful indeed are the believers"; "And those who strictly guard their worship such will be the honored ones in the Gardens of Bliss" (also 23: 9-11).

Significance of Prayer

This is very well stated by Muhammad Asad in his book, *The Road to Mecca* (1954, p. 88):

First we stand upright and recite from The Holy Qur'an remembering that it is His word, given to man he may be upright and steadfast in life. Then we say: "God is the Greatest" reminding ourselves that no one deserves to be worshipped but Him, and bow down deep because we honour Him above all, and praise His power and glory. Thereafter we prostrate ourselves on our forehead because we feel that we are but dust and nothingness before Him, and that He is our Creator and Sustainer on high. Then we lift our faces from the ground and remain sitting, praying that He forgive us our sins and bestow His grace upon us, and guide us aright, and give us health and sustenance. Then we again prostrate ourselves on the ground and touch the dust with our foreheads before the might and the glory of the One. After that, we remain sitting and pray that He bless the Prophet Muhammad (s) who brought His message to us, just as He blessed the earlier Prophets (as), and that He bless us as well, and all those who follow the right guidance; and we ask Him to give us the good of this world and the good of the world to come. In the end we turn our heads to the right and to the left saying, "peace and the grace of God be upon you" and thus greet all who are righteous wherever they may be. This is the nature, significance and the sum and substance of prayer in Islam.

In the Qur'an, ritual prayer (*salat*) is presented as the immediate and constant corollary of belief in Allah.

Kinds of Prayer

This subsection must be read along with the table, **Details of Rakah in Each Salat**, which appears at the end of Section 5.

Prayers may be divided into two broad categories: *Fard* and *Nafl*.

Fard Salat (Obligatory)

Fard salat, or obligatory ritual prayers, include the five daily prayers and the Friday's noon congregation. Failure to observe these prayers is a serious sin. Detailed discussion about *Fard* prayers appears in Section 6 below.

Funeral prayer is *Fard al-Kifaya*, i. e., the prayer of some suffices for performing the duty for all. The whole community, however, would be considered sinful if no one from the whole Muslim community prayed the funeral, or *Janajah*, prayer.

Nawafil Salat (Supererogatory Prayer)

According to *Fiqh* (v. 2, p. 3), "The nawafil prayers are those which are offered in addition to the *Fard Salat*, as prayed by the Prophet (s)." There are certain *nawafil* (singular: *nafl)* prayers which the Prophet (s) performed only occasionally.

The *Nawafil Salat* (prayer) can be divided into three categories:

(i) Sunnah Type : Nawafil Regularly Practiced by the Prophet (s)

They are the prayers (*salat*) observed along with the obligatory prayers, which include:
Two rakahs Salat al-Fajr
Four and two rakahs Salat al-Dhuhr
Two or four rakahs Salat al-'Asr
Two and two rakahs Salat al-Maghrib
Four and two rakahs Salat al- 'Isha
Discussion about these appears in Section 7 below.

(ii) Special Nawafil, which include:

Salat Lailat al-Qadr (Prayer at Night of Power)
Salat at-Tarawih (Special Prayer at Night in Ramadan)
Salat at-Tahajjud (Night Vigil Prayer)
Salat al-Ishraq wa Salat ad-Duha (Chast) (Morning and Forenoon Prayers)
Salat al-Kasuf (Prayer of the Solar and Lunar Eclipse)
Salat al-Istisqa (Prayer for Rain).
These are discussed in detail later.

(iii) General Nawafil

Generally speaking, *Nafl* is a voluntary prayer offered any time, any number of *rakahs* with or without being followed or preceded by regular or obligatory prayers. However, it is generally offered at the end of regular prayers except *Fajr*. Within the "General" category there are also specific types as listed below:
1. Salat ad-Dakhlil Masjid (Salutation for Mosque)
2. Salat at-Tahyat al-Wudu (Post-Ablution Prayer)
3. Salat at-Tasbih (Prayer of the Divine Glorification)
4. Salat al-Istikhara (Guidance Prayer)
5. Salat at-Tawbah wa al-Istighfar (Prayer of Repentance and Seeking Forgiveness).
Each one of these is discussed in detail later.

For the last fourteen centuries, Muslims, wherever they have been in the world, have performed the ritual prayer (*salat*) in accordance with the Qur'anic injunctions and the practice of Prophet Muhammad (s).

Times of (Salat) Prayer

Obligatory ritual prayer (*Fard salat*) times are all fixed. According to *The Life of Muhammad: a translation of 'Ishaq's sirat Rasul-Allah* (pp. 112-113), the apostle Jibril came to Prophet Muhammad (s) and showed him how to pray and informed him of the times of prayer. They are:

1. The Early Morning Prayer (Salat al-Fajr) is due to be offered anytime after the dawn and before sunrise, a total period of a little over an hour.

2. The Noon Prayer (Salat al-Dhuhr) is due to be offered anytime after the sun begins to decline from its zenith until it is about midway on its course to setting.

3. The Mid-Afternoon Prayer (Salat al-'Asr), which begins right after the expiration of the Noon Prayer time and extends to sunset. But no prayer is to be offered when the sun is setting.

4. The Sunset Prayer (Salat al-Maghrib). The time of this prayer begins immediately after sunset and extends until the red glow in the western horizon disappears. Normally it extends over a period of one hour and twenty-to-thirty minutes.

5. The Evening Prayer (Salat al-'Isha) begins after the red glow in the western horizon disappears (nearly one hour and thirty minutes after sunset) and continues until a little before the dawn. But it is best to perform the *Fard* (obligatory) prayers at the start of time.

There are calendars that tell the accurate time of each prayer. There are also watches available that are programmed to tell prayer time and qibla direction. If there is none available, one must resort to one's best judgment, and Allah (SWT) will forgive any unintentional mistake.

Forbidden Times of (Salat) Prayer

1. When the sun is rising or setting
2. When the sun is at its zenith
3. The times of personal impurity, partial or complete.
4. For a female, the period of menstruation or confinement due to childbirth.
5. No prayer may be offered after the following two prayers: after Asr prayer until sunset and after the morning prayer until the sun rises (Bukhari, No. 899 / 3)

Obligations and Prerequisites

Obligations

It is an obligation on every sane adult. Puberty is the age at which prayer becomes an obligation. However, to develop the discipline and commitment and to develop the habit of establishing prayers, the Prophet (s) recommended that children be ordered, by parents or guardians, to begin to pray at the age of seven.

Prerequisites

1. Knowledge that it is time to pray.
2. Purity of the whole body is needed. Ablution is a requirement.
3. Purity of the clothes worn is necessary; the ground used for prayers must be free from impurity.
4. Dress for men should be such that it covers them from the navel to the knees, at least; the shoulders should not be left uncovered. The dress of the woman should be such that it covers her whole body, leaving only the face, feet and hands

uncovered. A prayer offered in transparent clothing is not valid for either men or women. Also, tight fitting clothing, which shows the shape of the body, should be avoided.
5. The face must be towards the Kaaba. As has been mentioned, there are many ways to decide the right direction of *qiblah*.
6. Intent (*Niyyah*) for prayer.
7. Prayer must be offered at its appointed time.

Facing the Direction of Kaaba

All who perform the prayer must face towards the Kaaba. Generally, people know the direction. In a new place, one should ask. If there is no one to ask, then he must decide for himself. His prayer will still be correct and will not require repetition if it is discovered, after the prayer is completed that he was in error. However, if the mistake is pointed out while the prayer is in progress, he should turn towards the proper direction without interrupting his prayer. Remember, Allah says: "To Allah belong the East and the West; whithersoever you turn there is Allah's Face" (2: 115).

Section 3 : Purification

One cannot perform the prayer without fulfilling the prerequisites mentioned under "Obligation and Prerequisites" in the preceding page. First is cleanliness. This includes cleanliness of the body, garments, and the place where the prayer is performed. The purification of the body depends on circumstances that may necessitate bathing (*ghusl*). Even if the body is clean, ablution (*wudu*) or ritual of cleaning is required before performing *Salat*.

How to Perform Wudu

Qur'an spells it out:

$$\text{يَٰٓأَيُّهَا ٱلَّذِينَ ءَامَنُوٓاْ إِذَا قُمْتُمْ إِلَى ٱلصَّلَوٰةِ فَٱغْسِلُواْ وُجُوهَكُمْ وَأَيْدِيَكُمْ إِلَى ٱلْمَرَافِقِ وَٱمْسَحُواْ بِرُءُوسِكُمْ وَأَرْجُلَكُمْ إِلَى ٱلْكَعْبَيْنِ وَإِن كُنتُمْ جُنُبًا فَٱطَّهَّرُواْ}$$

O ye who believe! When ye prepare for prayer, wash your faces, and your hands (and arms) to the elbows: rub your heads (with water); and (wash) your feet to the ankles. If ye are in a state of ceremonial impurity, bathe your whole body ... (5: 6)

These are carried out as follows, according to the teachings of our Prophet (s):
1. Make *niyyah* (intention) that the act of performing *wudu* is for the purpose of purity. *Niyyah* should be made in the heart because it is an action of the heart, not of the tongue.
2. Then start *wudu* by saying: Bismillahir Rahmanir Rahim.
3. Wash the hands up to the wrists three times. If one so wishes, one may recite the following at this time:

$$\text{بِسْمِ اللهِ العَظيمِ والحَمْدُ لِلّهِ عَلى دينِ الإِسْلامِ}$$
$$\text{الإِسْلامُ حَقٌّ والكُفْرُ باطِلٌ}$$

Bismillahil-'Azimi walhamdu lillahi 'ala din-il-Islam. Al-Islamu haqqun walkufru batilu.

I begin with the name of Allah, Who is Great and I express gratitude to Allah for keeping me faithful to Islam. Islam is right and infidelity is wrong.

4. Rinse the mouth with water three times. Brushing teeth before doing *wudu* is Prophetic *sunnah*.
5. Cleanse the nostrils by sniffing water into them three times.
6. Wash the whole face three times with both hands, if possible, from the top of the forehead to the bottom of the chin and from ear to ear.
7. Wash the right arm three times up to the far end of the elbow, and then do the same with the left arm.
8. Wipe the whole head or any part of it with a wet hand once.
9. Wipe the inner sides of the ears with the forefingers and their outer sides with the thumbs. This should be done with wet fingers.
10. Wash both feet including the ankles three times, beginning with the right foot.

According to hadith, the following *du'a*s are highly recommended, but not required.

اَشْهَدُ أَن لاَّ اِلهَ إِلاَّ اللهُ وَحْدَهُ لاَّ شَرِيْكَ لَـهُ وَاَشْــهَدُ أَنَّ مُحَمَّـداً عَبُـدُه وَرَسُوْلُهُ ۞

Ashhadu an la ilaha illa-Allahu wahdahu la sharika lahu wa ashhadu an-na Muhammadan 'abduhu wa rasuluhu.

I testify that there is no deity except Allah alone. He is One and has no partner. And I testify that Muhammad (s) is His servant and messenger. (Muslim)

اَللّهُمَّ اجْعَلْنِيْ مِنَ التَّوَّابِيْنَ وَ اجْعَلْنِيْ مِنَ الْمُتَطَهِرِيْنَ ۞

'Ibadah : Salat

Allah humm aj 'alni minat taw-wabina, waj 'alni minal muta tahhirin.

O Allah, make me among those who are penitent and make me among those who are purified. (Tirmidhi)

At this stage the ablution is completed, and the person who has performed it is ready to start his prayer. When the ablution is valid, a person may keep it as long as he can and may use it for as many prayers as he wishes. But it is preferable to renew it as often as possible. There is a difference between everyday washing away of it and becoming purified for prayer. Purification (*taharah*) is a mental as well as physical cleansing. While external cleansing is essential, purification of heart is no less important.

Nullification of Wudu

Wudu becomes nullified by any of the following:
1. Natural discharges, i. e., urine, stools, gas, etc.
2. Unnatural discharges, i. e., vomiting a mouthful, inability to control urine, etc.
3. Sexual activity.
4. Flow of blood or pus and the like from any part of the body.
5. Falling asleep.
6. Losing one's reasoning by taking drugs or any other intoxicating substance (4: 43).

After the occurrence of any of these things, the ablution must be renewed for prayer. Also, after natural discharges, water should be applied because the use of toilet tissues may not be sufficient for the purpose of purity and worship.

Special Consideration in Wudu or Masah (Wiping Over Socks)

If socks or stockings are worn and were put on after performing an ablution, it is not necessary to take them off when renewing the ablution. (However, the socks must be thick enough so that the skin is not visible.) Instead of taking off the socks, the wet hand may be passed over them. They should be removed, however, and the feet washed at least once in every twenty-four hours. This special dispensation is based on the following hadith quoted by Tirmidhi, Ahmad, Abu Dawud and Ibn Majah. Mughirah ibn Shu'ban narrated that Rasulullah (s) performed *wudu* and only wiped over his socks and sandals.

As far as leather socks (shoes) are concerned, all concur that wiping may fulfill the conditions of *wudu*. But there is a difference of opinion regarding permissibility of wiping over the woolen, cotton, silken or nylon socks. Sayyid Abul A'la Maududi, in his *Rasa'il o masa'il*, Vol. II, p. 237, as quoted in *Everyday fiqh*, vol. 1, tr. by Abdul Aziz Kamal (published by Islamic Publications, Lahore, Pakistan, p. 74), says:

> The majority of the followers of the *Sunnah* are agreed that wiping over the leather socks is permissible, but as for the conditions prescribed by the jurists regarding the description of the woollen and cotton socks, I have been able to find no basis thereof. The *Sunnah* is explicit that the Holy Prophet (s) did sometimes wipe over the socks and shoes, but we do not find any specification or description of the socks anywhere. I am, therefore, satisfied that the conditions imposed by the jurists have no basis whatsoever, and if a person wipes over the socks without any regard for them, his *Wudu* will be complete and he will not be violating any injunction of the Shariah. The concession of

Tayammum (discussed later), which has been granted in special circumstances when keeping the feet covered up may be absolutely necessary and washing them every time harmful or involving unnecessary hardship. This concession is, in fact, a special favour of Allah Almighty and may be availed of as such. One may, therefore, wipe over any description of socks that one maybe wearing, with complete satisfaction of the heart, even over a bandage that one may have put on the feet to keep them safe from cold or dust, or to cover a wound.

Also *Sahih Muslim*, Vol. 2, pp. 162-163; *Mishkat*, no. 257; and *Fiqh*, Vol. 1, p. 44.

How to Wipe Over the Socks

According to *Fiqh* (Vol. 1, p. 46):
Islamic law prescribes that the top of the sock is to be wiped. Said al-Mughirah, "I saw the Messenger of Allah, upon whom be peace, wipe over the top of his socks." (Related by Ahmad, Abu Dawud and at-Tirmidhi, who called it *hasan*, i. e, close to authentic). 'Ali observed, "If the religion was based on opinion, the bottom of the sock would take preference in being wiped to the top of the sock." (Related by Abu Dawud and ad-Daraqutni with a hassan or sahih, i. e., authentic, chain.) What is obligatory in the wiping is what is meant by the lexicographical meaning of the word "wipe." There are no specifications authentically mentioned with respect to the wiping.

Time Limits for Wiping

A person resident at home is allowed to wipe over the socks for one day and one night (24 hours), but for a traveller the time limit is three days and three nights (72 hours), counting the limit for the time the *Wudu* breaks and not from the time the socks are put on.

As in the case of the socks, so is the case of a wound, whether covered by a bandage or not. If the wound is in any part of the body that needs to be washed for *wudu* and that washing is likely to cause harm, it is permissible to wipe over it, including the dressing, with a wet hand.

Tayammum (Dry Ablution)

The Qur'an ordains (5: 6) *Tayammum* (Dry Ablution) as the complete substitution for *wudu*:

$$\text{وَإِن كُنتُم مَّرْضَىٰٓ أَوْ عَلَىٰ سَفَرٍ أَوْ جَآءَ أَحَدٌ مِّنكُم مِّنَ ٱلْغَآئِطِ أَوْ لَمَسْتُمُ ٱلنِّسَآءَ فَلَمْ تَجِدُواْ مَآءً فَتَيَمَّمُواْ صَعِيدًا طَيِّبًا فَٱمْسَحُواْ بِوُجُوهِكُمْ وَأَيْدِيكُم مِّنْهُ مَا يُرِيدُ ٱللَّهُ لِيَجْعَلَ عَلَيْكُم مِّنْ حَرَجٍ وَلَـٰكِن يُرِيدُ لِيُطَهِّرَكُمْ}$$

Wa inkuntum-marda aw 'ala safarin aw ja'a ahadum minkum minal ghaiti aw lamastumun-nisa' a falan tajidu maan fatayammamu sa'idan tayyiban famsahu biwujuhikum wa aidikum-minhu; ma yuridullahu liyaj'ala 'alaikum min harajinu-walakiny-yuridu liyutahhirakum...

But if you are ill, or on journey or one of you cometh from offices of nature, or you have been in contact with woman, and you find no water, then take for yourselves clear sand or earth and rub therewith your faces and hands. Allah does not wish to place you in a difficulty, but to make you clean.

Tayammum is a symbolic demonstration of the importance of ablution, which is so vital for both worship and health. The procedure for *tayammum* is as follows:
1. Begin in the name of Allah and do the *niyyah*.
2. Strike both hands slightly on pure earth or sand or stone.
3. Shake the hands off and wipe the face with them once in the same way as done in the ablution.
4. Strike the hands again and wipe the right arm to the elbow with the left hand and the left arm with the right hand

According to *Fiqh* (Vol. 1, p. 66), it is enough to wipe the face and hands up to the wrists. Finish with the same *du'a* for ablution. Whatever invalidates *wudu* invalidates *tayammum*.

It must be remembered that the ideal means of purification is water. If *tayammum* is performed on account of unavailability of water, it will become void as soon as water is available. However, if one has already offered the prayer with *tayammum* and then the water is available, he need not repeat the prayer.

Physical Purity

It has been mentioned that purification of one's body, garments and place of prayer is a necessary preliminary to prayer. A well-known edict is cleanliness is next to godliness. According to a hadith, purification is half the faith. In other words, an essential requirements of being a Muslim is to be pure in body in order to be pure in mind and soul.

There is one aspect of purity that is emphasized by Afzalur Rahman (*Prayer: its significance and benefits*, 1979, pp. 49-51) and Muhammad Ali (*The Religion of Islam*, 1990, p. 293). The latter is quoted below:

In Tradition certain precautions are recommended in the case of natural evacuations, so that no part of the excrement of filth should remain on the body or defile the clothes. These consist in the use of pebbles--whose place may be taken by toilet paper--and water, after the passing of urine or stools, or simply water. These are apparently very minor details of life but they play an important part in the preservation of cleanliness and health. Similarly removal of superfluous hair, i. e., hair under the arm-pit or that of *regis pubis*, is enjoined for the same purpose, that is to say, for the sake of cleanliness and health.

Pure in body, the believer is all set to win the blessings of the Beneficent and the Merciful. There is, however, a mindset that is essential for the prayer.

Mindset for the Prayer

The prayer in Islam consists of three parts: (1) meditation, i. e., looking into oneself and to pray to Allah in the stillness of one's heart; (2) uttering Allah's words; and (3) bodily movements as ordained by Him and taught by Jibril to Prophet Muhammad (s).

Qur'an says (2: 177): "It is no virtue that you turn your faces East and West (in prayer)." In other words, by prayers, Qur'an simply does not mean standing up, facing Kaaba and making certain gestures with the body and the tongue; although they are an essential part, and without them there cannot be any prayer, they may become just a show if not performed with conviction and full concentration of mind. Allah says (4: 43): "Approach not prayer when you are in a drunken state until you know the meaning of what you utter." Imam Ghazzali observes (*Ihya* II, p. 34) that the drunken state applies by extension to those who are wholly preoccupied with temptations and worldly thoughts. He further writes: "You cover the private parts, i. e.,

'Ibadah : Salat

prevent certain areas of the body from being exposed to human view. But what about the shameful areas of your inner being, those unworthy secrets of your soul, that are scrutinized only by your Lord, Great and Glorious is He? Be conscious of these faults" (p. 44). So one has to prepare his heart also, besides the purity of the body, and let his soul be in fear of the Lord, for he is about to stand before the Master of Heaven and Earth.

Section 4 : Call to Prayer : Adhan and Iqamah

Adhan

Every congregational prayer is preceded by *adhan*, which is uttered in a sufficiently loud voice. It is the first call to prayer.

The Call to Prayer is itself an act of worship which precedes the prayer and, as such, is one of the most important religious ceremonies in Islam and the most widely recognized characteristic of the religion. The caller stands facing the *Qiblah*, raising both hands to his ears and says, in a loud voice, the following:

$$\text{اَللهُ أَكْبَرُ}$$

1. Allahu Akbar (God is the greatest) (repeated four times);

$$\text{أَشْهَدُ أَن لاَإِلَهَ إِلاَّ الله}$$

2. Ashhadu An La Ilaha Illallah (I bear witness that there is no got but the One God) (repeated twice);

اَشْهَدُ أَنَّ مُحَمَّداً رَسُوْلُ اللهِ

3. Ashhadu Anna Muhammadan Rasulu-l-lah (I bear witness that Muhammad is the Messenger of God) (repeated twice);

حَىَّ عَلَىَ الصَّلاةِ

4. Hayya 'Ala-s-Salah (Come fast to prayer) (repeated twice, turning the face to the right);

حَىَّ عَلَىَ الْفَلَاحِ

5. Hayya 'Ala-l-Falah (Come fast to success) (repeated twice, turning the. face to the left ;

اللهُ اَكْبَرُ

6. Allahu Akbar (God is the Greatest of all) (repeated twice);

لاَّ اِلهَ إِلاَّ اللهُ

7. La Ilaha Illa-l-lah (There is no god but the One and True God) (once).

When the call is made for the early Morning Prayer, the caller adds one sentence right after part (5) above. The required sentence is:

اَلصَّلاةُ خَيْرٌ مِنَ النَّوُمِ

As-Salatu khayrum Minan-nawm (prayer is better than sleep) (repeated twice).

'Ibadah : Salat

Then the caller continues with parts (6) and (7). This exception is made in the morning only because it is the time when people are asleep and in need of a reminder for prayer. *Fiqh* (v. 1, pp. 95-96) records some variations to the above formula of *Adhan*.

The *Adhan* should be listened to with great reverence and attention, and the words of the *Adhan* should be repeated in mind along with the Muadhdhin (the Caller), but when the Muadhdhin (the Caller) says:

$$حَيَّ عَلَى الصَّلاةِ$$

Hayya 'Ala-s- Salah ; and

$$حَيَّ عَلَى الْفَلَاحِ$$

Hayya 'Ala-l- Falah

we should say:

$$لاَ حَوْلَ وَلاَ قُوَّةَ إِلاَّ بِاللهِ$$

La-hawla wala quwwata illa billah.

There is no power or might except through Allah.

While responding to *Adhan*, one should stop all other activities. One should neither greet nor respond to greetings and should also stop recitation of the Qur'an.

Conditions When Adhan Should Not Be Responded To

1. Eating a meal;
2. Performing *Salat*;
3. Giving or receiving religious education;

4. In the toilet;
5. Women should not respond to *Adhan* while passing through menses or bleeding after child birth.

The traditional *Du'a* which is said after each call to prayer is:

اَللّٰهُمَّ رَبَّ هٰذِهِ الدَّعْوَةِ التَّامَّةِ وَالصَّلَاةِ الْقَائِمَةِ آتِ مُحَمَّداً الوَسِيْلَةَ وَالْفَضِيْلَةَ و اِبْعَثْهُ مَقَامًا مَّحْمُوْداً الَّذِيْ وَعَدْتَهُ

Allahumma rabba Hadhihid da'watit tammati was Salatil Qayimati āti Muhammadan al-wasilata wal Fadilata wab'ath-hu maqamam mahmuda nil ladhi wa 'adtahu.

Oh Allah! Lord of this complete prayer of ours. By the blessing of it, give Muhammad (s) his eternal rights of intercession, distinction and highest class (in paradise). And raise him to the promised rank you have promised him.

Iqamah : The Performance Call

Traditionally there is a short interval between *Adhan* and *Iqamah*. He who makes the call to prayer also, generally, makes this call. *Iqamah* begins when all he necessary conditions for performing the prayer are fulfilled. When all has become ready for prayer, stand facing the direction of the Kaaba. This call is made and then the prayer is performed. *Iqamah* is the same as the *adhan*, except that after Hayya 'Ala-l- Falah, the following words are added:

قَدْ قَامَتُ الصَّلَاةُ قَدْ قَامَتُ الصَّلَاةُ

Qad Qamatis Salah ; Qad Qamatis Salah

Salat has begun ; Salat has begun

One says the beginning and ending *takbir*, and the phrase "Qad Qamatis Salat" twice.
Iqamah is said in a faster voice than *Adhan* and also in a relatively low voice. *Iqamah* must be said before *Fard* part of each prayer.
Women who are praying together need not deliver the *Adhan* before praying but may recite the *Iqamah* (cf. *Reliance of the traveller*, p. 114).

Section 5 : Form and Parts of Prayer

Synopsis

Before we describe the actual performance of prayer. we would like to point out that for the uninitiated it might appear to be complex. *Salat* is not merely said; it is done. All readings or recitations have to be done from memory. In *Salat* extreme care is taken to pray exactly as the Prophet (s) said: "Pray as you have seen me praying."

The pattern of *Salat* may be divided into seven steps, as follows: (details of the prayer are given below):
1. The first step consists of facing the *qiblah* (Kaaba), raising one's hands to the ears, and pronouncing the *takbir*, or recitation of praise, "God is Great" (*Allahu Akbar*), and readying one's attention by affirming within the intention to say the prayer.

2. During the second step, known as the "standing," the chapter *al-Fatihah* is recited together with additional verses from the Qur'an.
3. With the recitation of another *takbir*, the worshiper bows, with his hands on his knees, and in this bent position praises God.
4. After resuming the standing position, the worshiper prostrates with the forehead touching the ground as a sign of humility and submission.
5. The fifth step involves raising oneself from prostration while reciting another *takbir* and remaining in a sitting position, praying.
6. There follows another act of prostration, when the praises of God are repeated.
7. The final step involves the sitting position and silent recitation, after which the individual worshipers turn their faces to the right and the left to greet their neighbors. This greeting, or *salam*, concludes the prayer proper. However, it must be noted that where additional *rakahs* are to be said, the first six steps are always repeated.

The pillars (*arkan*) of the prayer consist of seventeen items, as described by the thirteenth century Sunni jurist, Ahmad al-Naqib al-Misri (see the Article "*Salat*" in *Oxford encyclopedia of the modern Islamic world*), which summarizes the opinion of the majority of Muslim jurists, both Sunni and Shia, as follows:
1. Intention (*Niyyah*);
2. The Opening "God is the Greatest" (*Allahu Akbar*);
3. Standing (*Qiyam*) ;
4. Reciting *Surah al-Fatihah* (the Opening chapter of the Qur'an)
5. Bowing (*Ruku'*);
6. Remaining motionless for a short while therein (*Tuma'nina*);
7. Straightening back up after bowing (*I'itidal*);
8. Remaining motionless for a short while therein (*Tuma'nina*);

9. Prostration (*Sujud*);
10. Remaining motionless for a short while therein (*I'itidal*);
11. Sitting back between the two prostrations (*al-Julus bayina al-Sajadahtayin*);
12. Remaining motionless for a short while therein (*I'itidal*);
13. The Prayer's final Testification of Faith (*al-Tashahhud al-Akhir*);
14. Sitting therein (*Julus*);
15. The Blessings on the Prophet (s) (al-*Salat* 'ala al-Nabi);
16. Saying "Peace be upon you" (*"al-Salamu 'Alayikum"*), the first of the two times it is said at the end of the prayer; and
17. The Proper sequence of the above integrals.
[Also see table "Performance of Prayer" in this section.]

The above features of prayer have always made *Salat* a distinctive practice and defined Muslims in a unique way.

These tell us not just the multistage movements that combine bows, prostrations, and the recitation of prayer formulas, but also the inner dimension of prayer. These form the basis not just for obligatory (*fard*) prayers, but also for other forms of prayer (*sunnah* or *nawafil*).

Details of Prayer

Having fulfilled all the conditions for cleanliness, having done the *wudu*, and having been properly dressed, it is now time to pray. Physical preparation is necessary and it is a prerequisite for prayer, but equally if not more important is the mental readiness already discussed. Let your soul be in the fear of the Lord as you are about to stand before the Master of Heaven and Earth. Now stand on a prayer mat or the place where you are offering the prayer, facing towards the Kaaba and your heart facing Allah. At this time, silently recite the following:

آنِيْ وَجَّهْتُ وجهِيَ لِلَّذِيْ فَطَرَ السَّمَاوَاتِ والأَرْضَ حَنِيفًا مُسْلِمًا وَّ مَا أَنَا مِنَ الْمُشْرِكِيْنَ اِنَّ صَلَاتِيْ وَ نُسُكِيْ وَ مَحْيَاىَ وَ مَمَاتِيْ لِلّٰهِ رَبِّ الْعَـالَمِيْنَ لَا شَرِيْكَ لَهُ وَ بِذلِكَ أُمِرْتُ وَ أَنَا مِنَ الْمُسْلِمِيْنَ

Inni wajjahtu waj-hiya lilladhi fata-ras samaawaati wal arda hanifam muslimaw wa maa ana minal mushrikin inna salaati wa nu suki wa mah-yaya wa mamati lillahi rabbil 'alamin la sharika lahu wa bidhalika umirtu wa ana minal muslimin.

Verily I have turned my face earnestly Towards Him who created the heavens and the earth, And I am not of those who ascribe partners to Allah. Verily my prayer, my sacrifice, My life and death are for Allah, the Lord of the worlds. No partner has He. And am I commanded and I am among the Muslims.

You are now ready to begin the *Salat*. Make the *niyyah* (intention) for it. The intention is made within the mind, so think about the particular obligatory, optional or nafl prayer you intend to perform. You are not to utter the words of *niyyah* aloud as this is not authentic or approved by the Prophet (s). 'Abdul 'Aziz 'Abdullah bin Baz, former Grand Mufti in Saudi Arabia, has this to say on this subject (vide *Verifying and explaining many matters of Hajj, 'Umrah and Ziyarah in the light of the Qur'an and Sunnah*, 1996, p. 22):

> The expression of verbal intention is approved by Shariah only for *Ihram*, for there is a definite Hadith to this effect by the Prophet (s). However, there is no ruling for expressing verbal intention while performing prayers, any other worship act or *Tawaf*. For example, it should not be said: "I intend to perform *Tawaf*." To express such a verbal intention is a manifest heresy. In other words, to say any other worship intention aloud is a sinful act. Had a verbal

intention been approved by Shariah, the Prophet (s) would have definitely instructed so or demonstrated it through his deed or saying. And our righteous predecessors would have done the same.

After *niyyah* (intention), raise both hands up to the ears and say *Takbir* (*Takbir at-Tahrima*), i. e., "Allahu Akbar," meaning Allah is the Greatest. This particular glorification of Allah is the moment the prayer begins, and you are now in direct line with Allah and are talking to Him. From here on, only the words of prayer are permitted. There must be no interruption whatsoever; it must be a continuous uninterrupted performance. *Tahrim* means prohibition, and this name is given to the above *takbir* because with its utterance, attention to everything other than prayer is prohibited. One widely known hadith is that when a person stands in prayer, he stands with one foot in this world and the other in the grave.

In a standing position, after *takbir* is said, the right hand is put over the left and placed below the navel. This is called *qiyam*. However, the position of *qiyam* just described is according to Hanafi *Madhhab*. Followers of Maliki *Madhhab* leave hands to their sides, and Hanbali's place their hands on the chest. These are, however, minor differences, and one may follow any one of these. (For *Madhhab*, see the chapter on Shariah.)

Women, while saying "Allahu Akbar" for *takbir at-tahrima*, should raise their hands up to their shoulders, keeping only their hands covered. Then they should put their hands on the chest, keeping the palm of the right hand on the back of the left hand. *Takbir* is followed by *Du'a*, called *Thana* (see below); after that, *Surah al-Fatihah* is recited.

Recitation of Thana Before Surah al-Fatihah

There are several *du'a*s which Prophet Muhammad (s) used to recite before *Surah al-Fatihah*. Two are mentioned here:

اَللَّهُمَّ بَاعِدْ بَيْنِي وَ بَيْنَ خَطَايَايَ كَمَا بَاعَدْتَ بَيْنَ الْمَشْرِقِ وَ الْمَغْرِبِ ۞ اَللَّهُمَّ نَقِّنِي مِنْ خَطَايَايَ كَمَا يُنَقَّى الثَّوْبُ الْأَبْيَضُ مِنَ الدَّنَسِ ۞ اَللَّهُمَّ اغْسِلْنِىْ مِنْ خَطَايَايَ بِالْمَاءِ وَ الثَّلْجِ وَ الْبَرَدِ ۞

Allah humma ba`id bayni wa bayna khatayaya Kama ba`adta baynal mashriqi wal *Maghrib*i, Allah humma naq-qini min khatayaya kama yunaq-qath thatbul abyadu minad danasi, Allah hummaghsilni min Khatayaya bil mai wath thalji wal bardi.

O Allah, set me apart from my sins as East and West are apart from each other.
O Allah, cleanse me of my sins as a white garment is cleansed from dirt after thorough washing.
Oh Allah, wash my sins away with water, snow and hail.
(Bukhari and Muslim)

If a person does not know the *Du'a* just mentioned, then he should recite the following one. 'Umar (r) is reported to have used this *Du'a* after saying *Takbir at-Tahrima*. Hanafis normally recite this one:

سُبْحَانَكَ اَللَّهُمَّ وَ بِحَمْدِكَ وَتَبَارَكَ اسْمُكَ وَتَعَالَى جَدُّكَ وَلَا اِلٰهَ غَيْرُكَ

Subhanaka Allahumma wa bihamdika watabara kasmaka wata 'ala jadduka wa lailaha ghayruka.
Glory be to you, O Allah, and all praises are due unto you, and blessed is your name and high is your majesty and none is worthy of worship but you.

The *Thana* is followed by *Ta'wwudh*

$$\text{أَعُوذُ بِاللهِ مِنَ الشَّيْطَانِ الرَّجِيْمِ}$$

A'wudhubillahi min-ash-Shaitan nir- Rajim.
I seek the refuge of Allah to be saved from the accursed devil.

Then *Tasmiyah*

$$\text{بِاسْمِ اللَّهِ الرَّحْمَانِ الرَّحِيمِ}$$

"Bismillahir Rahman nir-Rahim", is recited. In subsequent *rakahs* in the same unit it is sufficient to say *tasmiyah* and skip thana and ta'wwudh. Now recite *Surah al-Fatihah*, reflecting and pondering over its meaning, and say "Amin" when finished. Amin in itself is a prayer which means "O Lord, accept my prayer."

Reciting Behind an Imam

As stated in *Fiqh* (Vol. 1, p. 146):
One's prayer is not accepted unless *Surah al-Fatihah* is recited in every *rakah*. But, one who is praying behind an imam is to keep quiet while the imam is reciting aloud, as Allah says in the Qur'an, "When the Qur'an is recited, listen and remain silent that you may attain mercy." The Prophet (s), upon whom be peace, also said, "When the imam makes the *takbir*, (you too) make the *takbir*. When he recites, be silent" (Related by Muslim). If the imam reads quietly, then all of the followers must also make their own recital. If one cannot hear the imam's recital, he must make his own recital ... It has become quite common nowadays

for imams to be silent for a period after reciting *al-Fatihah* in order to give those behind them a chance to recite it.

Recitation of *Surah al-Fatihah* is followed by a *Surah* or any portion of the Qur'an no fewer than three small verses. If the verse is long (e. g., 24: 35), then one verse is enough.

Note: In *Fajr, Maghrib* and *'Isha,* in *fard* part of the prayer Qur'an is recited loudly. However, in the third and / or fourth *rakah* of the *Fard* prayer recitation of *Surah al-Fatihah* is sufficient and is done silently. Women do all their recitation silently in all *rakahs. Surah al-Fatihah* is essential in all *raka hs*, and prayer is not valid without it.

After *Surah al-Fatihah* and some other verses are recited as mentioned above, then the worshipper says, "Allahu Akbar," lowering his head and placing the palms of his hands on the knees. This is called *Ruku'*, and in that position he repeats:

سُبْحَانَ رَبِّيَ الْعَظِيمِ

"Subhana Rabbiya-l-'Azim," "Glory to my Lord the Great," repeated three times or more. The practice has always been an odd number. During *Ruku'*, women have to bend only so much that their hands reach the knees. Rise upright from the *Ruku'*, saying:

سَمِعَ اللهُ لِمَنْ حَمِدَهُ

Sami'Allahu liman hamidah : May God hear he who worships Him

When you are upright, say:

رَبَّنَا لَكَ الْحَمْدُ

"Rabbana lakal hamad" (Our Lord be praised).

According to *Fiqh* (Vol. 1, p. 130):

'Ibadah : Salat

It is preferred to raise one's hands while going to bow and upon coming up from the bow ... Reported Ibn 'Umar, "When the Prophet (s), upon whom be peace, stood to pray, he would raise his hands until they were the same height as his shoulders and then he would make the *takbir*. When he wanted to bow, he would again raise his hands in a similar fashion. When he raised his head from the bowing, he did the same and said, "Allah hears him who praises Him." (Related by al-Bukhari, Muslim and al-Baihaqi.)

Hanafis, however, raise hands only once at the time of *takbir at-tahrima*.

The worshipper then says "Allahu Akbar," prostrating himself with the toes of both feet, both knees, both hands and the forehead touching the ground. This is the position of *Sujud*, or *Sajdah*, and is accompanied with these words:

سُبْحَانَ رَبِّيَ الأَعْلىٰ

Subhana Rabbiyal-A'La : Glory to my Lord the Most High repeated three times or more, as mentioned above.

Then with the utterance of "Allahu Akbar" comes the *Julus*, a short rest in a sitting posture: the outer side of the left foot and the toes of the right one, which are in an erect position, touching the ground and the two hands are placed on the knees. After this, the second prostration, *Sujud* is repeated in the same way with the same utterances as in the first one. This completes one *rakah* (unit) of the prayer.

In *sajdah*, women may keep their belly and armpits joined together and pressed against the thighs. They should not keep their feet standing on toes. They should place their elbows flat on the ground, while men keep them raised from the ground. For practical reasons, it may be necessary for women to have somewhat different physical positions or postures in prayer than men. Nevertheless, Prophet's (s) prayer applies equally to men and women, for there is nothing in the *Sunnah* to suggest the difference or exception for women. The generality of Prophet's (s) hadith, "pray as you have seen me praying," includes men and women alike. Imam Bukhari reported in *Tarikh Saghir* (p. 95) that Umm Darda, a renowned female narrator of hadith, used to sit during her prayer just as a man sits.

After the first *rakah* (unit) the worshipper rises, saying "Allahu Akbar," to assume a standing position for the second *rakah* (unit). After *Tasmiyah* he recites the Opening (*Surah al-Fatihah*), followed by a Qur'anic passage as in the first *rakah* (unit). When he has finished the second bowing and the two prostrations in the same way as the first, he takes a sitting position as in *Julus* and recites quietly

At-Tashahhud or Attahiyyat

اَلتَّحِيَّاتُ لله وَالصَّلَوَاةُ وَ الطَّيِّبَاتُ اَلسَّلَامُ عَلَيْكَ أَيُّهَا النَبِــــيُ ورَحْمَــةُ اللهِ وَبَرَكَاتُهُ اَلسَّلَامُ عَلَيْنَا وَعَلَى عِبَادِ اللهِ الصَّالِحِينَ . أَشْهَدُ أَنْ لاَّ اِلَهَ إِلَّـــا اللهُ وَاَشْهَدُ أَنَّ مُحَمَّداً عَبْدُهُ وَرَسُوْلُهُ .

At-Tahiyyatu Lillah Was Salawatu Wat Tayyhibatu As-Salamu 'Alaika Ayyuhannabiyyu Wa Rahmatullahi Wa Barakahuhu Assalamu 'Alaina Wa 'Ala 'Ibadillahis Salihin. Ash Hadu An Lailaha Illal Lahu Wa Ash Hadu Anna Muhammadan `abduhu Wa Rasuluhu.

All prayer is for Allah and worship and goodness Peace be on you, O Prophet (s) and the mercy of Allah and His blessings Peace be on us and on the righteous servants of Allah I bear witness that there is no god but Allah and bear witness that Muhammad is His servant and messenger.

'Ibadah : Salat

While saying "Ashhadu Allah Ilaha Illalahu," make a fist with the right hand and raise only the forefinger, denoting the oneness of Allah.

If the *Salat* consists of more than two *rakahs*, say *takbir* after the recitation of *Tashahhud* and stand up for the remaining part of *Salat*. If the prayer has only three *rakahs*, what would follow the fourth is done at third.

If the *Salat* consists of only two *rakahs* then, after the recitation of *Tasahhud*, recite as follows (for three or four *rakah Salat*, this will be done at the second of the final *rakah* and after reciting the **First part of** *Tasahhud* a second time):

اَللّٰهُمَّ صَلِّ عَلٰى مُحَمَّدٍ وَعَلٰى آلِ مُحَمَّدٍ كَمَا صَلَّيْتَ عَلٰى إِبْرَاهِيمَ وَعَلٰى آلِ إِبْرَاهِيمَ اِنَّكَ حَمِيدٌ مَجِيدٌ ۞

Allahumma Salli 'Ala Muhammadin Wa 'Ala Ali Muhammadin Kama Sallaita 'Ala Ibrahima Wa 'Ala Ali Ibrahima Innaka Hamidum Majid.

اَللّٰهُمَّ بَارِكْ عَلٰى مُحَمَّدٍ وَعَلٰى آلِ مُحَمَّدٍ كَمَا بَارَكْتَ عَلٰى إِبْرَاهِيمَ وَعَلٰى آلِ إِبْرَاهِيمَ اِنَّكَ حَمِيدٌ مَجِيدٌ ۞

Allahumma Barik 'Ala Muhammadin Wa 'Ala Ali Muhammadin Kama Barakta 'Ala Ibrahima Innaka Hamidum Majid

O Allah, let Your blessing come upon Muhammad and the family of Muhammad as You blessed Ibrahim and his family truly You are the Praiseworthy and Glorious. O Allah, bless Muhammad and the family of Muhammad As You blessed

Ibrahim and his family truly You are the Praiseworthy and Glorious.

These two together are known as the Words of Greeting and Blessing., or *Salat al-Muhammad wa Ibrahim*.

Finally, he turns his face to the right side, saying these words: "Assalamu 'Alaykum wa rahmatu-l-Lah" (peace be on you and the mercy of God). Then he turns his face to the left side, uttering the same greetings. This is known as the *salam*. This is how any prayer of two units (*rakahs*), whether obligatory or supererogatory, is performed.

Fard Salat, whether alone or in congregation, is inaugurated by *Iqamah*, which has been discussed in the section **Adhan and Iqamah**. When two or more persons perform obligatory prayers together, *Adhan* is highly recommended, and for a prayer in a mosque it is required.

Conditions for the Validity of Salat

Conditions that must be met before one starts the *Salat* (if any one of these is missing, the *Salat* will be invalid):
1. Knowledge that the time for a particular *Salat* has begun.
2. Cleanliness of one's body, clothing, and place of prayer.
3. Ritual purification.
4. Proper attire for *Salat* with the exception that women must cover the entire body other than the face and hands.
5. Face the *Qiblah*.
6. The *Niyyah* (intention)—the person about to pray should know what *Salat* he is going to pray, whether *Fard* (obligatory) or *Nafl* (Voluntary), and which prayer of the day, *Dhuhr* or *'Asr*, etc.

Basic Elements (Arkan) of Salat

If any one of the following is missing, the *Salat* is unacceptable:
1. *Takbir at-Tahrima* (to say Allahu Akbar at the beginning of the *Salat*).
2. *Qiyam* (Standing). However, if one is unable to stand for *Fard Salat*, he should pray sitting; if unable to pray sitting, he should pray on his side or as best he can.
3. Recite *Surah al-Fatihah* in every *rakah* of every *Salat*, whether obligatory or voluntary.
4. *Ruku'* (Bowing).
5. Resume standing after bowing. One should come to rest in an upright position.
6. Two *Sajdah* in each *rakah* and sitting up between them, coming to rest in each position.
7. The final sitting and recitation of *Tashahhud* while sitting.
8. *Taslim*. Say As-*Salamu 'alaikum* to the right, then the left.
9. The proper order.

In a nutshell: Start with *Takbir at-tahrim* standing, recite *Surah al-Fatihah*, then bow in *Ruku'*, then rise up from it to standing, then perform *Sajdah*, then rise up from it to sitting, then perform the second *Sajdah*. In the second *rakah* and in the final *rakah*, one should sit for *Tashahhud*, and in the final *rakah* make *Taslim*.

Invalidation of Prayers

Any prayer becomes invalid and nullified by any of the following acts:
1. To anticipate the Imam in any act or movement of prayer and be ahead of him.
2. To eat or drink during the prayer.

3. To talk or say something out of the prescribed course of prayers.
4. To shift the position from the direction of qiblah (Makkah).
5. To do any noticeable act or move outside the regular acts and movements of prayer without a proper reason.
6. To do anything that nullifies the ablution, e. g., discharge of urine, stool, gas, blood, etc.
7. To fail in observing any of the essential acts of prayer, like standing, reciting the Qur'an, *Ruku'*, *Sujud*, etc.
8. To uncover the body between the navel and the knees during the prayer in the case of males, or any part of the body, except the hands, face and feet, in the case of females.
9. Utterance of a cry of pain or trouble.

Any prayer which becomes invalidated must be repeated properly.

Prostration of Forgetfulness (Sajdah Sahw)

One should make a *sahw sajdah*:
1. If he is doubtful about the number of *rakahs* he prayed. According to a hadith (Muslim), the Prophet (s) said: "If you are uncertain in the prayer and do not know whether you have prayed three or four *rakahs*, then pray a *rakah* and make two prostrations while in sitting position before the *taslim*."
2. If he misses any of the *Fard* in prayer (see the table below, "Performance of Prayer"). However, forgetting any of the basic *Fard* units or steps such as *Takbir at-Tahrima*, Al-Fatihah, *Ruku'*, etc., requires repeat performance of the whole *rakah* in which the drop occurred. *Sajdah* Sahw is not enough in these cases.

No sahw *sajdah* is required in the cases of forgetting minor actions or sayings in the prayer such as "Allahu Akbar" (not

Takbir at-Tahrima, i. e., Allahu Akbar at the start), "Subhana rabbi al-'Azim," etc.

How the Sahw Sajdah is Performed

Since we are human beings, we are not above mistakes and errors. If we forget to do something in our *Salat*, we can make up for it by making two extra *sajdah* as we do in any *rakah* of *Salat*. This is called *Sajdah as-Sahw*. This is done at the end of the last *rakah* of *Salat*. What you have to do is to say *Tashahhud* and then turn your face to the right, saying *Assalamu 'alaikum wa rahmatullah* and make two extra *sajdah* with *tasbih* (*Subhana Rabbiyal 'ala* and then recite *Tashahhud* again with *Salat 'alan Nabiyy* (*Durud*) and *du'a*. Now you turn your face first to the right and then to the left, saying "Assalamu 'alikum wa rahmatullah."

Salat al-Jama'ah : Congregational Prayers

Although midday prayer on Friday is the only congregational *Fard* prayer, Muslims should take the opportunity to pray in congregation whenever possible. Imam Shafi held congregational prayer to be *Fard Kifaya*, while Imam Abu Hanifah and his disciples were of the opinion that it is *Sunnah Muakkadah*, coming close to *Wajib*. It is evident from both the Qur'an and hadith the great stress that has been laid on the necessity for us to try our utmost to join the congregational prayer. Abdullah bin 'Umar (r) narrates that he heard the Prophet (s) saying: "A *Salat* with *jama'at* is twenty-seven times superior to *Salat* performed at home."

In congregational prayer there is a prayer leader (Imam). He is not in any sense a priest, but simply a person who has volunteered or chosen to lead on his merits of religious knowledge and piety.

Most mosques have a regular Imam but it is not compulsory to have one, and any Muslim may lead the prayer in his absence based on his knowledge of the Qur'an.

The Imam of the congregation stands in front by himself while the followers (*Muqtadi*) stand behind him in straight lines, shoulder to shoulder, all facing the *qiblah*. After making the intention of prayer in heart, the Imam proceeds in manner similar to the steps described under "Details of Prayer" above. The *Muqtadi*s act likewise.

When the Imam recites the Qur'an aloud, the *muqtadi*s listen to him attentively and with humility. When the Imam concludes *al-Fatihah*, the followers say "Amin." After the Imam stands from the bowing posture he says: *Sami' Allahu liman Hamidah* (God accepts any who are thankful to Him), and the followers respond in these words: *Rabbana laka-l-Hamd* (our Lord praise be to You). The *muqtadi*s follow the Imam in all his ritual movements; should anyone supersede him, his prayer becomes void.

Latecomer in Congregation

If a person comes after the start of prayer and joins the congregation, he must, even if he has missed one *rakah* (unit) or more, follow the Imam. When the Imam completes the service by uttering the final peace greetings, this latecomer does not join in that, but takes a standing position to make up for the early *rakah* (units) he has missed. When a person joins the congregation in the bowing position, before rising, he is considered as having joined from the start of this particular *rakah* (unit). But if he joins in any position after bowing, he has missed the *rakah* (unit) and must make up for it individually right after the Imam concludes the prayer.

It must be remembered that whether praying in congregation or alone, it is a personal obligation to pray and fulfill the prayer requirements.

Concentration in Prayer

When we cannot concentrate in prayer, that should mean the *Shaytan* (Satan) is being successful in his efforts. (See Imam Ghazzali's plea on waging a war on Satan in "Overcoming Satan's Force" in the Appendix.) Afif A. Tabbarah gives the following advice on concentration in prayer in his The *Spirit of Islam*, pp. 129-130:

> When man hurries in prayer, turning himself to God through worship, he is occupied with various thoughts; yet he tries to drive them out, so as to give way to a summoning of God's Grace and of the bliss that springs from "conversing" with Deity. This mental activity the worshipper performs to push away his conflicting thoughts, needs considerable effort, patience and a fear of the Lord -- all leading to submission to God.
>
> [Imam] Fakhr ad-Din al-Razi ... [a distinguished Qur'ān commentator] theologian and scholar, interprets submission in prayer as an act of uniting one's effort in prayer and abstaining from everything else. It is a means of developing the faculty of mental concentration which bears a great effect on man's success in life.

No doubt attention can best be achieved when both the mind and body operate in complete harmony. This is exactly the case of joint activity between the mind and body during prayer; the worshipper bows and prostrates in performing his religious ritual.

Imam Ghazzali writes (*Ihya* II, pp. 35-36):

What is the point of praying "show us the straight path," if one is in a state of absentmindedness? If it is not intended as a humble entreaty and supplication, why bother the idle mouthing of the words, especially if it has become a habit? ... Far from seeing or witnessing Him, the heedless worshipper is not even aware Whom he is addressing, as his tongue moves purely from force of habit. How remote this is from the purpose of ritual Prayer, which was prescribed for the refinement of the heart, the renewal of Divine remembrance, and to secure the knot of faith!

From Whom Prayer Will Be Accepted

In order for a prayer to be acceptable to Allah, it must, above all, be offered correctly. *Salat* may be performed only in a prescribed form and under certain conditions as have been laid down in the Shariahs discussed in the preceding pages. But to please Allah, it has to be more than than merely correct. This is what Hadith Qudsi says on this point; these are the words of Allah:

I will accept the prayer of one who humbles himself before My greatness, who does not display arrogance towards my creatures, who does not constantly spend the night disobeying Me, who spends the day remembering Me, who has compassion for the wretched, the wayfarer, the widow, and the afflicted. That man's light is as the light of the sun. I will protect him with My might, guard him with My angels, give him light in the darkness, and understanding in ignorance. His likeness in my creatures is as paradise in the garden.

Allah reminds us in the Qur'an (23: 1-2):

> Successful indeed are the believers, those who offer *Salat* (prayers) with all solemnity and full submissiveness.

In a booklet entitled *Why do we pray?*, Suhaib Hasan (pp. 16-17) discusses the above verse and points out:

> The emphasis, in this verse, is on humility and concentration in the prayer (*Khushu*). There is no doubt that as *Shaytan* is the most bitter enemy of man, he always tries to disturb the believer's prayer. As soon as a person begins his prayer, he finds his mind suddenly engulfed with memories, problems, worries, work and his family. He may become so engrossed in his thoughts that he has no idea where he is and what he is doing. His prayer becomes a series of automatic actions, and he will often find himself wondering whether he has prayed three *rakahs* or four. This is how *Shaytan* steals the prayer.
>
> The Prophet (s) once said that only a tiny portion of the prayer, maybe as little as a tenth or an eighth, is accepted by Allah. The rest is lost because of the whisperings of *Shaytan*.

To summarize, there are many factors which make one's supplication acceptable. The sincerity, humbleness, complete submission to the will of Allah may lead to an acceptance as He asks (7: 55): "Invoke your Lord with humility and in secret." Although Almighty Allah assures us that He responds "to the prayer of every supplicant when he calleth on" Him (2: 186), no one can claim whether his prayer is accepted or not. As a servant of the Almighty ('Abd-Allah) one's duty is to offer his prayer with utmost devotion and wait with fear an hope for His acceptence. "Indeed it is He who is the Beneficent, the Merciful." (52: 28)

DETAIL OF RAKAH IN EACH SALAT

Name of Prayer	Period	Sunnah	Fard (Obligatory)	Fard rakah Aloud or Silent	Sunnah	Nafl	Witr	Total (Obligatory and Binding)
Fajr	Between dawn and sunrise	2*	2	Aloud	–	–	–	4
Dhuhr	Between just past noon and mid-afternoon	4*	4	Silent	2*	2	–	10
Asr	Between mid-afternoon and before sunset	4+	4	Silent	–	–	–	4
Magh-rib	Just after sunset	2+	3	Aloud (3rd silent)	2*	2	–	5
'Isha	Between dark and shortly before dawn	4+ (or 2+)	4	Aloud (3rd and 4th silent)	2*	2	3	9
Jum-uah	Between just past noon and mid-afternoon	2+(Greeting of Mosque) 4+	2	**Aloud**	4+ (and/ or 2+ at home)	2	–	10

* *Sunnah* Muakkada, i. e., binding
+ *Sunnah Ghair*, i. e., non-binding

Note: As can be seen from the table above, the observant Muslim must perform a minimum of 32 *rakah* every day. Out of these, 17 (2+4+4+3+4) are obligatory. If one give up any of these, he/she will be punished on Judgment Day. This is based on *The Prescribed Islamic Prayer: Salat*, compiled by Abdul Rahman Shad (p. 12).

PERFORMANCE OF PRAYER
Obligatory and Voluntary Acts
(Based on *Al-Salat* (Prayer))
(Edited by Abdel Warith M. Said, 1995, p. 79)

No	Fard	Sunnah	* Obligatory (*Fard*) Acts of Prayer x Voluntary (*Sunnah*) Acts of Prayer
1		X	*Sutrah* (Barrier for Passage)
2	*		Istiqbal al-Qiblah (Facing Kaaba)
3	*		*Al-Niyyah* (Intention)
4	*		Standing in *Fard* Prayer
5	*		*Takbir* at-Tahrim (at the start of prayer)
6		X	Du'a' al-Istiftah (in the first *rakah* only) Initiating Du'a' i. e., Inni Wajhatu ...
7		X	Al-Ista'dha (Audhubillah ... shaytanir rajim)
8	*		Reciting al-Fatihah
9	*		Recitation after al-Fatihah (except in $3^{rd}/4^{th}$ *Rakah*
10		X	*Takbir* for *Ruku'*
11	*		*Ruku'*
12		X	*Tasbih* in *Ruku'*, i. e., Subhana Rabbiyal-'Azim
13	*		Perfection of *Ruku'* (no rushing)
14	*		Standing from *Ruku'*
15		X	Du'a'
16		X	*Takbir* for first *Sajdah*
17	*		*Sajdah*
18		X X	*Tasbih* in *Sajdah* (Subhana Rabbi) *Takbir* of sitting from *Sajdah*
19	*	X X	Jalsah between the two *Sajdah* (Sitting between two *sajdahs* and also when saying Attahayyatu) Du'a' of this Jalsa (Allahummaghfirli ...) *Takbir* for the 2nd *Sajdah*
20		X X	The second *Sajdah'* *Tasbih* in *Sajdah* (subana Rabbi al-Ala) *Takbir* to sit down (or to stand up)
21	*		Al-Tashah-hud
22		X	Al-*Salat* al-Ibrahimiyyah, i. E., Part II of *Tasahhud*
23		X	Du'a' after Durud on Al-*Salat* al-Ibrahimiyyah (at the end of prayer only)
24	*		Al-*Salam* (peace) to end prayer
25		X	Khatam al-*Salat* (Du'a' after *Salat*) (Finishing of prayer)

Section 6 : Fard, Wajib and Witr, Qada and Qasr Prayers

Fard (Obligatory) Prayers

There are five daily compulsory prayers. These, along with the *Fard* components, are as follows:
Salat al-Fajr (The Dawn Prayer): 2 Rakahs
Salat adh-Dhuhr (The Early Afternoon Prayer): 4 Rakahs
Salat al-'Asr (The Late Afternoon Prayer): 4 Rakahs
Salat al-Maghrib (The Sunset Prayer): 3 Rakahs
Salat al-'Isha (The Night Prayer): 4 Rakahs.

Salat al-Witr (The Odd Prayer)

Witr means an odd number. *Witr* is a most desirable prayer to be performed after *'Isha* Prayer. It could be performed in any odd number, from one *rakah* to eleven rakahs. It is recommended that *Witr* should be the last prayer at night. Witr is performed in congregation in the month of Ramadan, after the Tarawih Prayers. In that case, the Imam should read the Qur'an audibly in all the rakahs. In the final *rakah* of *Witr* Prayer, reciting *Du'a al-Qunut* is recommended.

According to the Hanafis, *witr* is wajib, a duty without being *Fard*, but for the other *Madhhab*s it is a custom--a strong one, *sunnah muakkada*.

Nature and Number of Rakah

According to *Fiqh* (v. 2, pp. 13-14), it is permissible to pray all the three *rakah*s with two *tashahhud*s, i. e., one at the end of two *rakah*s and the second one at the end of the third Rakah, and

'Ibadah : Salat

one *taslim* after completion of both parts of *tasahhud*. It is also permissible to perform *witr* in two parts: (1) praying two *rakahs* and concluding them, and (2) then praying one *rakah* with a *tasahhud* and *taslim*. It is also allowed to offer a number of *rakahs* one after another, without making any *tasahhud*, save in the one before the last rakah, in which case one makes the *tasahhud* and then stands to perform the last *rakah* wherein one will make another *tasahhud* and end the prayer with the *taslim*. All of that is permissible and can be traced to the Prophet (s). It is permissible to recite any *Surah* after *al-Fatithah*.

Al-Qunut in the Witr

It is part of *sunnah* to supplicate with *qunut* in the *witr* prayer. The following *du'a*s are taken from *A Guide to Prayer in Islam* by M. A. K. Saqib, published by Revival of Islamic Heritage Society, Kuwait (pp. 61-63):

Hasan bin 'Ali (r) said, "The Messenger of Allah (s) taught me the words which I should say in the *du'a* of *witr*, and those are as follows:

اَللَّهُمَّ أَهْدِنِي فِيمَنْ هَدَيْتَ وَ عَافِنِي فِيمَنْ عَافَيْتَ وتولنى فيمن تَوَلَّيْتَ وَبَارِكْ لِيَ فِيمَا أَعْطَيْتَ وَقِنِي شَرَّ مَا قَضَيْتَ فَإِنَّكَ تَقْضِي وَلاَ يُقْضَى عَلَيْكَ انه لاَ يَذِلُّ مِنْ وَالَيْتَ وَلاَ يعِزُّ مَنْ عَادَيْتَ تَبَارَكْتَ رَبَّنَا وَ تَعَالَيْتَ نَسْتَغْفِرُكَ وَ نَتُوبُ إِلَيْكَ وصلىَّ الله عَلَىَ النَّبِي

Allah humma ahdini fiman hadyata, Wa 'afini fiman 'afayta, wata wal-lani fiman tawal-layta wa barik li fima a'taita, waqini shar-ra ma qadayta, fa-innaka taqdi wala yaqdi 'alayka, innahu la Yadhil-lu min walayta, wala ya'iz-zu man 'adayta, tabarakta rabbana wata 'alayta, nastaghfiruka wanatubu ilayka, wa sal-lal lahu 'alan-nabi.

O Allah, make me among those whom you have guided, and make me among those whom you have saved, and make me among those whom you have chosen, and bless whatever you have given me, and protect me from the evil which you have decreed; verily, you decide the things and nobody can decide against you; surely the person you befriend can't be disgraced, and the person you oppose can't be honoured. You are blessed, our Lord, and exalted, we ask for your forgiveness and turn to you. Peace and mercy of Allah be upon the Prophet. (Abu Dawud, Nasai, Ibn Majah, Tirmidhi)

The above quoted du'a reproduced in *Fiqh* version (v. 2, p. 16) is slightly shorter towards the end.

Another du'a is also quoted below:

اَللّٰهُمَّ اِنَّا نَسْتَعِينُكَ وَنَسْتَغْفِرُكَ ونُؤْمِنُ بِكَ و نَتَوَكَّلُ عَلَيْكَ و نُثْنِىُ عَلَيْكَ الْخَيْرَ وَنَشْكُرُكَ ولاَ نَكْفُرُكَ ونَخْلَعُ و نَتْرُكُ مَنْ يَفْجُرُكَ اللّٰهُمَّ اِيَّاكَ نَعْبُدُ ولَكَ نُصَلِّىُ ونَسْجُدُ و إِلِيك نَسْعَى و نَحْفِدُ ونَرْجُوُ رحْمَتَكَ و نَخْشَى عَذَابَكَ إنَّ عَذَابَكَ بِالْكُفَّارِ مُلْحِقٌ ۞

Allah humma in-na nasta'inuka wa nastaghfiruka wa numinubika wa natawak-kalu 'alayka wa nuthni 'alayk-al-khayr. Wa nashkuruka wala nakfuruka wa nakhla'u wa nat ruku' man-y yafjurka. Allah humma iyyaka na'budu walaka nusal-li wa nas-judu wa ilayka nas'a wa nahfidu wa narju rahmataka wa nakhsha 'adhabaka inna 'adhabaka bil kuf- fari mulhiq.

O Allah, we ask you for help and seek your forgiveness, and we believe in you and have trust in you, and we praise you in the best way and we thank you and we are not ungrateful to you, and we forsake and turn away from the one who disobeys you. O Allah, we worship you only and pray to you and prostrate ourselves before you, and we run towards you and serve you, and we hope to receive your mercy, and we fear your punishment. Surely, the disbelievers will receive your punishment.

This text, in a slightly shorter form, is found in Abu Dawud *Marasil, bab ma dja'a fi-man nama 'an al-Salat*, 12-13), according to whom it was reportedly taught to Muhammad (s) by Jibril himself.

A person may offer both or either of these. If one has not memorized any of these, it is permissible to render any recitation (supplication) similar in length until these are mastered.

How to Perform the Qunut

It is permissible to make the *qunut* before going into *Ruku'* (bowing), or it may be recited when one stands up straight after the *Ruku'*. According to Bukhari (Hadith No. 2. 115 as cited in Alim), Muhammad (s) recited *qunut* after bowing for some time (for one month). However, according to Hadith No. 116 in the same source, he used to recite *qunut* before bowing. Hanafis say *qunut* before bowing. Non-Hanafis split up *witr*: they first say two *rakahs*, after *salam* they offer the third rakah. According to *Encyclopedia of Islam* (p. 930), the Malikis deny that there is a *qunut* in the *witr* prayer. The followers of Imam Shaf'i recite the *Qunut* in the second *rakah* after *Ruku'* of *Fajr* Prayer daily.

Friday (Jumu'ah) Prayer

يَٰٓأَيُّهَا ٱلَّذِينَ ءَامَنُوٓاْ إِذَا نُودِيَ لِلصَّلَوٰةِ مِن يَوْمِ ٱلْجُمُعَةِ فَٱسْعَوْاْ إِلَىٰ ذِكْرِ ٱللَّهِ وَذَرُواْ ٱلْبَيْعَ ذَٰلِكُمْ خَيْرٌ لَّكُمْ إِن كُنتُمْ تَعْلَمُونَ ۝

O you who believe! When the call is heard for the prayer of the day of congregation, hasten unto remembrance of Allah and leave your trading. That is better for you if you did but know. (62. 9)

Friday is the day appointed by Muhammad (s) as the day of solemn, public and united prayer for Muslims. It rests on a direct command by Allah, as cited above. It is the bounden duty of every Muslim personally to attend this congregational prayer at the mosque. It is not obligatory for females, but they are allowed in the mosque for Friday *Salat*, as they are for all other prayers.

Imam Ghazzali writes (*Ihya*, p. 144), "Know that this is a great day, by which Allah has magnified Islam and by which He has given distinction to Muslims." According to *Fiqh* (v. 2, p. 131), "Whoever misses three Friday prayers in a row out of negligence will have a seal put over his heart by Allah." (Also *Ihya*, p. 144).

According to Imam Ghazzali (*Ihya*, p. 145), Muhammad (s) said, "The best day the sun shines upon is Friday." The Prophet (s) also said, "Whoever dies on Friday, or on the eve of Friday, has Allah decree him the reward of a martyr and preservation from the testing of the grave" (*Ihya*, p. 146). There is also a hadith which says that this day consists of blessed hour in which all prayers are accepted. Imam Ghazzali writes (*Ihya*, pp. 165-166):

There is disagreement for it is said, "It is the hour of the appearing of the sun," and it is said, "It is at the passing of the meridian," and it is said, "With the Call to Worship," and it is said, "When the imam mounts the pulpit and begins the address," and it is said, "When the people stand up for the Worship," and it is said, "The last part of the time of 'asr, mid-afternoon," I mean, in the "hour of preference," and it is said, "Before the setting of the sun."

Especially recommended for Friday is to clean and purify oneself, for there is a hadith:

The person who takes a bath on Friday, puts on the best possible clothes, uses perfume, if available, and comes for *Salat* (early), takes his place (in the mosque) quietly without disturbing other people, then offers the *Salat* that Allah has destined for him, and sits in perfect silence and peace from the time the Imam takes his place (for the sermon) until the completion of the *Salat*, he will have all the sins he committed since the previous Friday expiated (by Allah) on account of this (act).

According to another hadith, whoever pares his nails on Friday has Allah expel from him his disease and introduce into him healing.

Conditions for Friday Prayer

1. The time of this prayer is that of *Dhuhr* which it replaces.
2. It must be offered in congregation led by an Imam. No single person can offer it by himself.
3. It must be offered in a mosque, if there is one available. Otherwise, it may be offered at any gathering place, e. g., homes, parks, farms, etc.
4. If a person misses it, he cannot make up for it. Instead, he has to offer a regular *Dhuhr* prayer which it replaces.

5. All kinds of normal work are allowed on Friday before and after the prayer (62: 10).
6. When it is time for prayer, *adhan* is given.

The Highlights of the Prayer

1. It is customary to offer two or four *rakah*s of prayer on arrival at the mosque for prayer, not just for Friday prayer, as follows: (a) offer two *rakah*s of *Tahiyyatul Wudu*. Of course, this is performed after completion of *wudu*. According to a hadith in Muslim, whoever observes two *rakah*s with full devotion after performing *wudu* well becomes entitled to enter Paradise. According to another hadith (*Kashshaf*), our Prophet (s) recommended his followers to say this prayer.
2. It is much more common to offer *Dakhlil Masjid*, i. e., salutation upon entering a mosque. (One may offer both *Tahiyyatul Wudu* as well as *Dakhlil Masjid*.) According to a hadith in Bukhari, Rasullalah (s) said: "When any one of you enters the mosque, he should not sit until he has prayed two *rakah*s." According to another hadith (*Kashshaf*), Muhammad (s) said:

> Give the mosques their due. On being asked what that was, he replied: "When you enter a mosque, pray two *rakah*s; (according to another tradition) make two prostrations before you sit down."

Imam Ghuzzali writes: "It is a Confirmed Usage and is performed upon entering the mosque even if that happens to be when the imam is lecturing." According to *Fiqh* (v. 2, p. 130): "It is a *sunnah* to offer supererogatory prayers before al-Jumu'ah until the imam arrives."
3. When the second call to prayer is given, the Imam standing on the *minbar* gives a two-part sermon (*khutba*). Both praise Allah and call for his blessings on the Prophet (s) before urging

about religious practices or matters. The two sermons are separated by a short pause during which the Imam sits. When the Imam has stood up to deliver the sermon, no one should offer an individual prayer (other than *dakhlil masjid* or a missed prayer), nor engage in conversation, respond to greeting or even meditate. One may invoke Allah's blessings for the Holy Prophet (s) when his name is mentioned in the sermon.

4. After that, the *Iqamah* is made and the two obligatory rakahs (units) are offered under the leadership of the Imam who recites al-Fatihah and other Qur'anic passage in an audible voice. When this is done, the prayer is completed like any other regular *Salat*. As mentioned, Jumu'ah has two rakahs *Fard*. According to *Fiqh* (v. 2, p. 143), if a person catches only one rakah, he need only make up the one *rakah* he misses. However, whoever catches less than one *rakah* has not caught the Jumu'ah and is to pray *Dhuhr* according to the majority of the scholars.

5. It is a *sunnah* to pray four rakahs or two rakahs after Jumu'ah, as in the following *Sahih Muslim* hadith:

(1915) Abu Huraira (r) reported Allah's Messenger (s) as saying: When any one of you observes the Jumu'ah prayer (two obligatory *rakahs* in congregation), he should observe four (*rakahs*) afterwards.

(1916) Suhail reported on the authority of Abu Huraira (r) that the Messenger of Allah (s) said: When you observe prayer after (the two obligatory rakahs) of Jumu'ah, you should observe four *rakahs* (and 'Amr in his narration has made this addition that Ibn Idris said this on the authority of Suhail); And if you are in a hurry on account of something, you should observe two *rakahs* in the mosque and two when you return (to your home).

(1917) Abu Huraira (r) reported Allah's Messenger (s) as saying: When any one amongst you observes prayer after Jumu'ah, he should observe four rakahs.

(1918) Nafi reported that when 'Abudullah (b. 'Umar) (r) observed the Friday prayer and came back he observed two *rakahs* in his house, and then said: The Messenger of Allah (s) used to do this.

Imam Ghazzali records (*Ihya*, p. 163): "Ibn 'Umar has related that Muhammad (s) used, after the Friday observance, to perform a worship of two *rakahs* and Abu Huraira states four, and 'Ali and 'Abdullah bin 'Abbas six and all are valid."

In Islam there is no sabbath or day of compulsory rest and religious observance. Qur'an plainly speaks of daily business being conducted before and after the Friday prayer. Allah says (62: 10):

$$\text{فَإِذَا قُضِيَتِ ٱلصَّلَوٰةُ فَٱنتَشِرُوا۟ فِى ٱلْأَرْضِ وَٱبْتَغُوا۟ مِن فَضْلِ ٱللَّهِ وَٱذْكُرُوا۟ ٱللَّهَ كَثِيرًا لَّعَلَّكُمْ تُفْلِحُونَ}$$

And when the prayer is ended, disperse freely on earth [Muslims may devote themselves to worldly pursuits] and seek to obtain [something] of God's bounty; but remember God often, so that you might attain to a happy state!

Eid Prayers

Eid means festival, and there are two main festivals in the Muslim year. The first is *Eid al-Fitr*, celebrating the end of fasting during the month of Ramadan. The second is *Eid al-Adha*, the festival of sacrifice celebrated on the tenth day of the last month of the Muslim calendar, *Dhul-Hajjah*. It commemorates the sacrifice by Ibrahim (as) of his son. Both these festivals start with a congregational known as *Salat al-Eid*.

The time for Eid prayers is any time twenty minutes after sunrise until before noon. However, they are generally offered in the early part of the morning so that the rest of the day can be given over to rejoicing with family members and friends. Also for the second Eid, it allows time for sacrifice. In many places the Eid is performed in parks, plain fields or on common grounds rather than in mosques because it is Prophetical *sunnah*.

Eid Salat Prerequisites (Sunnah)

1. Rise early in the morning.
2. Clean teeth (with miswalk, brush)
3. Take a bath
4. Wear best possible clothes.
5. Use perfume.
6. Eat something sweet before going for *Eid-al-Fitr* prayer but not anything before going for *Eid al-Adha* prayer.
7. Give *sadqah al-fitr* (Eid charity) before *Eid al-Fitr Salat*.
8. Go for *Eid* early.
9. Use two different routes for going and returning from *Eid Salat*.
10. Offer Eid prayer in *Eidgah or Muslla* (Both *Eidgah* (Persian word) *Musllah* (Arabic word) mean open field where Eid prayers are held. Eid prayers are also held in mosques).
11. Bring the whole family to *Salat al- Eid*.
12. Recite the following on the way to *Eidgah*:

اَللهُ اَكْبَرُ ، اَللهُ اَكْبَرُ ، اَللهُ اَكْبَرُ لاَ اِلهَ اِلاَّ اللهُ . اَللهُ اَكْبَرُ ، اَللهُ اَكْــبَرُ وللهِ الحمد. اَللهُ اَكْبَرُ كَبِيرًا وَ سُبْحَانَ اَللهِ بُكْرَةً وَ أَصِيلاً

Allahu Akbar (thrice). La ilaha illa-L-Lah. Allahu Akbar (twice) wa lil-Lahi-l-hamd. Allahu Akbar Kabira. Wa subhana-l-Lahi bukratan wasila.

This *Takbir* means:
God is the Greatest (three times). There is no god but the One True God. God is the Greatest (twice) and His is the praise. Surely God is the Greatest. His is the abundant praise. Glory to Him, day and night.

Many people, however, recite the shorter version:

اَللهُ اَكْبَرُ اَللهُ اَكْبَرُ لاَّ اِلهَ إِلاَّ اللهُ وَاَللهُ اَكْبَرُ وَللهِ الحمد.

Allahu-Akbar, Allahu-Akbar, La ilaha-Illallahu-Wallahu-Akbar, Walillahilhamd

This is called *Takbir al-Tashriq*. It should be recited from the *Fajr* prayer of the 9th of *Dhulhajjah*, i. e., on the day of Arafat, up to the '*Asr* prayer of 13th *Dhulhajjah*. In all, there are 23 prayers in which this *takbir* should be recited aloud, but women recite it in a low voice.

There is no *Adhan* or *Iqamah* in Eid prayer. The Imam declares his intention to lead the prayer saying Allahu-Akbar. The worshippers follow the Imam silently saying the *Niyyah*. After intention and *Takbir*, he silently recites *Thana* (Subhanakallahumma or Allahumma Baid Baini until the end). At this point the Imam recites *Takbir* six times (number and time of its recitation varies according to different *Madhhabs*), raising his hands up to the ears and dropping them by his sides at the end of each utterance. On completion of these utterances, he puts his right hand over the left one under the navel or the chest as in other prayers. The worshippers follow the Imam in

'Ibadah : Salat

these movements step by step, doing exactly the same. Imam then recites *Surah al-Fatihah* followed by other verses, and the rest of the *rakah* is like any other *salat*.

At the end of the first unit (*rakah*) the Imam rises up for the second *rakah*, saying Allahu Akbar. Then he adds six such utterances, doing the same thing as he did in the first unit, followed by the congregation in like manner. The second *rakah* continues like any other prayer of two *rakah* unit.

After the prayer is completed in two units, the Imam delivers a sermon of two parts with a short recess in between. The first part is begun by saying Allahu Akbar, and the second by making the same utterance. The rest of the sermon goes along the lines of urging and advice like those of the Friday sermon.

In the sermon of the First Eid of the year, the Imam should draw the attention to the matter of *sadaqah* (charity to the poor).

In the sermon of the Second Eid, the Imam should draw the attention to the duty of sacrifice. This is related to what happens in *Hajj*. The 10th of *Dhulhajjah* is the day when the pilgrims, after spending a day in Arafat, return to Mina where they offer an animal in sacrifice to commemorate Ibrahim (as)'s obedience to Allah. Muslims all over the world conduct similar ceremonies in their homes. The sacrifice is preceded by the Eid prayer similar to the one previously mentioned.

The meat of the sacrificial animal is usually distributed as follows: one-third is for the family, another one-third is for relatives and friends, and the last third is for the poor. In Canada, one Muslim community, by donating the part for the poor to the homeless, created enormous good will in that society.

The significance of Eid prayers is great. They have all the benefits of daily prayers (they are in addition to the daily obligatory prayers), and in addition there is a sense of joy because of the festivities, annual reunion and comradeship and solidarity. Presents are often given and exchanged. This is also an occasion for the exercise of charity.

Janajah (The Funeral Prayer)

♦ مِنْهَا خَلَقْنَـٰكُمْ وَفِيهَا نُعِيدُكُمْ وَمِنْهَا نُخْرِجُـكُمْ تَارَةً أُخْرَىٰ

Thereof (the earth) We created you, and into it We shall return you, and from it We shall bring you out once again. (20. 55.)

    The prayer for the dead is a collective obligation. If it is performed by some, the others will be absolved of sin. When a Muslim dies, the whole dead body must be washed a few times with soap or some other detergent or disinfectant and cleansed of all impurities. A man washes a man, and a woman washes a woman. The washer should use a washcloth or wrap his or her hand with it because touching the private parts of the dead is *haram* (Fiqh, v. 4, p. 29). When the body is thoroughly clean, it is wrapped in one or more white cotton sheets of standard material, covering all parts of the body. Any extravagance in dressing up the body in fine suits or the like is contrary to Islamic practice. The body is then placed on a bier or in a coffin and carried to the place of prayer, a mosque or any other clean premises. The body is put in a position with the face towards the direction of Kaaba.

    Janajah prayer is different from other prayers in that there is no *Ruku'*, no *sajdah*, and no *tashahhud* in it. It has to be prayed in a standing position only. Other conditions like bodily purification, dress, facing the *Qiblah*, etc., have to be satisfied as in the usual prayers.

    According to Al-Ghazzali, this prayer has seven essential elements, consisting of (1) statement of Intention; (2) the

Standing Posture; (3) four *takbir*s, or possibly five; (5) after the *takbir*, al-Fatihah; (5) the Blessing upon the Prophet (s) after the second *takbir*; (6) the Supplication for the dead after the third *takbir*; and (7) the Salutation. Unlike other prayers, this involves no rakah. It is essentially a prayer of forgiveness of the dead and a means of reminding ourselves of our final end. This is a congregational prayer, and the whole funeral is offered in the standing position.

All participants in the prayer must perform an ablution unless they are keeping an earlier one. The Imam stands beside the body, facing the *Qiblah* with the followers behind him in lines. According to one hadith quoted in *The Religion of Islam* by Muhammad Ali (p. 330), the Imam is supposed to take the position in the middle of the bier in the case of a woman, and a position nearer the head in the case of a man. The Imam raises his hands to the ears, after making the intention in heart to pray to God for that particular deceased person and says *Allahu Akbar* (God is the Greatest). The *Muqtadi*s follow the Imam's lead and, after him, place their right hands over the left under the navel, as in other prayers. Then the Imam recites silently, or mildly loudly but clearly, what is usually recited in other prayers, i. e., the *Thana* and *Surah al-Fatihah* only (Bukhari and Mustadrak Hakim). At this stage he says *Allahu Akbar* without raising his hands (Hanafis do not raise their hands, but others do) and recites the second part of the *Tashahhud* (from "Allahumma salli 'ala Muhammad" to the end). Then he makes the third Takbeer, saying Allahu Akbar without raising the hands, and offers his supplication (*du'a*) in any suitable words he knows, preferably these:

اَللَّهُمَّ اَغْفِرْ لِحَيِّنَا وَمَيِّتِنَا وَشَاهِدِنَا وَغَائِبِنَا وَصَغِيرِنَا وَكَبِيرِنَا وَ ذَكَرِنَا وَٱنْثَانَا۔ اَللَّهُمَّ مَنْ أَحْيَيْتَهُ مِنَّا فَأَحْيِهِ عَلَى الإِسْلاَمِ۔ وَمَنْ تَوَفَّيْتَهُ مِنَّا فَتَوَفَّهُ عَلَى الإِيمَانِ اَللَّهُمَّ ۔ لاَ تَحْرِمْنَا أَجْرَهُ وَلاَ تُفْتِنَّا بَعْدَهُ۔

Allahumma aghfiru lihayyina wa mayyitina wa shahidina wa gha'ibina wa saghirina wa kabirina wa dhakirina wa unthana; Allahumma man ahyaitahu minna fa ahyihi 'ala al-Islami wa man tawaffaitahu minna fatawaffahu 'ala al-Iman. Allahumma la tahrimna ajrahu wa la taftinna ba`dahu

O Allah! Grant forgiveness to our living and our dead, present and absent, and our young ones and old ones, our males and females. O Allah! Whosoever among us is kept alive by You be kept alive in Islam and whomsoever You cause to die, make him die on iman. O Allah! Do not deprive us of the reward for patience on his loss and do not make us fall into a trial after him.

After this, the Imam should say the fourth *takbir* aloud and the *Muqtadi*s in a low voice. Last of all, the Imam turns his face to the right and then to the left, saying "As-salamu 'alaikum wa rahmatullah." The *Muqtadi*s must follow him.

If the deceased is a minor and a boy, the following *du'a* is recited:

اَللَّهُمَّ اجْعَلْهُ لَنَا فَرَطًا وَاجْعَلْهُ لَنَا أَجْرًا وَذُخْرًا وَاجْعَلْهُ لَنَا شَافِعًا وَمُشَفَّعًا

Allahumma aj`alhu lana faratan wa waj`al-hu lana ajran wa dhukhran waj`alhu lana shafi`an wa mushaffan.

O Allah! Make him our forerunner and the cause of reward and recompense for us in the world to come and let him be an intercessor for us on the day of compensation, and Thou grant him intercession.

If the deceased is a minor and a girl, the following *du'a* is recited.

اَللَّهُمَّ اجْعَلْهَا لَنَا فَرَطًا وَاجْعَلْهَا لَنَا آجْرًا وَذُخْرًا وَاجْعَلْهَا لَنَا شَافِعَةً وَمُشَفَّعَةً

Allahumm aj'alha lana faratan waj'alha lana ajran wa dhukhuran waj'alha lana shafi'atan wa mushaffa'atan.

O Allah! Make her our harbinger and the cause of reward and recompense for us in the world to come and let her be an intercessor for us on the day of compensation and her intercession be granted by You.

All Muslims should learn these invocations by heart because one may have to attend a funeral sometimes. However, if one does not remember these, he may only repeat the four *takbir*s along with others and recite the following:

اَللَّهُمَّ اَغْفِرُ لِلْمُؤْمِنِينَ وَ الْمُؤْمِنَاتِ

Allahumm aghfiru lil mu'minina wal mu'minat.

O Allah! Grant forgiveness to all Muslim men and all Muslim women.

After the prayer, the deceased is carried to his final resting place, escorted with dignity, respect and private prayer. At his final resting place it is required by tradition that those at the funeral repeat the private prayer for the dead, asking on behalf of the deceased for God's forgiveness and mercy.

After the prayer is completed, the body is lowered for burial with the face resting in the direction of qiblah (Makkah). When lowering the body, these words are said:

$$\text{بِسْمِ اللهِ وَبِاللهِ، وَ عَلَى مِلَّتِ رَسُولِ اللهِ صَلَّى اللهُ عَلَيْهِ وَسَلَّمَ}$$

Bismillahi wa billahi wa 'ala millati Rasulillahi salla Allahu 'alayhi wa sallam.

In the name of Allah and with Allah, and according to the *Sunnah* (Traditions) of the Messenger of Allah upon whom be the blessings and peace of Allah.

After the body is lowered into the grave, it should be turned on its right side so that it faces towards the *Qiblah*.

The body of a woman should be lowered into the grave under a curtain. If it is feared that a portion of the body might be exposed, it will be obligatory to have a curtain while placing it in the grave.

Filling the grave with earth should be started from the head side; each person should help fill the grave with both hands. While putting earth for the first time, one should say:

$$\text{مِنْهَا خَلَقْنَكُمْ}$$

Minha khalaqnakum.

Out of it We created you; on the second time:

$$\text{وَفِيهَا نُعِيدُكُمْ}$$

Wa fiha nu'idukum.

And into it We deposit you

$$\text{وَمِنْهَا نُخْرِجُكُمْ تَارَةً أُخْرَى}$$

Wa minha nakhrijukum taratan ukhra

And from it We shall take you out once again

After the burial, the people should stay for a while at the grave, make invocations for the forgiveness of the deceased and recite the Qur'an for his sake.

Visiting Graves and Supplication for the Dead

According to a report quoted by Ahmad and Nasai, Muhammad (s) said: "One is free to visit graves. Now onwards (Muhammad (s) had forbidden it at one time) you may visit these, for it would remind you of the Hereafter."

Abu Huraira reports that when the Prophet (s) went to a graveyard he said:

اَلسَّلَامُ عَلَيْكُمَ دَارَ قَومٍ مُؤْمِنِينَ وَ إِنَّا إِنْشَاءَ اللهِ بِكُم لَاحِقُونَ

Assalamu `alaikum dara qawmin Muminina wa inna insha Allahu bikum lahiqun.

O believers! Greetings be upon you. We will soon meet you if Allah wills.

With small variations, this prayer is offered. However, the following is found to be quite common and it is also one of the prayers Muhammad (s) used to offer:

اَلسَّلَامُ عَلَيْكُمَ أَهْلَ الدِّيَارَ مِنْ الْمُؤْمِنِينَ وَالْمُسْلِمِينَ وَ إِنَّا إِنْشَاءَ اللهِ بِكُم لَاحِقُونَ نَسْأَلُ اللهَ لَنَا وَلَكُمُ الْعَافِيَةَ

Assalamu `alaikum ahladdiyara minal muminina wal muslimina wa inna insha-Allah bikum la hiquna nasalu-llah lana wa lakumul `afiyah.

Peace be upon you all, O inhabitants of the graves, amongst the believers and the Muslims. Verily we will, Allah willing, be united with you, we ask Allah for well-being for us and you.

Innovations for the Benefit of the Dead

A large number of innovations has grown up about what may be done for the benefit of the dead. There is no mention of any tradition of distributing charity at the grave or having the Qur'an recited at the grave or elsewhere for the benefit of the dead. There are traditions speaking of the Qur'an being read to the dying person, but there is no mention at all of its being read over the dead body or over the grave. Muhammad (s) is reported as having prayed for the dead when visiting their graves, and the simple act of asking forgiveness for the deceased is not forbidden. As a matter of fact, supplication for the dead is mentioned in Qur'an, verse 59: 10. The preparation of food on the third or tenth or fortieth day after death is an innovation. In the Indo-Pakistan-Bangladesh subcontinent, Muslims in general have adopted several rites relating to the prayer for the dead and funeral banquet on various dates, especially on the fortieth after the death occurs. There is no basis for this in Sharia, and it may have been derived from local customs.

Salat al-Qasar
(Shortening Prayer In Journey)

وَإِذَا ضَرَبْتُمْ فِى ٱلْأَرْضِ فَلَيْسَ عَلَيْكُمْ جُنَاحٌ أَن تَقْصُرُوا۟ مِنَ ٱلصَّلَوٰةِ إِنْ خِفْتُمْ أَن يَفْتِنَكُمُ ٱلَّذِينَ كَفَرُوٓا۟ إِنَّ ٱلْكَٰفِرِينَ كَانُوا۟ لَكُمْ عَدُوًّا مُّبِينًا

And when you travel in the land, there is no sin on you if you shorten your prayer if you fear that the disbelievers may attack you, verily, the disbelievers are ever unto you open enemies. (4: 101)

God intends every facility for you; He does not want to put you to difficulties. (2: 185).

According to Hadith (Bukhari, Muslim and Tirmidhi), Rasulullah(s) said: "This is a favor of Allah to you, so you should accept His favor gratefully."

Our Prophet (s) always prayed Qasar *Salat* during travel, so it is mandatory on all Muslims to do likewise. Imam Malik is of the opinion that the minimum distance of the journey should be 48 miles, which is supported by Imam Shafi and Imam Ahmed. Imam Abu Hanifah is of the opinion that the journey should be a minimum of 54 miles. This is applicable to *Dhuhr*, *'Asr* and *'Isha* prayers which are reduced from four to two *rakahs* of *Fard*. The *Fajr* and *Maghrib* prayers remain unchanged, and the *witr* prayer being wajib must be offered in full. If a traveller offers four *rakahs* of *Fard* by mistake, he should offer sahw *sajdah*.

While traveling, he is exempt from all *sunnah* prayers except for the *Fajr sunnah*. He is also exempt from Friday Jama'at and Eid prayers. However, if he offers *Salat* in a congregation, the imam of which is a *muqim* (resident) he has no choice but to offer full (*Fard*) *Salat* along with the Imam. Should he lead the congregation, he should announce that he will pray *Qasar Salat*. He will thus complete his *Salat* after two rakahs, and the *Muqtadi*s will complete their *Salat* individually.

Qasar remains effective even after the traveller arrives at his destination so long as his stay there is for less than fifteen days. If the stay is for fifteen days or longer, he should then pray regular *Salat*. But under no circumstances may a prayer be missed.

Qada Salat Or Making Up For Missed Prayer

It must be emphasized that all prayers should be offered at their due time unless there are compelling reasons to do otherwise. The books on Hadith mention very severe punishment for those who neglect *Salat*. Jabir Bin 'Abdullah (r) narrates that he heard the Prophet (s) saying: "To discard *Salat* is to be linked with *Kufr* and *Shirk*."

Imam Ibn al-Qayyim al-Jawziyyah in his *Kitab as-Salat* (2d ed. Published by Wasi Muhammad al-Din al-Khatib) writes (p. 44) that if a Muslim delays in performing *Salat*, it will be *Makruh* or disliked by Allah unless it was due to forgetfulness or oversleeping. In the case of forgetfulness or oversleeping, he is expected to perform it just when he remembers or wakes up.

Imam Ibn al-Qayyim narrates an incident when Muhammad (s) was journeying with his companions. At night they pitched a tent but could not wake up for the *Fajr* prayer until the sun rose on the horizon. Then he commanded Bilal (r) to give *Adhan*. He then performed and led the two rakahs prayer. Failure to observe *Salat* within the prescribed time because of sleep or forgetfulness is further discussed in the following hadith quoted in *A manual of prayer* by Abu Bakr Fakir (pp. 224-225):

> Abu Qatadah reported that the Messenger of Allah said: There is no breach of duty in sleep. Verily breach of duty is in wakefulness. If any one forgets to perform a prayer or oversleeps at the appointed time, he should perform it as soon as he remembers it because Allah, the Almighty, said: "Keep up prayer to remember Me."

The last sentence signifies the spirit of Islamic prayer: the remembrance of Allah is its primary object. Anas ibn Malik reported that the Messenger of Allah said:

"He who forgets to pray or oversleeps shall pray when he remembers; there is no other atonement for it save that."

It is in this background and in consultation with the available prayer books including *Everyday fiqh*, vol. 1 by Yusuf Islahi, English version, Abdul Aziz Kamal (Lahore: Islamic Publications Ltd., 1975) and some ulamas that the following guidelines have been prepared:

Making Up for Missed Prayers

1. Anyone who has missed a prayer should offer it at the earliest opportunity and seek Allah's forgiveness. If anyone who has missed a prayer and did not offer it at the first opportunity and continued to postpone it from day to day and died before offering it, he would commit a double sin—one for missing the prayer and the second for not offering the missed prayer.
2. With the exception of women who are menstruating or in childbirth or are nursing mothers, and Muslims who are insane or unconscious for some time, every Muslim must make up his or her obligatory prayers.
3. If a person misses *Salat* for a valid reason, he should pray only the *Fard* and Wajib *Salat*. There is no Qada for *Sunnah* except for the *Fajr Sunnah*.
4. If the Qada *Fajr Salat* is offered before the decline of the sun, one should pray both for the *Sunnah* and the *Fard Salat*. If it is offered after the decline of the sun, one should only pray two *rakahs* of *Fard Salat*. If due to shortness of time, only *Fard* of *Fajr* is offered before sunrise, then *Sunnah* of *Fajr* should be offered after sunrise.
5. For valid reasons, if anyone has missed several prayers, he or she should offer all the missed prayers as soon as possible, preferably at one time. If there is any difficulty in doing so, only one missed prayer may be offered at a time.

6. There is no fixed or specific time for offering the missed prayers. Whenever one has time, make ablution and offer the prayer, but care should be taken that the time should not be the prohibited one.

7. If anyone has missed one prayer only, he should offer this prayer first, before the first regular *Salat*. However, if the time is such that if one offers the missed prayer and there would be no time left for the prescribed prayer of the time, then the prayer of the time should be offered first and the missed one thereafter.

8. If a person misses a total of five consecutive *Salat*s, his regular *Salat* will not be valid until he has offered the Qada *Salat*s. Furthermore, he should offer the Qada *Salat*s in their proper sequence; this is the Hanafi tradition. If a person has missed more than five *Salat*s, he does not have to follow the sequence while offering the Qada *Salat*s. Moreover, he may offer his regular *Salat* before offering the Qada *Salat*.

9. If a number of persons have missed their prayer of any time (e. g., traveling together), they should offer it in congregation with all its requisites—with loud or low recitation as is necessary for the prayer of that time.

10. If one has a prayer to make up and finds the current prayer being performed in a group, it is recommended to perform the makeup for oneself before praying the current one (*Reliance of the traveller*, p. 113).

11. The order between the delayed prayer and the regular obligatory prayer should be maintained (i. e., the first in sequence is offered first unless the missed prayers are too many to remember their exact dates, or the time available is not sufficient for both missed and present prayers). In this case, the present prayer comes first, and the missed ones may be offered later. At any rate, the Muslim must make certain that his record is clear to the best of his knowledge and that there are no missed prayers.

12. If a person is so sick as to be either unconscious or so weak that he cannot pray even by gestures and misses a total of six or more consecutive *Salat*s, he is then legally exempt from praying the Qada of these *Salat*s. (Islahi version, debatable)

13. *Salat* missed during a journey should be prayed as Qasr *Salat* even if one prays it after returning from the journey. There is no Qada for Friday congregational *Salat*. If missed, one should pray it as the *Dhuhr Salat*. Similarly, there is no Qada for the Eid *Salat*s. .

14. When making up at night (*layl*, from sunset to true dawn), one recites aloud. When making up in the daytime (*nahar*, from dawn to sunset), a prayer that one missed during the day or night, one recites oneself. At dawn, however, all makeup prayers are recited aloud. The upshot is that one recites aloud in all prayers that are made up at times when one normally recites aloud, and recites to oneself at the times one normally recites to oneself (*Reliance of the traveller*, p. 135).

15. Finish the prayer as one would any other prayer, and at the end ask for Allah's forgiveness for missing the prayer.

Section 7 : Nawafil (Additional) Prayers : Sunnah

Sunnah prayers are of two types: *Sunnah Mu'akkadah* and *Ghair Mu'akkadah*.

Sunnah Mu'akkadah (Stressed or Sort of Binding):

Those which are emphasized by the Holy Prophet (s) and offered regularly by him before or after the *Fard* prayer.

Sunnah Ghair Mu'akkadah (Optional)

Offered only occasionally by Muhammad (s). They may or may not be linked with regular prayer.

The *Sunnah* Prayers to be performed before and after obligatory daily prayers are called *Ar-Rawatib*. It is desirable to perform 22 *rakahs* of Rawatib as follows: two rakahs before *Fajr*, four rakahs both before and after *Dhuhr* Prayer, four rakahs before *'Asr*, two *rakahs* both before and after *Maghrib*, and two rakahs both before and after *'Isha* Prayer.

Sunnah Mu'akkadah include the following:
Fajr: 2 Rakahs. It is two rakahs before the *Fard* prayer. It is strongly recommended *Sunnah* and is supposed to be brief. Its importance can be appreciated by the fact that it is the only *Sunnah* that is required to be performed in journey.
Dhuhr: 6 Rakahs: This could be four before and two after *Fard*. The Prophet (s) said that he was fond of eight.
Maghrib: 2 Rakahs: It is two *rakah* after *Fard*.
'Isha: 2 Rakahs: It is two *rakah* after *Fard*.

For verification of types of *Nawafil* for a given prayer, consult Table at the end of Section 5 above.

Section 8 – Nawafil : Special

Salat at-Tarawih

Tarawi prayer is the special characteristic of the month of Ramadan. According to *Fiqh* (v. 2, p. 27), it is *sunnah* for both men and women, performed after the obligatory *'Isha* and before *witr*. In the same source it is reported that A'ishah (r) said that the Prophet (s) would not pray more than eleven rakahs [i. e.,

'Ibadah : Salat

including three rakah*s* of *witr*] during Ramadan. *Fiqh* (p. 28) also states that it is also true that during the time of 'Umar, 'Uthman and 'Ali the people prayed twenty rakah*s*. It also mentions that it is allowed to pray *tarawih* in a congregation, but one is allowed to pray them on an individual basis. The preference, however, is to pray them in congregation.

It is the practice in many places that the whole of the Qur'an is recited in the *tarawih* prayers. The name *tarawih* (meaning the act of taking rest) may have been taken from the fact that the worshippers take a brief rest after every two rakahs. During the interval after every four rakahs, it is customary for Hanafi people to offer the following *tasbih*:

سُبْحَانَ ذِي الْمُلْكِ وَالْمَلَكُوْتِ سُبْحَانَ ذِي الْعِزَّةِ وَ الْعِظْمَةِ وَالْهَيْبَةِ وَ الْقُدْرَةِ وَالْكِبْرِيَاءِ وَالْجَبَرُوْتِ سُبْحَانَ الْمَلِكِ الْحَيِّ الَّذِيْ لاَ يَنَامُ وَلاَ يَمُوْتُ سُبُّوْحٌ قُدُّوْسٌ رَبُّنَا وَرَبُّ الْمَلاَئِكَةِ وَالرُّوْحِ ❁

Subhana dhil-mulki wal-malakut; Subhana dhil 'izzati wal-'azmati wal-haibati wal qudrati wal- kibriya'i wal-jabarut; subhan al-maliki-il-hayy-illadhi la yanamu wa la yamutu subhuhun quddusun Rabbana wa Rabbul mala'ikati war-ruh.

Glory be to Allah Who is Pure. Glory be to Him Who is the King of the heaven and the earth. Glory be to Allah, the Possessor of Honor, Greatness, Grandeur, Glory and Majesty. Glory be to Him, the Sovereign, the Eternal, Who neither sleeps nor suffers death. He is Everlasting. Allah is Pure and Sacred. He is the Lord of us, of the Angels and the Souls.

It is quite common to offer the following Durud during the shorter break after two Rakahs:

$$\text{اَللّٰهُمَّ صَلِّ عَلَى سَيِّدِنَا مُحَمَّدٌ}$$

Allahumma salli 'ala sayyidina Muhammad

Oh Allah! Bless our leader Muhammad.

Du'a at-Tarawih

This may be offered at the end of every four *rakahs* or at the very end.

$$\text{اَللّٰهُمَّ إِنَا نَسْائِلُكَ الْجَنَّةَ وَنَعُوذُ بِكَ مِنَ النَّارِ يَا خَالِقَ الْجَنَّةِ وَالنَّارِ بِرَحْمَتِكَ يَا عَزِيزُ يَا غَفَّارُ يَا كَرِيمُ يَا سَتَّارُ يَا رَحِيمُ يَا جَبَّارُ يَا خَالِقُ يَا بَرِئُ اَللّٰهُمَّ أَجِرْنَا مِنَ النَّارِ يَا مُجِيرُ يَا مُجِيرُ يَا مُجِيرُ}$$

Allahumma inna nas'aluk al-jannata wa na'udhu bika min an-nari ya Khaliq-al-Jannati wa an-nar, bi-rahmatika ya 'Azizu ya Ghaffaru ya Karimu ya Sattaru ya Rahimu ya Jabbaru ya Khaliqu ya Bari'u Allahumma ajrina min an-nari ya Mujiru ya Mujiru ya Mujiru.

Oh Allah! We ask Thee for the reward of heaven and we seek Thy protection from the abode of misery, O Creator of Heaven and Hell! With Thy mercy O Sovereign One! O Forgiver! O Bountiful! O Coverer of human failings! O Compassionate! O the All-Compelling! O Creator! O the Elevated Creator! O Allah! Save us from the torment of Hell. O Savior! O Savior! O Savior!

Salat al-Lilat al-Qadr
(Prayer in the Night of Power)

إِنَّا أَنزَلْنَٰهُ فِى لَيْلَةِ ٱلْقَدْرِ ۝ وَمَآ أَدْرَىٰكَ مَا لَيْلَةُ ٱلْقَدْرِ ۝ لَيْلَةُ ٱلْقَدْرِ خَيْرٌ مِّنْ أَلْفِ شَهْرٍ ۝ تَنَزَّلُ ٱلْمَلَٰٓئِكَةُ وَٱلرُّوحُ فِيهَا بِإِذْنِ رَبِّهِم مِّن كُلِّ أَمْرٍ ۝ سَلَٰمٌ هِىَ حَتَّىٰ مَطْلَعِ ٱلْفَجْرِ ۝

(1) We have indeed revealed this message in the night of power (2) And what will explain to thee what the night of power is? (3) The night of power is greater than a thousand months (4) Therin come down the angels and the spirit by Allahs permission on every errand (5) Peace ! This until the rise of morn (5),

It is known as the "Night of Power or Honor" and is thus a most blessed night in the month of Ramadan. The Qur'anic *Surah* named after it, quoted above, says that it is better than a thousand months (97: 1-5). Revelation from Allah, the Qur'an, came down from the guarded or preserved tablet, i. e., *Lawhi Mahfuz*, to the sky above the earth, in the month of Ramadan and, more precisely, on the Night of Power or Destiny, which, however, has not been specified (44: 3). Statements from our Prophet (s) suggest that we should seek it during the odd nights of the last ten nights of Ramadan. Thus, the possibility is reduced to the nights of the 21st, 23rd, 25th, 27th and 29th, but the 27th night is considered more probable. Prophet Muhammad (s) said: "Whoever stands in prayer in the Night of Qadr with sincerity will have all his past sins forgiven" (Bukhari, 4: 217). It is the whole night from sundown to break of dawn that is the Night of Qadr. There is no fixed formula for prayer during this night. A'isha (r) asked our Prophet (s) what to recite on this night, and he replied:

Say as often as you can:

$$\text{اَللَّهُمَّ إِنَّكَ عَفُوٌّ تُحِبُّ الْعَفْوَ فَاعْفُ عَنِّي}$$

Allahumma innaka 'afuwwun tuhibbul 'afwa fa`fu 'anni.

O my Lord, You are the Great Forgiver and You love forgiveness, so forgive me. (Tirmidhi, No. 3760; Ibn Majah, No. 3850)

Pious Muslims spend the night in prayer, recitation of the Qur'an and offering *Du'a*.

Salat at-Tahajjud (Night Vigil Prayer)

$$\text{وَمِنَ ٱلَّيْلِ فَتَهَجَّدْ بِهِۦ نَافِلَةً لَّكَ عَسَىٰٓ أَن يَبْعَثَكَ رَبُّكَ مَقَامًا مَّحْمُودًا}$$

And as for the night, keep awake a part of it as an additional prayer for you; soon will your Lord raise you to station of praise and glory. (17: 79)

Although a voluntary prayer, the Qur'an has been so emphatic about Tahajjud, and so has the Prophet (s), that many Islamic scholars believe that this prayer was obligatory for our Prophet (s). According to *Mishkat al-Masabih*, v. 2, p. 318): *Tahajjud* prayer is optional but is considered to be very effective prayer for inculcating a true religious devotion and love for God.

Abu ad-Darda relates that Prophet (s) said that whoever goes to his bed with the intention of getting up and praying during the night, and sleep overcomes him until the morning comes, he will have recorded for him what he had intended, and his sleep will be a charity for him from his Lord. (See *Sahih Sunan al Nasa'i bi iktisar al-sanad / Sahha ahadith* Muhammad Nasir al-Din al-Albani (Riyadh, 1988), v. 2, p. 386, 63: 1686.)

Tahajjud occupies a high place in curbing the evil in man, consequently bringing him closer to Allah. The following hadith about voluntary prayers in general is worth noting for *Tahajjud* as well:

> Abu Hurairah told of hearing Allah's Messenger say, "The first of his deeds for which a man will be taken into account on the Day of Resurrection will be his prayer. If it is sound he will be saved and successful, but if it is unsound he will be unfortunate and miserable. If any deficiency is found in his obligatory prayer the Lord Who is Blessed and Exalted will issue instructions to consider whether His servant has said any voluntary prayers so that what is lacking in the obligatory prayer may be made up by it. Then the rest of his actions will be treated in the same fashion.

According to *Fiqh* (v. 2, pp. 24-25): "*Salat al-Layil* may be performed in the early part of the night, the middle part of the night, or the latter part of the night, but after the obligatory *Salat al-'Isha* [However,] it is best to delay this prayer to the last third portion of the night." 'Amr ibn Abasah reports that he heard the Prophet (s) say: "The closest that a slave comes to his Lord is during the middle of the latter portion of the night. If you can be among those who remember Allah, the Exalted One, at that time then do so." The recitation during this prayer is partly loud and partly in a low voice (*Mishkat*, No. 1202).

Tahajjud lasts until *Fajr* time. One way to do it is to offer *'Isha* prayer on time without *witr* and then have some sleep. After waking up in the early hours of the morning, do necessary purification including *wudu* and then offer this prayer and finally *witr* prayer before *Fajr* time.

There is no fixed number of *rakahs* in this prayer. According to *Mishkat al-Masabih* (No. 1191), the Prophet (s)

used to observe thirteen *rakahs* as a *Tahajjud* prayer, including *witr* and two *rakahs* of dawn prayer. However, in a footnote to this hadith, it is said:
> Hafiz Ibn Qayyim after reviewing most of the ahadith giving the number of *rakahs* of *Tahajjud* prayer says: There is a sort of agreement on eleven *rakahs* of *Tahajjud* prayer including *Witr* (Zad-ul-Ma'ad, Vol. I, p. 175).

Tahajjud is the only voluntary prayer spoken of in the Qur'an. As it is observed individually in the stillness of the night, the devotee is immersed in the remembrance of Allah, seeking nearness to Him. This is the time to establish communion with the Lord. Allah (SWT) says (73: 6):
> Truly the rising by night is a time when impression is more keen and speech more certain.

One should, however, stop praying and sleep if one is sleepy. Abu Huraira reported Allah's Messenger(s) as saying, "When anyone of you gets up at night [for prayer] and his tongue falters in [the recitation] of the Qur'an and he does not know what he is reciting, he should go to sleep.", *Sahih Muslim*, trans. by Abdul Hamid Siddiqui (Beirut, n. d.), Vol. 6, p. 378, CCLXXII: 1719).

Salat al-Ishraq wa ad-Duha (Chasht) (After Sunrise Prayer)

Pious Muslims offer these prayers as they find time to do so. These are *Mustahab* in status, i. e., recommended in *Sunnah* of the Prophet (s). The time for *Ishraq* is when the sun is just a little above the horizon until it reaches its zenith. Of course, no prayer is allowed when the sun is at its zenith. It is for four or twelve *rakahs* in units of four.

The time for *Duha* prayer overlaps with *Ishraq*. *Reliance of traveller* describes this prayer as follows (pp. 158-159):

It is recommended to pray the midmorning prayer (*duha*), which minimally consists of two rakah*s*, is optimally eight rakah*s*, and maximally twelve. One finishes each pair of rakah*s* with *Salam*s.

Its time is after the sun is well up until just before the noon prayer (*Dhuhr*). The preferable time for its performance is after a quarter of the day has passed.

According to *Fiqh* (v. 2, p. 31), the Prophet (s) prayed eight rakah*s* of *duha* and made *Taslim* after every two rakah*s*.

Salat al-Kasuf
(Prayer of the Solar and Lunar Eclipse)

The eclipses of the moon and the sun are two natural phenomena which frequently cause dismay and unrest in those who witness them. For this reason it is the tradition of Islam to perform a special prayer for these phenomena to which the faithful resort in order to confide in their Lord. They recite from His Book and, through this prayer and through confiding in God, calm their souls.

The Prayer of the Eclipse of the Moon and the Eclipse of the Sun differs in form from the other prayers. It consists of two rakas which are, preferably, performed in congregation although a person is permitted to perform the prayer alone. When it is performed in congregation, the Imam makes his recitations aloud and at the end of the prayer preaches a short sermon in which he speaks of the lesson to be learned from situations of this nature. The prayer is described as follows (*Reliance of the traveller*, p. 215):

The eclipse prayer consists of two rak'as. The minimum is:
(a) to open with *Allahu akbar*;
(b) to recite *Surah al-Fatihah*;
(c) to bow;

(d) to straighten up;
(e) to recite *Surah al-Fatihah* again;
(f) to bow again;
(g) to (straighten up and) remain motionless for a while;
(h) and to prostrate, then sit up, and then prostrate again.

This is one rakah, comprising standing twice, reciting (*Surah al-Fatihah*) twice, and bowing twice. One then prays the second *rakah* like the first.

Salat al-'Istisqa
(Prayer Asking for Rain)

The drought prayer is a confirmed *Sunnah* even for someone who is traveling and is recommended to be prayed in a group. It consists of two rakaahs like those of Eid. The Imam gives two sermons like those of Eid. During the sermons the Imam frequently asks Allah's forgiveness (*istighfar*), blesses the Prophet (s) and supplicates Allah. It can also be part of *Khutba* (sermon of Jumu'a Friday prayer). *du'a* for rainfall is as follows:

اَللّٰهُمَّ سُقْيَانًا نَافِعًا

Allahumma suqyanan nafi`an

O our Lord, give us plenty of the beneficial soaking (rain).

اَللّٰهُمَّ صَيِبًا نَافِعًا

Allahumma sayyiban nafi`an

O our Lord, rain for us plentifully and beneficially

If it rains so much that harm is feared, it is recommended to supplicate as has come in the *sunnah* (Bukhari, v. 2, No. 132). The following *du'a* is recommended (*Fiqh*, v. 2, p. 40):

اللّهُمَّ سُقْيَا رَحْمَة , وَلاَ سُقْيَا عَذَاب وَلاَ بَـــلاَء وَلاَ هَــدَم وَلاَ غَــرق
اللّهُمَّ عَلَي الظَرَابَ وَ مَنَابِت الشَّجَرَ , اَللّهُمَّ حَوَالَيْنَا وَلاَ عَلَيْنَا .

O Allah give us mercy and do not give us punishment, calamities, destruction or flooding. O Allah, make it upon the woods, farms and trees. Make it around us and not upon us.

Section 9 : Nawafil : General

Salat ad-Dakhlil Masjid (Prayer for Salutation for the Mosque)

The Prophet (s) said, "Nobody should enter the Mosque and sit down until he offers two *rakahs* prayer. However, it is offensive to begin any nonobligatory prayer when the imam has begun the prescribed prayer or the Muezzin has begun the *iqama* (*Umdat al Salik p.161*).

Salat at-Tahyat al-Wudu (Post-ablution Prayer)

The Prophet (s) encouraged Muslims to observe two *rakahs* Nawafil after the ablution. If one offers Dakhlil Masjid, one ordinarily does not offer this post-ablution prayer.

Salat at-Tasbih
(Prayer of Divine Glorification)

According to *The three abandoned prayers* by Shaykh Adnaan Ali Uroor, translated by Faraz Abdul-Haarith, this prayer is also called *Salat at-Tawbah* and also *Salat al-Ghufran* (prayer for forgiveness). Whatever its name, it refers to one prayer and is a great prayer for expiating the sins and for seeking salvation.

Prophet (s) recommended that this be offered daily. If one is unable to do so, then it should be done every Friday; if one is not able to do so, then once a month, failing which, once a year or, at the very least, once in a lifetime. This prayer consists of four *rakahs*, which may be offered two at a time, or all four with one salutation. It is called the *Tasbih* Prayer because in each of its four *rakahs* the following *Tasbih* has to be recited 75 times:

سُبْحَانَ اللهِ وَ الْحَمْدُ للهِ وَلاَ اِلهَ إِلاَّ اللهُ وَاللهُ اَكْبَرُ ۞

Subhan-Allah-i wa Alhamdul-Allahi wa la ila ha illa-Allahu wa Allahu Akbar.

Glory be to Allah; all praise is due to Him; there is no God but Allah; and Allah is the Greatest.

The procedure for this prayer is as follows:

1. Fold hands after *niyyahh* in the usual manner, saying *takbir* and reciting *thana* and then recite *Tasbih* 15 times;
2. Recite in every *rakah Surah al-Fatihah* and then some other *surah*. Then while still standing, recite *Tasbih* 10 times.
3. Bow down in *Ruku'* and recite "Subhana Rabb'i al Azim" in the usual manner and then again pronounce the *Tasbih* 10 times.

'Ibadah : Salat

4. Rise up from *Ruku'* in the usual manner and again say the *Tasbih* 10 times.
5. Go down for *Sajdah* and recite "Subhana Rabbi al A'ala" in the usual manner and then recite the *Tasbih* 10 times.
6. Sit down for Jalsah and recite the *Tasbih* 10 times.
7. Go down for the second *Sajdah* and recite the *Tasbih* ten times as in the first *Sajdah*.

In this manner, complete four *rakahs*. Observe the second, third and fourth *rakahs* in the same manner, thus completing the recitation of the *Tasbih* 300 times in the four *rakahs* of *Salats*. If one forgets to pronounce the required numbers of *Tasbih* in one place, he or she may make up the numbers in the next counting, e. g., the missed *Tasbih*s of *Jalsah* may be made up in *Sajdah*, and one of *Sajdah* in the Second *Sajdah*. It has no particular time, nor a specific *surah* besides *al-Fatihah*.

Salat al-Istikhara (Prayer for the Guidance)

The Prayer for God's Guidance is one of God's blessings. In it, the worshipper faces his Lord, seeking His guidance and asking from Him that which will be to his advantage, that which God would choose for him and that which would be in his best interest. It is a matter of tradition that the Prophet (s) customarily taught his Companions the private Prayer for Guidance, just as he taught them the verses from Qur'an (*Reliance of the traveller*, p. 161). The Prophet (s) said:
If one of you is concerned about something and is in need of guidance from Allah, you should make two *rakahs* optional *Salat*, then say [this supplication]:

اَللّٰهُمَّ إِنِي اسْتَخِيرُكَ بِعِلْمِكَ ، وَأَسْتَقْدِرُك بِقُدرِتِكَ وَ أَسْأَلُكَ مِن فَضْلِكَ

العَظيم ، فإنَّك تَقْدِرُ وَلاَ أقْدِرُ ، وَتَعلَمُ وَلاَ أعلَمُ ، وأنْتَ عَلَّامُ الغُيُوبِ. اَللّهُمَّ إنْ كُنتَ تَعلَمُ أنَّ هذا الأمرَ خَيرٌ لي في ديني ومَعَاشِي وَعَاقِيَةِ أمري عَاجِلِ أمري وآجِلِهِ فَاقْدُرْهُ لي وَيَسِّيرهُ لي ثم بَارِك لي فيـه ، وَإن كُنتَ تَعلَمُ أنَّ هذا الأمرَ شَرَّ لي في ديني ومَعَاشي وَعَاقِيَةِ أمـري فـي عَاجِلِ أمري وآجِلِهِ فَأصْرِفهُ عَني واصرفني عَنهُ وَ اقْدُرْ لـي الخَـيـر حَيثُ كَانَ ثُمَّ أرْضِيني بِهِ ۞

Allahamma inni astakhiruka bi 'ilmika wa astaqdiruka bi qudratika wa asaluka min fadlik al-'azim, fa innaka taqdiru wa la aqdiru wa ta'lamu wa la'alamu wa anta 'allamul ghuyub. Allahumma in kunta ta'lamu anna hadhal amra khairun li fi dini wa ma'ashi wa 'aqibati amri fi 'ajili amri wa ajilihi faqdurhu li wa yassirhu li thumma barik li fihi wa in kunta ta'lamu anna hadha al-amra sharrun li fi dini wa ma'ashi wa 'aqibati amri fi 'azli amri wa ajilihi faasrifhu 'anni wa asrifni 'anhu waqdur lil-khaira haithu kana thumma-raddini bihi.

O Allah, I ask You to show me what is best through Your knowledge, and bring it to pass through Your power, and I ask You of Your immense favor; for You are all-powerful and I am not, You know and I do not, and You are the Knower of the Unseen. O Allah, if You know this matter to be better for me in my religion, livelihood, and final outcome [or perhaps he said, "the short and long term of my case"], then keep it from me, and keep me from it, and bring about the good for me whatever it may be, and make me pleased with it," and then one should mention the matter at hand.

This prayer, or *du'a*, may be done more than once. Resorting to this "Guidance Prayer" for what is better does not mean that one should not consult with others or explore alternatives or find the best solution to the problem. Allah ordains consultation (3: 159; 42: 38).

Salat at-Tawbah wa al-Istighfar (Prayer for Repentance and Seeking Forgiveness)

Abu Bakr (r) reports:

I heard the Prophet (s) saying: "Allah forgives the man who commits a sin (then feels ashamed), purifies himself, offers a prayer (a two-rakah prayer) and seeks His forgiveness." (*Fiqh*, v. 2, p. 34)

In *Sahih al-Jami'i*, No. 5738 as quoted in *The three abandoned prayers* by Shaykh Adnaan Aaai Uroor, p. 110, the following is quoted:

From 'Ali (r) who said that Abu Bakr (r) told him that he heard the Messenger of Allaah (s) say: "There is no servant who commits a sin and then he purifies himself (performs *wudu*) and then prays two *rakahs* and then seeks forgiveness of Allah except that Allah forgives him."

Repentance leads to forgiveness. Divine forgiveness can be sought only through repentance. The repentance called for should come before it is too late because Allah says (4: 17-18):

God accepteth the repentance of those who do evil in ignorance and repent soon afterwards; to them will God turn in mercy: for God is full of knowledge and wisdom. Of no effect is the repentance of those who continue to do evil, until death faceth one of them and he saith, "Now have I repented indeed"; nor of those who die rejecting Faith. For them have We prepared a punishment most grievous.

Qur'an links repentance to deeds of righteousness for the attainment of Divine Forgiveness, as the following verse makes clear:

But without doubt, I am (also) He that forgives again and again, to those who repent, believe and do right--who, in fine, are ready to receive true guidance (20: 82).

Forgiveness must be sought, and sought from God. It is not just in dread, fear and despair that we seek forgiveness, but also in the consciousness of sin that we must seek His forgiveness, knowing full well that Allah knows all our wrongdoing and sins. According to Bukhari, Nasai, and Abu Dawud, the best prayer for forgiveness is this:

اَللّٰهُمَّ أَنْتَ ربي وَلاَ اِلٰهَ إِلاَّ أَنْتَ خَلَقْتَنِي وَ أَنَاْ عَبْدُكَ وَ أَنَاْ عَلَى عَـهْدِكَ وَوَعْدِكَ ما اسْتَطَعْتَ أَعُوذُ بِكَ مِنْ شَرِّ مَا مَنَعْتَ ، أَبُوءُ لك بِنِعْمَتِكَ عَلَـيَّ و أَبُوءُ بِذَنْبِي فَاغْفِرْ لِي فَإِنَّهُ لاَ يَغْفِرُ الذُّنُوبَ إِلاَّ أَنْتَ ۞

Allahumma anta rabbi waLa Ilaha illa ant. Khalaqtani wa ana 'abduk wa ana 'ala ahdik wa wa'dika ma asta'tatu. A'wudhubika min sharri ma mana't, abu' laka bini'matika 'alayya wa abu' bidhanbi faghfir li fa innahu la yaghfiru dhunuba. illa anta.

O Allah! You are my Lord, there is no deity but You. You created me and I am Your slave-servant. And I am trying my best to keep my oath (of faith) to You and to seek to live in the hope of Your promise. I seek refuge in You from my greatest-evil deeds. I acknowledge Your blessings upon me and I acknowledge my sins. So forgive me for none but You can forgive sins. (3 times)

This is known as the famous *du'a* for forgiveness (Sayyid al-istighafar).

The Prophet (s) used to say in prayer for forgiveness:

اَللَّهُمَّ اغْفِرْ لِي خَطِيئَتِي وَجَهْلِي وَإِسْرَافِي فِي أَمْرِي وَمَا أَنْتَ أَعْلَمُ بِهِ مِنِّي ، اَللَّهُمَّ اغْفِرْ لِي خَطِيئَتِي وَعَمْدِي وَهَزْلِي وَجَدِّي ، وَكُلُّ ذَلِكَ عِنْدِي ، اَللَّهُمَّ اغْفِرْ لِي مَا قَدَّمْتُ وَمَا أَخَّرْتُ وَمَا أَسْرَرْتُ وَمَا أَعْلَنْتُ ، أَنْتَ الْمُقَدِّمُ وَأَنْتَ الْمُؤَخِّرُ وَأَنْتَ عَلَى كُلِّ شَيْءٍ قَدِيرٌ 0

Allahumma aghfir li khatiati wa jahli wa israfi fi amri wa ma anta 'alamu bihi minni, Allahumma aghfir li khatiati wa 'amdi wa hazli wa jaddi, wa kullu dhalika indi, Allahumma aghfir li ma qaddamtu wa ma akhkhartu wa ma asrartu wa ma 'alantu, anta al-Muqaddimu wa anta al-Muakhkhiru wa anta 'ala kulli shayin qadir.

O God, forgive me my mistake, my ignorance and my intemperance in my affairs and what You know better than I. O God, forgive me my flippancy and my over-seriousness (*jidd*), my error, my [evil] intention, and anything like these I have. O God, forgive me what I did in the past and what I shall do in the future, what I did in secret and what I did in public, and what You know better than I. You are the Hastener (*Muqaddimu*) and the Postponer (*Mu'khiru*). You are powerful over everything. (Sahih Bukhari and *Sahih Muslim* narrated by Abu Musa (r.).)

When we confess in conscience, we have hope because Allah says (7: 156): "My Mercy extendeth to all things." He is *Ghafur* and *Ghaffar*, Forgiving and Forgiver and as in (6: 12) He has inscribed for Himself the rule of Mercy." After mentioning the eternal humiliation and punishment for those who commit the gravest sins, Allah in his unusual generosity says all past sins will be forgiven upon repentance. He says (25: 70):

> Excepted, however, shall be they who repent and attain to faith and do righteous deeds: for it is they whose [erstwhile] bad deeds God will transform into good ones-- seeing that God is indeed much-forgiving, a dispenser of grace.

The immediate fruit of repentance is a lesson learned and a new awareness and sensitivity. The believer's soul is purified by Allah's forgiveness, as Allah says (24: 21):

> And if not for the favor of Allah upon you, not one of you would have been pure. But Allah purifies whom He wills.

Thus there is comfort that in His mercy, Allah has made the believer aware of his wrongdoing so that he may repent and, after necessary repentance and seeking forgiveness, he can trust that all his sins will be forgiven because Allah says (39: 53):

> Say: O my Servants who Have transgressed against their souls! Despair not of the Mercy Of Allah: for Allah forgives All sins: for He is Oft-Forgiving, Most Merciful.

Section 10 : After Finishing Prayer After Prayer Supplication

Throne Verse

At the end of each prayer the Prophet (s) used to recite the verse of the Throne, which is:

ٱللَّهُ لَآ إِلَٰهَ إِلَّا هُوَ ٱلْحَىُّ ٱلْقَيُّومُ لَا تَأْخُذُهُ سِنَةٌ وَلَا نَوْمٌ لَّهُۥ مَا فِى ٱلسَّمَٰوَٰتِ وَمَا فِى ٱلْأَرْضِ مَن ذَا ٱلَّذِى يَشْفَعُ عِندَهُۥٓ إِلَّا بِإِذْنِهِۦ يَعْلَمُ مَا بَيْنَ أَيْدِيهِمْ وَمَا خَلْفَهُمْ وَلَا يُحِيطُونَ بِشَىْءٍ مِّنْ عِلْمِهِۦٓ إِلَّا بِمَا شَآءَ

'Ibadah : Salat

$$\text{وَسِعَ كُرْسِيُّهُ ٱلسَّمَٰوَٰتِ وَٱلْأَرْضَ وَلَا يَـُٔودُهُۥ حِفْظُهُمَا ۚ وَهُوَ ٱلْعَلِىُّ ٱلْعَظِيمُ ۝}$$

Allahu la ilaha illa huwal-Hayy-ul-Qayyum; la ta'khudhuhu sinatun wwalanaum; lahu ma fis-samawati wa ma fil-ard mandalladhi yashfa'u indahu illa bi-idhnih, ya'lamu ma baina adiihim wa ma khalfahum wala yuhituna bi sha-'im-min 'ilmihi illa bimasha'a; wasi'a kursiyyu-hus-samawati wal-arda, wala ya'kuduhu hifzuhuma wa huwal 'Aliyyul 'Azim.

God - there is no god but Him, the Living, the Self-sustaining Eternal. No slumber can seize Him, nor sleep. His are all things in the heavens and on earth. Who is there who can intercede in His presence except as He permitteth? He knoweth what (appeareth to His creatures as) before or after or behind them. Nor shall they bypass aught of his knowledge except as He willeth. His throne doth extend over the heavens and the earth, and He feeleth no fatigue in guarding and preserving them, for He is the Most High, the Supreme. (2: 255)

(This is the famous *Ayat al-Kursi*. For details, see Glossary in the Appendix.) You should memorize it well and recite it immediately after each prayer. Whoever recites it after his prayer is in God's protection until the next prayer.

Although this concludes the prayer, it is related that the Prophet (s) would then say a private prayer. It is therefore traditional to memorize and say the private prayer, which is:

$$\text{اَللّٰهُمَّ أَنْتَ السَّلَامْ وَ مِنْكَ السَّلَامْ وَاَلَيْكَ يَرْجَعُ السَّلَامْ حَيْنَا رَبَّنَا بِالسَّلَامْ وَأَدْخِلْنَا دَارَ السَّلَامْ تَبَارَكْتَ رَبَّنَا وَتَعَالَيْتَ يَـٰاذَالْجَلَالِ وَالْإِكْرَامْ 0}$$

Allahuma antassalam wa minkassalam wa ilaika yarja'ussalam, hayyina rabbana bissalam wa adkhilna darassalam tabarakta rabbana wa ta'alaita ya dhaljalali walikram.

O Allah, You are Peace; Peace always turns towards you, O Allah! Keep us alive with peace and let us enter the home of peace (Paradise). O Allah! O possessor of awe and honour, You are sublime and full of blessing.

Invocation after Salat

One may recite the following:

اَللَّهُمَّ أَنِّي ظَلَمْتُ نَفْسِيْ ظُلْمًا كَثِيْرًا وَّلاَ يَغْفِرُ الذُّنُوبَ إِلاَّ أَنْتَ فَاغْفِرْ لِي مَغْفِرَةً مِنْ عِنْدِكَ وَارْحَمْنِي اِنَّكَ أَنْتَ الْغَفُوْرُ الرَّحِيْمُ ۞

Allahumma inni zalam-tu nafsi zulm-an kathir-an wa la yagfir-udh dhunuba illa Anta: faghfir-li maghfiratan min 'indika warhamni innaka Antal-Ghafur-ur-Rahim.

O Allah! I have been greatly unjust to myself, and there is none beside You who can forgive me my sins. So favour me with forgiveness from You, and have mercy upon me. You are indeed most Forgiving and most Merciful.

Or the following invocation, or both:

اَللَّهُمَّ أَنِّي أَعُوْذُ بِكَ مِنْ عَذَابِ جَهَنَّمَ وَمِنْ عَذَابِ الْقَبْرِ وَ أَعُوْذُ بِكَ مِنْ فِتْنَةِ الْمَسِيْحِ الدَّجَّالِ وَ أَعُوْذُ بِكَ مِنْ فِتْنَةِ الْمَحْيَا وَالْمَمَاتِ اَللَّهُمَّ أَنِّي أَعُوْذُ بِكَ مِنَ الْمَأْثَمِ وَالْمَغْرَمِ ۞

Allahumma inni a'wudhubika min adhdhabi jahannama wa min 'adhab-il-qabr wa a'wudhubika min fitnat-ilmasih-id-dajjal-l wa a'wudhubika min fitnati mahya wa al-mamat. Allahumma inni a'wudhubika min al matham wa al-maghram.

O Allah! I seek Your protection from the torment of Hell and the grave, and from the mischief of the Antichrist, and I seek Your protection from the trials of life and death. O Allah! I seek Your protection from sin and debt.

Conclusion

It is worth mentioning here the following from Syed Abul A'la Mawdudi (*Let us be Muslims*, p. 153):

The Prayer prepares us for *'Ibadah*, for serving and obeying God. Even if you do not understand the full purport of the words you recite, it helps keep alive in your hearts the fear of God and the awareness that He is with you everywhere and He is watching over you; it helps remind you, too, that one day you, along with all mankind, will have to appear before God to give an account of your lives. The Prayer keeps ever-fresh the consciousness that you are the slaves of God, and of God only, and that it is only to God that obedience and worship are due.

It goes without saying that this faith is all the deeper when you fully appreciate the meaning of the words you are reciting in the Prayer. Then, the power of Prayer is capable of reshaping your entire lives in thoughts, in words and in deeds.

It is therefore important to know the meaning of what you say in your Prayers.

It should also be pointed out that prayer is the supreme form of *'Ibadah*.

Section 11 : Du'a and Dhikr (Supplication and Remembrance)

$$\text{يَٰٓأَيُّهَا ٱلَّذِينَ ءَامَنُوا۟ ٱذْكُرُوا۟ ٱللَّهَ ذِكْرًا كَثِيرًا}$$

O believers! Remember Allah with much remembrance. (33 : 41)

The ritual obligations of Muslims by no means exhaust the devotional life of the practicing Muslim. Liturgical *Salat* is followed by a practice of *Du'a*, or calling upon God. The *Du'a* is a prayer of supplication, a way of bringing one's needs, problems or wishes before Allah. Associated with *Du'a* is the term *Dhikr*. The word *Dhikr* generally means to remember. In a note in the Holy Qur'an, King Fahd edition, p. 62, it is pointed out that "the word 'remember' is too pale a word for *Dhikr*. In its verbal signification it implies to remember, to praise by frequently mentioning; to rehearse; to celebrate or commemorate; to make much of; to cherish the memory of a precious possession."

Prayer is also remembering Allah. The various poses assumed during prayers are the very embodiment of the spirit of submission. The various recitals are reminders to commitments to Allah. In order to bring man into obedience of Allah, continuous reminding is necessary because Allah is invisible and there are too many worldly distractions. To keep the realization that man is a servant of God and that he is to obey none but Him and to keep it fresh and alive, mere verbal

'Ibadah : Salat

confession of faith is not enough. It is absolutely essential that it must be continually strengthened. This is what prayer does, and *dhikr* solidifies it.

The term *dhikr* has very wide significance in both Qur'anic and devotional usage. *Dhikr* is a title of the Qur'an and a vital element in Muslim religious practice. Qur'an also uses the word *dhikr* to convey other meanings. Sometimes it is used to remind the believers of their duties and accountability on the Day of Judgment. On various occasions it is used for remembrance of Allah as in 26: 227: "Except those who believe, work righteousness, engage much in the remembrance of Allah."

The wide connotation of *dhikr* is clear from the following verses (63: 9): "O ye who believe! Let not your riches or your children divert you from the remembrance of Allah. If any act thus, surely they are the losers." The footnote to this verse (p. 1753 of the Holy Qur'an) is to the point:

> Riches and human resources of all kinds are but fleeting sources of enjoyment. They should not turn away the good man from his devotion to Allah."Remembrance of Allah" includes every act of service and goodness, every kind thought and kind deed, for this is the service and sacrifice which Allah requires of us. If we fail in this, the loss is our own, not anyone else's: for it stunts our own spiritual growth.

Man is commanded over and over again to remember Allah, His works, and His favors. For example (7: 205): "And do thou (O reader!) bring thy Lord to remembrance in thy (very) soul, with humility and remember without loudness in words in the mornings and evenings; and be not thou of those who are unheedful." And also (76: 25-26): "And celebrate the name of thy Lord morning and evening. And part of the night, prostrating thyself to Him, and glorify Him a long night through."

God praises people who are always, and in every situation, engaged in His remembrance. "Men who celebrate the praises of

Allah, standing, sitting, and lying down on their sides (i. e., in all postures, which again is symbolical of all circumstances)" (3: 191).

The benefits of *dhikr* are numerous. The medieval scholar Ibn al-Qayyim al-Jawziyyah mentioned more than 70 of these. Of course, on the top of these is that it pleases Allah, drives away Shaytan, and replaces pain and sorrow of the heart; it provides tranquility, happiness and contentment. According to this scholar, *dhikr* nurtures the love of Allah in the heart of the worshipper and draws him closer to Allah.

Dhikr also engenders the awe of Allah, invigorates the heart and cleanses it. By rehearsing the praise of Allah, the believer comes to know Allah's comfort in times of hardship, and hope of redemption from His wrath. *Dhikr* causes a feeling of assurance, a sense of well-being that emanates from Allah's mercy.

Of all the forms of *'Ibadah*, *dhikr* is the easiest and highly prized. Constant celebration of Allah's praise protects the believer from forgetfulness of Allah. *Dhikr* gives the worshipper the stamina and strength to do what would otherwise be beyond his reach. *Dhikr* is a mighty barrier between the believer and hellfire. The angels seek forgiveness on behalf of those who recite the praises of Allah. The practice of *dhikr* is commended in traditions of the Prophet (s), one of which states that "there is a way of polishing everything and removing rust and that which polishes the heart is the invocation of Allah." According to Hadith Qudsi, Allah says: "I am with my servant when he thinks of me." Seen this way, *dhikr* constitutes the very essence of religion. *Dhikr* can be practiced within, at any time, and complements the performance of formal ritual prayer. There is no set place or time for *dhikr*, it can be performed at any time, any place (except in the bathroom or when answering nature's call or things of that sort).

Dhikr has a wider connotation than that practiced in the *Sufi* Orders where it signalizes the art of concentration through various devices such as reciting the divine names. *Dhikr* as a *Sufi* concept most often involves rhythmic repetition in a group setting of one or more formulas containing the name of God. It has complex forms in different fraternities, often involving body movements, breathing techniques and chants. The great medieval theologian who is ever attentive to all details and to the needs of ordinary men writes (*Ghazali on prayer* by Kojiro Nakamura, The Institute of Oriental Culture, University of Tokyo, 1973, pp. 27-28):

> The best way to keep remembering God is to organize and regulate daily life for this single purpose with the practices of invocation (*Dhikr*), supplication (*du'a*), Qur'an recitation (*qira'a*) and meditation (*fikr*). Ghazzali elaborates these practices by dividing a whole day into twelve parts (*wird*), including the time for sleep. To each of these *wirds* he assigns specific exercises for the remembrance of God.

There are, however, many other occasions for *dhikr* which require special practices different from the regular daily pattern as on Friday among the weekdays during Ramadan and *Hajj* in the course of the year. Ghazzali also mentions *dhikr* formulas and *du'a* texts for such special occasions as traveling, marriage, funeral, drought, the eclipses of the sun and the moon, rain, thunder, wind, physical pain, anger, fear of people, grief, and others. Thus every moment of daily life is punctuated with the practice of *dhikr* and *du'a*.

The difference between the one who makes *dhikr* and the one who does not has been likened by the Prophet (s) to the difference between the living and the dead. And God gives the assurance in the Qur'an (2: 152): "As you remember me so shall I remember you." There is also this Hadith: "One who remembers Allah in seclusion and weeps will remain in the shadow of Allah on the day when there is no shade but His" (i.e., the Day of Resurrection).

Islamic Calligraphy: Allahu Akbar

Allah is the Greatest

11

ZAKAH (ALMS TAX OR COMPULSORY CHARITY TAX)

وَأَقِيمُوا۟ ٱلصَّلَوٰةَ وَءَاتُوا۟ ٱلزَّكَوٰةَ وَمَا تُقَدِّمُوا۟ لِأَنفُسِكُم مِّنْ خَيْرٍ تَجِدُوهُ عِندَ ٱللَّهِ إِنَّ ٱللَّهَ بِمَا تَعْمَلُونَ بَصِيرٌ ۝

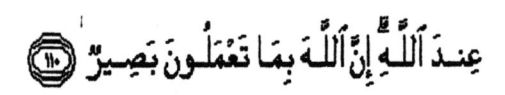

And be steadfast in prayer and give Zakah: and whatever good ye send forth for your souls before you, ye shall find it with Allah: for Allah sees well all that ye do. (2:110)
(Also verses: 2:43, 177; 4:162; 5:55; 92:18 and many others)

Zakah is an obligatory charity due on wealth with certain conditions, to be distributed to specific groups of people at a specific time. The word *Zakah* (variation *zakat*) means growth, purity, alms tax. According to *Reliance of the traveller* (the famous *Umdat al-Salik*), p. 246, "it is called *Zakah* because one's wealth grows through blessings of giving it and the prayers of those who receive it, and because it purifies its giver of sin and extols him by testifying to the genuineness of his faith." *Zakah* was made compulsory on the first of Ramadan in the second year of the *Hijra*.

Salah and *Zakah* are mentioned side by side in the Qur'an at least twenty-five times. Altogether they are mentioned thirty-two times in the Qur'an by the name of *Zakah*, seven times by *sadaqah* and several times as right of the poor and the needy and an obligatory spending by the well-to-do. According to *The Mysteries of almsgiving: a translation from the Arabic with notes of the Kitab asrar al-zakah of al-Ghazzali's Ihya' 'ulum al-din* by Nabih Amin Faris (American University of Beirut, 1966, p. 2), Allah has made almsgiving one of the pillars of Islam, placing it next to prayer which is the supreme duty of Islam. Imam Ghazzali writes: Allah said, "Observe prayer and pay alms." (2: 43) Then the Imam goes on to say, "Allah has strongly warned those who are remiss in the fulfillment of these duties" because Allah said (9:34): "And there are those who hoard gold and silver and spend it not in the way of Allah: announce unto them a most grievous chastisement."

Simply put, the word *Zakah* means purification. As stated, it also means growth, blessings, an increase in good, purification or praise. In Sacred Law it is the name for a particular amount of property that must be paid to certain kinds of recipients.

By an act of sharing, one's property, possessions and one's self are purified (9:103; 92:18). It purifies the believer's heart from greed, selfishness and from regarding what Allah has given him as his own. There is great wisdom in the institution of *zakah* as it fulfills many major aims of the *Shariah*, resulting in general benefits which should become clear as one ponders the Qur'anic verses and the *Sunnah* pertaining to it.

Islam is a community religion. Those who have must provide for the poor. In fact, Qur'an states that the poor and the needy have "in whose wealth [is] a recognised right" (70:24). From the very beginning of his mission, Muhammad(s) insisted on charity and later, in accordance with Allah's desire, he fixed the minimum by law. In early times this was collected by officials of the Islamic State and devoted to relief of the poor and other charitable and state purposes. M. Raquib-uz Zaman has a research publication entitled *Some administrative aspects of the collection and distribution of Zakah and the distributive effects of the introduction of Zakah into modern economies* (Jeddah: King Abdul Aziz University, 1987). However, nowadays the fulfillment of *zakah* obligation is left to the conscience of the individual believer. According to Imam Ghazzali in the work cited (p. 18), *zakah* is due as soon as the sun sets the last day of Ramadan, and if one wishes to be very prompt, he may pay it during the month of Ramadan, sometime between the first and the last day of the month. Whoever delays the payment of *zakah* although he is able to be prompt, sins. Incidentally, making the intention of *zakah* is a necessary condition for the validity of giving it.

System of Zakah

Qur'an exhorts believers to give (3:92), but no details are given as to what to give, when and how much. It was up to the jurists of later centuries to develop a precise system of donation and payment. Each Muslim's *zakah* is calculated individually, depending on the *Zakatable* wealth or property which include business, salaried and professional income, investments and other assets, gold, silver, jewelry, business, bank accounts, agricultural products, earned profits, and cash. *Zakah* is not to be paid on property which is for personal use such as clothing, household furniture, a house in which one lives, a car one drives and crops planted for domestic consumption. The amount of *zakah* varies from 10 percent to as low as approximately 2.5 percent on cash savings. It is to be paid once a year and is assessed on property only after a full year has passed since its acquisition. For calculation of *zakah* for North American residents, the following is recommended: Kaf, Monzer, *The*

Calculation of Zakah for Muslims in North America (Muslin Students Association of US and Canada, 2d ed., 1980), 20 pp.

Distribution of Zakah

It may be given to the following eight classes mentioned in the Qur'an (9:60):
1. The poor (*faqir*);
2. The destitute, the needy (*miskin*)
3. The debtors (*gharim*), i.e., those who are in debt so deep that they are unable to meet subsistence requirements;
4. Those whose hearts are won to Islam, i.e., new converts, allies;
5. Those engaged in the management of *Zakah* funds
6. For ransoming slaves and captives (*fi al-riqab*) who are in bondage both literally and figuratively and who must be redeemed;
7. For the purpose of promoting Islam (*fi sabil Allah*);
8. Traveler who is short of funds or otherwise in difficulty (*ibn al-sabil*).

Zakah marks the beginning, not the end, of charity. Allah (swt) urges Muslims to practice regular charity (98:5).

Sadaqah comprises everything that a believer freely gives to another person as a moral obligation without expecting any worldly return. This is in addition to *zakah*, which is obligatory. This payment also purifies a person's property from the taint of selfishness (e.g., 9:103).

Allah says (2:271): "If you disclose your *sadaqah* it is well; but if you conceal them and give them to the poor, that is better for you." Prophet(s) said: "The best *sadaqah* is that given by the right hand without the left hand knowing what the right hand has done." *Sadaqah* is a practical and tangible prayer of thanksgiving to Allah for His bounty.

12

FASTING

$$\text{يَٰٓأَيُّهَا ٱلَّذِينَ ءَامَنُواْ كُتِبَ عَلَيْكُمُ ٱلصِّيَامُ كَمَا كُتِبَ عَلَى ٱلَّذِينَ مِن قَبْلِكُمْ لَعَلَّكُمْ تَتَّقُونَ ۝}$$

O you who believe, decreed upon you is fasting as it was decreed upon those before you that you may become righteous. (2: 183).

As mentioned above, Qur'an prescribes fasting for all able, adult Muslims for the entire month of Ramadan, the ninth month of the Muslim calendar. The Qur'an continues (2: 185):

It was the month of Ramadan in which the Qur'an was [first] bestowed from on high as a guidance unto man and a self-evident proof of that guidance, and as the standard by which to discern the true from the false. Hence, whoever of you lives to see this month shall fast throughout it; but he that is ill, or on a journey, [shall fast instead for the same] number of other days. God wills that you shall have ease, and does not will you to suffer hardship; but [He desires] that you complete the number [of days required], and that you extol God for His having guided you aright, and that you render your thanks [unto Him].

Fasting is the fourth pillar of Islam. It is a form of *Ibadah* which is entirely private. The institution of fasting in Islam came after the institution of prayer. It was in Madinah in the second year of the Hijrah that fasting was made obligatory. Fasting begins at early dawn and ends after the setting of the sun. Ramadan is regarded as auspicious because, as referred to above, Qur'an was first revealed during this month. It also contains the "night of grandeur or majesty or power" called "Lailat al-Qadr," described in Qur'an (Surah 97) of the final ten nights, one of the odd-numbered ones is when the "Night of Power" falls (see section 8, Chapter 10, Lailat al-Qadr). It is marked by intensive devotions when people stay awake, praying, reading the Qur'an, contemplating and remembering Allah. While speaking of Ramadan, the Qur'an especially refers to nearness to Allah as if its attainment were an aim in fasting, as in verses 2: 186 and 188, as further emphasized in footnote 194 in the Yusuf Ali translation.

According to Bukhari (v. 3, no. 123), when the month of Ramadan starts, the gates of Heaven are opened and the gates of Hell are closed and the devils are chained. The Prophet (s) said (Hadith 118, same source) that fasting is a shield and Allah says, "He has left his food, drink and desires for My sake. The fast is for Me. So I will reward (the fasting person) for it and the reward of good deeds is multiplied ten times."

For Muslims, Ramadan is a month of reckoning with oneself, a unique month to take stock of one's moral and spiritual assets and liabilities. This is also the time to rededicate one's life to Allah's service and obedience with special determination.

Fasting is a spiritual discipline and also a moral one. It is a great moral lesson that one should be prepared to suffer the greatest privation and undergo the hardest trial rather than indulge in that which is not permitted to him. This lesson is repeated day after day for a whole month. It also teaches one to

Fasting

conquer his physical desires. There is also physical value in fasting. Refraining from food during stated intervals does no physical harm to a healthy person.; in fact, it does some good.. Nevertheless, we must realize that fasting was made obligatory as a way for us to worship Him.

With the twilight of the dawn appearing on the horizon, fasting begins with the Niyyah or intention for the obligatory fast before the appearance of the true dawn (*subh al-sadiq*). The place for the intention is the heart, and it is not necessary to pronounce it with the tongue (Abu Dawud, No. 2454 and Tirmidhi, No 730). This necessity of having intention is particular to obligatory fasts only, not for supererogatory (*nafl*) fasts.

During the fast it is forbidden to eat, drink or have any sexual activity. Smoking or even taking medicine is not allowed. The daily fast is broken after sunset with a light meal, *iftar*, with the supplication: "O Allah! For your sake have I fasted, and I break the fast with the food that comes from you." The common Arabic version is as follows:

اَللّٰهُمَّ صُمْتُ لَكَ وَ عَلَى رِزْقِكَ وَ أَفْطَرْتُ

Allahumma sumtu laka wa ala rijqeka wa iftartu.

The fast must be broken at sunset each day. Following *Maghrib* prayer and throughout the night, eating and drinking are permitted. A pre-dawn meal, *sahur* or *sehri*, is recommended.

In addition to meeting all the above necessities, Muslims also engage in increased devotional activities throughout the month. Besides the usual five prayers, an additional *salat* called *Tarawih* (for details, see the section 8, Chapter 10), which is observed during this whole month, is performed either individually or in congregation each night.

Exemptions from Fasting

The following people are exempt from fasting:

A. Sick people whose health is likely to be severely affected by the observance of fasting. They may postpone the fast as long as they are sick and make up for it later, a day for a day.
B. People who are traveling (i.e., they have left their homes and are on the road, or when reaching their destination they have the intention of returning in a few days). Such people may not fast temporarily during their travel days only. They are to make up later the days which are missed, a day for a day. But it is better for them, as Qur'an points out, to observe the fast during their travels if they can do so without extraordinary hardship.
C. Pregnant women and nursing mothers may also not keep the fast, but they must make up for it later, a day for a day.
D. Women during the period of menstruation (maximum of ten days) or of confinement after childbirth (maximum of forty days) should not fast. They must postpone the fast until these periods are over and then make up for it, a day for a day.
E. Men and women who are too old and feeble to undertake the obligation and to bear its hardships. Such people are exempt from this duty, but if they can afford it, they must offer to at least one needy Muslim an average full meal (or its value) for each day of Ramadan on which they have not fasted. Whenever they are able to fast, even it is for only one day of the month, they should do so and should compensate for the remainder.
F. Children under the age of puberty are exempt from the obligation of fasting.
G. The insane people who are not accountable for their deeds are also exempt.

Fasting

People in categories "F" and "G" are exempted fully. No compensation or substitution is required of them.

When for some reason the number of fasts is to be made up, it must be completed before the next Ramadan. Fasting on *Eid* days is strictly prohibited. When a person eats or drinks, forgetting that he is fasting, the fast is not broken. Gargling or rinsing the mouth (so long as water is not swallowed) and tasting of the food in the cooking pot do not break the fast. However, putting drops in nostrils breaks the fast.

Itikaf is another feature of Ramadan (2: 187). The Messenger (s) used to perform *itikaf* in the last ten days of every Ramadan in his lifetime (Sunani-i-Baihaqi: 4 /346). He would be in seclusion at the mosque during this time for the purpose of worshipping Allah. *Itikaf* is a period of intense reflection and devotion, seeking Allah's forgiveness and guidance.

Fasting in the month of Ramadan, along with *Salah* performed with greater intensity, being in a state of heightened devotion, brings us closer to our Creator. "Whoever fasts in the month of Ramadan out of faith (*Iman*) and with conviction of reward from Allah, all his past sins will be forgiven. Whoever stands for the prayers in the Night of *Qadr* out of faith (*Iman*) and conviction of reward from Allah,. all his past sins will be forgiven" (Bukhari, Muslim & Mishkat: Book III, 2nd ed., 1989, p. 514). As is obvious, through the fast there is an emphasis on deepened devotion and more frequent mosque attendance. The passage enjoining Ramadan (2: 187) refers to "retreat in mosques."

It has been observed that Ramadan is a yearly training program, a time of spiritual enrichment and discipline to reempower the Muslim for another year of Islam. It is a time when the spiritual and moral values, values of love, honesty, devotion and generosity, and social concern are deepened. Fasting also reminds the person who fasts that there are people in the world who are hungry even without fasting. It is the

Muslim's responsibility to share Allah's bounty with those hungry people.

Thus, Ramadan combines fasting and prayer and charitableness. In addition, it prescribes abstinence from falsehood in speech and action, slander, libel, lying, lustful looks, ill will towards others, etc. The Prophet (s) said that Allah does not require anybody to abstain from foods and drinks if he does not give up lying and deceitful action (Bukhari,v. 3, no. 127).

Imam Ghazzali insists that a fast which means only a consequent hunger and thirst is not a finally meaningful fast. For if only hunger results, the fast is only physically felt. It should be an occasion of that remembrance of God which is not a temporary, negative abstinence, but a positive preoccupation with God.

The discipline of fasting is different from dieting. What distinguishes fasting from dieting is that one diets to lose weight, but fasting is to please Allah. The month of Ramadan periodically falls during the summer because the Islamic calendar falls short by eleven days of the solar calendar. Fasting in the summer adds more strain to the already arduous fast. Although Ramadan may appear to be a hard and difficult month, it is in fact an enjoyable time because of the special atmosphere that prevails at home, at mosques and in Muslim communities.

Islam teaches that fasting nurtures self-discipline and compassion as well as a sense of our own frailty and dependence on God. Kemal A. Faruqi states it very well in his *Islam Today and Tomorrow* (Karachi, 1974, p. 265):

> The benefit of fasting is primarily in terms of character. The abstention from food, drink and other material pleasures for the long hours between dawn to dusk during the month of Ramadan is an act of self-discipline by which an individual asserts his or her ability to gain control over material pleasures and habits. There is a triumph of mind over

Fasting

matter. The desire to quench the thirst, to soften the pangs of hunger, or to light a cigarette are placed in their proper perspectives as things which can be postponed, and in some cases given up altogether if necessary. This, in itself, constitutes a victory for the human being over his or her material environment.

The end of the month is celebrated by Eid al-Fitr (see Chapter 10, Section 6) (Eid means a recurring happiness), a time of rejoicing, feasting and sharing.

Besides obligatory fasting in Ramadan, there are three other categories of fasting: redeeming or atoning fast, vowed fast, and supererogatory (additional) fast. Atoning or redeeming fast has the notion of *kaffara* for duties omitted which have been stipulated in the Qur'an; for example, fasting is the penalty for killing an animal while on *hajj* (5: 95). Some people distinguish between redemptive (*fidyah*) and expiatory (*kaffarah*) fasts, making them two separate categories.

Vowed fast, that is, the fast one has vowed to keep, is one when a believer has vowed a fast to Allah under certain circumstances. They may be the specified type, i.e., the date on which one will fast is specified, or they may be of the unspecified type, i.e., the day on which one will fast is unspecified.

Supererogatory fast includes all kinds of voluntary or additional fasts. There are certain days of the month when it is considered praiseworthy and meritorious to observe as days of fasting such as any six days of Shawwal, the 9th, 10th and 11th of Muharram, the 15th of Sha'ban, etc. These were recommended and practiced by the Prophet (s) but are not obligatory.

Baitul Mukarram, Dhaka, Bangladesh *(top)* believed to have been constructed on the pattern of the Kaaba.

Al-Azhar *(bottom)* is a venerable institution combining a mosque and a major university.

13

HAJJ AND 'UMRAH (PILGRIMAGE)

$$\text{فِيهِ ءَايَـٰتٌ بَيِّنَـٰتٌ مَّقَامُ إِبْرَٰهِيمَ وَمَن دَخَلَهُ كَانَ ءَامِنًا وَلِلَّهِ عَلَى ٱلنَّاسِ حِجُّ ٱلْبَيْتِ مَنِ ٱسْتَطَاعَ إِلَيْهِ سَبِيلًا وَمَن كَفَرَ فَإِنَّ ٱللَّهَ غَنِىٌّ عَنِ ٱلْعَـٰلَمِينَ}$$

In it are Signs manifest; the Station of Abraham; whoever enters it attains security; Pilgrimage thereto is a duty men owe to Allah,-- those who can afford the journey; but if any deny faith, Allah stands not in need of any of His creatures. (3: 97).

Hajj

The religious pilgrimage is familiar to people of all traditions, oriental or occidental. The Muslim pilgrimage (Arabic Hajj), however, is unique among sacred journeys because it is obligatory and not simply an act of special piety or devotion. It is obligatory on every adult Muslim, male or female, who is of sound mind and body to perform the Pilgrimage to Makkah once in his or her life time provided that one has the means to do so.

Hajj cannot be performed on credit. Muslims prepare for it as if they were leaving this world altogether. After they have paid their debts, paid zakat due on their wealth; returned whatever was given to them in trust; and provided for their families and dependents during their absence, they prepare for their trip. They must have earned enough, in an honest way to cover the expenses of the journey and the sacrifice it includes. The duty of Hajj rests on special commands of the Qur'an. The Prophet (s) exhorted his companions to perform it, and taught the specific way in which each of the rituals involved was to be done. Hajj is one of the five pillars of Islam and the Sunnah raised the religious and ethical value of pilgrimage so high that it became the ultimate worldly hope of the Muslim life. For the Muslims, the journey to and presence in Makkah Al-Mukkarramah (the Honored) is the highest act of worship. It is an opportunity to re-enact the founding of Islam and renew links with Prophet Ibrahim (as), his deserted wife, Hajar, their son Prophet Ismail (as), and of course Prophet Muhammad (s). Hajj is a return to the origins, roots and beginnings of Islam. It is also a self-presentation before Allah. In a sense, it is rehearsal of the Day of Judgment when all human beings will return to Allah.

It is not intended to give the details of Hajj rites here because there are many Hajj guides and, some rites are fairly long and consist of numerous details, and these can also be found in many writings on Hajj. An attempt will be made here to highlight the main ones and to an extent explain their significance. The sequence of ritual actions performed in Hajj are based on revelations in the Qur'an and the practice of the Prophet(s).

Before one leaves the house for Hajj, it is highly recommended that he/she prays and makes the intention to go to the Holy land to visit the Holy Places and to perform *Umrah* (little pilgrimage) and the Hajj. Before entering Miqat (designated areas in Saudi Arabia) that one cannot cross without putting on pilgrim's dress (*Ihram*), one must declare his or her intention for Hajj and for that one must be physically clean and pure.

The *Ihram* consists of two unseamed lengths of white cloth for the men and a simple modest gown and head covering for the women indicating that they are entering a state of consecration and casting off what is ritually impure. Putting on the *Ihram* is the beginning of a great change, becoming genuinely conscious about Allah, seeking a new direction for oneself, in fact, forget about one's own self; as an example, one is not supposed to look at the mirror in the state of *Ihram*.

The *Ihram* is also a reminder that before Allah there are neither rich nor poor, neither Kings nor beggars, neither refined nor crude- all are equal. Hajj allows the participant to experience the egalitarian nature of Islam. It is also a reminder that on the Day of Judgment one can avail oneself of nothing else- but the record of his / her deeds on earth.

The Hajj to Makkah and its surrounding area is a ritual lasting up to seven days. One arrives Makkah preferably by the seventh day of Dhul- Hajjah the twelfth month of the Muslim year but no later than the noon of the 8th of the month. On arrival at Makkah, the first thing one does is take a bath and ablution, and then visit the Kaaba and circumambulate (*tawaf*) it seven times. This is a reenactment of what Prophet Ibrahim (as), Ishmail (as) and Prophet Muhammed (s) did. Of course, it has been ordained in the Qur'an. It is also symbolic of the ideal of the unity of humankind. The essential meaning of this rite is brought out well by the late Iranian philosopher Ali Shariati:

> As you circumambulate and move closer to the Ka'ba, you feel like a small stream merging with a big river. Carried by a wave you lose touch with the ground. Suddenly, you are floating, carried on by the flood. As you approach the center, the pressure of the crowd squeezes you so hard that

you are given a new life. You are now a part of the People; you are now a Man, alive and eternal... The Kaaba is the world's sun whose face attracts you into its orbit. You have become part of this universal system. Circumambulating around Allah, you will soon forget yourself... You have been transformed into a particle that is gradually melting and disappearing. This is absolute love at its peak.

The circumambulation of the Kaaba is followed by performing the sa'y, i.e., running (actually brisk walks at points) between the two hillocks known as Safa and Marwa to commemorate Hajar's search for water when she and her son Ismail were abandoned in the desert by Prophet Ibrahim(as) commanded by Allah. Imagine a lonely woman with her only child cast into the depth of this barren waterless valley! Wandering, homeless, shelterless. deprived of support, isolated from her society, a lonely slave, a victim, a stranger, exiled, rejected, hated by her family, this black maid is all alone in this fearful valley of Makkah with her child in her arm in desperate search for water for the baby! Rituals of Hajj are memories of Hajar. By running and hurrying, the Haji's try to act as Hajar again. Remember, she was restless but hopeful and determined in her search for water. It is also a tribute to motherhood—a mother's struggle for her child. She submitted totally to the will of Allah, an example of submission and obedience and a great champion of faith. Consequently, she is buried near the noblest and most ancient sanctuary, Kaaba. Islam honors her, coining the word Hijra from her name because she was the ultimate refugee! And, of course, her search resulted in the appearance of the sacred well of Zam Zam whose waters are believed to posses special powers.

After Sa`yi, the pilgrims then travel several miles from Makkah to Mina, and pass the night there. It is Sunnah to go to Mina before noon on the 8th. When one leaves for Mina, his/her

Hajj and 'Umrah (Pilgramage)

Hajj has begun, (what has been done prior to this is *'Umrah*). First the pilgrim(Hajee) left the house and the worldly comfort, then at Miqat gave up his/her dress, put on *Ihram* and joined the eternal human migration to Hajj. The Hajee then comes to Kaaba, House of God. But Kaaba is the direction not the destination. The Hajee leaves Kaaba to go to Arafat, by way of Mina - to approach Allah, to be closer to Him! (Arafat is about 12 miles East of Makkah.)

The central event of the pilgrimage is the *Wuquf* (halting or standing still) on the 9th anywhere in the area surrounding the Jabal al-Rahma (the Mount of Mercy) a small rocky eminence in the valley of Arafat itself. It is called the Mount of Mercy because it is where Adam and Eve were re-united, where they prayed and were forgiven by Allah. This Mount is also significant for Muslims because Prophet Mohammed (s) gave his farewell address from here.

The rite of standing before Allah takes place beginning at high noon. The hours until sunset are dedicated to prayerful repentance during which the mass of pilgrims seek and receive from Allah His merciful forgiveness. This is the central rite of the pilgrimage, its omission nullifies the validity of Hajj. It is also a sin if one doesn't think, having been in Arafat on the 9th, that he or she was not forgiven.

The plain of Arafat is a city of tents, no houses; people from all over the world no matter what color or race or language are clad in the all equalizing *Ihram*, beseeching, Allah, shedding tears, sobbing and murmuring for forgiveness for past sins and seeking His blessings. During *Wuquf*, time seems to stand still. Life with all its allurements, frustrations, hopes, fears and achievements are all left behind as the mammoth crowd of several million stand before Allah A Muslim is taught to hold communion with God in solitude. in the dead of night; and thus he goes all alone through the experience of drawing nearer to

God. But there is yet a higher spiritual experience which he can attain in that vast concourse of men in the plain of Arafat. To concentrate not in solitude all one's ideas on God but in the company of others, is an object of Hajj. Muhammad Ali writes (*The Religion of Islam*, p. 389):

> Take the case of hundreds of thousands of people, all inspired by the one idea of feeling the presence of the Divine Being, all concentrating their minds on the One Supreme Being Who for the time is their sole object; and add to this the mighty effect of the outward unity of them all clad in the same two sheets, crying in one language what is understood by all, *Labbaika Allah-umma labbaik*—"Here we are, O Allah! Here are we in Thy august presence." Their appearance, as well as the words which are on their lips, show that they are standing in the Divine presence, and are so engrossed in the contemplation of the Divine Being that they have lost all ideas of self.

It is also the time to reflect on the "Farewell Sermon" given by the Prophet (s) the same day and place centuries ago. This reflection may help comprehend the relationship between his farewell sermon and the essence of Hajj. The guidance contained in the words of the Prophet (s) is a legacy that continues to exist for us. (For the "Farewell Sermon," see the chapter: Muhammed (s).

The mass of Pilgrims leaves Arafat when the sun has set to return to Muzdalifa, about half way back to Mina where the night is spent. The prayers of *Dhuhr* and *'Asr* are performed combined at Arafat. Later it is time for *Maghrib* (sunset) prayer: this prayer has been performed throughout one's life exactly at the time fixed for it, and this prayer cannot be delayed. But not today. Today it has to be offered late at Muzdalifah, for there is no virtue in any prayer offered by the force of habit, the merit lies in doing what Allah ordains, the prayer is for Him. Hence *Maghrib* and *'Isha* are prayed together, as ordained by Allah.

The next day, the 10th, Pilgrims return to Mina where they stone the devils represented by three heaps of stone (jamra). The devil is said to have appeared to Prophet Ibrahim (as) here to stop him from sacrificing his son and was driven away by him by throwing stones at him. Every act of Hajj symbolizes an act of Prophet Ibrahim (as). The sacrifice of his son is symbolized by the animal sacrifice at the conclusion of the Hajj which falls on this day. This day, the 10th, is a great moment of Hajj because it is the day of *Eid al-Adha* (the Festival of sacrifice.) While the *Eid al-Adha* is being celebrated at Mina, Muslims throughout the world are conducting similar ceremonies in their homes and towns.

The 10th is a busy day for the Hajis. They also return to Makkah to repeat the circumambulation. This circumambulation is considered more meritorious than all those performed before and after and it is considered the most important one.

The pilgrimage is now over and the male Hajis now shave or trim, wash and change while the females shorten their hair. They must, however, spend three days in Mina although two days is permissible. Each day, while at Mina, normally between midday and sunset, every pilgrim has to throw seven stones at each of the three fixed places known as *ramy al-jumar* constructions. Pilgrims finally return to Makkah for final prayers and before leaving town, it is the custom to circumambulate the Kaaba. Muslims can go to Makkah any time of the year but the real pilgrimage is the one performed during the month of *Dhul-Hajjah*. A minor pilgrimage (which does not count towards fulfillment of the religious obligation Hajj), called *'Umrah* in Arabic, may be made at any time in the year and is less ceremonial, as discussed below.

The Hajj itself is the life experience of the individual pilgrim in an intense experience of several days. The first important act of the Hajj is to answer both individually and collectively, Allah's call:

$$\text{لَبَّيْكَ اللهُمَّ لَبَّيْكَ}$$

$$\text{لَبَّيْكَ لاَ شَرِيكَ لَكَ لَبَّيْكَ}$$

$$\text{إِنَّ الحَمدَ وَالنِعمَةَ لَكَ وَالمُلكَ}$$

$$\text{لاَ شَرِيكَ لَكَ .}$$

Labbayik Allahumma Labbayik
Labbayik La sharika lak Labbayik
Innal hamda wan ni'mata laka wal mulk
Laa sharika lak

Here I am O Allah here I am
There is none who is Thy associate
All praise and blessing belong to Thee
Though art the Sovereign
There is none associated with Thee

From the time he is still at a distance of several miles from Makkah to the time he leaves the Holy city, there is but this phrase on his tongue, this one idea in his heart.

The second and highly symbolic act of the pilgrim is his total isolation from all worldly concerns as he or she enters into the state of *Ihram*, or dedication to Allah. The sacrifice of the security and comfort of one's home and family for the sake of religion is symbolized in the *hijrah*, the migration of the Prophet and his Makkan companions to Madinah. The Hajj is an ever-recurring *hijrah* to Allah in answer to His call.

Beyond all this symbolism, there is yet another significance of the Hajj. The days of the pilgrimage witness the largest gatherings of human beings from all around the world. No religious rite has done more to unite the Muslims than the pilgrimage. Here, hundreds of thousands of pilgrims meet and are incidentally able to exchange ideas and experiences. The days of Hajj represent a way of reaffirming one's commitment and sense of belonging and an opportunity to renew one's faith while in the largest gathering of Muslims. Participation in the Hajj becomes a way of sharing in the founding experiences of the *Ummah*. Reflecting on the many and significant lessons in the Hajj, one must not forget its most important aspect. The Hajj is above all one of the pillars of Islam. It is an act of worship. The most important factor of the Hajj is to have the intention of performing it solely for the purpose of pleasing Allah and for seeking His mercy. It should not be mixed up with any worldly interest.

The life of the pilgrim after the pilgrimage is bound to change. The Prophet(s), declared, 'A man who performs the Hajj returns to his home as though he was created anew, as on the day when his mother gave birth to him'. This means that Hajj gives the pilgrim a new and pure life. The entire journey of Hajj is a complete *'ibadah* (worship) and one must do everything to keep it up. Hajj is indeed a reformation and transformation of the person in the path of Allah and he or she should strive to make it permanent. The experiences and lessons of Hajj should never leave the Hajees. Each time a Hajee makes a salat, his heart and soul should again see the Kaaba in all its splendor and, through his mind's eye, he should revisit it and renew his Hajj commitment to his Creator.

'Umrah (the Little Pilgrimage)

Allah says in Qur'an (2:196): "And complete the Hajj or 'Umrah in the service of Allah." According to a report of Abu Hurairah(r), Prophet (s)said: "To perform *'Umrah* after *'Umrah* serves as the expiation for the lapses committed between them and the reward for Hajj *Mabrur* (accepted) is nothing but Paradise" (Bukhari, 3:1). Prophet (s)also said that (Bukhari, 3:10) '*Umrah* in Ramadan is equivalent to Hajj in reward.

'*Umrah* differs from Hajj in two respects. In the first place, Hajj cannot be performed except at the fixed time, while '*Umrah* may be performed at any time. The actual devotions of Hajj are limited from the 8th through the 13th of Dhul-Hajjah. Ceremonies of Hajj have to be performed on the sacred precincts of Makkah and the two neighboring places Mina and Arafat on the fixed dates; '*Umrah* is performed in the sanctuary of Makkah. Another difference is the sacrifice of an animal as the concluding act is essential to Hajj, but not for '*Umrah*.

'*Umrah*, like the Hajj, can only be performed in a state of ritual purity. On assuming this state, the pilgrim must make up his mind whether he is going to perform the '*Umrah* by itself or in combination with the Hajj and must express his intention. If he combines the two, he can assume the *ihram* for both pilgrimages at once; in the other case, the *ihram* must be especially assumed for the '*Umrah* in the unconsecrated area outside of the sacred area of Makkah.

The actual ceremony of the '*Umrah* begins as with Hajj with the utterance of the formula "at Your service" (Arabic labbayka). The pilgrim enters the mosque of Makkah through the north door of the northeast side, goes to the Black Stone and, turning right, begins the seven-fold circumambulation of the Kaaba. The first three circumambulations are performed at a rapid pace, the four last at an ordinary rate. He then prays behind the Maqam Ibrahim, drinks a draught of the holy Zamzam water. Leaving the mosque through the great al-Safa door, he then performs the second essential part of the '*Umrah*, namely, running seven times between al-Safa and al-Marwa. After having his hair cut or shaved, the ceremony of the '*Umrah* is completed.

Hajj and 'Umrah (Pilgramage)

Fundamentals (Arkan) of Hajj

Note: If any of these is missing, Hajj will not be valid.

1. Entering the state of *Ihram*, pronounce the intention (*niyyah*) of Hajj, wear *Ihram* (at a designated station) and recite *talbiyah*.
2. Stay at Arafat: *Wuquf* (standing still or halting), i.e., Arafat; staying at Arafat on the 9th of Dhul-Hajja from noon until sunset. Prophet (s)said: "The pilgrimage is Arafat."
3. Perform *Tawaf* (circumambulation) around Kaaba; perform *Tawaf Ifadah* (also called *Ziarah*) any time after *Fajr* on the 10th after returning from Arafat and Mina.
1. Fast walk between As-Safa and Marwah (near Kaaba). The walk known as sa`yi is seven passages back and forth (3.5 round trips) between the two points.
2. Carrying out these rites at the prescribed times, prescribed places and in the prescribed sequence

Other Hajj Rituals

Staying the night at Muzdalifa;
Staying the nights preceding Arafat and following Eid al-Adha at Mina;
Casting pebbles at Mina;
Sacrificing an animal;
Cutting or shortening the hair;
Circumambulation including farewell;

Fundamentals of 'Umrah

Entering the State of *Ihram*;
Perform circumambulation around Kaaba;

Fast walk between As-Safa and Marwah.

Obligations During Ihram (for Hajj or 'Umrah)

1. Observe, as always, all that Allah has made obligatory, such as the daily prayers. Every Muslim must bear in mind that if his belief (*aqidah*) is not sound, Hajj or any other '*ibadah* is not accepted.
2. Avoid all that Allah has prohibited, such as wrongdoing, committing sins.
3. Guard against injuring Muslims by deed or word.
4. Abstain from what is prohibited in *Ihram*.

   (a) do not cut nails, remove hair by shaving or clipping, or any other way;

   (b) do not kill, frighten or assist in hunting any land animals;

   (c) within the precincts of the Grand Mosque, no one is allowed to cut trees, pluck vegetables or collect lost property except for the purpose of identifying it or its owner.

   (d) Do not propose to a woman or contract marriage either for yourself or on behalf of others. Sexual intercourse is prohibited; so is touching of the opposite sex with desire

   (e) Wearing sewn clothes for men is prohibited; so is covering the head with a cap, turban or shawl. However, an umbrella (seamless) is allowed.

   (f) It is forbidden for a woman to wear gloves on her hands or to cover her face with a veil (*niqab*) or drape (*burqah*).

Note: It is permissible to wear sandals, a ring, a pair of glasses, a hearing aid, a watch and a belt (without stitches) or a girdle to protect one's money or documents. It is also permissible to change one's clothes to wash them as well as to wash one's hair and body, and it is acceptable if some hair inadvertently falls out during washing.

14

FIVE PILLARS : A SUMMARY

قَالَ رَسُولُ اللَّهِ ﷺ بُنِيَ الإِسْلامُ عَلى خَمْسٍ: شَهَادَة أَنْ لاَ إِلَهَ إِلاَّ اللَّه ، وَأَنَّ مُحَمَّدًا رَسُولُ اللَّهِ ، وَاَقَام الصَّلاَوةِ ، وَاَيْتَاءِ الزَّكَاةِ ، وَالحَجّ ، وَصَوْم رَمَضَانَ .

Rasul-Allah (s) said, foundation of Islam [stands] upon five: testify that there is no god but Allah, and that Muhammad (s) is the messenger of Allah, and establishment of prayer (*salah*), and payment of alms tax (*zakah*), and the performance of the pilgrimage (*hajj*) and fasting in the month of Ramadan (*sawm*). (Bukhari : 7)

The basic devotional duties of Islam are conventionally classified under five pillars. (Each of the individual pillars has been described previously in its proper place. Here is a summary view of it.) They are easily remembered as a summary of rituals and doctrines. They are the first duties owed by humanity to God; they are the essence of a life in Islam. Although Qur'an gives specific instructions about observing these obligations, "five pillars" as such are not mentioned in the Qur'an. However, according to Bukhari and Muslim, Prophet (s) did state that Islam is based on five things. The five pillars are intended as the focus of a total life orientation and they are understood as gateways to Allah.

Islam is built on submission to Allah with the five pillars as its foundation. They are *Iman* (Faith), *Salat* (Prayer), *Zakah* (Obligatory almsgiving), *Sawm* (Fasting) and *Hajj* (Pilgrimage). Each one of these formed a chapter in the book.

As we stated, these five pillars are the basic practices of Islam. They are relevant to every Muslim although *Zakah* and *Hajj* may not be required of some. Highly important is also the question of ritual purity, since without it the prayers of the worshipper are rendered invalid.

Of the five pillars of Islam, *Iman* or Faith is most important. It demands the confession of a sincere double belief, namely, the unity of Allah and the truth of the message of Muhammad (s). Every Muslim makes this confession by saying *Shahada*, i.e., testifying that none has the right to be worshipped but Allah and Muhammad (s) is the Messenger of Allah. The Confession must be said intentionally, thoughtfully and with full understanding of its truth. The pious Muslim will recite the *Shahadah* several times a day in prayer. *Salat*, or prayer, in Islam is a direct link between the worshipper and Allah. Prayer is an expression of glorification of Allah and supplication to Him; its ritual is very precisely determined and unites Muslims with Islam. There are five obligatory prayers a day for Muslims. *Zakah*, or legal almsgiving, purifies the giver by bestowing on him victory over selfishness and the moral satisfaction of participation in the creation of a just society. Fasting in the month of Ramadan every year is an act of pure submission to Allah's command. Fortifying the will, it frees man from passion and purifies him spiritually through self-denial and deprivation. *Hajj*, or Pilgrimage, for able-bodied who has the means to do so, is an act of answering Allah's call; it also purifies one from all kinds

Five Pillars

of pride and prejudices. It is the most explicit representation of the solidarity of the Muslim community gathering in an assembly annually.

The five pillars, however, can give a very narrow view of Islam as pillars themselves do not make a house. In fact, a building or a construction with pillars only is not a building at all, and is far less a house. In the same way, in order to be a Muslim, a number of things will need to be added to the pillars. Worship in Islam is not only observance of the prescribed rites (Prayer, Almsgiving, Fasting, Pilgrimage), but living one's entire life in obedience to God, doing His will and seeking His pleasure, exactly in the way He has laid down. But the rites of worship are the essential and only key to that full life of worship. This book is concerned with all that. All the qualities that are essential for a Muslim are discussed throughout the book.

"O Prophet! Truly We have sent thee as a witness, a bearer of glad tidings, and a warner." (33:45)

Qur'anic callighaphy by Ottoman Sultan Mahmud II ca. 1838

Islamic Calligraphy: Articles of Faith
The hull and rudder represent the Articles of Faith *(Allah, His Angel, His Books, His Prophets, the Last Judgment, Preordination, Resurrection after death)*. The Shahadah forms the sail.

Part IV

BEYOND PRAYER

15

ISLAM : A WAY OF LIFE

وَلْتَكُن مِّنكُمْ أُمَّةٌ يَدْعُونَ إِلَى ٱلْخَيْرِ وَيَأْمُرُونَ بِٱلْمَعْرُوفِ وَيَنْهَوْنَ عَنِ ٱلْمُنكَرِۚ وَأُو۟لَٰٓئِكَ هُمُ ٱلْمُفْلِحُونَ ۝

And that there might grow out of you a community [of people] who invite unto all that is good, and enjoin the doing of what is right and forbid the doing of what is wrong: and it is they who shall attain to a happy state (3: 104).

Islam is not just a religion; it is a way of life. It has been mentioned that Islam is a set of beliefs, but it is more than that. It is the basic blueprint by which man should live. Islam is an all-encompassing religion. It encompasses not only how one must pray, but how one must do all his other activities, viz., how one must behave, dress, work, marry and die. Qur'an, the center of Islam, is the foundation of an ideal society. It is an accompaniment to life. It provides guidance, it warns, it chastises and it exhorts.

Islam is a practical system in every way, but its practicality is derived from its ideals. These ideals are reflected in everyday life. No problem of life is outside the scope of Islam. It includes religious, spiritual, physical, economic, social and political affairs. Qur'an contains principles of religion and ethics as well as prescriptive legislation for everyday living. Laws of marriage and divorce, of dependence and inheritance are all laid down there. They govern the family which is the essence of human life. Islamic community is that community which works to implement God's will in Qur'an here on earth. The communal duty in Islam is commanding the good and forbidding the evil. This will result in a healthy, moral environment. If this is done, order and peace will prevail in the community. This duty is based upon an injunction in Qur'an which says: "and that there might grow out of you a community [of people] who invite unto all that is good, and enjoin the doing of what is right and forbid the doing of what is wrong: and it is they who shall attain to a happy state" (3: 104, Muhammad Asad's translation). All Muslims are expected to exercise this ethical judgment for their society. This shows the concern in Islam for social ethics.

The preservation of social order depends on families as a unit of the society, with every member in the family freely adhering to the same moral principles and practices. Islam is founded on individual and collective morality and responsibility. Collective morality in Qur'an is expressed in such terms as equality, justice, fairness, brotherhood, mercy, compassion and solidarity. The essence of all human rights is the equality of the entire human race; Qur'an obliterated all distinctions among men except goodness and virtue. Allah says (49: 11, 12):

> O you who have attained to faith! No men shall deride [other] men: it may well be that those [whom they deride] are better than themselves. And no women [shall deride other] women: it maybe that those [whom they deride] are better than themselves. And neither shall you defame one another, nor insult one another by [opprobrious] epithets: evil is all imputation of iniquity after [one has attained to] faith: and they who [become guilty thereof and] do not repent—it is they, they who are evildoers! (11) ✿

O you who have attained to faith! Avoid most guesswork [about one another]—for, behold, some of [such] suspicion is [in itself] a sin; and do not spy upon one another, and neither allow yourselves to speak ill of one another behind your backs. . . . Would any of you like to eat the flesh of the dead brother? Nay, you would loathe it! And be conscious of God. Verily, God is an acceptor of repentance, a dispenser of grace! (12) ❁

As already mentioned, Islam does acknowledge a fundamental equality of all men, and a fundamental justice among all, but over and above that it leaves the door open for achievement of preeminence (cf. 13: 11; 53: 39-41) through hard work, just as it lays in the balance values other than the economic. "... Verily, the noblest among you in Allah's eye is the most pious who has *At-Taqwa*" (49: 13). The Islamic view of life goes beyond merely economic values to those other values which are nobler and that make the Islamic faith the more powerful to provide equity and justice in society, and to establish justice in the whole of the human sphere. There is no doubt that a central aim of the Qur'an is to establish a viable social order on earth that is just and ethically based.

The Islamic way is to link the fundamentals of Islam in our daily life with a future that offers hopeful promise in this world as well as the hereafter. Islam as a faith is built on five palpable pillars or cornerstones, each of which has its spiritual values along with its physical aspects. A Muslim's first duty is to declare and publicly confess the *Shahadah*. Such declaration in the absolute Oneness of Allah and in the Prophethood of Muhammad (s) must be continuously borne in mind and translated into the Muslim's daily activities. *Salat* is a combination of physical and spiritual exercise aimed at disciplining and religious uplifting. In advance of *salat*, the individual must undergo ablution, which is a physical purification and spiritual preparation for being in the presence of

God. The prescribed *salat* is the minimum that a Muslim must perform. Through *salat*, Muslims communicate with God, confirm their submission to Him, and foster the power of good ingrained in them. *Zakah* means the right of God to a Muslim's wealth, and the beneficiaries are the poor and the needy. Fasting is a practical exercise of will, of self-control, a sure method of subduing the passion. Pilgrimage is a most impressive and great experience in a Muslim's life during which he gives all his body and soul to the ritual. Pilgrimage inspires a Muslim to think of Islam as a religion initiated in ancient times by Ibrahim(as) and perfected during the lifetime of Muhammad (s).

Adherence to the five pillars is a requirement for all Muslims. But Islam is not just what one formally or ritualistically performs. Linking these practices with performing deeds that enhance and preserve basic ethical and moral values of Islam has to be an ongoing effort. A Muslim is accountable for what he does and what he fails to do in accordance with not only the Islamic law, but also the spirit of it. Morality rates high even in economic life which is based on a solid foundation of divine instructions. To earn a living by honest labor is not only a duty, but a great virtue comparable to acts of worship (cf. 23: 51).

Islam demands honesty in all business dealings, which should be concluded with frankness, justice and honor (cf. 83: 1-3). It condemns cheating and forbids usury or taking interest in return for lending money to the needy (cf., 2: 275).

Islam is what Qur'an defines, directs or, rather, enjoins. It is noble and pious to have Qur'an in one's heart, but it is equally pious to live by it. Every Muslim's religious world must be coextensive with the outside world. Islamic way of life means being religious in personal life, being Islamic in the world, and the way Qur'an has laid it out. Qur'an is a finality and has to be understood in its own terms."This is a book with verses fundamental [of established meaning] ..." (11: 1) and "... in it are verses basic or fundamental clear [in meaning]; they are the foundation of the Book; others are not entirely clear ..." (3: 7). Hence, some of the verses, especially those that are allegorical, are subject to different interpretation. However, as already mentioned, this does not affect the decisive verses that are the basis of the Book and contain fundamental principles of Islam. In regard to the verses that are subject to interpretation, such as "And such are the parables we set forth for mankind, but only those understand them who have knowledge" (29: 43). Muhammad Ali (*The Religion of Islam*, p. 35) lays down an important principle:

> The important principle to be borne in mind in the interpretation of the Qur'an, therefore, is that the meaning should be sought from within the Qur'an, and never should a passage be interpreted in such a manner that it maybe at variance with any other passage, but more essentially with the basic principles laid down in the decisive verses. Allah has indeed said, "a Book consistent with itself" (39: 23).

It should be pointed out that there are libraries of commentaries interpreting every passage as to its theological and juristic, philosophic and linguistic aspects. The learned men sought the meaning of the Qur'an according to their understanding and circumstances. The same right accrues to every generation.

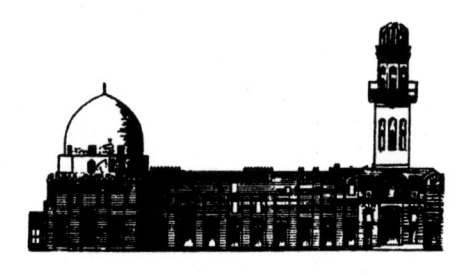

Islamic Architecture: **The Taj Mahal (circa 1632-43)**

This is a tomb built by Emperor Shah Jahan for his wife, Mumtaz Mahal. Its superb proportions create a unique architectural achievement, considered to be one of the wonders of the world.

Catherine B. Asher, in Architecture of Mughal India (1992 pp 214-215) writes: *The interior, like the exterior, bear Qur'anic verses ... The number of Qur'anic verses and their emphasis on the Day of Judgment is reinforced by the location of the mausoleum, not only at the end of the paradisical gardens, but also on the platform above them. That position matches the very location of God's Throne, which, according to Islamic tradition, will be above the gardens of Paradise. ... illustrated in a diagrammatic drawing that Shah Jahan owned, depicting the assembled on the Day of Judgment. ... (the edifice) is intended not only as a tomb ... but also as a visual replica of the throne of God on that momentous day. ... the designers were highly educated, not only in mathematics, engineering and astrology, but also in literature and of course theology. (and thus) well prepared to formulate the tomb's symbolic program as the ultimate vision of Paradise on Earth.*

Included in the calligraphy are the final verses from the chapter entitled Daybreak (89:28-30) that invites the faithful to enter Paradise.

16

RIGHTEOUSNESS

وَٱلَّذِينَ ءَامَنُواْ وَعَمِلُواْ ٱلصَّٰلِحَٰتِ أُوْلَٰٓئِكَ أَصْحَٰبُ ٱلْجَنَّةِۖ هُمْ فِيهَا خَٰلِدُونَ ﴿٨٢﴾

But those who believe and do righteous deed those are companions of Paradise; therein shall they abide for ever (2:82).

Righteousness has been briefly touched upon in the chapter "Islam as a Way of Life." In this chapter, this is the main focus.

"Righteous" is the translation for the word *salih*, also sometimes translated as "good." Whatever the translation, *salih* is one of the most common words for ethico-religious excellence used in the Qur'an."Those who believe and do good deeds" is a phrase used many a time in the Qur'an. In other words, faith is inconceivable without good deeds. It is fair to say that believers are not believers in the true sense unless they are also *salihin*, i.e., they have done some good deeds. What, then, are good deeds? In short, they are:

(2: 83). Worship none but Allah; treat with kindness your parents and kindred, and orphans and those in need; speak fair to the people; be steadfast in prayer; and give *Zakah*.

Later in that *Surah*, Allah says:

(2: 277). Those who believe, and do deeds of righteousness, and establish regular prayers and give *Zakah*, will have their reward with their Lord: On them shall be no fear, nor shall they grieve.

He further assures:

(18: 110). [W]hoever expects to meet his Lord, let him work righteousness, and in the worship of his Lord, admit no one as partner.

Yet another definition of *salih* men (*salihin*) as in Muhammad Asad's translation (3: 114-115): "Among the followers of earlier revelation there are upright people, who recite God's messages throughout the night, and prostrate themselves [before Him]. They believe in God and the Last Day, and enjoin the doing of what is right and forbid the doing of what is wrong, and vie with one another in doing good works; and these are among the righteous."

God commands and commends righteousness and the doers of righteousness. In many places He rebukes evil and doers of it. Qur'an links faith and good works intimately by pronouncing (2: 25): "Give you good tidings to those who believe and do deeds of righteousness." In considering the scope of what is good and what is evil, the criteria of the Divine Law must be applied. Good deeds must be done in sincerity and must be done right. If either is lacking, it is not a good deed. Sincerity means it is done for the sake of Allah; done right means in accordance with the laws of *Sharia*. As long as a man is able to submit to the texts of the law, he must not deviate from them. When an issue is complicated, the believer should seek enlightenment until the true interpretation becomes clear. It is by means of justice that all affairs may be kept in order. Justice is the principle, and the criteria may have been laid down in the *Sharia*.

Very similar to *salih* is the word *birr*, another Qur'anic moral term. The usual translation of *birr* is piety, but it does not convey the full meaning of it. It means carrying out the commandments of religion; it stands for genuine belief as against empty ritual. Thus it compliments *salih*. A good definition of *birr* and an excellent exposition of the topic of righteousness will be found in the following verse (2: 177):

> The *birr* (righteousness) does not consist in turning your faces towards the East or the West but (true) *birr* is this that one believes in God, and the Last Day, and the angels, and the Scripture, and the prophets; that one gives one's own wealth howsoever cherished it may be, to kinsfolk, orphans, the needy, the wayfarer, and beggars, and also for the sake of slaves; that one performs the ritual prayer, pays the alms. And those who keep their covenant when they have once covenanted and are patient in distress and hardship: these are they who are sincere; these are they who are godfearing.

In *Salat al-Tahajjud*, Muhammad Imran underscores the excellence of *Tahajjud* prayer, but he also makes the point that *Tahajjud* and all other acts of devotion will be meaningless unless the source of livelihood of the devotee is a lawful one (p. 12).

There is practically nothing to distinguish *birr* or *salih* from Iman in the true sense of the term. Allah says (2: 92): "You attain not to righteousness (*birr*) until you expend what you love. And whatever you expend, Allah knoweth it all."

Both *salih* and *birr* are interrelated to *taqwa*. *Taqwa* is sometimes translated as "piety," sometimes as consciousness of Allah, sometime as fear of Allah. It is derived from *wiqayah*, for shield, which really means to shield oneself from Allah's wrath by doing what He ordered to be done and by avoiding what He has prohibited. Fazlur Rahman, in *Major themes of the Qur'an* (1980, p. 29), explicates it this way:

> *Taqwa* means to protect oneself against the harmful or evil consequences of one's conduct. If, then, by "fear of God" one means fear of the consequences of one's actions— whether in this world or in the next (fear of punishment of

the Last Day)—one is absolutely right. In other words, it is the fear that comes from an acute sense of responsibility, here and in the hereafter. ... When a man or a society is fully conscious of this while conducting himself or itself, he or it has true *taqwa*. This idea can be effectively conveyed by the term "conscience," if the object of conscience transcends it. This is why it is proper to say that "conscience" is truly central to Islam. . . .

Qur'an often mentions *taqwa* together with a complimentary positive virtue; for example, "those who have *taqwa* and do good deeds (righteous," as in the following verse (7: 35):

> O children of Adam! Whenever there come to you Messengers from amongst you, rehearsing My Signs unto you—those who are righteous and mend (their lives)—on them shall be no fear nor shall they grieve.

Thus, Iman, *taqwa*, *birr* and *salih* are all linked. True faith and ritual worship, on the one hand, and a life lived the Islamic way which leads to justice and compassion in society, on the other, are clearly established in the Qur'an; for example (107: 1-7):

> Seest thou one who denies the Judgment (to come)? Then such is the one who repulses the orphan, and encourages not the feeding of the indigent. So woe to the worshippers who are neglectful of their Prayers, those who (want but) to be seen, but refuse (to supply) (even) neighbourly needs.

17

HALAL AND HARAM
(PERMITTED AND FORBIDDEN)

يَٰٓأَيُّهَا ٱلَّذِينَ ءَامَنُوا۟ لَا تُحَرِّمُوا۟ طَيِّبَٰتِ مَآ أَحَلَّ ٱللَّهُ لَكُمْ وَلَا تَعْتَدُوٓا۟ إِنَّ ٱللَّهَ لَا يُحِبُّ ٱلْمُعْتَدِينَ ۝

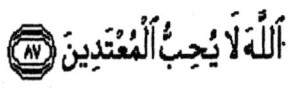

O you who believe! Do not make *Haram* the good things which Allah has made *Halal* for you, and do not transgress; indeed Allah does not like the transgressors. And eat of what Allah has provided for you, lawful and good, and fear Allah, in Whom you are believers. (5: 87-88)

Halal and *Haram* are very difficult topics, and the material on them in English is scant. The best and most comprehensive work is *The Lawful and prohibited in Islam: Al-Halal walharam fil Islam* by Yusuf al-Qaradawi (trans. By: Kamal El-Helbawy, M. Moinuddin Siddiqui and Syed Shukry, 1993). This work is sponsored and published by the General Institute of Islamic Culture at Al-Azhar University. This chapter is primarily based on that publication.

Halal is defined as that which is permitted where no restrictions exist, and the doing of which the Law-Giver, Allah, has allowed.

Haram is defined as that which the Law-Giver has absolutely prohibited. Anyone who engages in it is liable to incur the punishment of Allah in the Hereafter and will likely incur legal punishment in this world. *Haram* is applied to things, places, persons, and actions other than acts of worship.

Principles Pertaining to Halal and Haram

1. Principle of natural permissibility

The first principle established by Islam is that those things which Allah has created and the benefits derived from them are essentially for man's use, and thus are permissible. Allah says (2: 29): "It is He who created for you all things that are on earth." He further says (2: 168): O mankind! Eat of that which is lawful and good on the earth, and follow not the footsteps of Shaytan." The general principle, then, would be: what is lawful and good, and not what is evil or shameful.

According to Sahih Hadith, Prophet (s) said: "What Allah has made lawful in His Book is *Halal* and what He has forbidden is *Haram*, and that concerning which He is silent is allowed as His favor. So accept from Allah His favor, for Allah is not forgetful of anything."

2. To make lawful and to prohibit is the Right of Allah

The second principle is that Islam has reserved the authority of the Almighty to legislate the *Haram* and *Halal* of human beings alone. Allah says:

(16: 116): Hence, do not utter falsehoods by letting your tongues determine [at your own discretion], "this is lawful and that is forbidden," thus attributing your own lying inventions to God: for, behold, they who attribute their own lying inventions to God will never attain to a happy state!

3. Prohibiting the Halal and permitting the Haram is similar to committing Shirk

While Islam reprimands all those who may on their own authority declare what is lawful and what is prohibited, it is more strict with respect to those who voice prohibitions. As stated earlier, Allah says :

(5: 87): Do not make *Haram* the good things which Allah has made *Halal* for you, and do not transgress; indeed Allah does not like the transgressors. And eat of what Allah has provided for you, lawful and good, and fear Allah, in Whom you are believers." (Also verses 7: 32-33).

4. The prohibition of things is due to their impurity and harmfulness

It is the right of Allah, the One who created us and bestowed innumerable gifts on us, to legalize or prohibit as He deems proper, and to place obligations and responsibilities upon us as He sees fit. However, Allah is not arbitrary in what He commands because He is merciful to His servants and He makes things *Halal* and *Haram* for a reason, with people's well-being in view. In Islam, things are prohibited only because they are impure or harmful. (5: 3-4; 7: 32-33).

5. What is Halal is sufficient, while what is Haram is superfluous.

Islam has prohibited only such things as are unnecessary and dispensable while providing alternatives which are generally better and which give greater ease and comfort to human beings. For example, Allah has prohibited usury but has encouraged profitable trade.

6. Whatever is conducive to Haram is itself Haram

Another Islamic principle is that if something is prohibited, things which leads to it are also prohibited. Thus, secondary effects which lead to things which are *Haram* are also prohibited. For example, Islam has prohibited sex outside marriage; it has also prohibited anything which leads to it or makes it attractive, such as seductive clothing, private meetings, casual mixing between men and women, the depiction of nudity, pornographic literature, obscene songs, etc.

7. False representation of Haram as Halal is prohibited

It is just as unlawful to find devious means or develop technical excuses to justify what is *Haram* as to what is in fact *Haram*.

Calling something *Haram* by a name other than its own or changing its form while in essence it remains the same is a devious tactic not acceptable. Since a change of name or of form is of no consequence as long as the thing basically or principally remains the same, it is still *Haram*. Thus when some people invent new terms in order to deal in usury or to consume alcohol, the sin of dealing in usury and drinking remains.

8. Good intentions do not make Haram acceptable

Something remains *Haram* no matter how good the intention. Islam can never allow employing a *Haram* means to achieve a praiseworthy end. Indeed, it demands that not only the aim be honorable but also that the means as well. The maxim of Shariah is not that the end justifies the means. Shariah requires that the right be secured through just means only. In Islam good intentions have no effect on the sinfulness of what is *Haram*. According to Hadith, if a person earns property through *Haram* means and then gives charity, it will not be accepted (by Allah). Allah commanded the believers with what He commanded His messengers saying: "O, Messenger, eat of good things and do righteousness: surely I know the things you do." (23: 51).

9. Doubtful things are to be avoided

There is a gray area between clearly *Halal* or clearly *Haram*. This is the area of what is doubtful. Some people may not be able to decide whether a particular matter is permissible or forbidden. Such confusion may be because of doubt concerning the applicability of the text to the particular circumstance or matter in question (this is known as *Mushtabahat*). In such matters Islam considers it an act of piety for the Muslim to avoid doing what is doubtful in order to stay clear of doing something *Haram*. This principle originates from the following Sahih Hadith: "*Halal* and *Haram* -- both are clear and distinct. Borderline and midway between them are things which many people do not know whether they are *Halal* or *Haram*." (Bukhari and Muslim).

In Islam there are no privileges enjoyed by certain class or group of people allowing them to do whatever they like. For example, theft is *Haram* whether the thief or his victim is a Muslim or non-Muslim.. The thief will face the charge and pay the penalty whatever his status. This is what the Prophet (s) meant when he said: "By Allah, had Fatima (his daughter) committed theft, I would have cut off her hand."

10. Necessity dictates exception

Islam is a very practical religion. It is not unmindful to circumstances where adjustments may be necessary. It has, therefore, formulated a principle whereby necessity removes restrictions. However, it must be understood that the individual experiencing the necessity should not desire to relish it nor go beyond the limit by more than the amount needed to satisfy his hunger. Allah says (2: 173):

But if one is driven by necessity--neither coveting it nor exceeding his immediate need--no sin shall be upon him.

In Islam the number of prohibited things is rather small, whereas the number that is permissible is extremely vast.

Highlights of the Discussion of Halal and Haram

- There are categories of *Halal* and the classification may be as *Fard* (compulsory), *mustahab* (recommended), *mubah* (tolerated) and *makruh* (disliked).
- If one understands or knows the principles that govern *Haram*, it is going to be helpful.
- Anything that has been declared *Haram* is for a reason; basic reason is its impurity and/or harmfulness.

Halal and Haram

- Good intentions are not an excuse for indulging in *Haram* activities.
- In case of necessity, the *Haram* thing may be allowed but only so long as the necessity lasts.
- Hardships give rise to relaxation of laws. As for example, laws relating to salat and fasting are relaxed for persons who are sick or travelling.
- There are areas where there are no precise pronouncements in the Shariah; it is better to avoid these areas which may indeed be unlawful.

Food and Drink

All vegetable foods, with the exception of what is fermented (whether grapes, dates, barley, or any other substance), are *Halal*. Foods and substances which intoxicate or affect the functioning of the brain or harm the body are *Haram*. In this regard Qur'an says (2: 173):

> He has only forbidden you dead meat, and blood, and the flesh of swine, and that on which any other name has been invoked besides that of God...

And even in greater detail (5: 4):

> They ask you (O Muhammad (s)) what is lawful for them (as food). Say: "Lawful unto you are *At-Tayyibat* [all kind of *Halal* (lawful-good) foods which Allah has made lawful (meat of slaughtered edible animals, milk products, fats, vegetables and fruits, etc.]. And those beasts and birds of prey which you have trained as hounds, training and teaching them (to catch) in the manner as directed to you by Allah; so eat of what they catch for you, but pronounce the Name of Allah over it, and fear Allah. Verily, Allah is swift in reckoning."

Thus the prohibited foods are:

1. Those which die of themselves, including strangled animals, and those that are beaten to death, killed by a fall or eaten by wild beasts;
2. Blood;
3. Flesh of swine (pork);
4. Any kind of food over which any other name than that of Allah has been invoked at the time of slaughtering;
5. All unclean things repugnant to health and morality, such as dogs, cats, mules, horses, asses, lizards, swine, etc.
6. The Prophet (s) forbade all beasts of prey with canine teeth and all birds of prey with claws

Condemned Professions and Trade

Conducting business which involves injustice, cheating, making exorbitant profits, or the promotion of something that is *Haram* is prohibited by Islam. Doing business in alcoholic beverages, intoxicants, drugs, swine, idols, statues, or anything similar whose consumption and use Islam has prohibited is *Haram*. Any earnings from such business are sinful earnings.

Defrauding the customer is condemned in Islam. Qur'an emphasized this aspect of business transactions and included it among the ten obligations described in last part of Surah al-Anam in verses 151-152. These verses are relevant as to what is *Haram* (6: 151-152):

> Say: Come, let me convey unto you what God has [really] forbidden to you: Do not ascribe divinity, in any way, to aught beside Him; and [do not offend against but, rather,] do good unto your parents; and do not kill your children for fear of poverty, [for] it is We who shall provide sustenance for you as well as for them; and do not commit any shameful

deeds, be they open or secret; and do not take any human being's life--[the life] which God has declared to be sacred--otherwise than in [the pursuit of] justice: this has He enjoined upon you so that you might use your reason; and do not touch the substance of an orphan--save to improve it--before he comes of age. And [in all your dealings] give full measure and weight, with equity. We do not burden any human being with more than he is well able to bear; and when you voice an opinion, be just even though it be [against] one near of kin.

All unlawful means of acquiring property are denounced:

O you who believe, devour not your property among yourselves by illegal methods except that it be trading by your mutual consent (4: 29). And swallow not up your property among yourselves by false means (in any illegal way, e.g., stealing, robbing, deceiving), nor seek to gain access thereby to the judges, so that you may swallow up a part of the property of men wrongfully while you know by right it belongs to others (2: 188).

Misappropriation is forbidden."Behold, God bids you to deliver all that you have been entrusted with unto those who are entitled thereto, and whenever you judge between people, to judge with justice ..." (4: 58).

Islam absolutely rejects, condemns and forbids any male or female to earn money by selling sexuality. Islam does not permit sexually exciting dance or any other erotic activity. Islam is against any kind of sexual contact and relationship outside marriage. Allah warns (17: 32): "Nor come nigh to adultery, for it is an indecent (deed) and an evil way." While Islam forbids adultery, it urges Muslims to get married when they are able to support a family. Allah always guides His people towards good (4: 26-28).

Halal and *Haram* can also be looked at in terms of holiness and pollution. Everything that is profane or contemptuous of God, is *Haram*; everything separated from the world of the profane qualifies as being *Halal*. *Haram* and *Halal* are most intimately connected with God as immediate expression of His will. Allah says:

> (7: 31). O Children of Adam! Beautify yourselves for every act of worship, and eat and drink [freely], but do not waste: verily, He does not love the wasteful! •
>
> (32). Say: Who is there to forbid the beauty which God has brought forth for His creatures, and the good things from among the means of sustenance?" •
>
> Say: "They are [lawful] in the life of this world unto all who have attained to faith - to be theirs alone on Resurrection Day." •

Muhammad Asad gives a beautiful commentary on these verses as follows (*The Message of the Qur'an,* p. 207):

> By declaring that all good and beautiful things of life, i.e., those which are not expressly prohibited are lawful to the believers, the Qur'an condemns, by implication, all forms of life-denying asceticism, world-renunciation and self-mortification. While in the life of this world, those good things are shared by believers and unbelievers alike, they will be denied to the latter in the hereafter.

There is a lot that has not been covered in this section. For example, asceticism and matters relating to the soul have not been discussed. One case in point is backbiting. Imam Ghazzali, in *Muslim's Character* (p.185), writes:

> Islam has declared backbiting as *Haram*, so that man's life may continue and the factors of strength may remain in it, for the man who states the defects of a person in his absence

and derives satisfaction from it is undoubtedly very mean and low.

Allah says (49: 12):

O you who believe! Avoid much suspicions, indeed some suspicions are sins. And spy not, neither backbite one another. Would one of you like to eat the flesh of his dead brother! You would hate it (so hate backbiting). And fear Allah. Verily, Allah is the One Who accepts repentance, Most Merciful. ✦

About jealousy, Imam Ghazzali writes (p.165):

Islam has declared jealousy as *Haram* (forbidden). Allah has commanded His Messenger to seek shelter from the mischief of jealous people, because jealousy is a spark that burns inside the bosom and hurts the jealous person as well as others.

Imam Ghazzali says that Islam declared cursing and abusing and exchange of vulgar and obscene words and acts as *Haram*.

Although the preceding discussion of *Halal* and *Haram* is not complete, it is hoped that this will raise consciousness among Muslims. These ethical values are shared by other religions although the degree may vary. These are universal values, but in Islam they are laid down as a duty. Life's experience shows that man has greater inclination to sin than to do good. His ability or propensity to fall deep into sin, while Satan is always there to help, appears to be greater than to reach up to the heights of virtue. This is why we need guidance and, in particular, divine guidance. We need to be constantly reminded to stay on track doing right; we need a standard and Qur'an is the standard. By telling us about *Halal* and *Haram*, Allah lets us choose our path.

Symbols of Islam: Star and Crescent
These are the most recognizable symbols of the Islamaic faith *(not the sword, as commonly misconstrued.)*.

18

MANNERS, MORALS AND SYMBOLIC EXPRESSIONS OF ISLAM

يَٰٓأَيُّهَا ٱلَّذِينَ ءَامَنُواْ ٱتَّقُواْ ٱللَّهَ وَكُونُواْ مَعَ ٱلصَّٰدِقِينَ ۝

O you who believe! Be afraid of Allah, and be with those who are true (in words and deeds). (9: 119).

Manners

Manners are the way people behave and treat others. Manners reflect upbringing, values and religious teaching. A pious Muslim has a formidable list of social vices to avoid and a daunting list of social virtues to cultivate.

Patience (As-Sabr)

Patience is defined as the bearing of provocation without complaint, an ability to suppress restlessness or a quiet perseverance. The Arabic *as-sabr* is much more inclusive.

Yusuf Ali, in footnote 61 (p. 19) of his translation of the Qur'an, explains it this way:

> The Arabic word *Sabr* implies many shades of meaning, which it is impossible to comprehend in one English word. It implies (1) patience in the sense of being thorough, not hasty; (2) patient perseverance, constancy, steadfastness, firmness of purpose; (3) systematic as opposed to spasmodic or chance action; (4) a cheerful attitude of resignation and understanding in sorrow, defeat, or suffering, as opposed to murmuring or rebellion, but saved from mere passivity or listlessness, by the element of constancy or steadfastness.

He further explicates it in footnote 501 (p. 203):

> The full meaning of *Sabr* is to be understood. viz.: patience, perseverance, constancy, self-restraint, refusing to be cowed down. These virtues we are to exercise for ourselves and in relation to others; we are to set an example, so that others may vie with us, and we are to vie with them, lest we fall short; in this way we strengthen each other and bind our mutual relations closer, in our common service to Allah.

Patience and perseverance were inculcated again and again in the early revelations as well as later ones. The word *as-sabr* is mentioned ninety times in the Qur'an. Allah commended the patient when He said (2: 177):

> ... it is righteous ... to be firm and patient, in pain or suffering and adversity, and throughout all periods of panic. Such are the people of truth, the God-fearing.

Ibn Qayyim al-Jawziyyah, in his *Patience and Gratitude* (trans. by Nasiruddin al-Khattab, 1997, 32), highlights the need for patience. Following are two examples:

> At any given moment, a person is in a situation where he has to obey a command of Allah, or he has to stay away from something which Allah has prohibited, or he has to accept a decree of Allah, or he has to give thanks (show

gratitude) for a blessing which he has received from Allah. All of these situations demand patience, so up until the time of death, no one can do without patience. Whatever happens to us in life is either in accordance with our wishes and desires, or against them. In both cases, patience is required".

He further states (p. 42):

Allah has given a general ruling that whoever does not have faith and does not belong to the people of truth and patience, is in a state of loss. This means that the only true winners are people of patience. "By (the Token of) Time (through the Ages), verily Man is in loss, except such as have Faith, and do right actions, and (join together) in the mutual teaching of Truth, and of Patience and Constancy" (al-'Asr 103: 1-3). Commenting on this surah, Imam ash-Shafi'i said: "If people thought deeply enough about this surah, it would provide enough guidance, as man cannot attain perfection without perfecting these two things, his knowledge and his actions, i.e., his faith and right actions. As he is required to perfect himself, so he is required to perfect others, which is joining together in mutual teaching of the truth. The foundation of all this is patience".

The learned author lists five categories of patience and gives a detailed discussion of them (pp. 19-20). For the sake of brevity, a slightly different categorization is given below. From a religious point of view, patience is generally divided into three categories:

1. Patience to obey Allah in what He has ordered. Patience in obedience is required, whether it is prayer or any other activity. Allah says (18: 28):

And keep yourself patient with those who call upon their Lord morning and evening, seeking His face.

2. Patience to refrain from disobedience, especially for those who have been accustomed to living a lifestyle away from the religious path. Men who enjoy the good things of life have

special cause for gratitude. Patience is required after repentance in order to straighten oneself.

3. Patience in the face of problems or suffering and patience that is content with the ordering of Allah's world.

Allah says (2: 155-157):

> Be sure we shall test you with something of fear and hunger, some loss in goods, lives and the fruits (of your toil), but give glad tidings to those who patiently persevere ✦ Who say, when afflicted with calamity: "To Allah we belong, and to Him is our return."✦ They are those on whom (descend) blessings from their Lord, and Mercy. And they are the ones that receive guidance. ✦

A believer faces all such trials from Allah in good faith. He also must bear in mind the following hadith which is in Bukhari and Muslim:

> There is no disaster which befalls the Muslim to which Allah does not remove sins from him--even [as little as] the thorn that pricks him.

Patience in the face of mishaps, difficulties and disasters is a great virtue and a proof of faith. This is not to minimize the feeling of loss, suffering and frustration. At the death of his son, Ibrahim, Prophet Muhammad (s) said: "The eyes send their tears and heart is saddened, but we do not say anything except that which pleases our Lord." (Muhammad Husayn Haykal, *The Life of Muhammad*, p. 453).

Even when confronted with difficulties and ordeals, the believer does not turn away from God, but finds strength in the quality of *sabr* and steadfastness which He recommends (3: 17):

> And bear with patient constancy whatever befalls you for this is firmness [of purpose] in the [conduct of] affairs. Reward is gained by praising Allah under all circumstances and realizing that the blessings after a loss might eventually be far greater than the loss sustained. Remember that appreciation of blessings is complementary to patience. Ibn

Qayyim al-Jawziyyah states (p. 5) that patience or patient perseverance is half of faith, the other half of which is gratitude. By the way, both *as-Sbr* and *as-Sakur* are the two attributes of Allah. And He has told us that only those who are grateful to Him truly worship Him, for He says (2: 172): "and be grateful to Allah, if it is Him you worship." And the reward of gratitude is unlimited. (14: 7): "If you are grateful, I will add more (favors) unto you".

Cleanliness

Islam lays great emphasis on the purity of body and soul. Clean eating, clean drinking, clean dressing, clean appearance and clean habits of all kinds are of great moral value. It is obligatory for every Muslim to take a bath in case of grave impurity. Qur'an says (9: 108): "Allah loveth those who make themselves pure." He emphasizes this again in (2: 222): "He loves those who keep themselves pure and clean." There is a hadith which says "cleanliness is half the faith."

Cleanliness and personal hygiene are maintained as part of religious devotion. The link is *wudu* (ablution), partial or full as may be necessary. Prayers have been made compulsory five times a day, and a Muslim must be clean and pure before he can say his prayers. If necessary, he must wash his whole body, i.e., do full wudu or otherwise do partial *wudu*, which cleans part of the body and at the same time serves as ritual purification. Cleanliness of mind, body and clothes is called *taharah*, or purification, which is a precondition for prayer. Islam also requires cleaning of teeth with *siwak* or other means, as discussed under "Preparation for Prayer." Allah says (5: 6): "O you who have attained faith! When you are about to pray, wash your face, and your hands and arms up to the elbows, and pass your [wet] hands lightly over your head, and [wash] your feet up to the ankles. And if you are in a state requiring total ablution [meaning *ghusl*], purify yourself."

Ghusl involves washing the private parts, dirty parts first. This is followed by *wudu* and then washing of the entire body from head to toe. *Ghusl* is compulsory after sexual contact between spouses, after menstruation, childbirth, and after emission of semen. It is recommended for congregational prayer on Friday and for Eid.

In regard to the hairs over private parts and under armpits, Abu Bakr has this to say in his *Manual* (p. 55):

> The hairs under the armpits and over the private regions should be shaved off regularly, or shortened at least once in parts every forty days. This can easily become a breeding place for germs and lice, and a source of unhealthy smells.

Cleanliness is also an act of consideration for others. Prophet (s) used to love perfumes. Imam Ghazzali mentions (Muslim's Character, pp. 273-274) the following hadith: "The person who would be keen and desirous in this world of keeping his body clean, his parts and person neat and his face shining, when such a man will be made to rise on the Doomsday then his face will be shining, beams of light will be emanating from his forehead, and his body and parts of the body will be clean."

Qur'an and Hadith leave little uncovered to make a Muslim full of manners. Qur'an says (49: 13): "Lo! the noblest of you, in the sight of Allah, is the best in conduct."

Respect and Duty to Parents

There is a most famous hadith about this. Abu Huraira recorded that a person asked Allah's Messenger:

> "Who of all people is the most deserving of the best treatment from my hand?" He said: "Your mother." The man said again: "Then who is next?" He said: "Again, it is your mother." He said: "Then who?" He said: "Again, it

is your mother." He said: Then who? Thereupon, he said: "Then it is your father." (Muslim)

Similar commandment is also given in verse 29: 8. Two ahadith underscore the point very well:

> May his nose be rubbed in dust who found his parents approaching old age and lost his right to enter Paradise because he did not look after them.(Tirmidhi)
> Allah defers the punishment of all your sins until the Day of Judgement except one--disobedience to parents. For that, Allah punishes the sinner in this life, before death. (Baihaqi)

Parents have every right to expect that their children treat them with kindness, obedience and honor. Allah says (31: 14):

> And We have enjoined upon man goodness towards his parents: his mother bore him by bearing strain upon strain, and his utter dependence on her lasted two years; [hence, O man,] be grateful towards Me and towards thy parents, [and remember that] with Me is all journeys' end.

He reiterates it in 46: 15.

> We have enjoined on man kindness to his parents: In pain did his mother bear him, and in pain did she give him birth. The carrying of the (child) to his weaning is (a period of) thirty months...

In addition to parents, Allah ordains kind treatment to orphans and those in need (2: 83). To treat orphans kindly, to meet their needs, and to safeguard their future from ruin is an excellent kind of worship. Kindness is a basic quality of human nature. Kindness does not mean spending monetarily. Allah says (2: 263): "Kind words and covering of faults are better than charity." Muslims are enjoined to be pious and "speak right, appropriate words" (4: 9).

Morals

Some aspects of morality have been touched upon in the chapter "Halal and Haram." Here this topic is taken up in detail.

Islamic morality has many dimensions. It deals with the relationship between man and God, man and man, man and the creatures of the universe,, and man and his innermost self. Generally speaking, his role is to champion what is right and stand up against wrongs, seek what is true, abandon what is false, cherish what is beautiful and wholesome, and avoid what is indecent. According to the Qur'an and Sunnah, good morals and good manners are the real test of a man's excellence. Allah says (49: 13): "the noblest of you, in the sight of Allah, is the best in conduct" (trans. by Pickthall). Imam Ghazzali writes (*Muslim's Character*):

> Islam expects of its followers that they will be masters of live hearts and wakeful conscience, which would ensure the protection of rights of God and humanity and which would also protect their actions from the commission of excesses. Therefore it is necessary that every Muslim should be *amin* [trustworthy]. The holy Prophet (s) said: "I have been sent only for the purpose of perfecting good morals."

These precepts go back to the foundations of Islam. As an historical perspective, the following is mentioned (Marcel A. Boisard, *Humanism in Islam*, American Trust Publications, p. 39):

> According to tradition, Ja'far ibn Abu Talib, leader of the first group of Muslims to flee, in answer to Negus of Ethiopia who had offered them hospitality, defined Islam as follows: "The Prophet sent by God asked us to give up our idols and worship Allah, the only God. He commanded us to speak the truth, to remain true to our promise, to act benevolently toward our parents and neighbors, to avoid evil, not to spill the blood of the innocent, not to lie, not to

lay hold of the belongings of orphans, and not to violate the honor of women. We believed in him; we were eager to make our lives conform to the precepts he taught."

One cannot overemphasize the importance of morality in Islam for a practicing Muslim. Every Muslim scholar deals with paramount importance of morality. In our own time, Hamudah Abdalati puts it very clearly (*Islam in Focus*, p. 40):

For in his relationship with his fellow men, the Muslim must show kindness to the kin and concern for the neighbor, respect for the elderly and compassion for the young, care for the sick and support for the needy, sympathy for the grieved and cheer for the depressed, joy with the blessed and patience with the misguided, tolerance toward the ignorant and forgiveness of the helpless, disapproval of the wrong and rise above the trivial. Moreover, he must respect the legitimate rights of others as much as he does his own.

He goes on to say (p. 41):

The Muslim moral obligation is to be a vivid example of honesty and perfection, fulfill his commitments and perform his tasks well, seek knowledge and virtue by all possible means, correct his mistakes and repent his sins, develop a good sense of social consciousness and nourish a feeling of human response, provide for his dependents generously without extravagance and meet their legitimate needs.

Thus we see that the essence of Islam is to serve Allah and do good to our fellow creatures. Morality is such an integral part of Islam that this tone pervades throughout the Qur'an. Here are some verses that set up clear moral standards for us (4: 36-38; 16: 90-91):

Serve Allah, and join not any partners with Him; and do good to parents, kinsfolk, orphans, those in need. Neighbours who are of kin, neighbours who are strangers, the companion by your side, the way-farer (ye meet) and what your right hands possess: For Allah loveth not the arrogant, the vainglorious ✦ (Nor) those who are niggardly, enjoin niggardliness on others, hide the bounties which Allah hath bestowed on them; for, We have prepared, for those who resist Faith, A Punishment that steeps them in contempt; ✦ Nor those who spend of their substance, to be seen of men, and have no faith in Allah and the Last Day: If any take the Shaytan for their intimate, what a dreadful intimate he is! ✦

Allah commands justice, the doing of good, and giving to kith and kin, and He forbids all indecent deeds, and evil and rebellion: He instructs you, that you may receive admonition. ✦ Fulfill the Covenant of Allah when you have entered into it, and break not your oaths after you have confirmed them; indeed you have made Allah your surety; for Allah knoweth all that you do. ✦

The concept of morality pervades every aspect of Muslim life. Morality rates highly in economic life and is based on a solid foundation of divine instructions. To earn a living by honest labor is not only a duty, but a great virtue, to be valued on an equal standing with acts of worship and to complement the Muslim's belief (cf. 23: 51; 41-33).

Although these are but a few of the many verses in Qur'an on morality, hadith abound in discussion about it. It is all meant to help the individual to develop his character and enrich his association with God. The moral element and how one conducts his life above all is what defines and distinguishes what is a true Muslim. His awareness of the absolute and his religious makeup urge him to be a better person in this world and in the Hereafter.

As already stated, the notion of morality pervades every aspect of human existence. It is the touchstone of how one relates to other human beings, to the physical universe around us, and to one's relationship to the concept of God. The following are a number of essential areas where the Qur'an refers to man's existence in leading a moral life.

Truthfulness

Truthfulness is one of the highest moral qualities that man or woman can possess. It is necessary for good social relationships and is highly regarded by God. The Qur'an says (9: 119): "O you who believe! Fear God and be with those who are true [in word and deed]." Also (33: 35): "For Muslim men and women ... for true men and women ... for them has Allah prepared forgiveness and great reward." The Qur'an lays down the basis of a society in which everyone is required to enjoin truth upon those with whom he comes in contact (103: 2, 3) and states repeatedly that it is with truth that falsehood can be challenged and quashed. It exhorts again and again that truth is to be adhered to at all costs, even if it goes against one's own interest or the interest of one's near and dear ones. For example (4: 135):

O you who have attained to faith! Be ever steadfast in upholding equity, bearing witness to the truth for the sake of God, even though it be against your own selves or your parents and kinsfolk. Whether the person concerned be rich or poor, God's claim takes precedence over [the claims of] either of them. Do not, then, follow your own desires, lest you swerve from justice: for if you distort [the truth], behold, God is indeed aware of all that you do!

Further, the principle of truth is not to be deviated even if it went in favor of an enemy (5: 8):

O you who have attained to faith! Be ever steadfast in your devotion to God, bearing witness to the truth in all equity; and never let hatred of anyone lead you into the sin of deviating from justice. Be just: this is closest to being God-conscious. And remain conscious of God: verily, God is aware of all that you do.

According to a hadith narrated by Abdullah (Bukhari, v. 8, No. 116), the Prophet (s) said: "Truthfulness leads to righteousness (*Al-Birr*) and righteousness (Al-Birr) leads to Paradise. He also said: "Falsehood pulls a man to sin and sin throws him into hell." More to this point, he said: "Adhere to truth, for truth leads to good deeds and good deeds lead to Paradise" (Tirmidhi). Further, he said: "Falsehood, on the contrary, leads to wickedness and wickedness leads to hell-fire" (Bukhari, Muslim and Mishkat). In addition, he said: "My *ummah* will keep on flourishing so long as they retain the characteristics of speaking the truth when they talk" (Bukhari and Muslim).

Honesty and Keeping Promises

This quality is most treasured by the Qur'an and highly rewarded by God. The Qur'an commands people to be honest and just in their dealings with other people.

Most people are tempted to avoid the truth if it is detrimental to themselves or their family, but the Qur'an points out that it is best to tell the truth at all times if we want to live in harmony with our fellow men and women. Honesty is considered one of the basic foundations on which societies are built. Through, honesty, right is established, and people have confidence in one another. In this connection, the Prophet explains: "Be honest because honesty leads to goodness, and goodness leads to Paradise. As long as a man is honest and clings to honesty, God will consider him among the Truthful."

Keeping a promise is another type of honesty. A Muslim's word is his bond and he must keep his promise. Prophet (s) said: "One who does not keep his word is not a man of faith." Allah says (2: 177): "Fulfill the contracts which you have made." He also says (5: 89): "He will take you to task for oaths which you have sworn in earnest." The Prophet (s) said: "To take a false oath is a major sin, like associating someone with God."

Trustworthiness

Trust is a form of honesty, and one of the noblest qualities in individuals and groups. Trust leads to goodness, and to this effect Islam considers it among the traits of true believers.

The Prophet (s) gave the best example of trustworthiness. Even in his youth, before he was called to the Prophethood, he was called *al-Amin* (the trustworthy) by all the Makkans. The Qur'an lays great stress on the importance of returning to their owners things which have been entrusted to their care. "God commands you to render back your trusts to those to whom they are due" (4: 58).

Forgiveness

Forgiveness is one of the commendable virtues which often springs from a generous heart and a sensible mind that keeps patience against offense and harm from others. In many places in the Qur'an, Allah praises forgiveness; for example (64: 14): "If you forgive and overlook, and cover up [their faults], verily God is Oft-Forgiving, Most Merciful." In another place, God says (42: 40, 43):

The recompense of an injury is an injury equal thereto (in degree). But whosoever forgiveth and maketh reconciliation, his reward is due from God: for (God) loveth not those who do wrong.✦ But indeed if any show patience and forgive, that would truly be an exercise of courageous will and resolution in the conduct of affairs.

The Qur'an says that God is always forgiving: "If any of you did evil in ignorance and thereafter repented (his conduct), lo!

He is Oft-Forgiving, Most Merciful" (6: 54). The Prophet always forgave people, even his worst enemies. At the victory of Makkah, when he had complete power over all those who had persecuted him and his companions for many years, he did not punish anybody, but forgave them all and succeeded in building a new and better community. He often said that he had been sent as a mercy for mankind.

Kindness and Compassion ; Benevolence and Generosity

For the sake of simplicity and brevity, we will simply call all of these terms together as beneficence. It denotes charity and kindness, but it covers a wide range, including doing good as opposed to doing evil.

Good deeds include all kinds of virtuous and humane treatment that discipline one's character and bring him closer to the Creator. In this sense, the Commandments of the Qur'an call for beneficence and induce people to practice it in their daily living. The Qur'an says (28: 77): "Do good to others as God has been good to you."

The Prophet himself was very kind and compassionate, even though other people often did wrong through lack of knowledge. He said, "God will not show mercy to him who does not show mercy to others" (Bukhari and Muslim).

The Qur'an gives a special worth to beneficence and links it with devotion to God, describing both as the noblest qualities of a pious person: "Who can be better in religion than he who submits his whole self to God, does good, and follows the tradition of Abraham" (4: 125). God commands people to be benevolent and generous to others. The Qur'an says (2: 196): "Do good (be generous) to others, for God loves those who do good (and are benevolent)." It also says (2: 177): "It is righteousness ... to spend of your substance, out of love for

Him, for your kin, for orphans, for the needy, for the wayfarer." The Prophet used to offer food to anybody who came to his door, even if there were none left for his family.

Immoral Characteristics

There are immoral or evil characteristics into which a man has a tendency to fall. These immoral qualities represent the negative side of human behavior and encroach upon the rights of others and do harm to oneself and to others as well. One of Islam's objectives is to curb man's harmful passions and prevent him from being swayed by them. The Qur'an specifically addresses the following:

Hypocrisy

According to *Mishkat*, the signs of hypocrisy are three: speaking falsely, promising and not performing, and being treacherous when trusted. There are four qualities which, being possessed by anyone, constitute a complete hypocrite, and whoever has one of the four has one hypocritical quality until he discards it: perfidy when trusted, breaking agreements, speaking falsely, and prosecuting hostility by treachery. Hypocrisy has been condemned in the Qur'an in the severest terms. For example (9: 67-68):

> The hypocrites, both men and women, are all of a kind: they enjoin the doing of what is wrong and forbid the doing of what is right, and withhold their hands [from doing good]. They are oblivious of God, and so He is oblivious of them. Verily, the hypocrites—it is they, they who are truly iniquitous!♦ God has promised the hypocrites, both men and women—as well as the [outright] deniers of the truth—the fire of hell, therein to abide: this shall be their allotted

portion. For God has rejected them, and long-lasting suffering awaits them.

Also 4: 145:

The hypocrites will be in the lowest depths of fire: no helper will thou find for them.

The hypocrites have been condemned again and again, and the Arabic word for it—*Munafiqin*—appears over a hundred times in the Qur'an.

Lying

Lying is a grave social evil and may be the origin of all vices. Prophet (s) warns:

Beware of falsehood because it leads to immorality, and immorality leads to Hell. As long as a man is false and clings to falsehood. God will consider him among the deceptive.

People need the confidence of others. Dishonesty and lying uproot this confidence, and that is why, concerning liars, God says: "God guides not one who transgresses and lies" (40: 28). "God guides not such as are false and ungrateful" (39: 3).

Backbiting

Backbiting means speaking ill of others behind their back. In its call for respect of others, the Qur'an says (49: 12):

You who believe! Avoid much suspicions, indeed some suspicions are sins. And spy not, neither backbite one another. Would one of you like to eat the flesh of his dead brother? You would hate it (so hate backbiting). And fear Allah. Verily, Allah is the One Who accepts repentance, Most Merciful.

Arrogance

Arrogance means pride. Those who take pride in themselves refuse to listen to others advice. So they cannot benefit from the knowledge or expectations of others. The result is falling into ignorance and delusion. Arrogance is a hateful thing in the sight of God. He says (31: 18):
And turn not your cheek (in pride) at people, nor walk in insolence through the earth; for God does not love any arrogant boaster.

Ridicule

Ridiculing others means laughing at them out of a sense of superiority or pride. One of the aims of Islam is the establishment of respect among people and to eliminate the reason for discord and aversion. Allah says (49: 11):
O ye who believe! Let not some men among you laugh at others: it may be that the (latter) are better than the (former); nor let some women laugh at others; it may also be that the (latter) are better than the (former; nor defame nor be sarcastic to each other, nor call each other by (offensive) nicknames (to be used of one) after he hath believed. And those who do not desist are (indeed) doing wrong.

Drinking and Gambling

Islam prohibits all alcoholic drinks, drugs and gambling because they lead to so many other social evils. God calls wine and gambling "an abomination of Satan's handiwork" (5: 90). By abomination is meant utmost disgrace and wickedness. Allah also says that they prevent the person from performing remembrance of God and prayer to Him (5: 91).

Corruption

Corruption literally means the breaking down of anything. Islam is a religion of peace and order, and any act which causes the breakdown of peace and order is repugnant to Islam. The decline of societies and downfall of man is corruption.

Obscenity

Obscenity means speaking or doing things which are disgusting and repulsive and cause displeasure to others. Islam condemns all forms of obscenity, and one of the worst forms of it is adultery. Adultery is not just obscene; it is heinous. It drowns one's moral standard. Allah says (17: 32): "Nor come near to adultery, for it is a shameful act and an evil, opening the way (to other evils.)" The Prophet said, "Obscenity is part of hardness of heart and hardness of heart is in Hell" (Ahmad and Tirmidhi).

Homosexuality

Male and female homosexuality has no place in Islam. Private consent to sexual intimacy outside of marriage is not allowed. "Living together" or "temporary unions" do not constitute a family in the Islamic sense.

Symbolic Expressions of Islam

Most of the phrases listed below are part and parcel of daily conversation in a Muslim community, and these are, by and large, Qur'anic verses and remembrance of Allah. These tell of the attitude and determine the framework of the spiritual life of a Muslim.

Tasmiyah

$$\text{بِسْمِ اللَّهِ الرَّحْمَٰنِ الرَّحِيمِ}$$

Bismillahir-Rahmanir Rahim

"In the name of Allah, the Beneficent, the Merciful."

Literal meaning of *Tasmiyah* is giving a name. It is also known as *Basmalah*. Religiously speaking, before beginning any action that is necessary and legitimate, *tasmiyah* or *basmala* is pronounced. Before meals or drinks (legitimate), *Basmala* is uttered; an extended one is preferable:

$$\text{بِسْمِ اَللهِ وَ عَلَى بَرَكَةِ اللهِ}$$

Bismillahi wa'ala barakati'llah

Basmala is not just a symbolism; it is also a supplication. All the *Surah* in Qur'an (except *Surah Tawbah*), begin with *Basmala*. It is placed at the heads of books, as an ornamental inscription on buildings, and used as a wall decoration in homes, shops and offices.

Takbir

The expression is:

اَللهُ اَكْبَرُ

Allahu Akbar

"Allah is the Most Great," or sometimes translated as "greater" because Muslims believe that God is greater than anyone or anything else. All ritual prayer and call for them begin with this phrase. The most common watchword of Islam is Allahu Akbar. It is the declaration of the kernel of Islamic belief. (Constance E. Padwick, Muslim Devotions, p. 30; see in the reiterated *takbir* of the *adhan*, a shout of defiance, a word of power, against the dethroned heathen gods.)

Tahmid

Tahmid is said as follows:

اَلْحَمْدُ لِلَّهِ

Al-hamdu-lillah *

"Praise be to Allah" is said at the end of every action, to express gratitude or to return thanks for kindness. Our Prophet (s) said: If when God grants a grace to one of His servants, he says al-hamdulillah. A good Muslim will utter this phrase at the end of a meal, even better to say the following:
Al-Hamdu lillahi-lladhi at'amana, wasaqana, wa ja'alana Muslimiin.
All praise is due to God Who has given us to eat and to drink, and Who has made us Muslims.
Thankfulness leads to greater humanity in one's dealings with others; being thankless means being discourteous and mean. There is reward to come in being thankful and punishment in

afterlife in being thankless. This phrase is the proclamation that all praise belongs to God for all His favors. Allah says (14: 7):
If you are thankful [to Me], I will add more [favors] unto you; but if you are thankless [or show ingratitude], truly My punishment is terrible indeed.
Whenever a believer sneezes, it is desirable to say al-hamdu-lillah to praise Allah. Then it becomes incumbent upon the adjacent listeners to reply by uttering Yarhamuka Allah (may Allah show mercy to thee)

Tasbih

سُبْحَانَ اللَّهِ

Subhan-Allah *

I proclaim "the glory of God" is known as *tasbih*. It is a proclamation that God is completely free from every impurity and imperfection. It is used in Qur'an to express the impression made by God's overwhelming greatness and His wondrous deeds, or to deny anything contradictory to His absolute perfection and superiority. This *tasbih* may be used to express astonishment at some strange sight; in other words, this is to say that His wondrous activity shows itself through His creatures or creation.

Congratulatory Greetings

مَا شَاءَ اَللَّهِ

Masha Allah

"What God has willed" is said when there is occasion for happiness or to congratulate others. The idea is to attribute all achievements to the power of God.

Istithna'

إنْ شَاءَ اَللَّهِ

Insha-Allah

Insha-Allah mean God willing. Perhaps a better translation is "if it should please God." It is taken from Qur'an where it says (18: 23-24):

> And never say about anything, "behold, I shall do this tomorrow" without adding "if God so wills."

By uttering this *istithna*, a Muslim recognizes his total dependence upon the divine will. It is an acknowledgment that he can only hope for Allah's blessings in whatever he plans but cannot commit himself irrevocably to any course since he is not the master of his destiny. Allah also says (2: 224): "Make not Allah's name an excuse.."

Taslim

اَلسَّلَامُ عَلَيْكُمْ

As-Salamu 'Alaikum

"Peace be upon you." Among Muslims all over the world, this is the customary greeting. It is also required by the religion. The reply is *Wa Alaikum Salam*, "On you be peace." It is even better to add the words wa *Rahmatuliah wa Barakatuhu* (and Allah's mercy and blessings) in greeting as well as when responding. Allah says in Qur'an (4: 86):

> When a [courteous] greeting is offered you, meet it with a greeting still more courteous, or [at least] of equal courtesy. God takes careful account of all things.

Jazak-Allah

جَزَاكَ اللَّهُ

Jaza-ka-llah

جَزَاكُمُ الله خَيْرَ

Jaza-kumu-llahu khaira

May Allah reward thee. May Allah give you a goodly reward. This is an expression of thanks or appreciation to a Muslim.

Inna lillah

إِنَّا لِلَّهِ وَإِنَّا إِلَيْهِ رَاجِعُونَ

Inna lillahi wa inna ilaihi raji'un

"We all belong to Allah and unto Him shall we return" is said on hearing the news of death or to express resignation when one has sustained a loss.

Tamjid

لَا حَوْلَ وَلَا قُوَّةَ إِلا بِالله

La haula wa la quwwata illa Billah *

"No power or might except Allah's" is a very powerful Qur'anic formula considered next to the Shahada. It is used to scare away Satan. It is also used to express resignation when one has sustained a loss.

Istighfar

أَسْتَغْفِرُ اللّٰه

Astaghfirullah

"I seek the protection of Allah" is a prayer to which one should resort as often as possible, and the words are also used when one sees a thing which he would wish to avoid.

Sallah-Nabi or Durud

صَلَّى اللّٰهُ عَلَيْهِ وَسَلَّم

Sallallaho 'Alaihe wa Sallam

"May Allah's blessings and peace be upon him [Prophet Muhammad (s)]" is the shortest and most generally used expression of Divine blessing and peace of our Prophet (s).

Sahadah

لَا إِلٰهَ إِلَّا اللّٰهُ مُحَمَّدٌ رَسُولُ اللّٰه

La Ilaha Illallahu Muhammadur Rasulullah

This is the Muslim profession of faith and the first of the five pillars of Islam. It means there is no god but God, and Muhammad (s) is the Messenger of God. This formula resounds five times a day in the call to prayer in every town or village in Arabia or in a Muslim country. It is whispered into the ear of the newborn and is the farewell to the dying. Its continuous litany-like repetition is an essential part of the religious service (dhikr) of most Sufi orders.

The phrases above that are marked with an asterisk (*) can be very good instruments for getting into the mold of *Ibadah*, or worship, of God by mere conscious repetition of any or all of them. Of course, every work that is done deliberately in accordance with Allah's wishes is *Ibadah*. However, these phrases are like instruments that activate the remembrance of Allah. This can be considered *Dhikr* which is discussed in detail in the section called *Du'a* and *Dhikr*. Besides the phrases mentioned, there are many others, including all of Allah's beautiful names that can be silently recited any time anywhere (except when answering nature's call or taking a bath), including traveling, driving, studying, working, etc.

The Sultanahmet Mosque, Istanbul Turkey
Constructed between *1609 and 1617,* by Sultan Ahmet I, and built by Sedefkar Mehmet Aga. Also called the Blue Mosque, because of the wide use of blue tile in the interior.

19

MUSLIM LIFE CYCLE

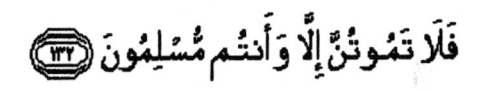

فَلَا تَمُوتُنَّ إِلَّا وَأَنتُم مُّسْلِمُونَ ﴿١٣٢﴾

...So die not unless you are Muslim (2: 132)

Birth and Childhood

When a child is born, a call to prayer is recited in the baby's right ear, and *iqamah* in the left ear. When his grandson Husain *(r)* was born, the Prophet *(s)* himself had done it (*Tabarani-Zaadul Maad* by Imam Ibn Qayyim). Although the baby is unaware of this chanting, the idea is that he should first hear the name of Allah and the Muslim confession of faith. A traditional ceremony called *aqiqa* is usually performed on the seventh day when the child is formally given a name, the head is shaved, and an animal is sacrificed. Part of the flesh is given to the poor and also distributed among relatives. It is in order for the child's family to eat *aqiqa* meat. The *aqiqa* is, however, neither obligatory nor essential, nor is the sacrifice binding on parents; it is sunnah. On this occasion it is not uncommon to give to the poor and the needy the equivalent of the weight of the hair in gold or silver for invocation of a blessing of Allah on the child (Muwatta 26: 1(2), (3)).

According to Muslim tradition, the circumcision of boys is a universal requirement. It is a sunnah of earlier prophets. It can take place at birth, especially if the baby is born in a hospital; otherwise, at the time of aqiqa. In some countries the culture of the land leaves it until the boy is 7-10 years old. It should be done anytime before the child attains maturity. In some parts of the Islamic world, girls are also circumcised, which is a practice without any religious basis.

Children are taught to read Qur'an at an early age, actually at the age of 7, so that they become familiar with the holy book and its teachings. By the age of 10, every child should know enough to perform and be regular in the five daily prayers.

The Permanence of Marriage

Islam considers marriage to be a very serious commitment; it has prescribed certain measures to make the marital bond as permanent as humanly possible. The parties must meet the condition of proper age, general compatibility, good will, honorable intentions, judicious discretion and reasonable dowry. Marriage is a social contract which brings rights and obligations to both men and women, and which can only be successful when these are mutually respected and cherished. As a good and devout home life is essential to Islam, making a good marriage is of the utmost importance. The Creator, Qur'an asserted, creates for you mates of your own kind so that you may incline towards them, and He engenders love and tenderness between you (30: 21, trans. by Muhammad Asad).

Allah encourages marriage, for he says (16:72) : And Allah has made for you mates of your own nature and made for you, out of them, sons and daughters and grandchildren and provides for your sustenance out of the good things of life. . . .

There is also marital advice (24: 32):

Marry those among you who are single, and the virtuous ones among your slaves, male or female.

In a footnote to this, Allama Yusuf Ali states that single here means anyone not in the bond of wedlock, whether unmarried or lawfully divorced or widowed.

In regard to the above verse, Muhammad Asad comments in a footnote (p. 539):

As most of the classical commentators point out, this is not an injunction but a recommendation to the community as a whole.

Family life is a vital part of the Muslim social order and, based on Qur'anic injunctions, the Sharia defines in great detail the rules affecting marriage, orphans, inheritance and other aspects of family life. "When the servant of God marries," declared the Prophet (s), "he perfects half of his religion."

Delivery of a sermon at the marriage ceremony serves the double purpose of giving it a sacred character and making it an occasion for the education of the community. The following are some of the verses that form an essential part of the marriage sermon:

4: 1. O mankind! Be careful of your duty to your Lord Who created you from a single soul and from it created its mate and from them twain hath spread abroad a multitude of men and women. Be careful of your duty toward Allah in Whom ye claim (your rights) of one another, and toward the wombs (that bore you). Lo! Allah hath been a Watcher over you.

3: 102. O ye who believe! Observe your duty to Allah with right observance, and die not save as those who have surrendered (unto Him).

33: 70. O ye who believe! Fear Allah, and Make your utterance Straight forward.

33: 71. That He may make your conduct whole and sound and forgive you your sins; He that obeys Allah and His Messenger, has already attained the great victory.

Muslim parents are enjoined in the Qur'an to meet their family obligations with kindness and justice. The ideal Muslim family is one in which there are basic necessities of life, where meals are eaten together and all pray together. The idea of remaining voluntarily celibate is alien to Muslims. However, continence is the rule before marriage. If a man cannot marry for the time being because of financial or other difficulties, he must exercise self-control. Allah says (24: 33): "Let those who find not the wherewithal for marriage keep themselves chaste, until Allah gives them means out of His grace."

Pure religion demands chastity. Muslim society is lax on man in this regard, but the Islamic law is the same for men and women. Chastity is a prerequisite on the path to God, and it involves purity of thoughts and actions, resulting in a life spent according to God's commands. Chastity in relation to one's actions involves restraints; physical chastity thus implies that people refrain from sexual activities outside of bonds of marriage.

Polygamy (Plurality of Wives)

The standard dictionary meaning of polygamy is plurality of mates. It is, however, used here to mean a man having more than one wife at the same time. Contrary to all the misconceptions, Islam recognizes only the union of one man and one woman as a form of marriage. The Qur'anic passage--the only passage, in fact--that speaks of polygamy, says (4: 3): And if you have reason to fear that you might not act equitably towards orphans, then marry from among [other] women such as are lawful to you--[even] two, or three, or four; but if you have reason to fear that you might not be able to treat them with equal fairness, then [only] one.

The above passage was revealed after the Battle of Uhud in which many Muslims were killed, leaving widows and orphans for whom due care was incumbent upon the Muslim survivors. Marriage was one way of protecting those widows and orphans. Qur'an does not enjoin polygamy. It only permits it, and that, too, conditionally. Permission to marry more than one wife (up to the maximum of four) is restricted by the condition "if you have reason to fear that you might not be able to treat them with equal fairness, then [marry only] one." It also must be borne in mind that Allah says (4: 129): "And it will not be within your power to treat your wives with equal fairness, however much you may desire it."

The notion that Muslims are at liberty to shift from one wife to a number of them is a myth. Polygamy has been made permissible with certain conditions and under certain circumstances. This permission is an exception to the ordinary course. This permission is not an article of faith. The second or third or fourth wife, if ever taken, enjoys the same rights and privileges as the first one. Equality between the wives in treatment, provisions and kindness is a prerequisite of polygamy and a condition that must be fulfilled by anyone who maintains more than one wife. This equality depends largely on the inner conscience of the individual involved. In the whole of contemporary Islamic society, monogamy is the norm; polygamy is the exception.

Divorce

One of the most distorted concepts of Islam is the real meaning of marriage. It is something solemn, something sacred; it is not merely physical or material. It is a decent human companionship and a sign of Allah's blessings, as He says (30: 21):

He creates for you mates out of your own kind, so that you might incline towards them, and He engenders love and tenderness between you: in this, behold, there are messages indeed for people who think!

When a marriage does not function properly, it may be terminated by divorce. However, all means of conciliation and

arbitration must be exhausted. Allah says (4: 35):

If you fear a breach between the two of them, appoint an arbiter from his folk and arbiter from her folk. If they desire amendment, Allah will make them of one mind.

It is clear that divorce is permitted only as a last resort. "Of all things permitted by Law," said the Prophet, "divorce is the most hateful in the sight of Allah" (Abu Daud Sunan, xiii, 3).

The seriousness of the matter of divorce is evident from the fact that a whole Surah named for it is devoted to this topic. Divorce is mentioned in 2: 228-233, but it is amplified and elucidated in Surah 65. Before the marriage is finally dissolved, Allah cautions (65: 1-2):

O Prophet! When you [the plural "you" indicates the whole community] [intend to] divorce women, divorce them with a view to the waiting-period appointed for them, and reckon the period [carefully], and be conscious of God, your Sustainer. Do not expel them from their homes; and neither shall they [be made to] leave unless they become openly guilty of immoral conduct.

These, then, are the bounds set by God--and he who transgresses the bounds set by God does indeed sin against himself: [for, O man, although] thou knowest it not, after that [first breach] God may well cause something new to come about. And so, when they are about to reach the end

Muslim life cycle

of their waiting-term, either retain them in a fair manner or part with them in a fair manner.

It is obvious that when divorce is deemed inevitable, it must be carried out in a decent and kind way. To revoke it, Allah says (2: 229):

> A divorce may be [revoked] twice, whereupon the marriage must either be resumed in fairness or dissolved in a goodly manner.

Three pronouncements of divorce make it final and irrevocable; it must be made singly, i.e., spaced over a waiting period of three months.

After the divorce takes place, there is a waiting period, normally three months, during which the divorce is supported and maintained by her former husband. When the waiting period expires, the divorcée is free to marry another man.

Concept of Life

Allah is the Creator of life which is a demonstration of His wisdom and knowledge. Allah is the Giver of life, and He is the only Rightful One to take it back. No one else has the right to destroy it. This is why Islam forbids all kinds of suicide and self-destruction. Life is a trust from God, and man should deal with this trust with care, honesty, mindful of God and with consciousness of responsibility to Him.

Twilight Years

Life is God's gift, the length of one's life is His grant. Time and place of death is not of anyone's choosing, but Allah's. For a devout Muslim, death is not something to be feared.

Last Wish

Every Muslim who is knowledgeable, pious or not, wishes to die with *Kalimah Shahadah* on his lips (see in the chapter Iman). Practically everyone knows that there is virtue in reciting the *Shahada* as an act of faith in the Unity of God. As soon as family members foresee or sense that death is nearing a near and dear one , they should recite *Kalimah Shadahah* in order to encourage him to recite it in turn. But they should not press or urge or request him to do it because that is the most painful time of one's life. However, if the person is too seriously ill to speak or utter the words, the relatives and/or friends around him should recite the *Kalimah* or engage themselves in the remembrance of Allah. It is also recommended that at that critical time, the people around should recite Sura Yasin. For those tending the dying, a tactful, respectful and sympathetic atmosphere is recommended as the best way. When the person has breathed his last, his face should be turned towards the Qibla, the eyes and mouth gently closed, and the body straightened.

Burial Ceremony

Soon after a Muslim dies, preparations start for the washing (*ghusal*) of the dead body and the provision of a shroud (kafan) for him. Muslims believe that final washing should not be done by strangers. After washing the dead body thoroughly with soap and water and drying it well, it is dressed in the shroud. Those who have performed the Hajj usually bring back the ihram which is their shroud.

Funeral Service

After the dead body is washed and shrouded, it is customary to show the face to those who have gathered for the service or to show respect to the deceased. After that, it is time for the funeral service, which is an act of great merit for the deceased as well as for those participating in it. The funeral service, or *Salat al-Janaza* is offered in congregation and is described in the prayer section.

ALLAH

اللّٰه

THE PROPHET
MUḤAMMAD

محمد ﷺ

Supplication at the Grand Mosque, Makkah

Part V

LIFE AFTER DEATH

20

JUDGMENT DAY AND LIFE AFTER DEATH
(YAUM AL-DIN WA AL-AKHIRAH)

كُلُّ نَفْسٍ ذَآئِقَةُ ٱلْمَوْتِ وَإِنَّمَا تُوَفَّوْنَ أُجُورَكُمْ يَوْمَ ٱلْقِيَٰمَةِ ۖ فَمَن زُحْزِحَ عَنِ ٱلنَّارِ وَأُدْخِلَ ٱلْجَنَّةَ فَقَدْ فَازَ ۗ وَمَا ٱلْحَيَوٰةُ ٱلدُّنْيَآ إِلَّا مَتَٰعُ ٱلْغُرُورِ ۝

Every human being is bound to taste death; but only on the Day of Resurrection will you be requited in full [for whatever you have done]. (3: 185)

The Day of Judgment is a basic article of Islamic faith. Qur'an discusses in detail what happens on that day, and the hadith has more details and specifics on that subject. In many passages, Qur'an gives a minute description of Death, Resurrection, the Judgment, Paradise and Hell. When the hour comes for man to die, Azrail, the angel of death, appears with his assistants and the spirit is drawn out of the body. Allah says (32: 11): "The Angel of Death put in charge of you will take out your souls, then shall you be brought back to your Lord."God determines the life span of every individual (3: 145). Man's helplessness before death's approach is understandable. But it has to be understood that it is He who brought us into being in the first place, so we will return unto Him (7: 29). Death is mentioned in Qur'an at least thirty-five times. The process of death is frightful, especially for the disbeliever. The Prophet (s) called death "the only preacher you need."While Muslims are exhorted to follow God's will out of obedience and gratitude to their Creator, the specter of the Last Judgment, with its reward and punishment, serves as a reminder of the ultimate consequences of life. Death is not the end, but the passage into a new existence. According to the Prophet (s), "the grave is one of the plots of Garden (Paradise) or one of the pits of the fire."The waiting between death and Day of Resurrection is known as the *barzakh* (barrier). As the Qur'an says (23: 100): "behind those (who leave the world) there is a barrier until the day they will be resurrected.":

At a moment known only to God (31: 34), Resurrection, rising of the dead, will take place. Qur'an refers to this as the Day of Retribution, Day of Wrath, Day of Decision. Day of Reckoning, and Day of Truth. Imam Ghazzahi lists over one hundred names for this event, derived from the Qur'an and Hadith. This event is eloquently described in a number of places in the Qur'an; of particular significance are *suras* 81, 82 and 84. A summary appears below, taken from F. A. Klein., *The Religion of Islam* (1956, p. 86):

> At the first blast of the Trumpet the earth will be shaken, and all buildings and mountains will be leveled; the heavens shall melt, the sun be darkened, the stars fall and the sea be troubled and dried up. Women who suck shall abandon their infants and even the she-camels which have gone ten months with young shall be utterly neglected. This first blast shall be followed by the second blast, when nothing shall survive except God alone, with Paradise and

Judgment Day and Life After Death

hell and the inhabitants of these two places and the throne of glory. The last who will die is the Angel of death.

At that time the dead will be resurrected but "no ties of kinship will on that day prevail among them, and neither will they ask about one another" (23: 101). In that awful moment, men stand alone before God. The very moment of resurrection and judgment climaxes the absolute power of God over human destiny. God alone is the Master and the Judge. And "on that day you shall be brought to judgment: not (even) the most hidden of your deeds will remain hidden" (69: 18).

In its reference to the Last Judgment, Qur'an repeatedly talks of weighing the deeds of all adults and responsible humans. Allah says (21: 47):

> But we shall set up just balance-scales on Resurrection Day, and no human being shall be wronged in the least: for though there be [in him but] the weight of a mustard-seed [of good or evil], We shall bring it forth; and none can make count as We do!

Also in verses 7: 8-9, it is further emphasized:

> (8) And true will be the weighing on that Day: and those whose weight [of good deeds] is heavy in the balance--it is they, they who shall attain to a happy state; (9) whereas those whose weight is light in the balance--it is they who will have squandered their own selves by their willful rejection of Our messages.

It is believed that Prophet Muhammad (s) will intervene on behalf of Muslims. J. L. Esposito, in *Islam: the Straight Path* (p. 35), observes:

> While the Qur'an teaches that intercession belongs to God alone (39: 44; 6: 54, 70), belief in Muhammad (s)'s role as a divinely designated intercessor did develop and was justified by the text. "There is no intercessor [with God] unless He gives permission" (10: 3).

Hadith literature, however, refers clearly to Muhammad (s) as intercessor for his community. Qur'an leaves no question whatsoever that divine justice will prevail on the Day of Judgment, that the distribution of rewards and punishments will correspond in direct proportion to the degree of one's faith (*Iman*) and the nature of one's religious response (*Ibadah*).

The very linking of human ethical responsibility in this world with the full accounting in the next reveals the unity of God's overall plan. The ultimate object of the life of man is that he shall live in the service of God. "I have only created Jinns and men, that they may serve Me" (51: 56). *Dunya*, this world, is the power or the attraction which can divert humans from the hereafter (cf. 87: 16). Those who prefer it (cf. 2: 86; 4: 74) to the after life or love it more "chose the life of this world as the sole object of their love" (14: 3), or "hold this world's life in greater esteem than the life to come" (16: 107) are warned and called upon to repent.

Death is where this world (*dunya*) meets the next (*akhirah*). The word *akhirah* appears in the Qur'an 115 times, which is an indication of its significance for humans. The concept of these two world is very well explained in *The Islamic Understanding of Death and Resurrection* by Jan Idleman Smith and Yvone Yazbeck Haddad (1981, p. 6):

> The terms *dunya* and *akhira* themselves are related both to time and space: *dunya* is the earth in the physical sense but at the same time refers to the period every individual spends on earth, related to its activities, as well as to the total time frame continuing until the coming of the hour of judgment. *Akhira* correspondingly refers both to the heavens, *samawat*, as the specific abodes of the angels and the saved, and to the antithesis of *dunya*, the hereafter or eternity. The very term used repeatedly in the Qur'an for eternity is the *dar al-akhira*, the "abode" of the hereafter, in itself illustrating the coincidence of the spatial and the temporal.

Judgment Day and Life After Death

Life after death takes two forms: life in Paradise or life in Hell. It is the word "garden" (*jannah*) that is generally used in the Qur'an to indicate the abiding place for the righteous. Blessings of the Paradise cannot be conceived of in this life, not being things of this world. Allah says (32: 17): "no human being can imagine what blissful delights, as yet hidden, await them." Muhammad Asad, in his translation of the Qur'an in reference to the above verse, points out (p. 635, footnote 15):

The impossibility of man's really "imagining" paradise has been summed up by the Prophet (s) in the well-authenticated Hadith: "God says, 'I have readied for My righteous servants what no eye has ever seen, and no ear has ever heard, and no heart of man has ever conceived'" (Bukhari and Muslim, on the authority of Abu Hurayrah; also Tirmidhi).

In reference to the Qur'anic verse 13: 35, Muhammad Asad elaborates it further (p. 367, footnote 65): "Qur'anic description of what awaits man after resurrection are, of necessity, metaphorical, since the human mind cannot conceive of anything that is--both in its elements and its totality--entirely different from anything that can be experienced in this world.

Muhammad Ali similarly says (*The Religion of Islam*, pp. 219-220): "All descriptions of the blessing of next life are only a **likeness** or a **parable** (*mathal*) as is explained in the Qur'an" and then he gives a reference to the verse cited above, in talking about men and women in paradise, he points out, citing Raghib (famous lexicologist of the Qur'an) that the relations there will not be as they are known in this life (p. 221). He further goes on: "no reader of the Qur'an can fail to see that the real picture of paradise, therein portrayed, has no implication whatsoever, of any sensual pleasure" (p. 224).

However, the fundamental message is that Paradise holds the means to satisfy man's deepest relationships and most profound spiritual needs. Muhammad Ali in his introduction to the *Holy Qur'an*, writes (p. xxx):

Paradise, according to the Holy Qur'an, is not a place for simple enjoyment or rest; it is essentially a place for advancement to higher and higher stages.

Thus the idea of rising higher and higher is connected with Paradise, that of falling down in immeasurable depth is essentially connected with Hell. Naturally, the ideas of contentment and happiness are associated with paradise, and the idea of burning is associated with Hell, which is itself but the result of being subservient to passion in this life. All this is the result of man's own deeds.

In contrast to Paradise, Hell is an evil place. Qur'an says it is an ambush (78: 21). Life in Hell is the worst imaginable. It is a life of punishment, torture and persecution. No one knows the exact condition of Hell except the Creator. Hell is described by seven different names in the Qur'an, and these are supposed to be the seven divisions of Hell. The most frequently used name of Hell is *Jahannam*, which signifies great depth. God describes the agony in Hell in a frightening manner. Words such as "the most terrible," "burning winds and boiling water and shadow of a smoking blaze," : "unshading and giving no relief against flames" are used to describe Hell. When it catches the glimpse of sinners from a distance, here is what Qur'an says (25: 12) about Hell: "When it sees them from a place far off, they will hear its fury and its raging sigh."

Muhammad Ali is of the opinion that Hell is meant for purification. He writes (in the same introduction already mentioned): "The idea underlying hell is that those who wasted their opportunity in this life shall, under the inevitable law which makes every man taste of what he has done, be subjected to a course of treatment for the spiritual diseases which they have brought about with their own hands."

Judgment Day and Life After Death

As to whether suffering in Hell will be unending or not, and whether the happiness in Paradise will be everlasting, the messages are in the following verses (11:107-108): (Muhammed Asad, *The Message of the Qur'an*, pp. 331-332):

> (107) therein to abide as long as the heavens and the earth endure--unless the Sustainer wills it otherwise: for, verily, thy Sustainer is a sovereign doer of whatever He wills♣

> (108) But as for those who [by virtue of their past deeds] will have been blest with happiness, [they shall live] in paradise, therein to abide as long as the heavens and the earth endure--unless the Sustainer wills it otherwise--as a gift unceasing ♣

As a footnote 135, to the translated text above Asad comments:
> Unless God wills to bestow on them a yet greater reward--which to my mind is more probable--unless He opens up to man a new, yet higher stage of evolution.

Heaven and Hell all balance in justice. They appear not for their own sake, but as signs of Allah's mercy and wrath. No religious book gives as vivid a picture of heaven and hell as does the Qur'an.

The idea of life after death may appear to be strange to some, but the Qur'an leaves no doubt (cf. 14:21;17:51, 99; 50: 15). The Qur'an tells us that man's life in this world is but the first stage (cf. 17: 99). Death or end of this world does not signify an annihilation, i.e., reduction to nothingness, of the physical universe but, rather, its fundamental, cataclysmic transformation into something men cannot visualize as Muhammad Asad explicates (p. 482) in reference to verse 20: 105. He also raises the question, "How can man be made to understand the nature of these consequences, and thus the quality of life that awaits him?" (p. 990). The answer lies in referring back to the Prophetic differentiation between man's life in this world and in the hereafter, referred to above.

**Islamic Architecture: Suleymaniye Mosque
Istanbul, Turkey (circa 1549-57)**
Built by Suleyman The Magnificent, and designed by Sinan the greatest architect of the time. This is counted as the finest of Sinan's work in Istanbul.

Part VI

MISCELLANEOUS

21

HOLY PLACES

KAABA

وَإِذْ يَرْفَعُ إِبْرَاهِيمُ الْقَوَاعِدَ مِنَ الْبَيْتِ وَإِسْمَاعِيلُ رَبَّنَا تَقَبَّلْ مِنَّا إِنَّكَ أَنْتَ السَّمِيعُ الْعَلِيمُ ﴿١٢٧﴾

And remember Abraham and Isma'il raised the foundations of the House (with this prayer): "Our Lord! Accept (this service) from us: For Thou art the All-Hearing, the All-Knowing. (2: 127)

Kaaba is the most sacred spot on earth for Muslims. It is also called "the house of God" (Bayit Allah). It is situated almost in the center of the Great Mosque (*al-Masjid al-Haram*) in Makkah. Muslims everywhere direct their prayers to the Kaaba, and every year millions of them make pilgrimage to it.

The Kaaba is a cubic stone structure which is approximately fifty feet high, forty feet long and thirty-five feet wide. Its single door (there are no windows) is at about seven feet above ground level. On the infrequent occasions when the Kaaba is opened, a wooden staircase running on wheels gives access to its interior.

According to Qur'an, as in the verse mentioned above, the foundations of the Kaaba were laid by Ibrahim (as) and Ismail (as). Muslim tradition locates the Kaaba just below the heavenly

Kaaba, i.e., *Bayit al-Mamûr*. It is, however, the building as a whole, not its contents, that is sacred to Muslims, and the most important object at the Kaaba is the Black Stone (*al-hajar al-aswad*) which is believed to have come down with Adam (as) from Paradise (for further details about Black Stone, see Glossary). The Kaaba is covered by the *kiswah*, a black brocade cloth decorated with gold-embroidered passages from the Qur'an, including the *Shahada*.

After conquering Makkah for Islam (c. 630 C. E.), Prophet Muhammad(s) made it his first order of business to cleanse the Kaaba of its idolatrous trappings and rededicate to Allah.

According to hadith, praying in the sacred Mosque is 100000 times better than any mosque other than the Prophet's Mosque. Offering a prayer in Masjid al-Nababi (another name for Prophet (s)'s Mosque) is a thousand times better than praying in mosques except the Al-Masjid al-Haram in Makkah.

Makkah

Usually referred to as al-Mukarramah (the Honored), Makkah (also Mecca, since this spelling is a wrong transliteration of the word Makkah, its use is prohibitted in Saudi Arabia) lies in a hot rocky valley, about forty miles from the Red Sea, in a rugged Western Arabian area of the Hijaz, a term that means barrier, the barrier between the coast and the deserts of the interior. The population of Makkah is estimated at 750000, which is greatly mixed in origin, consisting of the descendants of pilgrims who settled in over the centuries. This means that virtually all ethnic groups of Islam are represented although the overwhelming majority of them speak Arabic. A ban on non-Muslims entering the city and its environs accentuates the Islamic character of the city.

The heart of Makkah is the Haram (Sanctuary), the Grand Mosque and in the center of its courtyard stands the holy Kaaba.

Haram is at the center of the old city. Served by the seaport and airport facilities of Jedda, and transformed into a modern city, Makkah is well equipped to serve millions of Muslims who arrive during the Hajj from all over the world.

Madinah

It is also known as Madinah al-Munawwarah and Madinah al-Rasul Allah (Town of the Messenger of Allah). This is the second holiest city of Islam. It is about 250 miles north of Makkah and was known as Yathrib in pre-Islamic times. As the site of the Great Mosque, called the Prophet's Mosque, which contains the tombs of the Prophet, and Khalifa Abu Bakr (r) and 'Umar (r), Madinah emerged as the second holiest place in Islam. Most pilgrims combine their visit to Makkah with one to Madinah. The nearby area is the site of the first mosque in Islam.

Makkah al-Mukarramah and Madinah al-Munawwarah : Islamic Centers

These two cities are the centers of the world of Muslim scholars. Apart from their importance as shrines, these two cities have been meeting grounds for ideas in Islam since many prominent Muslims pass through these cities on the pilgrimage. Scholars often stay for relatively long periods, teaching and studying, and some settle permanently. As a result, al-Haramayin wa al-Sharifayin (the two sanctuaries) are the key points in the international exchange of Islamic ideas and inspiration.

Noble Sanctuary in Jerusalem

Built on Mount Moriah in the Old City of Jerusalem (currently annexed by Israel) is the Noble Sanctuary which houses the Dome of the Rock (Qubbat al-Sakhra) and al-Aqsa Mosque (the Farthest Mosque, 17: 1). It was from this spot that, having arrived there in the course of his night journey (*isra*) and having prayed at the Rock of Foundation, Prophet Muhammad (s) ascended into the Heavens (*mi'rāj*), he met the Almighty Allah.

In reference to the Qur'anic verse mentioned above, *The Holy Qur'an*, King Fahd edition, in a footnote (p. 774), supplies the following information about Masjid al-Aqsa:

The Farthest Mosque must refer to the site of the Temple of Solomon in Jerusalem on the hill of Moriah, at or near which stands the Dome of the Rock, called also the Mosque of Hadhrat 'Umar. This and the Mosque known as the Farthest Mosque (Masjid-al-Aqsa) were completed by the Amir 'Abd-ul-Malik in A. H. 68. Farthest because it was the place of worship farthest west which was known to the Arabs in the time of the holy Prophet: it was a sacred place to both Jews and Christians, but the Christians then had the upper hand, as it was included in the Byzantine (Roman) Empire, which maintained a Patriarch at Jerusalem. The chief dates in connection with the Temple are: it was finished by Solomon about B. C. 1004; destroyed by the Babylonians under Nebuchadnezzar about 586 B. C. ; rebuilt under Ezra and Nehemiah about 515 B. C. ; turned into a heathen idol-temple by one of Alexander's successors, Antiochus Epiphanes, 167 B. C. ; restored by Herod, B. C. 17 to C. E. 29; and completely razed to the ground by the Emperor Titus in C. E. 70. These ups and downs are among the greater Signs in religious history.

Holy places

The above may be read along with the footnote supplied by Muhammad Asad in his translation of the Qur'an (p. 417):

The Remote [lit., "farthest"] House of Worship," on the other hand, denotes the ancient Temple of Solomon--or, rather, its site--which symbolizes here the long line of Hebrew prophets who preceded the advent of Muhammad and are alluded to by the phrase "the environs of which We had blessed." The juxtaposition of these two sacred temples is meant to show that the Qur'an does not inaugurate a "new" religion but represents a continuation and the ultimate development of the same divine message which was preached by the prophets of old.

Al-Aqsa is a grand mosque with numerous Qur'anic verses inscribed both inside and outside; the most prominent one in translation reads (17: 1):

In the name of God, the Compassionate, the Merciful, glory to the one who took His servant for a journey by night from the masjid al-haram to the masjid al-aqsa whose precincts we have blessed.

Jerusalem is Islam's next most holy city after al-Haramayn Sharifain, i. e., Makkah and Madinah.

TASBIḤ

Masjid Al-Aqsa
Jerusalem (705 C.E.)

This mosque is of major significance to Muslims, religiously, historically, architecturally and culturally.

Karen Armstrong in *Islam, A Short History*, *(2000 pp 44-45)* writes: *"The Dome laid the foundations of the unique architectural and artistic style of Islam. The inside of the Dome was decorated with Qur'anic verses. The Dome itself ... is a towering symbol of the spiritual ascent to Heaven to which all believers aspire, but it also reflects the perfect balance of Tawhid. Its exterior, which reaches towards the infinity of the sky, is a perfect replica of its internal dimension. It illustrates the way in which the human and the divine, the inner and the outer worlds, complement one another as two halves of a single whole."*

This sanctuary commemorates the Prohet(s)'s Night Journey *(isra')* and is where he ascended to Heaven. Jerusalem is also Holy for being the first *qiblah* (direction for prayer) and the domicile of many of the great prophets. It is the third most holy place after Makkah and Madinah.

The great significance of the Al-Aqsa Mosque to Muslims explains why so much unrest has accompanied its history when held by non-Muslims.

Jonathan Bloom and Sheila Blair state: *(Islamic Arts*, 1997 p. 30) Building the structure on the site of Adam's burial, Abraham's sacrifice and Solomon's Temple, and copying the Domed form of the Holy Sepulcher that Constantine had erected over Christ's burial place on Golgotha, also suggests an effort to symbolize the role of Islam as a worthy successor to earlier revealed religions.

22

FEASTS AND FESTIVALS
MAJOR ISLAMIC FESTIVALS

وَأَنَّ هَـٰذَا صِرَٰطِى مُسْتَقِيمًا فَٱتَّبِعُوهُ ۖ وَلَا تَتَّبِعُوا۟ ٱلسُّبُلَ فَتَفَرَّقَ بِكُمْ عَن سَبِيلِهِ ۚ ذَٰلِكُمْ وَصَّىٰكُم بِهِۦ لَعَلَّكُمْ تَتَّقُونَ ۝

And, [moreover], this is my path, which is straight, so follow it; and do not follow [other] ways, for you will be separated from His way; this has He instructed you that you may become reighteous. (6: 153)

12th Rabi' al-Awwal	Mawlid wa wafat al-Nabi : Prophet's birth and death day
27th Rajab	Laylat al-Isra wa Mi'raj: The Night Journey and Ascent
15th Sha'ban	Laylat nisf Sha'ban: Night of half-Sha'ban
27th Ramadan	Laylat al-Qadr: The Night of Power
1st Shawwal	Eid al-Fitr: Feast of Fast-breaking
10th Dhul-Hajjah	Eid al-Adha: Festival of Sacrifice (celebration of Abraham's readiness to sacrifice his son, Ismael)

There are local feasts and holy days and holidays observed in every Muslim country. These differ widely from country to country, and even in different sections of the same country. Celebration of the above are more or less common. Because these events depend on the sighting of the moon, the observance may not take place the same day even in a country or locality. The reason for this is that sighting of the moon varies with longitude and latitude and besides, according to tradition, the sighting must be reported by at least two trustworthy witnesses.

Mawlid wa Wafat al-Nabi

The birth and death anniversary of Prophet Muhammad(s) is on 12 Rabi al-Awal. According to Sheikh Abdul Aziz Ibn Abdullah Ibn Baz, *Admonition Against Heresies: Four Helpful Treatises* (Riyadh, 1400 A.H.), p. 3:

> It is inadmissible to celebrate the anniversary birthday of the Prophet-- peace and blessings of Allah be unto him--nor that of anyone else, since it is one of the heretic evils brought about in religion, as the Apostle--peace and blessings of Allah be unto him -never did so, and neither did his true Caliphs, nor others of his companions--may Allah be pleased with all of them--nor those who followed them with good faith in the pre-eminent centuries; let alone the fact that they were more versed in Sunnah, and more perfect than their descendants in revealing their affection to the Apostle--peace and blessings of Allah be unto him--as well as in observing his tradition.

He further writes (p. 5):

> If birthday celebrations (mawalid) were considered religious, and sanctioned by Allah--praise be to Him--the Apostle--peace be unto him--would have expounded the matter to the people, or done it himself in his lifetime; or his companions--may Allah be pleased with them--would have

performed it themselves at least. Since celebrations such as these were never performed, it has become known that they have absolutely nothing to do with Islam.

The outpouring of the love of the Prophet(s) is such that people have an insatiable desire to celebrate the *Mawlid*. It has been mentioned that Muhammad(s) did not celebrate his own birth. However, there are those who feel it is wrong not to commemorate the birth and death of such a great Prophet. It can be a significant socio-religious function that provides an opportunity to remind the young and old alike of what the Prophet taught and learn lessons from his life. It is also an occasion to send blessings on the soul of the Prophet.

Lailat al-Isra wa al-Mi'raj (the Night Journey of the Prophet(s) and his Ascent into Heaven)

It is commemorated on the 27th of Rajab, in the tenth year of Muhammad's(s) prophethood, when Archangel Jibril conducted him from Makkah to Masjid al-Aqsa in Jerusalem, then up to the Seven Heavens (53: 18). Prophet Muhammad(s) was allowed to see both Paradise and Hell and to be in the presence of God. He returned the same night with instructions that included the institution of the five daily prayers. Many Muslims spend the night reading the Qur'an and praying.

Muhammad Asad in *Message of the Qur'an*, "Appendix IV: Night Journey" (pp. 996-998), describes the Prophet's mystic experience this way:

> The Prophet's "Night Journey (*isra'*) from Mecca to Jerusalem and his subsequent "Ascension" (*mi'raj*) to heaven are, in reality, two stages of one mystic experience, dating almost exactly one year before the exodus to Medina (cf. Ibn Sa'd I/1, 143). According to various well-

documented Traditions--extensively quoted and discussed by Ibn Kathir in his commentary on 17: 1, as well as by Ibn Hajar in *Fath al-Bari* VII, 115 ff.--the Apostle of God, accompanied by the Angel Gabriel, found himself transported by night to the site of Solomon's Temple at Jerusalem, where he led a congregation of many of the earlier, long since deceased prophets in prayer; some of them he afterwards encountered again in heaven. The Ascension, in particular, is important from the viewpoint of Muslim theology inasmuch as it was in the course of this experience that the five daily prayers were explicitly instituted, by God's ordinance, as an integral part of the Islamic Faith.

In conclusion, it should be noted that the Prophet's Night Journey from Mecca to Jerusalem, immediately preceding his Ascension, was apparently meant to show that Islam is not a *new* doctrine but a continuation of the same divine message which was preached by the prophets of old, ,who had Jerusalem as their spiritual home. This view is supported by Traditions (quoted in *Fath al-Bari* VII, 158), according to which the Prophet, during his Night Journey, also offered prayers at Yathrib, Sinai, Bethlehem, etc. His encounters with other prophets, mentioned in this connection, symbolize the same idea. The well-known Traditions to the effect that on the occasion of his Night Journey the Prophet led a prayer in the Temple of Jerusalem, in which all other prophets ranged themselves behind him, expresses in a figurative manner the doctrine that Islam, as preached by the Prophet Muhammad (s), is the fulfillment and perfection of mankind's religious development, and that Muhammad (s) was the last and the greatest of God's message-bearers.

Lailat Nisf Shaban
(the Night of 14th Shaban)

It is celebrated, as obvious from the above, on the 14th of Shaban, the night of the full moon before the start of Ramadan. There is another side to the celebration of this night which is not sanctioned in the Sharia. In some Muslim countries it is celebrated as *Laylatul Baraat* (Persian: Night of the Decree or Fate). Annemarie Schimmel, the well-known Harvard professor, describes it as follows (*Oxford Encyclopedia of the Modern Islamic World* (p. 455):

A non-Qur'anic [event] but very popular feast is the Laylat al-Bara'ah (Pers., Shab-i Barat), celebrated on the night of the full moon. Historically this is the night when the Prophet entered Mecca triumphantly, but in Muslim folklore it is considered to be the night when the "writing conferring immunity is written in heaven" or, more generally, the night during which the fates for the coming year are fixed. Therefore pious Muslims fast, pray, and keep vigils. On the whole, however, and especially in Indo-Pakistan, the night is celebrated with illuminations and fireworks. Orthodox critics object to such displays as symptoms of Hindu influence, even though the Shab-i Barat is mentioned in a non-Indian environment as early as the twelfth century, in a poem by Sana i of Gahaznah (d. 1131).

Muslims of the South Asian subcontinent celebrate this night by staying awake in prayer most, if not all, of the night Sometimes a special meal is eaten, sweets are made, and sweets and loaves of bread are distributed among the poor. As already alluded to, these are not supported or proven by Sahih Ahadith (cf. 15: 27, also Musnad Ahmad, Abu Dawud and Tuhfa Tirmidhi, Vol. 2, p. 53).

Laylat al-Qadr

This celebration of the Night of Power (Surah 97) is on one of the last ten (odd-numbered) nights of Ramadan. Many believe it is on the 27th night of the month. It commemorates the first appearance of the angel Jibril to Muhammad (s) and the beginning of the revelation of the Qur'an. Thus is it considered a particularly holy night. Most people keep the night of the 27th as an all-night of prayer, preferably at the mosque. (For details about prayer see "Lailatul Qadr" in Chapter 10.)

Eid al-Fitr (Feast of Fast Breaking)

This Eid brings release from the month-long fast of Ramadan and is called the "lesser feast" (the other *Eid* being a greater one). However, so great is the joy at the end of Ramadan that Muslims have come to celebrate it with much more festivity and rejoicing than the other *Eid*. *Eid* means festival or a time of happiness in Arabic, and it is celebrated universally throughout the Muslim world. At the time of both *Eids*, Muslims send each other wishes for a happy occasion. These festivals are oriented on the family and the community. Remembering the poor and being generous with those less fortunate is characteristic of these occasions. (For *Eid* prayers and other related religious obligations, see "*Eid* Prayers" in Section 10.)

Eid al-Adha (Feast of Sacrifice)

This Eid differs from *Eid al-Fitr* in that sacrifice is also offered up on this occasion. The origins of this festival go back to Prophet Abraham(as) who demonstrated his willingness to sacrifice his son to obey Allah, which act is commemorated in the last rite of the pilgrimage to Makkah. Muslims throughout the world celebrate the day at the same time as those fortunate enough to be in Makkah. They begin the festival by attending communal prayer (for details about prayer, see under appropriate section) as in *Eid al-Fitr* and then sacrifice a sheep, a goat, a cow or a camel, usually keeping one-third of the meat and giving away the rest which must include the poor for one-third. The distribution of the offering enjoined by the Islamic law is designed to provide a healthy and hearty meal on this festive occasion. Vernon James Schubel, writing about this in *The Oxford Encyclopedia of the Modern Islamic World* (p. 303), points out that animal-rights activists in Europe have objected to the animal sacrifice of *Eid al-Adha*. He further states that in India, Hindus have long objected to animal sacrifice, particularly of cows.

Eid al-Adha is also known as *Eid al-Kabir* (the Major Festival). Both festivals, major or minor, are times of celebration and joy, and the faithful wear their best clothes, visit friends and relatives and exchange gifts. The aims of *Eid* are basically to praise and thank Allah for his many blessings, especially those connected with the feast. This is also a great occasion for family and friends to get together and cultivate friendship in the Muslim community to have a strong sense of fellowship with the whole *Ummah*.

Qutb-Minar

Delhi, India (595 / 1199 C.E.)
After the Taj Mahal, perhaps the most famous Islamic monument in India, attached to the *Quwwat Al- Islam* mosque. Begun in 1199, completed in 1368. The 238 foot minaret is more than a monument to 'call for prayer' it is a spectacular symbol of Islam.

23

ISLAMIC CALENDAR

وَجَعَلْنَا ٱلَّيْلَ وَٱلنَّهَارَ ءَايَتَيْنِ ۖ فَمَحَوْنَآ ءَايَةَ ٱلَّيْلِ وَجَعَلْنَآ ءَايَةَ ٱلنَّهَارِ مُبْصِرَةً لِّتَبْتَغُواْ فَضْلًا مِّن رَّبِّكُمْ وَلِتَعْلَمُواْ عَدَدَ ٱلسِّنِينَ وَٱلْحِسَابَ ۚ وَكُلَّ شَىْءٍ فَصَّلْنَـٰهُ تَفْصِيلًا ۝

And We have made the night and day two signs, and We erased the sign of the night and made the sign of the day visible that you may seek bounty form your Lord and may know the number of years and the account [of time] and everything We have set out in detail. (17: 12)

The Islamic year (*Hijra*), is lunar. The lunar calendar is comprised of twelve lunar months. Since each month begins and ends with the new moon--a period lasting 29 days, 12 hours, 44 minutes and 2.8 seconds--each lunar year contains only 354 days (plus 8 hours and 4.8 minutes) as opposed to 365 and 1/4 days for the solar or astronomical year. Since a lunar year is shorter than a solar one by about 11 days, it takes roughly 34 lunar years to equal 33 solar years. As a consequence of the fewer number of days in the lunar year, the Islamic calendar passes through all the seasons every 33 years. The calendar, however, operates on a 30-year cycle in which an extra day is added to the last month of years 2, 5, 7, 10, 13, 16, 18, 21, 24, 26 and 29. The Islamic calendar was devised in the seventh century in response to the exigencies of governing the vast empire. It was also created to glorify the triumph of the new religion. There were other calendars in use at the time, but those were tied to other religions and states. According to historian al-Biruni, it was Khalifa 'Umar (r) who decided to develop a new calendar beginning with the Great Event of the Hijra from Makkah to Madinah or the Emigration of Prophet Muhammad (s) and his companions to Madinah, taking July 16, 622 C.E. as the starting point of the Islamic calendar. We are now in the Islamic year 1421 which began April 6, 2000, and written as 1421 A.H. (Anno Hegirae). The Hijri calendar is used for religious purposes throughout the Islamic world and is the official calendar in Saudi Arabia. Most Muslim countries follow the Western (Gregorian) calendar; the Hijra calendar is continued alongside. A rule of thumb is that the date of any Islamic holiday will advance eleven days from one year to the next.

The Islamic year begins with the month of Muharram. Its tenth day Ashura as also the 11th were suggested as days for fasting by Prophet Muhammad (s) but subsequently became associated with the death of his grandson, Hussain ibn Ali, who was killed in the Battle of Karbala on 10 Muharram 81 A.H. (680 C.E.). Although it is a day of mourning for all Muslims, Shias attach great significance to Hussain's martyrdom and to the entire month of Muharram. The Islamic months and their duration are roughly as follows, subject to the sighting of the moon:

Muharram   (30 days)
Safar   (29 days)
Rabi' I   (30 days) (also Rabi' al-Awwal)

Islamic Calendar

Rabi' II   (29 days (also Rabi' al-Akhir)
Jumada I   (30 days) (also Jumada al-Ula)
Jumada II   (29 days) (also Jumada al-Akhir)
Rajab   (30 days)
Sha'ban   (29 days)
Ramadan   (30 days)
Shawwal   (29 days)
Dhu'l-Qa'da   (30 days)
Dhu'l-Hajjah (29 days) (and in leap years 30 days)

As can be seen, the months alternate in length between 29 and 30 days. The days begin and end at sunset. The night of a day, which ends at dawn, is that which precedes, not what follows it.

The month of Ramadan is especially sacred; complete fasting is practiced during daylight hours, and pious behavior prevails throughout. Dhul-Hajjah is the month of pilgrimage in Makkah and its suburb.

Mosques in the Far East
Some far eastern countries have large numbers of Muslims. (above) A Malaysian mosque in Kuala Lampur (circa 1897), and (below) a mosque in East Sumatra, Indonesia.

Part VII

APPENDICES

APPENDIX A

SOME SHORT SURAHS OR PASSAGES FOR PRAYER

Qur'an is always recited during prayer. *Surah al-Fatiha* is recited in every *rakah* (unit) of the prayer. In addition, any *Surah* or part of a *Surah* (minimum of three verses) must be recited depending on the individual's preference. Some of the most used passages are the al-*Fatiha*, *Surah* 112 : *Surah al-Ikhlas* (The Oneness of God), 114: *Surah al-Nas* (Humankind), 2:255: Ayat al-Kursi (the famous "Throne Verse" (reprinted under "After Prayer Supplication" in Chapter 10, Section 10) and 59:22-24 (some wonderful names of God). These and a couple of more short *Surahs* are appended. For each one, a brief note about its significance is given.

Al-Fatihah (Al-Hamd or The Opening)

Introduction

First comes that beautiful Surah,
The Opening Chapter of Seven Verses,

Rightly called the Essence of the Book.
It teaches us the perfect Prayer.
For if we can pray aright, it means
That we have some knowledge of Allah
And His attributes, of His relations
To us and His creation, which includes
Ourselves; that we glimpse the source
From which we come, and that final goal
Which is our spiritual destiny
Under Allah's true judgment: then
We offer ourselves to God and seek His light.
(Abdullah Yusuf Ali, the Holy Qur'an, p. 13)

Surah Al- Fatiha No. 1

بِسْمِ ٱللَّهِ ٱلرَّحْمَٰنِ ٱلرَّحِيمِ ۝ ٱلْحَمْدُ لِلَّهِ رَبِّ ٱلْعَٰلَمِينَ ۝ ٱلرَّحْمَٰنِ ٱلرَّحِيمِ ۝ مَٰلِكِ يَوْمِ ٱلدِّينِ ۝ إِيَّاكَ نَعْبُدُ وَإِيَّاكَ نَسْتَعِينُ ۝ ٱهْدِنَا ٱلصِّرَٰطَ ٱلْمُسْتَقِيمَ ۝ صِرَٰطَ ٱلَّذِينَ أَنْعَمْتَ عَلَيْهِمْ غَيْرِ ٱلْمَغْضُوبِ عَلَيْهِمْ وَلَا ٱلضَّآلِّينَ ۝

1. Bismil-llahir-Rahmani-r-Rahiim.
2. Al-Hamdu li-llahi Rabbi-l-'ala-miin;
3. Ar-Rahmani-r-Rahiim;
4. Maliki yawmi-d-Diin.
5. Iyyaka na'budu wa iyyaka nasta'iin.
6. Ihdinas Siratal Mustqiim;
7. Sirata-l-ladhiina an'amta 'alayhim, ghayri-l maghdubi 'alayhim wala-d-dalliin. (Amin)

Some Short Surahs or Passages for Prayer

This may be translated as follows:

1. In the name of Allah, Most Gracious, Most Merciful
2. All praise be to God, the Lord of all beings.
3. The All-Merciful, the Compassionate.
4. Master of the Day of Judgment.
5. You alone do we worship, and You alone do we beseech for help.
6. Guide us on the straight way.
7. The way of those upon whom You have bestowed Your favor, not of those who have incurred Your wrath or those who have gone astray.

Abu Hurairah (r) said, "Rasulullah (s) informed us about this *Surah*: Allah (swt) says, "I have divided up this *Surah* into two parts. The first half of it is for Me, and the second half of it is for My servant. Whatever My servant asks Me for will be given to him."

Surah Ali 'Imran No. 3

3:26

قُلِ ٱللَّهُمَّ مَٰلِكَ ٱلْمُلْكِ تُؤْتِى ٱلْمُلْكَ مَن تَشَآءُ وَتَنزِعُ ٱلْمُلْكَ مِمَّن تَشَآءُ وَتُعِزُّ مَن تَشَآءُ وَتُذِلُّ مَن تَشَآءُ بِيَدِكَ ٱلْخَيْرُ إِنَّكَ عَلَىٰ كُلِّ شَىْءٍ قَدِيرٌ

Quilillahumma Maalik al-Mulki tu'til Mulka man-tashaaa-u wa tanzi-'ul-Mulka mimman-tashaaa'. Wa tu-'izzu man-tashaaa-'u wa tuzillu man-tashaaa': bi-yadi-kal-Khayr, 'Innaka 'alaa kulli shay-'in-Qadiir.

Say: O Allah, Owner of the Kingdom, Thou givest the kingdom to whom Thou pleasest, and takest away the kingdom from whom Thou pleasest, and Thou exaltest whom Thou pleasest and abasest whom Thou pleasest. In Thine hand is the good. Surely, Thou are Possessor of power over all things.

3:27

$$تُولِجُ ٱلَّيْلَ فِى ٱلنَّهَارِ وَتُولِجُ ٱلنَّهَارَ فِى ٱلَّيْلِ وَتُخْرِجُ ٱلْحَىَّ مِنَ ٱلْمَيِّتِ وَتُخْرِجُ ٱلْمَيِّتَ مِنَ ٱلْحَىِّ وَتَرْزُقُ مَن تَشَآءُ بِغَيْرِ حِسَابٍ ۝$$

Tuulijul-layla fin-nahaari wa tnulijun-nahaara fil-layl: wa tukhrijul-hayya minal-mayyiti wa tukhrijul mayyita minal-hayyi wa tarzuqu man-tashaaa-'u bi-gayri hisaab

Thou makest the night to pass into the day and Thou makest the day to pass into the night; and Thou bringest forth the living from the dead and Thou bringest forth the dead from the living; and Thou givest sustenance to whom Thou pleasest without measure These glorious passages are popular in recitation in *salat*.

Surah Al-Hashr No. 59

59: 22.

$$هُوَ ٱللَّهُ ٱلَّذِى لَآ إِلَٰهَ إِلَّا هُوَ عَٰلِمُ ٱلْغَيْبِ وَٱلشَّهَٰدَةِ هُوَ ٱلرَّحْمَٰنُ ٱلرَّحِيمُ$$

Huwallaa-hulladhi Laa-i-laaha illaa Huu;-'Aaalimulgaybi wash-shahaadati Huwar-Ra hmaanur-Rahiim.

59:22. He is Allah besides Whom there is no God: The Knower of the unseen and the seen; He is the Beneficent, the Merciful.

Some Short Surahs or Passages for Prayer

59: 23

هُوَ ٱللَّهُ ٱلَّذِى لَآ إِلَٰهَ إِلَّا هُوَ ٱلْمَلِكُ ٱلْقُدُّوسُ ٱلسَّلَٰمُ ٱلْمُؤْمِنُ ٱلْمُهَيْمِنُ ٱلْعَزِيزُ ٱلْجَبَّارُ ٱلْمُتَكَبِّرُ سُبْحَٰنَ ٱللَّهِ عَمَّا يُشْرِكُونَ ۝

Huwallaa-hulladhi Laaa-'I laaha illaa Huu;-Al Malikul-Qudduusus-Salaamul-Mu'minul-Muhay-minul- 'Aziizul-Jabbaarul-Mutakabbir: Subhaanallaahi 'ammaa yushri-kuun

He is Allah, besides Whom there is no God; the King, the Holy, the Author of Peace, the Granter of Security, Guardian over all, the Mighty, the Supreme, thePossessor of greatness. Glory be to Allah from that which they set up (with Him).

59: 24

هُوَ ٱللَّهُ ٱلْخَٰلِقُ ٱلْبَارِئُ ٱلْمُصَوِّرُ لَهُ ٱلْأَسْمَآءُ ٱلْحُسْنَىٰ يُسَبِّحُ لَهُۥ مَا فِى ٱلسَّمَٰوَٰتِ وَٱلْأَرْضِ وَهُوَ ٱلْعَزِيزُ ٱلْحَكِيمُ ۝

Huwa-laahul-Khaaliqul-Baari-'ul-Musawwiru lahul-Asmaaa'-ul-Husnaa: yusabbi-hu lahuu maa fis-samaawaati wal-arz: wa Huwal-`Aziizul-Hakiim

He is Allah; the Creator, the Maker, the Fashioner: His are the most beautiful names. Whatever is in the heavens and the earth declares His glory; and He is the Mighty, the Wise.

According to some scholars, these are the most beautiful passages in the Qur'an. Here is a summary of the most beautiful attributes of Allah; these give us the fundamental basis on which to form some idea of Allah.

Surah al-Qadr No. 97

بِسْمِ اللَّهِ الرَّحْمَٰنِ الرَّحِيمِ

إِنَّآ أَنزَلْنَٰهُ فِى لَيْلَةِ ٱلْقَدْرِ ۝ وَمَآ أَدْرَىٰكَ مَا لَيْلَةُ ٱلْقَدْرِ ۝ لَيْلَةُ ٱلْقَدْرِ خَيْرٌ مِّنْ أَلْفِ شَهْرٍ ۝ تَنَزَّلُ ٱلْمَلَٰٓئِكَةُ وَٱلرُّوحُ فِيهَا بِإِذْنِ رَبِّهِم مِّن كُلِّ أَمْرٍ ۝ سَلَٰمٌ هِىَ حَتَّىٰ مَطْلَعِ ٱلْفَجْرِ ۝

Bismillaahir-Rahmaanir-Rahiim
1. 'Innaaa 'anzalnaahu fii Layla-til-Qadr:
2. Wa maaa 'adraaka maa Laylatul-Qadr?
3. Laylatul-Qadri khayrum-min alfi Shahr.
4. Tanazzalul-malaa-ikatu war-Ruuhu fiihaa bi-'izni-Rabbihim-min-kulli 'amr:
5. Salaamun Hiya hattaa matla-'il-Fajr

In the name of Allah, Most Gracious, Most Merciful
1. Verily, We sent it down on the Glorious Night!
2. And what Will make thee know What the Glorious Night is?!
3. The Glorious Night is the benediction of a thousand months:
4. Therein do angels And revelations Waft down by the grace of their Lord: In every way
5. 'Tis full of peace until the rising of the Dawn!

Tradition has interpreted the "night" as one of the last ten odd

Some Short Surahs or Passages for Prayer

nights of the month of Ramadan when the essence of Qur'an was revealed to Muhammad (s) on this night. Consequently, this *Surah* enjoys great devotion among Muslims. The beauty and the majesty of enlightenment is presented here in the charming and rhetorical form. This *Surah* embodies in it a spiritual enlightenment. "Peace" (*salam* as contained in the last verse) is the distinctive mark of this blessed night. This peace comes to the hearts of the true devotees in the form of a tranquillity of mind which makes them fit to receive divine blessings.

Surah al-'Asr No. 103

بِسْمِ ٱللَّهِ ٱلرَّحْمَٰنِ ٱلرَّحِيمِ

وَٱلْعَصْرِ ۝ إِنَّ ٱلْإِنسَٰنَ لَفِى خُسْرٍ ۝ إِلَّا ٱلَّذِينَ ءَامَنُواْ وَعَمِلُواْ ٱلصَّٰلِحَٰتِ وَتَوَاصَوْاْ بِٱلْحَقِّ وَتَوَاصَوْاْ بِٱلصَّبْرِ ۝

Bismillaahir-Rahmaanir-Rahiim
1. Wa al-'Asri,
2. Innal Insaana lafii khusrin,
3. Illa-lladhiina aamanuu wa 'amilus-saalihaati wa tawaasaw bil-Haqqi wa tawaasaw bis-Sabr

In the name of Allah, Most Gracious, Most Merciful
1. By the Time (fleeting) surely,
2. Man is in a state of loss.
3. Except those who believe and do noble deeds and exhort one another to (accept) truth and exhort one another to endurance.

This is one of the shortest and also one of the earliest of Makkan Qur'anic *Surahs*. '*Asr* means afternoon, and the word has subsequently been associated with the afternoon prayer. The word '*asr* also means time generally and presents the idea of loss except those who do righteous good deeds. Time is always in favor of those who have faith, live clean and pure lives, and know how to wait in patience when needed.

Surah al-Kauthar No. 108

بِسْمِ ٱللَّهِ ٱلرَّحْمَٰنِ ٱلرَّحِيمِ

إِنَّآ أَعْطَيْنَٰكَ ٱلْكَوْثَرَ ۝ فَصَلِّ لِرَبِّكَ وَٱنْحَرْ ۝ إِنَّ شَانِئَكَ هُوَ ٱلْأَبْتَرُ ۝

Bismillaahir-Raḥmaanir-Rahiim
1. Innaa a-'ataynaakal-Kauthar.
2. Fa-salli li-Rabbika wanhar.
3. Inna shaani-'aka huwal-'abtar.

In the name of Allah, Most Gracious, Most Merciful
1. Verily, we have given thee abundance.
2. So pray unto Thy Lord, and make sacrifice.
3. Verily, it is thy insulter (and not thou) who is without posterity.

This briefest of all the Qur'anic *surahs* is regarded by many as the finest example of Qur'anic comprehensiveness, construction and language. The most significant word in this *surah*, according to most scholars, is the word *kauthar*, which means abundance, as also inexhaustible blessings. This suggests spiritual riches through devotion and sacrifice. As Muhammad Asad explains in his commentary of Qur'an (p. 980), it relates to the abundance bestowed on the prophet of all that is good in an abstract, spiritual sense, like revelation, knowledge, to do good works, to be kind towards all living beings, and thus to attain inner peace and dignity.

Surah al-Kafirun No. 109

بِسْمِ اللَّهِ الرَّحْمَٰنِ الرَّحِيمِ

قُلْ يَٰٓأَيُّهَا ٱلْكَٰفِرُونَ ۝ لَآ أَعْبُدُ مَا تَعْبُدُونَ ۝ وَلَآ أَنتُمْ عَٰبِدُونَ مَآ أَعْبُدُ ۝ وَلَآ أَنَا۠ عَابِدٌ مَّا عَبَدتُّمْ ۝ وَلَآ أَنتُمْ عَٰبِدُونَ مَآ أَعْبُدُ ۝ لَكُمْ دِينُكُمْ وَلِيَ دِينِ ۝

Bismillaahir-Rahmaanir-Rahim
1. Qul yaa-ayyuhal-Kaa-firuun
2. Laaa 'a-budu ma ta 'buduun,
3. Wa laaa antum 'aabiduuna maaa 'a-bud.
4. Wa laaa ana 'aabidum-maa 'abattum,
5. Wa laaa 'antum 'aabiduuna maaa 'a-bud.
6, Lakum Diinukum wa li-ya Diin.
   In the name of Allah, Most Gracious, Most Merciful
1. Say, O disbelievers!
2. I worship not that which you worship.
3. Nor worship you what I worship.
4. And I shall not worship that which thou worship.

5. Nor will thou worship what I worship.
6. Unto you is your religion and unto me is my religion.

The subject matter of this *Surah* has a deep connection with that of the S*urah* preceding it. In *Surah Al-Kauthar*, it was stated that spiritual and material blessings will be bestowed upon the holy Prophet. In this *Surah*, those disbelievers against whom a divine decree had gone forth that they will not accept Islam are admonished.

In view of the importance of this *surah*, Prophet Muhammad (s) enjoined its frequent recital. He is reported to have said that *Surah Ikhlas* was equal to one-third of Qur'an and this *surah* one-fourth of it.

Surah al-Ikhlas No. 112

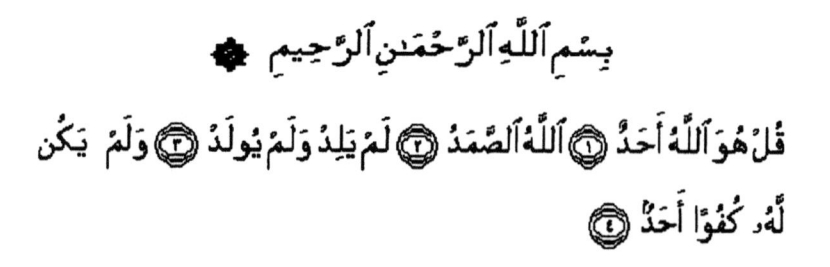

بِسْمِ ٱللَّهِ ٱلرَّحْمَٰنِ ٱلرَّحِيمِ ۝

قُلْ هُوَ ٱللَّهُ أَحَدٌ ۝ ٱللَّهُ ٱلصَّمَدُ ۝ لَمْ يَلِدْ وَلَمْ يُولَدْ ۝ وَلَمْ يَكُن لَّهُۥ كُفُوًا أَحَدٌۢ ۝

Bismillaahir-Rahmaanir-Rahiim
1. Qul Hu-wallaahu 'Ahad;
2. 'Allaahus-Samad;
3. Lam yalid, wa lam yuulad;
4. Walam yakul-la-Huu kufu-wan 'ahad.

In the name of Allah, Most Gracious, Most Merciful
1. Say: "He is Allah, the One
2. Allah, the Eternal, Absolute

Some Short Surahs or Passages for Prayer

3. He begetteth not, nor is He begotten
4. And there is none Like unto Him.

This *Surah* is considered to be second in importance and popularity in the daily prayers only to *Surah al-Fatiha*. It has been called *al-Ikhlas*, meaning purity, i.e., purity in faith. Muhammad Ali's note on this *Surah* in his translation of the Qur'an is very helpful. A portion of his commentary appears as follows:

This, a very early Makkan revelation, points out the fundamental errors of many religions, including Christianity, in its four short sentences. The first verse proclaims the absolute Unity of the Divine Being, and deals a death-blow to all forms of polytheism, including the doctrine of the Trinity. In the second verse Allah is said to be *Samad*, which the Holy Prophet is reported to have explained as meaning *the Lord to Whom recourse is had in every need*, so that all have need of Him and He has need of none.

The third verse points out the error of those religions which describe God as being father or son, such as the Christian religion.

The fourth verse negates such doctrines as the doctrine of incarnation, according to which a mere man is likened to God.

Thus four kinds of *shirk* are rejected here, a belief in the plurality of gods, a belief that other things possess the perfect attributes of the Divine Being, a belief that God is either a father or a son, and a belief that others can do that which is ascribable only to God.

As has been mentioned before, according to Bukhari, Ibn Hanbal, Abu Dawud, Nasai, Tirmidhi and Ibn Majah, this *Surah* is equivalent to one-third of the whole Qur'an.

Surah al-Falaq No. 113

بِسْمِ اللَّهِ الرَّحْمَٰنِ الرَّحِيمِ ۝
قُلْ أَعُوذُ بِرَبِّ الْفَلَقِ ۝ مِن شَرِّ مَا خَلَقَ ۝ وَمِن شَرِّ غَاسِقٍ إِذَا وَقَبَ ۝ وَمِن شَرِّ النَّفَّاثَاتِ فِي الْعُقَدِ ۝ وَمِن شَرِّ حَاسِدٍ إِذَا حَسَدَ ۝

Bismillaahir-Rahmaanir-Rahiim
1. Qul 'a-'uudhu bi-Rabbil-Falaq,
2. Min-sharri ma khalaq;
3. Wa min-sharri gaasiqin idhaa waqab,
4. Wa min-sharrin-Naffaasaati fil- 'waqad,
5. Wa min-sharri haasidin 'idhaa hasad.

In the name of Allah, Most Gracious, Most Merciful
1. Say, I seek refuge in the Lord of the dawn,
2. From the evil of created things.
3. And from the evil of the darkness when it overspreads.
4. And from the evil of malignant witchcrafts (those who blow into knots)
5. And from the evil of the envier when he envies.

Rasulullah (s) informed the Muslims that this *Surah* and the next, *Surah an-Nas*, has no equal in any other revealed book. He advised Muslims to recite them each night at the time of going to sleep and in the morning too.

Some Short Surahs or Passages for Prayer

Surah an-Nas No. 114

بِسْمِ ٱللَّهِ ٱلرَّحْمَٰنِ ٱلرَّحِيمِ ۞

قُلْ أَعُوذُ بِرَبِّ ٱلنَّاسِ ۞ مَلِكِ ٱلنَّاسِ ۞ إِلَٰهِ ٱلنَّاسِ ۞ مِن شَرِّ ٱلْوَسْوَاسِ ٱلْخَنَّاسِ ۞ ٱلَّذِى يُوَسْوِسُ فِى صُدُورِ ٱلنَّاسِ ۞ مِنَ ٱلْجِنَّةِ وَٱلنَّاسِ ۞

Bismillaahir-Rahmaanir-Rahiim

1. Qul-a-'uudhu, bi-Rabbin Naas,
2. Malikin-Naas,
3. Ilaahin-Naas,
4. Min-sharril-waswaasil khan-Naas,-
5. Allladhi yuwas-wisu fii suduu-rin-Naas,-
6. Minal-Jinnati wan-Naas.

In the name of Allah, Most Gracious, Most Merciful
1. Say, I seek refuge with the Creator and Nourisher of Mankind,
2. The King of Mankind,
3. The God of Mankind,
4. From the evil of the sneaking whisperer
5. Who whispers into the hearts of Men,
6. From among the Jinn and Mankind.

These verses are a complement to the previous *surah*. They also relate to the opening verses of Qur'an in which God is spoken of as *Rabb*. These three *surahs* numbered 1, 113 and 114, along with *Surah al-Ikhlas* (No. 112), bring out the essence of Qur'an. Their 22 verses epitomize Islam in its origin (genesis) and history.

Calligraphic design of Allah
By Emin Berin, Istanbul, Turkey

APPENDIX B

SELECTED DU'AS AND DURUD

I. Selected Qur'anic Du'as

40: 60.

وَقَالَ رَبُّكُمُ ٱدْعُونِىٓ أَسْتَجِبْ لَكُمْ إِنَّ ٱلَّذِينَ يَسْتَكْبِرُونَ عَنْ عِبَادَتِى سَيَدْخُلُونَ جَهَنَّمَ دَاخِرِينَ ۝

Wa qaala Rabbukum ud-'uni astajib lakum. Innal-ladhina yastakbiruuna 'an 'ibaadati sayad-khuluuna Jahannama daakhiriin!

And your Lord says: Pray to Me, I will answer you. Those who disdain My service will surely enter hell, abased.

2: 201

... رَبَّنَآ ءَاتِنَا فِى ٱلدُّنْيَا حَسَنَةً وَفِى ٱلْءَاخِرَةِ حَسَنَةً وَقِنَا عَذَابَ ٱلنَّارِ ۝

Rabbana aatina fiddunya hasanah wa fil aakhirati hasanah wa qina 'adhaban naar.
O our Lord! Grant us the good in this life and in the Next Life and save us from the penalty of Fire.

2: 128.

رَبَّنَا وَٱجْعَلْنَا مُسْلِمَيْنِ لَكَ وَمِن ذُرِّيَّتِنَآ أُمَّةً مُّسْلِمَةً لَّكَ وَأَرِنَا مَنَاسِكَنَا وَتُبْ عَلَيْنَآ إِنَّكَ أَنتَ ٱلتَّوَّابُ ٱلرَّحِيمُ ۝

Rabbana waj'alna-Muslimyni-laka wa min-dhurriyyatina-Ummatam-Muslimatai-laka-warina-manasikana-watub 'alayna-innaka Antat-tawabur Rahiim.

Our Lord! make of us Muslims, bowing to Thy (Will); And of our progeny a people, Muslim, bowing to Thy (Will) And show us our places for, The celebration of (due) rites; And turn unto us (in Mercy); For Thou art the Oft-Returning, Most Merciful.

2: 285

ءَامَنَ ٱلرَّسُولُ بِمَآ أُنزِلَ إِلَيْهِ مِن رَّبِّهِۦ وَٱلْمُؤْمِنُونَ كُلٌّ ءَامَنَ بِٱللَّهِ وَمَلَٰٓئِكَتِهِۦ وَكُتُبِهِۦ وَرُسُلِهِۦ لَا نُفَرِّقُ بَيْنَ أَحَدٍ مِّن رُّسُلِهِۦ وَقَالُوا۟ سَمِعْنَا وَأَطَعْنَا غُفْرَانَكَ رَبَّنَا وَإِلَيْكَ ٱلْمَصِيرُ ۝

Āmana-r rasûlu bimā unjila ilayihi min rabbihi wa al-mu'mnûna

Selected Du'as and Durud

kullu āmana billahi wa malaikatihi wa kutubihi wa rusulihi lā nufarriqu bayina ahadim min rusulihi wa qālū sami'nā wata'anā gufrānaka rabbanā wa ilayikal masîr

The Messenger believeth in what hath been revealed to him from his Lord, as do the men of faith, each one (of them) believeth in Allah, His angels, His books, and His Messengers. "We make no distinction (they say) between one another of His Messengers." And they say: "We hear, and we obey: (We seek) Thy forgiveness, Our Lord, and to Thee is the end of all journeys."

2: 286

$$\text{لَا يُكَلِّفُ ٱللَّهُ نَفْسًا إِلَّا وُسْعَهَا ۚ لَهَا مَا كَسَبَتْ وَعَلَيْهَا مَا ٱكْتَسَبَتْ ۗ رَبَّنَا لَا تُؤَاخِذْنَآ إِن نَّسِينَآ أَوْ أَخْطَأْنَا ۚ رَبَّنَا وَلَا تَحْمِلْ عَلَيْنَآ إِصْرًا كَمَا حَمَلْتَهُۥ عَلَى ٱلَّذِينَ مِن قَبْلِنَا ۚ رَبَّنَا وَلَا تُحَمِّلْنَا مَا لَا طَاقَةَ لَنَا بِهِۦ ۖ وَٱعْفُ عَنَّا وَٱغْفِرْ لَنَا وَٱرْحَمْنَآ ۚ أَنتَ مَوْلَىٰنَا فَٱنصُرْنَا عَلَى ٱلْقَوْمِ ٱلْكَـٰفِرِينَ ۝}$$

La yukallifullahu nafsan will us'aha laha ma kasabat wa 'alayha maktasabat Rabbana la tuakhejna inna sina awakhtana Rabbana wala tahmil 'alayina isran kama hamaltahu 'ala lladhina min qablina Rabbana wa laa tuhammilnaa maa laa taqata lanaa bih. Wa'afu 'annaa, waghfirlana wa arhamna anta mawlana faansurna 'alal qawmil kafirin.

On no soul doth Allah place a burden greater than it can bear. It gets every good that it earns, and it suffers every ill that it earns. (Pray:) "Our Lord ! Condemn us not if we forget or fall into error; our Lord! Lay not on us a burden like that which Thou didst lay on those before us; Our Lord! Lay not on us a burden greater than we have strength to bear. Blot out our sins. And grant us forgiveness. Have mercy on us. Thou art our Protector; Grant us victory Over the unbelievers.

7: 23

قَالَا رَبَّنَا ظَلَمْنَآ أَنفُسَنَا وَإِن لَّمْ تَغْفِرْ لَنَا وَتَرْحَمْنَا لَنَكُونَنَّ مِنَ ٱلْخَٰسِرِينَ ﴿٢٣﴾

Qala Rabbana zalamna anfusana wa inlam taghfirlana wa tarhamna lana kunanna min al-khasirin.

They said: "Our Lord we have Wronged our own souls: If Thou forgive us not and bestow not upon us Thy Mercy, we shall Certainly be lost.

3: 16

ٱلَّذِينَ يَقُولُونَ رَبَّنَآ إِنَّنَآ ءَامَنَّا فَٱغْفِرْ لَنَا ذُنُوبَنَا وَقِنَا عَذَابَ ٱلنَّارِ ﴿١٦﴾

Alladhina yaquluna Rabbana innana amanna faghfirlana dhunubana wa qina 'adhab al-nar.

(Namely), those who say: "Our Lord! We have indeed believed: forgive us, then, our sins, and save us from the agony of the Fire".

3: 191.

$$\rbrace$$ رَبَّنَا مَا خَلَقْتَ هَٰذَا بَٰطِلًا سُبْحَٰنَكَ فَقِنَا عَذَابَ ٱلنَّارِ

Rabbana ma khalaqta hadha batilan subhanaka faqina 'adhab an-naar.

Our Lord! not for naught Hast Thou created (all) this! Glory to Thee! Give us salvation from the penalty of the Fire.

3: 193.

رَبَّنَا إِنَّنَا سَمِعْنَا مُنَادِيًا يُنَادِى لِلْإِيمَٰنِ أَنْ ءَامِنُوا۟ بِرَبِّكُمْ فَـَٔامَنَّا رَبَّنَا فَٱغْفِرْ لَنَا ذُنُوبَنَا وَكَفِّرْ عَنَّا سَيِّـَٔاتِنَا وَتَوَفَّنَا مَعَ ٱلْأَبْرَارِ

Rabbana innana sami'ina munadiyan unadi lil eimani an aminu bi Rabbikum fa amanna. Rabbana faghfir lana dhunubana wa kaffir anna sayyietina wa tawaffana ma 'al abrar.

Our Lord! Verily we have heard the call of one [Muhammad (s)] calling to Faith: "Believe in your Lord," and we have believed. Our Lord! Forgive us our sins and remit from us our evil deeds, and make us die in the state of righteousness along with *Al-'Abrar* (those who are obedient to Allah and follow strictly His Orders).

3: 194

$$\rm رَبَّنَا\ وَآتِنَا\ مَا\ وَعَدتَّنَا\ عَلَىٰ\ رُسُلِكَ\ وَلَا\ تُخْزِنَا\ يَوْمَ\ الْقِيَامَةِ\ ۗ إِنَّكَ\ لَا\ تُخْلِفُ\ الْمِيعَادَ ۝$$

Rabbana wa atina ma waadtana 'ala rusulika wala **tu**khzina yawmal qiamati innaka la tukhliful mi'aad.

Our Lord! Grant us what You promised unto us through

Your Messengers and disgrace us not on the Day of Resurrection, for You never break (Your) Promise.

7: 143

$$\rm ...سُبْحَانَكَ\ تُبْتُ\ إِلَيْكَ\ وَأَنَا\ أَوَّلُ\ الْمُؤْمِنِينَ ۝$$

Subhanaka-Tubtu-Ilayika Wa ana awwal-ul-Mu'miniin.

Glory be to Thee! To Thee I turn in repentance, and I am the first to believe.

14: 40-41

$$\rm رَبِّ\ اجْعَلْنِي\ مُقِيمَ\ الصَّلَاةِ\ وَمِن\ ذُرِّيَّتِي\ ۚ رَبَّنَا\ وَتَقَبَّلْ\ دُعَاءِ ۝$$
$$\rm رَبَّنَا\ اغْفِرْ\ لِي\ وَلِوَالِدَيَّ\ وَلِلْمُؤْمِنِينَ\ يَوْمَ\ يَقُومُ\ الْحِسَابُ ۝$$

Selected Du'as and Durud

Rabbij'alni muqiimas-salati wamin-dhurriyyati. Rabbana-wa taqabbal-du'a. Rabbana-gh-firli wa liwalidayya walilmu miniina-yawma yaquum al-hisaab.

40. O my Lord! make me one who establishes regular Prayer, and also (raise such) among my offspring O our Lord! And accept Thou my Prayer.

41. O our Lord! cover (us) with Thy Forgiveness-- me, my parents, and (all) believers, On the Day that the Reckoning will be established!

17: 24

رَّبِّ ارْحَمْهُمَا كَمَا رَبَّيَانِي صَغِيرًا ﴿٢٤﴾

Rabbir-hamhumaa kamaa Rabbayanii saghiira'

My Lord! bestow on them, Thy Mercy even as they cherished me in childhood.

20: 114

وَقُل رَّبِّ زِدْنِي عِلْمًا ﴿١١٤﴾

Waqur-rabbi-zidni-'Ilman.

O my Lord! advance me in knowledge.

23: 94

رَبِّ فَلَا تَجْعَلْنِي فِي الْقَوْمِ الظَّالِمِينَ ﴿٩٤﴾

Rabbi falaa taj'alni fil qawmiz zalimiin.

My Lord! Then (save me from Your punishment), and put me not amongst the people who are the Zalimun (polytheists and wrong-doing).

23: 118

$$وَقُل رَّبِّ ٱغْفِرْ وَٱرْحَمْ وَأَنتَ خَيْرُ ٱلرَّاحِمِينَ$$

Waqur-rabbi-gh-fir wa rham wa anta khayrur rahimiin

So say: "O my Lord!, Grant Thou forgiveness and mercy. For Thou art the Best Of those who show mercy!"

26: 83.

$$رَبِّ هَبْ لِى حُكْمًا وَأَلْحِقْنِى بِٱلصَّٰلِحِينَ$$

Rabbi-habli hukmaw wa alhiqni bi ssalihiin..

O my Lord! bestow wisdom on me, and join me with the righteous.

46: 15

...رَبِّ أَوْزِعْنِي أَنْ أَشْكُرَ نِعْمَتَكَ الَّتِي أَنْعَمْتَ عَلَيَّ وَعَلَى وَالِدَيَّ وَأَنْ أَعْمَلَ صَالِحًا تَرْضَاهُ وَأَصْلِحْ لِي فِي ذُرِّيَّتِي إِنِّي تُبْتُ إِلَيْكَ وَإِنِّي مِنَ الْمُسْلِمِينَ

Selected Du'as and Durud

Rabbi awzi'ni an-ashkura ni'matakal-lati An'amta 'alayya wa 'ala walidayya wa 'amal salihan tardahu wa aslih-li fi-dhurriyyati. inni tubtu ilayika wa inni min al-muslimiin.

O my Lord! Grant me that I may be Grateful for Thy favour which Thou hast bestowed upon me, and upon both My parents, and that I May work righteousness such as Thou mayest approve; and be gracious to me in my issue. Truly have I turned to Thee and truly do I bow (To Thee) in Islam.

59: 10

رَبَّنَا اغْفِرْ لَنَا وَلِإِخْوَٰنِنَا ٱلَّذِينَ سَبَقُونَا بِٱلْإِيمَٰنِ وَلَا تَجْعَلْ فِى قُلُوبِنَا غِلًّا لِّلَّذِينَ ءَامَنُوا۟ رَبَّنَآ إِنَّكَ رَءُوفٌ رَّحِيمٌ ۝

Rabbana-gh-fir-lana. wa al-ikhwanin al-ladhina Sabaquuna bil-iman wa la-taj'al fi quluubina ghillal-lilladhina amanu. Rabbanaa innaka Ra 'uufur-Rahiim.

Our Lord! Forgive us, and our brethren who came before us into the Faith, and leave not, in our hearts, rancour (or sense of injury) against those who have believed. Our Lord! Thou art indeed Full of kindness, Most Merciful.

71: 28

رَّبِّ ٱغْفِرْ لِى وَلِوَٰلِدَىَّ وَلِمَن دَخَلَ بَيْتِىَ مُؤْمِنًا وَلِلْمُؤْمِنِينَ وَٱلْمُؤْمِنَٰتِ وَلَا تَزِدِ ٱلظَّٰلِمِينَ إِلَّا تَبَارًۢا ۝

Rabbigh-fir li-waliwalidayya wa liman dakhala baytiya Mu'minaw walilmu'miniina wa al-Mu'minati-Wala-tazidizzalimiina illa abara.

O my Lord: forgive me, my parents, all who enter my house in faith, and (all) believing men and believing women; and to the wrong-doers Grant thou no increase But in Perdition!

110: 3.

$$\text{فَسَبِّحْ بِحَمْدِ رَبِّكَ وَاسْتَغْفِرْهُ إِنَّهُ كَانَ تَوَّابًا}$$

Fasabbih bihamdi-rabbika-wastaghfirh innahu kana Tawwaba.

Celebrate the Praises of thy Lord, and pray for His Forgiveness: for He is Oft-Returning (in Grace and Mercy)

II. Selected Du'as from Sahih Hadith

Some of the supplications as reported from the Holy Prophet (s) are as follows:

It is reported that one day the Holy Prophet held Mu'adh bin Jabal's (r) hand and remarked: "O Mu'adh, I have great love for you: I exhort you to make the following supplication after every salat (prayer), without fail:

1

$$\text{اللَّهُمَّ أَعِنِّي عَلَى ذِكْرِكَ وَشُكْرِكَ وَحُسْنِ عِبَادَتِكَ}$$

Allahumma a'inni 'ala dhikrika wa shukrika wa husni 'ibadatika.

O Allah! Help me so that I may remember Thee, express my gratitude to Thee, and adore Thee in the best way.

2

لاَ إلهَ إلاَّ اللهُ وَحْدَهُ لاَشَرِيكَ لَهُ، لَهُ الْمُلْكُ وَلَهُ الْحَمْدُ وَهُوَ عَلَى كُلِّ شَيْئٍ قَدِيرٌ. اللَّهُمَّ لا مَانِعَ لِمَا أَعْطَيْتَ وَلاَمُعْطِيَ لِمَا مَنَعْتَ ولاَيَنْفَعُ ذَاالْجَدِّ مِنْكَ الْجَدُّ

La ilaha ill-Allah-u wahda-hu la sharika-lahu, lahul-mulku wa lahul hamdu wa huwa 'ala kull-i shayin Qadir. Allahumma la mani'a lima a'atayita wa la mu'tiya lima mana'ta wa la yanfau'dhalj-addi minka-l jadda

There is no god but Allah: He alone is God, and has no partner; sovereignty is for Him and He alone is worthy of all praise and gratitude: He has full power over everything. Oh Allah! no one can give anything which Thou willest not to give: the glory and greatness of no one can be of any avail against Thee. (*Bukhari and Muslim*)

3

Shadad bin Aus (r) reported that the Prophet of Allah used to say in his prayer:

اللَّهُمَّ إِنِّي أَسْئَلُكَ الثَّبَاتَ فِي الأَمْرِ والعَزِيمَةَ عَلَى الرُّشْدِ وَأَسْئَلُكَ شُكْرَ نِعْمَتِكَ وَ حُسْنَ عِبَادَتِكَ وَأَسْئَلُكَ قَلْبَاً سَلِيمَاً وَلِسَاناً صَادِقاً وَأَسْئَلُكَ مِنْ خَيْرِ مَا تَعْلَمُ وَ أَعُوذُ بِكَ مِنْ شَرِّ مَا تَعْلَمُ وَ أَسْتَغْفِرُكَ لِمَا تَعْلَمُ.

Allah humma inni as-alu kath thubata fil amri, wal 'aziimata 'alar rushdi, wa as-aluka shukra ni'matika, wa husna 'ibadatika, wa as-aluka qalban saliman, wa lisanan sadiqan, wa as-aluka min khayri ma ta'lamu, wa a'udhubika min Shar-ri ma ta'lamu, wa as taghfiruka, lima ta'lamu.

O Allah, I ask you for strength in every matter of din and a strong willpower to be on the right path. And I ask you to make me thankful for your bounties and give me ability to worship you perfectly. And I ask you to make my heart sincere and my tongue truthful. I ask you for every goodness known to you and I seek refuge in you from everything bad that you know is bad. I ask your forgiveness for all mistakes you know. (Nasai)

4

Follow closely his thoughts in this du'a:

اَللَّهُمَّ بِعِلْمِكَ الْغَيْبَ ، وَ قُدْرَتِكَ عَلَى الْخَلْقِ أَحْيِنِيْ مَا عَلِمْتَ الْحَيَاةَ خَيْرًا لِّي ، وَتَوَفَّنِيْ إِذَا عَلِمْتَ الْوَفَاةَ خَيْرًا لِّي .

Allahumma bi 'ilmikal ghaiba, wa qudratika 'alal khalqi, Ahyini ma 'alimtal hayyata khayran li, wa tawaffani idha 'alimtal wa fata khayiran li.

Our Lord, by Your Knowledge of the Unseen, and by Your Power over Your creation, grant me life so long as You know life to hold good for me, and grant me death when You know death to hold good for me!

III. Selected Durud

1

اَللَّهُمَّ صَلِّ عَلَى مُحَمَّدٍ وَعَلَى آلِ مُحَمَّدٍ ۰

Selected Du'as and Durud

Allahumma salli `ala Muhammadi n wa ala `ali Muhammad

O Allah! let Your blessings shower upon Muhammad and the family of Muhammad.

2

اَللّٰهُمَّ صَلِ عَلَى مُحَمَّدٍ وَعَلَى آلِ مُحَمَّدٍ عَبْدِكَ وَ رَسُولِكَ *

Allahumma salli `la Muhammadin `abdika wa rasulika

Oh Allah! bless and exalt Your slave and Your apostle Muhammad

3

اَللّٰهُمَّ صَلِ عَلَى مُحَمَّدٍ وَعَلَى آلِ مُحَمَّدٍ وَ عَلَى آلِهِ وَاَصْحَبِهِ وَبَارِكْ وَسَلَمْ *

Allahumma salli `ala Muhammadin wa `ala alihi wa ashabihi wa barik wa sallam

O Allah! bless and give reward to Muhammad, his family and to all his companions.

4

يَأَيُّهَا اَلَذِينَ عَلَمَنُواْ صَلُّواْ عَلَيْهِ وَسَلِمُواْ تَسْلِيمًا *

Ya ayyuhalladhina amanu salliu `alaihi wa sallimu taslima.

O you who believe! Send your *Salat* on (ask Allah to bless) him Muhammad (s), and (you should) greet (salute) him with the Islamic way of greeting (salutation, i.e., *As-Salaam-o-'Alaikum*). (33:56)

5

الصَّلواتُ وَالسَّلَامُ عَلَيْكَ يَا رَسُوْلُ اللهِ *

Assalatu wassalamu `alaika ya rasul-Allah

The salutations and greetings be on you, O the Messenger of Allah.

6

اَللَّهُمَّ صَلِّ عَلَى مُحَمَّدٍ وَعَلَى آلِ مُحَمَّدٍ كَمَا صَلَّيْتَ عَلَى إِبْرَاهِيمَ وَعَلَى آلِ إِبْرَاهِيمَ اِنَّكَ حَمِيْدٌ مَّجِيْدٌ اَللَّهُمَّ بَارِكْ عَلَى مُحَمَّدٍ وَعَلَى آلِ مُحَمَّدٍ كَمَا بَارَكْتَ عَلَى إِبْرَاهِيمَ وَعَلَى آلِ إِبْرَاهِيمَ فِي العَالَمِينَ اِنَّكَ حَمِيْدٌ مَّجِيْدٌ *

Allahumma salli `ala Muhammadin wa `ala ali Muhammadin kama sallayta `ala Ibrahima wa `ala ali Ibrahima innaka hamidum Majid. Allahamma barik `ala Muhammadin wa `ala `li Muhammadin kama barakta `ala Ibrahima wa `ala ali Ibrahima innaka hamidum Majid.

Selected Du'as and Durud

O Allah, bless and exalt Muhammad and his family as you blessed and exalted Ibrahim and his family. Truly you are the Praiseworthy and Glorious. O Allah, bless Muhammad and his family as you blessed Ibrahim and his family. Verily you are the Praiseworthy and Glorious and magnified.

7

السَّلامُ عَلَيْكَ يَا نَبِيَّ الله ، السَّلامُ عَلَيْكَ يَا خِيْرَةَ الله مِنْ خَلْقِهِ ، السَّلامُ عَلَيْكَ يَا سَيِّدَ الْمُرْسَلِيْنَ وَ إِمَامَ الْمُتَّقِيْنَ ، أَشْهَدُ أَنَّكَ قَدْ بَلَّغْتَ الرِّسَالَةَ وَأَدَّيْتَ الأَمَانَةَ ، وَنَصَحْتَ الأُمَّةَ ، وَجَاهَدْتَ فِي الله حَقَّ جِهَادِهِ

Assalamu 'alaika ya Nabi-Aallah, assalaamu 'alaika ya khyirat-Allah min khalqihi, assalaamu 'alaika ya sayyid al-mursalin wa imam al-muttaqin, ashadu annaka qad ballaght ar-risalata, wa addaital a-manata, wa nasaht al- ummata, wa jahadta fi Allahi haqqa jihadihi.

Peace be upon you, O Prophet of Allah! Peace be upon you, O the best of Allah's creation. Peace be upon you, O the leader of the Messengers and of the pious. I testify that you conveyed the Message and discharged the assignment, guided the Ummah and strove in the way of Allah with all due struggle.

8

اَللَّهُمَّ صَلِّ وَسَلِّمْ وَ بَارِكْ عَلَى سَيِّدِنَا مُحَمَّدٌ وَعَلَى آلِ سَيِّدِنَا مُحَمَّدٌ كَمَا صَلَّيْتَ وَسَلَّمْتَ وَ بَارَكْتَ عَلَى سَيِّدِنَا إِبْرَاهِيمَ وَعَلَى آلِ سَيِّدِنَا إِبْرَاهِيمَ فِي العَالَمِينَ اِنَّكَ حَمِيدٌ مَجِيدٌ ❈

Allahumma salli wa sallim wa barik `ala sayyidina Muhammadin wa `ala ali sayyidina Muhammadin kama sallayita wa sallamta wa barakta `ala sayyidina Ibrahima wa `ala ali sayyidina Ibrahima fi-l`alamina innaka himidum majid.

O Allah salute, send peace and blessing upon our leader Muhammad as you sent salution, peace and blessing on our leader Ibrahim, and on the family of our leader Ibrahim. Verily you are the Praised and Majestic in all the worlds.

IV. Dua's for Various Situations

There are du'as for every occasion in life--in personal life, in distress, in travel and on social occasions. Only a couple are mentioned below:

Recite the following when you sleep:

$$\text{اَللّٰهُمَّ بِاسْمِكَ أَمُوَاتُ وَ أَحْيى}$$

Allahumma bi ismika amwatu wa ahya.

O Allah! In your name do I die and with your name I shall live again.

The Prophet (s) said: "when you are about to sleep, recite *Ayat al-Kursi* (2:255) till the end of the verse for there will remain over you a protection from Allah and no devil will draw near you until morning."

For text, transliteration and translation of Ayat al-Kursi or Throne Verse see pp. 176-177, Section 10 of Chapter 10.

The Prophet (s) also said: "Whoever recites the last two verses of *Surah Al-Baqarah* at night, these two verses shall be sufficient for him".

For text, transliteration and translation of the last two verses of *Surah Al-Baqarah* see pp. 320-321.

On waking up in the morning, recite:

$$\text{اَلْحَمْدُ لِلّٰهِ الَّذِيْ أَحْيَانَا بَعْدَ مَا أَمَا تَنا وَ إِلَيْهِ النُّشُوْرُ}$$

Al-hamdu lillahil-ladhi ahyana ba'ada ma amatana wa ilayhin nushur.

All praise to Allah who restored us to our life, having caused us to die (sleep is resemblance to death) and unto Him shall be the resurrection.

With the first signs of the coming day, the Prophet and his Companions used to say:

أَصْبَحْنَا عَلَى فِطْرَةِ الإِسْلاَمِ وَكَلِمَةِ الإِخْلاَصِ وَعَلَى دِينِ نَبِيِّنَا مُحَمَّدٍ ، وَعَلَى مِلَّةِ أَبِينَا إِبْرَاهِيمَ حَنِيفاً ، وَمَا كَانَ مِنَ الْمُشْرِكِينَ

Asbahna ala fitratil islami wa kalimatil ikhlasi wa 'ala deeni nabiyyina Muhammad wa 'ala millati abiina Ibrahima hanifan wa ma kana minal mushrikin

We have begun the day in the way of Islam and with the word of devotion, in the religion of our Prophet Muhammad, in the nation of our father. Ibrahim, the True Unitarian who was never an idolater. Also, at every pre-dawn time when the Prophet (s) used to wake up for Tahajjud, he performed ablution; then looking at the celestial twinkling stars, he would recite the last section of Surah Ali 'Imran.

When one boards a car or a plane or mounts a carriage, he should, as our Prophet (s) used to on a journey, start with "Bismillahhir Rahmanir Rahim." Then say, "Allahu Akbar" three times, then the following *du'a*: {43: 13}

سُبْحَانَ الَّذِي سَخَّرَ لَنَا هَذَا وَمَا كُنَّا لَهُ مُقْرِنِينَ ۝ وَإِنَّا إِلَى رَبِّنَا لَمُنْقَلِبُونَ ۝

Subhanalladhi sakhkhara lana hadha wa ma kunna laha muqriniin, wa inna ila Rabbina lamunqalibuun.

Selected Du'as and Durud

Limitless is His glory is He who has made [all] this subservient to own use – since [out for Him.] we would not have been able to attain to it. However verily. It is unto Him that we must always turn.

The following du'a is also quite common:

اَللّٰهُمَّ إِنِي أَسْئَلُكَ فِي سَفَرِي هَذَا الْبِرُ وَالتَّقْوَى وَمِنْ الْعَمَلِ مَا تَرْضَى . اَللّٰهُمَّ هَوَّنْ عَلَيْنَا سَفَرَنَا هَذَا ، وَاَطْوِ عَنَّا بُعْدَهُ ، اَللّٰهُمَّ أَنْتَ الصَّاحِبُ فِي السَّفَرْ وَالْخَلِيْفَةُ فِي الأَهْلِ ، اَللّٰهُمَّ إِنِي أَعُوذُ بِكَ مِنْ وَعْثَاءِ السَّفَرِ وكَآبَةِ الْمَنْظَرِ ، وَسُوْءِ الْمُنْقَلَبِ فِي الْمَالِ وِالأَهْلِ

Allahumma inni asaluka fi safari hadha, al birra wat taqwa wa minal 'amali ma tarda, Allahumma hawan 'alaina safarana hadha, watwi 'anna bu'dahu, Allahyumma antas sahibu fis safari, wal khaliifatu fi- lahli. Allahumma inni a'udhubika min aghthaissafari wa ka'aabatil manzari wa su'il munqalabi filmali wal ahli

A translation of the above *du'a* given on page 7 of *Hajj, 'Umrah and Zirayah* by 'Abdul 'Azîz 'Abdullah Bin Baz is quoted below:

Glory be to Him, Who has subjugated this to us, and we were not capable of doing it. and certainly we would return to our Lord. O Allah! I ask You in this journey of mine, piety and goodness and such deeds that please You. O Allah! Make this journey of ours easy for us, and reduce its distance for us. O Allah! You are my Companion in journey and the Successor for my family behind. O Allah! I seek refuge with you against the hardship of travel, bad sight, and any harm that may occur to my family and my belongings.

According to Imam Ahmad, Imam Tirmidhi, Imam Nasai, Imam Ibn Majah and Hakim, the following *dua* is said at the time of seeing someone off, and it is said holding hands (Imam Ibn Qayyim, *Kitab al-Salat*, p. 104):

أَسْتَوْدِعُ اللهَ دِيْنَكَ وَأَمَانَتِكَ وَخَوَاتِيْمَ عَمَلِك ۞

Astaudiullah dinaka wa amanataka wa khawatima 'amalika

I hereby put you in the trust of Allah in your religion of Islam up to your last deed. When one returns from a journey, he should, as the Prophet (s) did, recite the following *dua*:

آئِبُوْنَ تَائِبُوْنَ عَابِدُوْنَ لِرَبِّنَا حَامِدُوْنَ ۞

Aibuna taibuna 'abiduna li Rabbina hamiduna.

We return unto Allah (swt), penitents, adorers and worshippers.

There are very many *du'as* which Prophet Muhammad (s) used to say, and he taught them to his companions. These can be found in famous Books of Hadith.

In case of danger, recite the following:

1

لاَ إِلَهَ إِلاَّ أَنْتَ سُبْحَانَكَ إِنِّي كُنْتُ مِنَ الظَّالِمِين ۞

La Ilaha illa Anta Subhanaka inni kuntu minaz zalimiin

There is no deity except you, so glory and praise be to you. Verily, I am among the oppressors and evil-doers.(21: 87)

2

حَسْبُنَا اَللهُ نِعْمَ الوَكِيلِ نِعْمَ المَولَى وَ نِعْمَ النَّصِيرُ ۞

Hasbunallahu ni'mal wakil ni'mal mawlaa wa ni'man nasiir. (cf. 22: 78, 8: 40)

Allah is enough for us. He is the best Supporter, the best Guardian and the best Helper.

When haunted by dreams:

أَعُوذُ بِكَلِمَاتِ اللهِ التَّامَّاتِ مِنْ غَضَبِهِ وَعِقَابِهِ وَمِنَ شَرِ عِبَادِه وَمِنَ هَمَزَاتِ الشَّيطَانِ وَانْ يَحْضُرُونْ ۞

A'uwdhu bikalimatillahi attamarati min ghadabihi wa iqabihi wa min sharri 'ibadihi wa min hamazatish shayatiini wa ain yahduruun.

I seek refuge with Allah's perfect words
From His displeasure and His chastisement, and from the evil of His creatures and from the evil suggestions of the Satan and from their coming near me.

V. Miscellaneous

The following two after-prayer supplications are very common:

1

اَللّهُمَّ اغْفِرْ لِي وَلِوَا لِدَىَّ وَلِأُسْتَاذِي وَلِجَمِيْعِ الْمُؤْمِنِيْنَ وَلِمُؤْمِنَاتِ وَالْمُسْلِمِيْنَ وَالْمُسْلِمَاتِ بِرَحْمَتِكَ بَا اَرْحَمُ الرَّاحِمِيْنَ

Allahumm aghfirli wa liwalidyya wa li ustadhi Wa li jami'il muminiina walmuslimiina wal muslimate birahmatika ya arhamarrahmiin

O Allah, forgive me and my parents and my teachers and all the believing men and women and obedient men and women with your mercy. O Most Merciful of (all) those who show mercy.

2

اَللّهُمَّ أنت السَّلَامْ وَ مِنْكَ السَّلَامْ وَالَيْكَ يَرْجِعُ السَّلَامْ حَيِّنَـا رَبَّنَـا بِالسَّلَامْ وَأَدْخِلْنَا دَارَ السَّلَامْ تَبَـارَكْتَ رَبَّنَـا وَتَعَـالَيْتَ يَـاذَالْجَلَالِ وَالْإِكْرَامِ

Allahuma antassalam wa minkassalam wa ilaika yarja'ussalam, hayyina rabbana bissalam wa adkhilna darassalam tabarakta rabbana wa ta'alaita ya dhaljalali walikram.

O Allah, You are Peace; Peace always turns towards you, O Allah! Keep us alive with peace and let us enter the home of

Selected Du'as and Durud

peace (Paradise). O Allah! O possessor of awe and honour, You are sublime and full of blessing.

Merit of Tasbih, Tahmid and Other Invocations

The Messenger of Allah said:
If a man says "Glory be to God!"(i) after ritual prayer thirty-three times and says "Praise be to God!"(ii) thirty-three times and says "God is most great"(iii) thirty-three times and finishes the hundredth with the formula "There is no god but God, Who is alone; He has no associate; to Him belongs sovereignty and to Him belongs praise; He is powerful over everything"(iv), then his sins are forgiven, even though they are like the foam of the sea.

He said:
If one says "Glory be to Him, and praise be to Him!" a hundred times a day, his sins fall off from him, even though they are like the foam of the sea.

The first invocation is quoted below, along with transliteration:

(١) سُبْحَانَ اللهِ. (٢) اَلْحَمْدُ لله. (٣) اَللهُ أَكْبَرُ. (٤) لاَ اِلهَ إلاَّ اللهُ وَحْدَهُ لاَ شَرِيكَ لَهُ لَهُ الْمُلْكُ وَلَهُ الْحَمْدُ وَهُوَ عَلَى كُلِّ شَيْءٍ قَدِيرٌ.

(i) Subhan-Allah-i! (ii) Al-hamd-u-lillah-i! (iii) Allah-u-Akbar! (iv) La ilaha ill-Allah-u wahda-hu la sharika lah, lahul-mulk-u wa lahul hamd-u wa-huwa 'ala kull-i-shai'in Qadir.

(a) "Glory be to Allah!" – 33 times (*Tasbih*)

(b) "All praise is only due to Allah"-33 times (*Tahmid*)
(c) "Allah is Great!"-33 times (*takbir*)
(d) "There is no god but Allah. He is One and has no partner, sovereignty and praise are only for Him; and He has full authority over everything"-1 time.

Dua for prostation after reciting sajdah verses:

سُبحانكَ اللّهم وبحَمدكَ أشهَدُ الاّ إله
إلاّ أنتَ استَغفِرُكَ وأتوبُ إلَيك.

اللّـهمَّ زِد بها لي عِندكَ زُخرا،
و دَع بها لي عِندكَ وزرا،
وتَقبَّلها مِنّي، كما تَقبَّلتَ
مِن داوود عَلَيهِ السلام!

Subhanaka-llahumma wa behamdika ashhadu alla ilaaha illa antas taghfiruka wa atoubu ilaik.

Allahumma zid biha li 'indaka zukhra, wa da' biha li 'indaka wizra. wa taqabbalha minni kama taqabbalta min Dawood alaihis salaam

Glory to You. I thank You and testify that there is no god except You. I seek your forgiveness and repent to You. O' Allah! Increase with it a treasure for me and wipe out a sin of mine with it and accept it (this dua) from me as You accepted it from Dawd (as).

APPENDIX C

LORD'S (JESUS) PRAYER

From: *Book of Common Worship* by the Theology and Worship Ministry Unit for the Presbyterian Church (U.S.A.) and the Cumberland Presbyterian Church (Louisville, Ky.:Westminster/John Knox Press, 1993), p. 73.

>Our Father in heaven
>hallowed be your name,
>your kingdom come
>your will be done,
>on earth as in heaven.
>Give us today our daily bread.
>Forgive us our sins
>as we forgive those who sin against us.
>Save us from the time of trial
>and deliver us from evil.
>For the kingdom, the power, and the glory are yours
>now and forever. Amen.

Chinese Mosques
China has a large Muslem population. (top) A mosque in Shanghai. (bottom) A mosque in Beijing (circa1362)

APPENDIX D

IBN SINA ON PRAYER

It is prayer which causes the human, rational soul to resemble the heavenly bodies, eternally worshipping Absolute Truth, and seeking the imperishable reward. The Prophet of God declared, "Prayer is the foundation-stone of religion"; and religion is the purifying of the human soul of all devilish impurities and carnal suggestions, turned away from mean worldly interests. Prayer is the worship of the First Cause, the One Supreme and Mightiest Worshipful; adoration is to know Him Whose Being is Necessary. It needs not that we should interpret the text *And jinns and men were not created save to worship Me* (Qur'an 51: 56) as meaning "to know Me," for worship is knowledge, and to be aware of the existence of One Whose Being is necessary and absolute, being seized of His Being with a pure heart, a spirit undefiled, and a soul wholly devoted to Him. The real nature of prayer is therefore to know Almighty God in His Uniqueness, as a Being wholly Necessary, Whose Essence is infinitely exalted and Whose Qualities are infinitely holy, with habits of sincerity in prayer; by which sincerity I mean, that one should know the Qualities of God in such a manner that there remains no opening to a multiplicity of gods, no intent to join others to His worship.

(From: *Avicenna On Theology* by Arthur J. Arberry Hyperion Press, Inc. Westport, Connecticut (1979, p.55)

The Alhambra,
Granada, Spain
(circa 1300s)

This is one of the great masterpieces of Islamic Architecture. Located in southern Spain, the area was part of the Islamic world for more than seven centuries.

According to John D. Hoag *(Western Islamic Architecture, 1963 p. 29)* "*This palace corresponds closely to the Quar'anic description of Paradise.*"

The Alhambra;
The Court of the Lions
(Top) and
Courtyard Fountain

APPENDIX E

THE QUR'ANIC DESCRIPTION OF A PIOUS MUSLIM

AL-FURQĀN 25: 63-76
(Yusuf Ali translation, pp. 1050-1054)

وَعِبَادُ ٱلرَّحْمَٰنِ ٱلَّذِينَ يَمْشُونَ عَلَى ٱلْأَرْضِ هَوْنًا وَإِذَا خَاطَبَهُمُ ٱلْجَٰهِلُونَ قَالُوا۟ سَلَٰمًا ۝

63. And the servants of (Allah) Most Gracious are those who walk on the earth in humility, and when the ignorant address them, they say, "Peace!"

وَٱلَّذِينَ يَبِيتُونَ لِرَبِّهِمْ سُجَّدًا وَقِيَٰمًا ۝

64. Those who spend the night in adoration of their Lord prostrate and standing;

$$\text{وَٱلَّذِينَ يَقُولُونَ رَبَّنَا ٱصْرِفْ عَنَّا عَذَابَ جَهَنَّمَ إِنَّ عَذَابَهَا كَانَ غَرَامًا ﴿٦٥﴾}$$

65. Those who say, "our Lord!" avert from us the wrath of

$$\text{إِنَّهَا سَاءَتْ مُسْتَقَرًّا وَمُقَامًا ﴿٦٦﴾}$$

hell, for its wrath is indeed an affliction grievous,--

66. "Evil indeed is it as an abode, and as a place to rest in";

$$\text{وَٱلَّذِينَ إِذَآ أَنفَقُوا۟ لَمْ يُسْرِفُوا۟ وَلَمْ يَقْتُرُوا۟ وَكَانَ بَيْنَ ذَٰلِكَ قَوَامًا ﴿٦٧﴾}$$

67. Those who, when they spend, are not extravagant and not niggardly, but hold a just (balance) between those (extremes);

$$\text{وَٱلَّذِينَ لَا يَدْعُونَ مَعَ ٱللَّهِ إِلَٰهًا ءَاخَرَ وَلَا يَقْتُلُونَ ٱلنَّفْسَ ٱلَّتِى حَرَّمَ ٱللَّهُ إِلَّا بِٱلْحَقِّ وَلَا يَزْنُونَ وَمَن يَفْعَلْ ذَٰلِكَ يَلْقَ أَثَامًا ﴿٦٨﴾}$$

The Qur'anic Description of A Pious Muslim

68. Those who invoke not with Allah, any other god, nor slay such life as Allah has made sacred, except for just cause, nor commit fornication;--and any that does this (not only) meets punishment

$$\text{يُضَٰعَفْ لَهُ ٱلْعَذَابُ يَوْمَ ٱلْقِيَٰمَةِ وَيَخْلُدْ فِيهِۦ مُهَانًا ۝}$$

69. (But) the chastisement on the Day of Judgment will be doubled to him, and he will dwell therein in ignominy,--

$$\text{إِلَّا مَن تَابَ وَءَامَنَ وَعَمِلَ عَمَلًا صَٰلِحًا فَأُو۟لَٰٓئِكَ يُبَدِّلُ ٱللَّهُ سَيِّـَٔاتِهِمْ حَسَنَٰتٍ ۗ وَكَانَ ٱللَّهُ غَفُورًا رَّحِيمًا ۝}$$

70. Unless he repents, believes, and works righteous deeds, for Allah will change the evil of such persons into good, and Allah is Oft-Forgiving, Most Merciful.

$$\text{وَمَن تَابَ وَعَمِلَ صَٰلِحًا فَإِنَّهُۥ يَتُوبُ إِلَى ٱللَّهِ مَتَابًا ۝}$$

71. And whoever repents and does good has truly turned to Allah in repentance:

$$\text{وَٱلَّذِينَ لَا يَشْهَدُونَ ٱلزُّورَ وَإِذَا مَرُّوا۟ بِٱللَّغْوِ مَرُّوا۟ كِرَامًا ۝}$$

72. Those who witness no falsehood And, if they pass by futility, they pass by it with honourable (avoidance);

وَٱلَّذِينَ إِذَا ذُكِّرُواْ بِـَٔايَٰتِ رَبِّهِمْ لَمْ يَخِرُّواْ عَلَيْهَا صُمًّا وَعُمْيَانًا ۝

73. Those who, when they are admonished with the signs of their Lord, droop not down at them as if they were deaf or blind;

وَٱلَّذِينَ يَقُولُونَ رَبَّنَا هَبْ لَنَا مِنْ أَزْوَٰجِنَا وَذُرِّيَّٰتِنَا قُرَّةَ أَعْيُنٍ وَٱجْعَلْنَا لِلْمُتَّقِينَ إِمَامًا ۝

74. And those who pray, "our Lord! grant unto us wives and offspring who will be the comfort of our eyes, and give us (the grace) To lead the righteous."

أُوْلَٰٓئِكَ يُجْزَوْنَ ٱلْغُرْفَةَ بِمَا صَبَرُواْ وَيُلَقَّوْنَ فِيهَا تَحِيَّةً وَسَلَٰمًا ۝

75. Those are the ones who will be rewarded with the highest place in heaven, because of their patient constancy: therein shall they be met with salutations and peace,

خَٰلِدِينَ فِيهَا حَسُنَتْ مُسْتَقَرًّا وَمُقَامًا ۝

76. Dwelling therein,--how beautiful an abode and place of rest!

The Qur'anic Description of A Pious Muslim

AL-MA 'ĀRIJ 70: 19-35
(Yusuf Ali translation, pp. 1817-1819)

$$\text{﴾ إِنَّ ٱلْإِنسَٰنَ خُلِقَ هَلُوعًا ۝}$$

19. Truly man was created, very impatient;

$$\text{إِذَا مَسَّهُ ٱلشَّرُّ جَزُوعًا ۝}$$

20. Fretful when evil touches him;

$$\text{وَإِذَا مَسَّهُ ٱلْخَيْرُ مَنُوعًا ۝}$$

21. And niggardly when good reaches him;--

$$\text{إِلَّا ٱلْمُصَلِّينَ ۝}$$

22. Not so those devoted to Prayer:--

$$\text{ٱلَّذِينَ هُمْ عَلَىٰ صَلَاتِهِمْ دَآئِمُونَ ۝}$$

23. Those who remain steadfast to their prayer;

$$\text{وَالَّذِينَ فِي أَمْوَالِهِمْ حَقٌّ مَّعْلُومٌ ﴿٢٤﴾}$$

24. And those in whose wealth is a recognised right

$$\text{لِلسَّائِلِ وَالْمَحْرُومِ ﴿٢٥﴾}$$

25. For the (needy) who asks and him who is deprived (for some reason from asking);

$$\text{وَالَّذِينَ يُصَدِّقُونَ بِيَوْمِ الدِّينِ ﴿٢٦﴾}$$

26 And those who hold to the truth of the Day of Judgment;

$$\text{وَالَّذِينَ هُم مِّنْ عَذَابِ رَبِّهِم مُّشْفِقُونَ ﴿٢٧﴾}$$

27. And those who fear the punishment of their Lord,--

$$\text{إِنَّ عَذَابَ رَبِّهِمْ غَيْرُ مَأْمُونٍ ﴿٢٨﴾}$$

28. For their Lord's punishment is not a thing to feel secure from:--

The Qur'anic Description of A Pious Muslim

$$وَالَّذِينَ هُمْ لِفُرُوجِهِمْ حَافِظُونَ ﴿٢٩﴾$$

29. And those who guard their chastity,

$$إِلَّا عَلَىٰ أَزْوَاجِهِمْ أَوْ مَا مَلَكَتْ أَيْمَانُهُمْ فَإِنَّهُمْ غَيْرُ مَلُومِينَ ﴿٣٠﴾$$

30. Except with their wives and the (captives) whom their right hands possess,-- for (then) they are not to be blamed,

$$فَمَنِ ابْتَغَىٰ وَرَاءَ ذَٰلِكَ فَأُولَٰئِكَ هُمُ الْعَادُونَ ﴿٣١﴾$$

31. But those who trespass beyond this are transgressors;--

$$وَالَّذِينَ هُمْ لِأَمَانَاتِهِمْ وَعَهْدِهِمْ رَاعُونَ ﴿٣٢﴾$$

32. And those who respect their trusts and covenants;--

$$وَالَّذِينَ هُم بِشَهَادَاتِهِمْ قَائِمُونَ ﴿٣٣﴾$$

33. And those who stand firm in their testimonies;

$$وَالَّذِينَ هُمْ عَلَىٰ صَلَاتِهِمْ يُحَافِظُونَ ﴿٣٤﴾$$

34. And those who (strictly) guard their worship;--

$$أُو۟لَـٰٓئِكَ فِى جَنَّـٰتٍ مُّكْرَمُونَ ﴿٣٥﴾$$

35. Such will be the honoured ones in the gardens (of bliss).

AL-MU'MINÛN 23:1-11
(Yusuf Ali translation, pp. 977-978)

$$قَدْ أَفْلَحَ ٱلْمُؤْمِنُونَ ﴿١﴾$$

1. Successful indeed are the believers,--

$$ٱلَّذِينَ هُمْ فِى صَلَاتِهِمْ خَاشِعُونَ ﴿٢﴾$$

2. Those who humble themselves in their prayers;

The Qur'anic Description of A Pious Muslim

$$وَٱلَّذِينَ هُمْ عَنِ ٱللَّغْوِ مُعْرِضُونَ ﴿٣﴾$$

3. Who avoid vain talk;

$$وَٱلَّذِينَ هُمْ لِلزَّكَوٰةِ فَاعِلُونَ ﴿٤﴾$$

4. Who are active in giving zakat;

$$وَٱلَّذِينَ هُمْ لِفُرُوجِهِمْ حَافِظُونَ ﴿٥﴾$$

5. Who guard their modesty,

$$إِلَّا عَلَىٰٓ أَزْوَٰجِهِمْ أَوْ مَا مَلَكَتْ أَيْمَٰنُهُمْ فَإِنَّهُمْ غَيْرُ مَلُومِينَ ﴿٦﴾$$

6. Except with those joined to them in the marriage bond, or (the captives) whom their right hands possess,-- for (in their case) they are free from blame,

$$فَمَنِ ابْتَغَىٰ وَرَاءَ ذَٰلِكَ فَأُولَٰئِكَ هُمُ الْعَادُونَ ۝$$

7. But those whose desires exceed those limits are transgressors;--

$$وَالَّذِينَ هُمْ لِأَمَانَاتِهِمْ وَعَهْدِهِمْ رَاعُونَ ۝$$

8. Those who faithfully observe their trusts and their covenants;

$$وَالَّذِينَ هُمْ عَلَىٰ صَلَوَاتِهِمْ يُحَافِظُونَ ۝$$

9. And who (strictly) guard their prayers;--

$$أُولَٰئِكَ هُمُ الْوَارِثُونَ ۝$$

10. These will be the heirs,

The Qur'anic Description of A Pious Muslim

$$\text{ٱلَّذِينَ يَرِثُونَ ٱلْفِرْدَوْسَ هُمْ فِيهَا خَٰلِدُونَ ﴿١١﴾}$$

11. Who will inherit paradise: they will dwell therein (for ever)

AT-TAWBAH 9: 112
(Muhammad M. Pickthal translation)

$$\text{ٱلتَّٰٓئِبُونَ ٱلْعَٰبِدُونَ ٱلْحَٰمِدُونَ ٱلسَّٰٓئِحُونَ ٱلرَّٰكِعُونَ ٱلسَّٰجِدُونَ ٱلْءَامِرُونَ بِٱلْمَعْرُوفِ وَٱلنَّاهُونَ عَنِ ٱلْمُنكَرِ وَٱلْحَٰفِظُونَ لِحُدُودِ ٱللَّهِ وَبَشِّرِ ٱلْمُؤْمِنِينَ ﴿١١٢﴾}$$

112. (Triumphant) are those who turn repentant (to Allah), those who serve (Him), those who praise (Him), those who fast, those who bow down, those who fall prostrate (in worship), those who enjoin the right and who forbid the wrong and those who keep the limits (ordained) of Allah--and give glad tidings to believers!

AL-AHZĀB 33: 35
(Muhammad Asad translation)

إِنَّ ٱلْمُسْلِمِينَ وَٱلْمُسْلِمَٰتِ وَٱلْمُؤْمِنِينَ وَٱلْمُؤْمِنَٰتِ وَٱلْقَٰنِتِينَ وَٱلْقَٰنِتَٰتِ وَٱلصَّٰدِقِينَ وَٱلصَّٰدِقَٰتِ وَٱلصَّٰبِرِينَ وَٱلصَّٰبِرَٰتِ وَٱلْخَٰشِعِينَ وَٱلْخَٰشِعَٰتِ وَٱلْمُتَصَدِّقِينَ وَٱلْمُتَصَدِّقَٰتِ وَٱلصَّٰٓئِمِينَ وَٱلصَّٰٓئِمَٰتِ وَٱلْحَٰفِظِينَ فُرُوجَهُمْ وَٱلْحَٰفِظَٰتِ وَٱلذَّٰكِرِينَ ٱللَّهَ كَثِيرًا وَٱلذَّٰكِرَٰتِ أَعَدَّ ٱللَّهُ لَهُم مَّغْفِرَةً وَأَجْرًا عَظِيمًا ۝

35. Verily, for all men and women who have surrendered themselves unto God, and all believing men and believing women, and all truly devout men and truly devout women, and all men and women who are true to their word, and all men and women who are patient in adversity, and all men and women who humble themselves [before God], and all men and women who give in charity, and all self-denying men and self-denying women, and all men and women who are mindful of their chastity, and all men and women who remember God unceasingly: for [all of] them has God readied forgiveness of sins and a mighty reward.

APPENDIX F

OVERCOMING SATAN'S FORCE

Satan obtained Allah's permission to tempt man, and this was implied in such free will as granted to man by Allah. Satan's boast is that the portion of mankind seduced by him will be so corrupted in their nature that they will bear a sort of brand that will mark them off as his own; or that they will be like a portion assigned to himself. Satan's deceptions are with false desires, false superstitions, and false fears. According to verses 4:118-119, Allah did curse Satan and rejected him for having said:

> Verily, of Thy servants I shall most certainly take my due share, and shall lead them astray, and fill them with vain desires; and I shall command them--and they will cut off the ears of cattle [in idolatrous sacrifice]; and I shall command them--and they will corrupt God's creation!

Imam Ghazzali gives a stern warning against Satan in the following words which are taken from his *Minhaj al-'Abidin* (Cairo, 1337 A.H. = 1918 A.D.), pp. 21-22, quoted in *Islam: Muhammad and His Religion*, edited with an Introduction by Arthur Jeffery, pp. 115-116. (This has been edited by the author.):

> It is your duty, O my brother Muslim, to make war on Satan and to overcome him, and that for two very good reasons.

The first of them is that he is an enemy who manifestly leads astray, and there is no hope that he will be reformed or will ever spare you. Nay, rather, the fact is that he will be contented with nothing less than your complete destruction. So there is no means of being safe from such an enemy as this or of being neglected by him. Ponder now on two verses from the Book of Allah--exalted be He. One of them is His saying:

(36:60): Did I not enjoin on you, O ye children of Adam, that ye should not worship Satan; For that he was to you an enemy avowed?

35:6): Verily Satan is an enemy to you: so treat him as an enemy. He only invites his adherents, that they may become companions of the Blazing Fire.

No warning could possibly go further than that.

The second reason is that there was given him an innate disposition to be inimical to you, so he is ever alert to make war with you, and during the watches of the night and at all hours of the day he is shooting his arrows at you while you are heedless of him. So how will the state of things be?

Then there is another point for you [to consider]. You are busied with your service of Allah, Most High, and with summoning creatures to the gate of Allah--glory be to Him--by your actions and your words, and all this is the very antithesis of Satan's work, of his efforts, his desires, his crafty schemes, so that it is as though you have taken your stand and girt your loins to provoke, to stir the rancor, and to oppose Satan. For this very reason he also is girding his loins to treat you as an enemy, to fight you, to circumvent you until he succeeds in doing some mischief. Thus it is up to you to take refuge with Allah with regard to your affair, lest he go so far as to destroy you completely. Never can you consider yourself secure on your side, for he is one who does evil to, and aims at the destruction of,

Overcoming Satan's Force

even those who do not rouse his anger or go against him but who are friendly to him and agree with him, such as the unbelievers and the people of error and the people of desire in certain circumstances. [If this is how he treats them], what must be his purpose toward those who take a stand which arouses his rage and who definitely set themselves in opposition to him?

He has leave [from Allah] to indulge in general enmity against folk as a whole, but has a special enmity against you who are diligent in worship and in seeking knowledge. To him your case is one of importance, and against you he has certain helpers, the strongest among whom are your own soul and your passions. He has methods, and a way of access, and openings of which you are heedless.

Author's note: Also remember, Allah says (24:21):

O ye who believe! Follow not Satan's footsteps: If any will follow the footsteps of Satan, he will (but) command what is indecent and wrong.

Mosques in Iran and Pakistan
(top left) Minaret of the Gauhar Shad Mosque, Mashhad, Iran. *(top right)* Detail of the base showing Qur'anic calligraphy of the *Surah Ya-Sin*. *(bottom)* Badshahi Mosque, Lahore, Pakistan. Built by Mogul Emperor Aurangzeb, from red sandstone and marble. It is the largest mosque in the subcontinent.

APPENDIX G

ALLAH'S MOST BEAUTIFUL NAMES

Allah, the Most Exalted, said:

وَلِلَّهِ ٱلْأَسْمَآءُ ٱلْحُسْنَىٰ فَٱدْعُوهُ بِهَا وَذَرُوا۟ ٱلَّذِينَ يُلْحِدُونَ فِىٓ أَسْمَٰٓئِهِۦ ۚ سَيُجْزَوْنَ مَا كَانُوا۟ يَعْمَلُونَ ﴿١٨٠﴾

The most beautiful names belong to Allah: So call on Him by them; But shun such men as distort His names: For what they do, they will soon be requited (7: 180).

There are many names of Allah: some say 300, some say 1001, while others say 124000, which is the number of prophets that were sent by Allah, and each one of them might have called Allah by a specific name. According to Ibn 'Abbas, the number is endless! But the names that have come down to us through Abu Musa Al-Tirmidhi from Abu Huraira (R) that Rasulillah (s) said, "Allah has 99 names, 100 less one; and he who memorizes them all by heart will enter Paradise) (vide *Al-Jami' al Sahih wa* hua Sunan al-Tirmidhi (Cairo: n.d., 5, pp. 530-531, Hadith Nos. 3506 and 3507. Translation from Bukhari, translated by Muhsin Khan, Vol. 9, p. 363, Hadith No. 489).

The Names of Allah Almighty : These names occur in the Qur'an and are listed by Imam Tirmihdi in his collection of Hadith.

$$هُوَ اللّٰهُ الَّذِى لَا إِلٰهَ إِلَّا هُوَ$$

He is Allah besides whom there is no God

الرَّحْمٰنُ	1. Ar-Rahman	the Merciful One
الرَّحِيمُ	2. Ar-Rahîm	the Compassionate
الْمَلِكُ	3. Al-Malik	the King
الْقُدُّوسُ	4. Al-Quddus	the Holy One
السَّلَامُ	5. As-Salãm	the Peace
الْمُؤْمِنُ	6. Al-Mu'min	the Faithful
الْمُهَيْمِنُ	7. Al-Muhayimin	the Overseer
الْعَزِيزُ	8. Al-'Azîz	the Mighty
الْجَبَّارُ	9. Al-Jabbãr	the Almighty

Allah's Most Beautiful Names

الْمُتَكَبِّرُ	10. Al-Mutakabbir	the Justly Proud
الْخَالِقُ	11. Al-Khāliq	the Creator
الْبَارِئُ	12. Al-Bāri	the Maker
الْمُصَوِّرُ	13. Al-Musawwir	the Fashioner.
الْغَفَّارُ	14. Al-Ghaffār	the Pardoner
الْقَهَّارُ	15. Al-Qahhār	the Overcomer
الْوَهَّابُ	16. Al-Wahhāb	the Bestower
الرَّزَّاقُ	17. Al-Razzāq	the Provider
الْفَتَّاحُ	18. Al-Fattāh	the Opener
الْعَلِيمُ	19. Al-'Alīm	He Who knows
الْقَابِضُ	20. Al-Qābid	the Restrainer
الْبَاسِطُ	21. Al-Bāsit	the Extender
الْخَافِضُ	22. Al-Khāfid	the Humbler
الرَّافِعُ	23. Ar-Rāfi'	the Exalter
الْمُعِزُّ	24. Al-Mu'izz	the Empowerer
الْمُذِلُّ	25. Al-Mudhill	the Abaser

السَّمِيعُ	26. As-Samî'	the Hearer
الْبَصِيرُ	27. Al-Basîr	He Who sees
الْحَكَمُ	28. Al-Hakam	the Judge
الْعَدْلُ	29. Al-'Adl	the Just
اللَّطِيفُ	30. Al-Latîf	the Kindly One
الْخَبِيرُ	31. Al-Khabîr	the Well-informed
الْعَظِيمُ	32. Al-'Azîm	the Great One
الْحَلِيمُ	33. Al-Halîm	the Forbearing
الْغَفُورُ	34. Al-Ghafûr	the Forgiving
الشَّكُورُ	35. Ash-Shakûr	the Grateful
الْعَلِيُّ	36. Al-'Alî	the High One
الْكَبِيرُ	37. Al-Kabîr	He Who is great
الْحَفِيظُ	38. Al-Hafîz	the Guardian
الْمُقِيتُ	39. Al-Muqît	the Nourisher
الْحَسِيبُ	40. Al-Hasîb	the Reckoner
الْجَلِيلُ	41. Al-Jalîl	the Majestic

Allah's Most Beautiful Names

الْكَرِيمُ	42. Al-Karîm	the Generous
الرَّقِيبُ	43. Ar-Raqîb	the Watcher
الْمُجِيبُ	44. Al-Mujîb	He Who answers
الْوَاسِعُ	45. Al-Wasi'	the Comprehensive
الْحَكِيمُ	46. Al-Hakîm	the Wise
الْوَدُودُ	47. Al-Wadûd	the Loving One
الْمَجِيدُ	48. Al-Majîd	the Glorious
الْبَاعِثُ	49. Al-Bã'ith	the Raiser (of the dead)
الشَّهِيدُ	50. Ash-Shahîd	the Witness
الْحَقُّ	51. Al-Haq	the Truth
الْوَكِيلُ	52. Al-Wakîl	the Trustee
الْقَوِيُّ	53. Al-Qawî	the Most Strong
الْمَتِينُ	54. Al-Matîn	the Firm One
الْوَلِيُّ	55. Al-Walî	the Protecting Friend
الْحَمِيدُ	56. Al-Hamîd	the Praiseworthy
الْمُحْصِى	57. Al-Muhsî	the Reckoner

الْمُبْدِئُ	58. Al-Mubdî	the Originator
الْمعيد	59. Al-Mu'îd	the Restorer
الْمُحْيِي	60. Al-Muhyyi	the Giver of Life
الْمُمِيتُ	61. Al-Mumît	the Creator of Death
الْحَيُّ	62. Al-Hayyyi	the Alive
الْقَيُّومُ	63. Al-Qayyûm	the Self Subsisting
الْوَاجِدُ	64. Al-Wājid	the Finder
الْمَاجِدُ	65. Al-Mājid	the Noble
الْوَاحِدُ	66. Al-Wāhid	the Unique
الأحد	67. Al-Ahad	the One
الْصَّمَدُ	68. As-Samad	the Eternal
الْقَادِرُ	69. Al-Qādir	the Able
الْمُقْتَدِرُ	70. Al-Muqtadir	the Powerful
الْمُقَدَّمُ	71. Al-Muqaddim	the Expediter
الْمُؤَخِّرُ	72. Al-Mu'akhkhir	the Delayer
الأوَّلُ	73. Al-Awwal	the First

Allah's Most Beautiful Names

الأَخِيرُ	74. Al-Akhîr	the Last
الظَّاهِرُ	75. Az-Zāhir	the Manifest
الْبَاطِنُ	76. Al-Bātin	the Hidden
الْوَالِي	77. Al-Wālî	the Governor
الْمُتَعَالِي	78. Al-Muta'ālî	the Most Exalted
الْبَرُّ	79. Al-Barr	the Source of All Goodness
التَّوَّابُ	80. At-Tawwāb	the Acceptor of Repentance
الْمُنْتَقِمُ	81. Al-Muntaqim	the Avenger
الْعَفُوُّ	82. Al-'Afwu	the Pardoner
الرَّؤُوفُ	83. Ar-Raûf	the Compassionate
مَالِكُ الْمُلْكِ	84. Mālik-al-Mulk	the Eternal Owner of Sovereignty
ذُو الْجَلَالِ وَالْإِكْرَامِ	85. Dhul-Jilāl wa al-Ikrām	the Lord of Majesty and Bounty
الْمُقْسِطُ	86. Al-Muqsît	the Equitable
الْجَامِعُ	87. Al-Jāmi'	the Gatherer

الْغَنِيُّ	88. Al-Ghanî	the Self-Sufficient
الْمُغْنِي	89. Al-Mughnî	the Enricher
الْمَانِعُ	90. Al-Māni'	the Preventer
الضَّارُّ	91. Al-Dārr	the Distresser
النَّافِعُ	92. An-Nāfi'	the Propitious
النُّورُ	93. An-Nûr	the Light
الْهَادِي	94. Al-Hādî	the Guide
الْبَدِيعُ	95. Al-Badi'	the Incomparable
الْبَاقِي	96. Al-Bāqî	the Everlasting
الْوَارِثُ	97. Al-Wārith	the Supreme Inheritor
الرَّشِيدُ	98. Ar-Rashîd	the Guide to the Right Path
الصَّبُورُ	99. As-Sabûr	the Patient

APPENDIX H

PROPHETS OF ALLAH
(with an English equivalent, if applicable)

1. Adam
2. Idris (Enoch)
3. Nuh (Noah)
4. Hud
5. Salih
6. Ibrahim (Abraham)
7. Isma'il (Ishmael)
8. Ishaq (Isaac)
9. Lut (Lot)
10. Ya'qub (Jacob)
11. Yusuf (Joseph)
12. Shu'aib
13. Ayyub (Job)
14. Musa (Moses)
15. Harun (Aaron)
16. Dhu'l-kifl (Ezekiel)
17. Dawud (David)
18. Sulaiman (Solomon)
19. Ilias (Elias)
20. Al-Yasa

21. Yunus (Jonah)
22. Zakariyya (Zacharias)
23. Yahya (John)
24. 'Isa (Jesus)
25. 'Uzair (Ezra)
26. Muhammad

Qur'anic References: 2: 31,136; 6: 84-6; 7: 65, 73, 85; 19: 56; 21: 85 and Surah Muhammad.

Note: All prophets are not mentioned in the Qur'an (cf. 4: 164; 40: 78).

Contemporary calligraphic design representing the word Allah many times

APPENDIX I

BIOGRAPHICAL NOTES
(a selected list)

Abu Dawud, Sulaiman bin Al-Ashath (817-889)
　　He studied ahadith under Imam Ahmad bin Hanbal along with al-Bukhari and taught many of the later scholars of Hadith like At-Tirmidhi and An-Nasai. He ranks as one of the six compilers of Hadith. He adopted a more critical approach in his collection of Hadith than many others of his time and before him. Though he collected 500,000 ahadith, he compiled only 4,800 of them in his book entitled As-Sunan.

Abu Hanifah (700-767)
　　His real name is al-Numan ibn Thabit. He was the leading fiqh scholar and theologian in Iraq after whom the madhhal of the Hanafites was named. The Imam was a Hadith expert who had all the ahadith of the companions of Makkah and Madinah in addition to those of Kufa and only lacked the relatively few channels of narrators who were in Damascus.
　　His *Musnad* (ascribed traditions) is comparable in size to the *Muwatta* of Imam Malik and the *Musnad* of Shafi'i. The Imam was of an age that was plagued by Hadith forgers, he was moved by his extreme piety to reject any Hadith that he was not reasonably sure was authentic, for which reason he applied a relatively selective range of Hadith evidence in Sacred Law. His school does not accept qualifications or modifications of any

ruling established by Qur'anic verse when such qualification comes through a Hadith with but one, even if rigorously authenticated (*sahih*), channel of transmission, but only if it comes through a Hadith with three separate channels of transmission. So despite Abu Hanifah's being a Hadith specialist, his school reflects a legacy of extensive use of analogy and deduction from specific rulings and general principles established by primary texts acceptable to the Imam's rigorous standards, as well as the use of inference and juridical opinion as to what conforms to the human interests in general protected and furthered by Sacred Law.

With his legal brilliance, he was equally well known for his piety and asceticism. He shunned sleep at night, and some called him the Peg because of his perpetual standing for prayer therein, often reciting the entire Qur'an in his nightly *rakahs*. He performed the dawn prayer for forty years with the ablution (*wudu*) made for the nightfall prayer, would only sleep a short while between his noon and mid-afternoon prayers, and by the end of his life had recited the Holy Qur'an seven thousand times. (*Reliance of Traveler*, pp. 1027-1028).

Abu Hanifah made his living as a cloth merchant. Most of his biographers relate that he persistently refused to accept the office of a *Qadi* (judge) which the Umayad governor in Kufa and later the Caliph al-Mansur wanted him to accept. By his refusal he is said to have incurred corporal punishment and imprisonment. He died in prison.

Abu Hurayra (d. 678)

He was one of Muhammad(s)'s companions and the greatest of them in memorizing and relating ahadith. He oversaw affairs at Madinah for a time. In the Caliphate of Umar(r) he was made governor of Bahrain. He was known as a very pious man.

Biographical Notes

Ahmad Ibn Hanbal

He is Abu 'Abdullah, Ahmad bin Muhammad bin Hanbal Ash-Shaibani, known by the name Ibn Hanbal. He was a celebrated theologian, jurist and a Hadith scholar. He is also one of the four *Fiqh Imam* and the founder of what later came to be known as Madhhab Al-Hanbaliya (the Hanbal's juristic school).

He was born in Baghdad where he grew up as an orphan. For sixteen years he traveled in pursuit of the knowledge of Hadith to Kufa, Basra, Makkah, Madinah, Yemen, Damascus, Morocco, Algeria, Persia and Khurasan, memorizing one hundred thousand hadith, about thirty thousand of which he recorded in his Musnad. He was among the most outstanding students of Shafii. Like his teacher, the Imam used to recite the entire Qur'an daily. He was, perhaps, the most persecuted and most firm among the Imams.

Al-Baihaqi, Ahmad bin al-Husain (994-1066)

Abu Bakr Al-Baihaqi Ahmad bin al-Husain ibn Ali was his full name. He was considered to be a learned *Hafiz* among the eminent Imam of Hadith and a jurisprudence scholar specializing in *Shafi'i madhhab*. He wrote many books like *As-Sunan al-kubra* and *As-Sunan as-sughra*. It is said that his books exceed one thousand volumes, treating hadith, Qur'anic exegesis, sacred law, tenets of faith and other subjects. It is stated that every Shafii scholar is indebted to the Master except Baihaqi, to whom Shafii is indebted for his writing so many works strengthening the school, expanding questions on which the Imam had been brief, and supported the Iman's positions.

Al-Bukhari, Muhammad bin Ismail (810-870)

He is the Amir-ul-Mu'minin (Commander of the Faithful) in the knowledge of Hadith, and his full name is Abu 'Abdullah, Muhammad bin Isma'il bin Ibrahim bin Al-Mughira bin Bardizbah Al-Ju'fil Al-Bukhari. He studied Ahadith at an early age and traveled widely over the Muslim world collecting

Ahadith. It is said that he collected some 600,000 ahadith and memorized 200,000 of them. In his selection he showed the greatest critical ability, and in editing texts he sought to obtain the most scrupulous accuracy. Yet it was impossible wholly to prevent the appearance of variants. It was a great task for him to sift the forged ahdith from the authentic ones. He finally chose approximately 7,725 with repetition and about 2,230 without repetition, about which there is no doubt of their authenticity. It has been unanimously agreed that his work is the most authentic of all the works of hadith.

Al-Ghazzali, Abu Hamid Muhammad (also Ghazali, 1058-1111)

A towering figure in Islam, he was born at Tus near Mashad in Iran in the early Seljuq era and studied theology and law at Nyshapur. His formidable intellectual abilities soon won him honor and respect at the Court of the famous Seljuq Prime Minister Nizam al-Mulk. He was nicknamed Shafii the Second in recognition of his legal virtuosity.

In *Reliance of the Traveller* (pp. 1047-1048), the following is a partial description of this brilliant intellectual:

His worldly success was something of a mixed blessing, and in mid-career, after considerable reflection, he was gripped by an intense fear for his soul and his fate in the afterlife, and he resigned from his post, traveling first to Jerusalem and then to Damascus to purify his heart by following the way of Sufism. In Damascus he lived in seclusion for some ten years, engaged in spiritual struggle and the remembrance of Allah, at the end of which he emerged to produce his masterpiece *Ihya' 'ulum al-din* (giving life to the religious sciences], a classic among the books of the Muslims about internalizing godfearingness (*taqwa*) in one's dealings with Allah, illuminating the soul through obedience to Him, and the levels of believers' attainments therein. The work shows how deeply Ghazali personally realized what he wrote about, and his masterly treatment of hundreds of questions dealing with the inner life that no one had previously discussed or solved is a performance of sustained excellence that shows its author's well-disciplined legal intellect and profound appreciation of human psychology. He also wrote nearly two hundred other works, on the theory of government, Sacred Law, refutations of philosophers, tenets of faith, Sufism, Qur'anic exegesis, scholastic theology, and bases of Islamic jurisprudence.

Ibn Majah, Muhammad bin Yazid (824-887)

He studied under Imam Malik and others. Many people narrated ahadith from him. He was one of the eminent scholars of Hadith and the author of Sunan, one of the six principal collections of Hadith.

Ibn Taimiyah, Ahmad bin Abdul Halim (1263-1328)

A famous Hanbali scholar in Qur'anic exegesis, Hadith and jurisprudence, he was the son of a leading scholar of the Hanbali school of Islamic law. Endowed with a penetrating intellect and wonderful memory, he mastered the various disciplines of Islamic study at an early age and read extensively the books of the various sects and religions in existence at the time.

He was a great reformer who fought relentlessly against the heretic beliefs and innovative practices that crept into the body of Islam. He endeavored to revive the religion of Islam in its pristine purity and revolutionary spirit. Much of his time and effort was spent defending the orthodox Islamic position against a tidal wave of deviation which had swept over the Muslim nations. In all his writings and reformative efforts, he accepted the Qur'an and the Sunnah as the basic criteria. In matters where there was no clear guidance from these basic sources, he ventured into rational thought and took the path of ijtihad. Consequently, he was imprisoned much of his life.

He left behind a voluminous and influential written legacy, and his influence was felt not only in his own time but ever since. It is believed that he had a profound impact on the most prominent reformer of the eighteenth century, Muhammad ibn Abdul Wahhab (1691-1792).

Malik bin Anas (d. 795)

One variation of Malik's full name is Abu 'Abdullah, Malik bin Anas bin Malik bin Abu 'Aamir Al-Asbahi. According to a tradition preserved by al-Tirmidhi, the Prophet(s) himself is said to have foretold his coming as well as that of the Abu Hanifah and al-Shafii. He is the Imam of the madhhab of Malikis which is named after him, and frequently called briefly the Imam of Dar Al-Hijra, i.e., Imam of Madinah. He is also the *faqih* of the Ummah and the leader of Ahl Al-Hadith. He studied under more than nine hundred professors, and innumerable people learned from him, among them Imam Ash Shafi'i, the founder of the Shafi'i madhhab. His great work is the *Muwatta*.

Muslim bin Hajjaj (817-875)

Muslim's full name is Muslim bin Al-Hajjaj Al-Qushairi An-Nishapuri (also spelled Naisaburi). Muslim is considered second only to Al-Bukhari in the science of the methodology of Hadith. He started the study of Hadith at an early age and traveled to Iraq, Hijaz, Ash-Sham and Egypt and studied under the scholars of Hadith at that time like Al-Bukhari, Ahmad bin Hanbal and Ibn Abu Shaiba. He also taught the famous Hadith scholars like At-Tirmidhi and Ibn Abu Hatim. Muslim compiled the Hadith book Al-Musnad As-Sahih, which became known as Sahih Muslim. This book is considered by the Muslim 'Ulama as the second most authentic Hadith book after Al-Bukhari. His sahih is also said to have been composed out of 300,000 traditions (like that of Al-Bukhari) and contains 9,200 Ahadith. However, unlike other collectors of traditions, he did not subdivide his work into chapters.

Biographical Notes

Al-Nasai (830-915)

His full name is Abu 'Abdur-Rahman, Ahmad bin 'Ali bin Shu'aib bin 'Ali Al-Hafiz. Very little is known about him. He became famous for the study of the methodology of Hadith, memorizing and mastering it. His book, known as *Sunan an-Nasa'i*, is third to *Sahih al-Bukhari* in terms of containing the least weak Ahadith. He lived in Egypt, then moved to Damascus in Syria and died in Makkah. He specialized in Hadith dealing with acts of devotion (*ibadat*) to God.

An-Nawawi, Imam Abu Zakariya Yahya bin Sharaf (631-676)

He is known as Imam Nawawi for short. He was not only an accomplished scholar, litterateur par excellence, but also as a devout dervish. He took pains to select about 1,900 traditions from Bukhari and Muslim, and one or two other standard books on Hadith like *Muwatta*. He supplemented these with appropriate verses from the Qur'an and arranged these as different topics.

He is the author of a large number of books, particularly on traditions and their commentaries. His *Riyadh as-Salihîn* (Garden of the Virtuous Persons is one of the most important, very useful and popular.

Al-Shafi'i, Muhammad bin Idris (767-820)

A shortened version of his name is Abu Abdullah Muhammad bin Idris al-Shafi. He is considered to have been one of the most brilliant and original legal scholars that mankind has ever known. He was an orphan brought to Makkah when he was 2 years old and raised there by his mother in circumstances of extreme poverty and want. He memorized the Qur'an at age.7 and the *Muwatta* at age 10 and was authorized to give formal legal opinion (*fatwa*) at age 15.

The Imam and his legacy are monumental. He paved the way for the enormous importance attached to subsequent generations of Muslims to study prophetic Hadith as reflected by the fact that most of the Imams in the field were from his school. It is said that if the scholars of Hadith speak, it is in the language of Shafii. No wonder that Bukhari, Muslim, Daud, Tirmidhi, Nasai, Majah, Baihaqi and all the other luminaries of the time came from his school. He was the founder of *Shafi'i Madhhab*.

Imam reflected that knowledge is not what is memorized, but only what benefits. It is said that he recited the entire Qur'an each day at prayer and twice a day in Ramadan. He studied and taught Sacred Law in Cairo until his death.

Al-Tirmidhi, Abu Isa Muhammad bin Isa (824-892)

He was a student of Al-Bukhari and compiled 4,000 Ahadith in his book called Al-Jami', which later came to be known as *Sunan at-Tirmidhi*. Although this contains far fewer traditions than those of Bukhari or Muslim, it is also less repetitious. He also contributed tremendously to the methodology of Hadith and composed a book on it called *al-'Illal* (the discrepancies). He was famous for his piousness and asceticism. It is said that he was born blind but also that he lost his eyesight in later years.

APPENDIX J

SHORT HISTORICAL CHRONOLOGY OF ISLAM

c. 570*	52 years before Hijra	Birth of Muhammad(s)
c. 595	27 years before Hijra	Marriage of Muhammad(s) to Khadija
610	12/13 years before Hijra	Muhammad(s)'s call to be a prophet and the beginning of the revelations of Qur'an
620	2 years before Hijra	Isra (night journey) and Miraj or ascension of Muhammad(s)
		Prayers five times daily made obligatory during Miraj
		Year of Sorrow: Uncle Abu Talib and wife Khadijah died
622	July 15/16 Start of Hijra	The Hijra or "emigration" of Muhammad(s) and his followers from Makkah to Madinah, which marked the founding of the *Umma* and the beginning of the Islamic

		lunar calendar
624	2 years after Hijra	Battle of Badr Adhan and Zakah introduced Revelation about the change of *Qiblah* Ramadan prescribed
26	4th year of Hijra	Order of Hijab (Veil) for women revealed Revelation about the Prohibition of drinking wine
630	8 years after Hijra	Muhammad(s)'s conquest of Makkah and the rededication of the *Kaaba* sanctuary as a purely Islamic worship center
631	10th year of Hijra	Farewell Address, 9 Dhu'l-Hijjah
632	11 years after Hijra	Muhammad(s)'s death; election of Abu Bakr(r) as Caliph
632-656	10-34 years after Hijra	First four caliphs (*Khulafaye* and *Rashidin*)
650	28 years after Hijra	Written text of Qur'an established

*The Prophet's biographers differ about the exact year of his birth. Some have taken it to be 570 C.E., and others 569 C.E. Shibli Nu'mani, in Siratun Nabi, puts it as 571 C.E.

GLOSSARY

(Unless otherwise indicated the words are Arabic)

Adab. The term has a wide connotation of meanings. In its practical aspect aspect, it can refer to qualities necessary for proper personal behavior, upbringing and mode of conduct of daily life and social interaction.

Ahkam. "Orders." According to Islamic law, there are five kinds of orders: (1) compulsory (Fard); (2) order without obligation (Mustahab); (3) forbidden (Muharram); (4) disliked but not forbidden (Makruh); (5) legal and allowed (Halal).

Ahal al-Bayt. "People of the House." This is a term given to the family of the Prophet (s). Among the Shia it is applied to the Prophet, his daughter Fatima, her husband Ali, and their children Hasan and Husayn.

Ahal al-Kitab. The People of the book (ahl al-kitab) are those to whom a sacred book has been revealed by God; the Qur'an names the Jews, Christians and Sabians. According to some, Zoroastrians also fall into this category.

'Alim. See 'Ulama.

Ansar. The original residents of Madinah who, after embracing Islam, helped those Muslims who had migrated from Makkah under the instructions of the Holy Prophet (s).

Aqiqah. It is the sacrificing of two sheep or goats for a boy and one sheep or goat for a girl on the occasion of the birth of a child, as a token of gratitude to Allah. It is also a ceremony of shaving the head of a baby on the seventh day after its birth and naming the baby.

Al-Aqsa Masjid or Masjid al-Aqsa. "The Furthest Mosque" or "the Furthest Sanctuary." This is the name given to one of Islam's holiest mosques, traditionally regarded as having been built by 'Abd al-Malik b. Marwan, which stands on the Temple Square in Jerusalem. The name of the mosque, al-Masjid al Aqsa, derives from Surah al-Isra in the Qur'an.

'Arafah or 'Arafat. Plain about 13 miles from Makkah, which is a major focal point of the Hajj. On the ninth day of the Islamic month of Dhul-Hajja, pilgrims make a solemn "staying" (wuquf) at 'Arafah and a special sermon is preached. If the wuquf at 'Arafah is omitted, the entire pilgrimage is considered to be invalid. Legend derives the name 'Arafah or 'Arafat from the encounter and mutual recognition between Adam and Eve at this place after they were expelled from Paradise and initially separated.

'Ashurah. Literally the "tenth". A nafle fast day, observed on the tenth of the month of Muharram. Prophet Muhammad (s) observed it, and said it was a day respected by Jews and Christians (ref. *Mishkat*). Shii Muslims commemorate the day as the day of martyrdom of Imam Husayn at Karbala.

Awliyah. A word (sing., wali), referring to Muslim individuals who, through their devotion and spirituality, have become reference points for others. In mystical and devotional literature, they are referred to as "friends of God."

Glossary

Ayat. The term for a verse of Qur'an; it also denotes the "signs" in the natural order and prophetic story by which mankind is alerted to the truths of God.

Ayat al-Kursi. The Throne Verse: one of the most famous and beloved of the verses of the Qur'an, frequently recited as a protection against harm or evil. It is v. 255 of Surah al-Baqara.

Basmala. The formula bismillahir rahman ar rahim. Also called Tasmiyah.

Bida'a. Lit. A novelty and "innovation" in religion. Denotes all things, ideas and usage were not in practice during the life time of Prophet (s) or early generations of Muslims. A bida'a when does not contradict Qur'an and Sunnah is known as bida' al-hasana whereas, when it goes against their principle it is known as sayyiah.

Black Stone or al-Hajar al-Aswad. Stone built into the outside wall of the Kaaba at Makkah, in the Eastern corner, a little above the ground. Formerly broken into three pieces and several fragments, it is now held together by a ring of stone mounted in a silver band. The surface is hollowed out irregularly. Its diameter is around 30 cm., and its color is reddish black with red and yellow particles. In 930 it was carried off by the Carmathians who sent it back in 950. According to popular Islamic legend, the stone was given to Adam on his fall from paradise and was originally white but has become black by absorbing the sins of the pilgrims who have kissed and touched it. The stone is sometimes described as lava or basalt, but its real nature is difficult to determine because its visible surface is worn smooth by touching and kissing.

Circumcision. Arabic: Khitan, Khitanah or Khatnah. The practice of circumcision of male children, while not mentioned in the Qur'an, is generally accepted as being in accord with Prophetic practice. Most modern Muslims oppose and condemn female circumcision, which they argue represents historically an indigenous custom in some parts of the world to which Islam has spread, but one which has no Islamic sanction.

Dar al-Islam. Land of Islam. It is a country in which Islamic laws are fully promulgated In Dar al-Islam, the citizenry abide by the ordinances, rules, edicts, and assembly of Islam. The Muslim state guarantees the safety of life, property and religious status (only if the religion is not idolatrous) of minorities (ahl al-dhimma), provided they have submitted to Muslim control.

Daw'a. Invitation or call. In the Qur'an and by certain Muslim groups, it came to signify a call to others to return to the straight path or to the practice of true Islam.

Dhikr. "Remembering" God, reciting the names of God; a religious service common to all the mystical fraternities, performed either solitarily or collectively.

Din. The core meaning of din is obedience. As a Qur'anic technical term, din refers to the way of life and the system of conduct based on recognizing God as one's sovereign and committing oneself to obey Him. According to Islam, true din consists of living in total submission to God, and the way to do so is to accept as binding the guidance communicated through the Prophets.

Du'a. Appeal, invocation (addressed to God) either on behalf of another or for oneself, or against someone; hence, prayer of invocation.

Glossary

Durud. A benediction. A Persian word for Blessings on the Prophet (s). In Arabic it is as-Salat or Salla 'ala Nabi.

Fard. Something which has been apportioned, or made obligatory; as a technical term in religious law, is a religious duty or obligation, the omission of which will be punished and the performance of which will be rewarded.

Fatwa. This is a formal opinion rendered by a Muslim scholar having appropriate status and training. Such opinions may be sought from scholars who are known as mufti in the Sunni tradition and as mujtahid among the Shia, but are not necessarily binding. The practice of issuing a fatwa has continued in modern times as a mechanism for dealing with personal, social, legal and religious issues.

Fiqh. This is the science of jurisprudence, including its logic, methodology and applicability. The composite body of law produced by the science is referred to as Sharia. An expert in jurisprudence is called a faqih (pl. fuqaha).

Fitnah. A significant term meaning hostility, overt or covert, to Islam and Muslims.

Hadith. Literally means communication or narration. In the Islamic context it has come to denote the record of what the Prophet (peace be on him) said, did or tacitly approved.

Hadith Qudsi. A sacred, or holy, tradition. This is the name given to a tradition which records God's own utterances as opposed to those of the Prophet Muhammad (s).

Hadrat. Presence, dignity, a title applied to any great person.

Halal. The Qur'anic term for that which is lawful or allowed. In general, it connotes that which is appropriate for use or practice and in particular refers to the permitted categories of food and drink. Halal food includes the meat of permitted animals that have been ritually slaughtered, hunted game over which the divine name has been invoked and praised, fish and marine life.

Hanafi. Referring to the Sunni legal madhhab ascribed to Abu Hanifah (699-767).

Hanbali. Referring to the Sunni legal madhhab ascribed to Ahmad ibn Hanbal (780-855).

Haram. The Arabic word indicates an area of a particularly sacred nature. Examples include Makkah and Madinah, both of which are forbidden to non-Muslims.

Haram. That which is forbidden and unlawful, also sinful.

Al-Haram al-Sharif. The Noble Sanctuary. This is the third holiest sanctuary in Islam after Makkah and Madinah. Situated in the Temple area of Jerusalem, the Haram contains, inter alia al-Aqsa Mosque, and the Qubbat al-Sakhra.

Hashr. (lit., gathering) Signifies the Islamic doctrine that, with the blowing of the second Trumpet, all those who were ever created will be resurrected and will be brought forth to the Plain where all will be made to stand before God for His judgment.

Hijab. Veil. Worn by many Muslim women. The Qur'an enjoins women to dress modestly. The extent of veiling, and the size of the veil, varies from Muslim country to country in accordance with local custom. It may be a plain piece of cloth or

Glossary

highly colored and decorated, again depending on both local custom and the wish of the wearer.

Hijra. Signifies migration from a land where a Muslim is unable to live according to the precepts of his faith to a land where it is possible to do so. The hijrah par excellence for Muslims is the hijrah of the Prophet (s) and his Companions to Madinah in 622 C.E. This provided not only refuge from persecution, but also an opportunity to build a society and state according to the ideals of Islam.

'Ibadah (pl 'Ibadat). Worship, devotional action, observance required by the Islamic faith, e.g., salat or any other ritual enjoined by Islamic law. All actions of a person which are in accordance with the will of God and intended for His pleasure are regarded as Ibadat.

Iblis. The Devil. Made out of fire, he was cast down by God for refusing, alone of all the angels, to bow down and acknowledge God's new creation Adam, who was made out of clay. He also asked God to allow him a term during which he might mislead and tempt mankind to error. The term was granted to him by God, where after he became the chief promoter of evil and prompted Adam and Eve to disobey God's order. He is also called al-Shaytan (Satan).

Ijma'. Refers to the consensus of eminent scholars (mujtahidun) of Islam in a given age. Ijma' comes next to the Qur'an and the Sunnah as a source of Islamic doctrine.

Imam. Leader of mosque prayers, or the leader of the Muslim community. Among Sunnis, any great alim might be called imam. Among Shias, one of the twelve successors of the

Prophet, descended from Ali, the legitimate leaders of the Muslim community.

It'ikaf. Seclusion in a mosque for the purpose of worshipping Allah only during the last ten days of the month of Ramadan.

Jibril. He is one of the greatest of all the Islamic angels since he was the channel through which the holy Qur'an was revealed from God to the Prophet Muhammad (s).

Jinn. Genie. This is one of the classes of beings created by God. Whereas humankind was created of clay and divine spirit and angels out of light, the jinn are created out of smokeless fire.

Kaffarah. Making atonement (amends for uttering or committing an unlawful act in Islam.

Kafir. He who does not believe in God or His Prophets or in any of the Articles of Faith.

Khutbah. Sermon, address; in particular, the sermon delivered during the Friday prayer in the mosque and Eid prayer in open field in good weather.

Lailat al-Mi'rāj. The night of the Ascension (of the Prophet Muhammad (s)) on the 27th of the Muslim month of Rajab. In its Persian form, it is known in Iran, Afghanistan and South Asian countries and communities as Shab-i Mi'raj (meaning of the word shab being night.)

Lailat al-Qadr. The Night of Power (or Decree) which is believed to be the night between the 21st and 29th of Ramadan, or the 27th night. The Night has a very special significance in the Muslim calendar because it is the anniversary of that night

Glossary

when the Qur'an was first revealed to the Prophet Muhammad (s). In Surah al-Qadr, this Night is described as "better than 1000 months." Tradition holds that requests made to God during Laylat al-Qadr will be granted. In its Persian form, it is known in Iran, Afghanistan and South Asian countries and communities as Shab-i Qadr (meaning of the word shab being night.)

Madhhab. One of the four equally legitimate schools of law among Sunni Muslims : Hanafi, Maliki, Hanbali and Shafi'i. (For details, see text in the Sunnah section.)

Madrasah. A school designed for religious education, usually associated with a mosque in Non-Arab countries. In Arab countries any school is a madrasah.

Maliki. Referring to the Sunni legal Madhhab ascribed to Malik b. Anas (715-795 A.D.).

Masjid. Place of prostration, of worship, mosque. Another name, jami', was originally reserved for a mosque in which the Friday prayer was said.

Mawlana. "Our Lord." South Asian 'ulama assume this title as an Arabic equivalent of Shaikh.

Muhajirun. A term used for those of the first converts to Islam who migrated with, before or after Prophet (s) and later made up a considerable portion of the population of Madinah.

Mujaddid. A reformer commissioned to remove errors that have crept in among the Muslims, and to shed new light on the great religious truths of Islam in the new circumstances which the Muslim community will be called upon to face.

Mukabbir. One who pronounces loudly Takbir, etc., following Imam.

Muttaqi. Pious and righteous person who fears Allah.

Na'at. A melodic recitation of devotional verse about the Prophet Muhammad (s) in Arabic and other languages.

Naqsabandi. A Sufi path of those initiated into a chain of succession of Baha'u'd-Din Naqshbandi (d. 1389), the mujdaddidi (mujaddidi) branch has initiation from Shaikh Ahmad Sarhindi, called the mujaddid, of the second millennium.

Nation of Islam. The name used to describe a group of African Americans who have converted to Islam through the teachings of Elijah Muhammad. The name is currently retained by the followers of Louis Farrakhan.

Qada. Missed or lost prayer or fast, postponed.

Qibla. Direction of prayer towards the Kaaba in Makkah.

Rabb. Has at least three meanings: (I) Lord and Master; (ii) Sustainer, Provider, Supporter, Nourisher, Guardian, (iii) Sovereign and Ruler, He who controls and directs. God is Rabb in all the three meanings of the term.

Sadaqat al-Fitr or Zakat al-Fitr. Compulsory amount paid by the head of a household at the end of the fast of Ramadan for the benefit of the poor.

Sahaba. Companions of the Prophet (s), a title originally given to the men belonging to Muhammad (s)'s immediate entourage and having participated with him in battle. Gradually the term

Glossary

extended to every Muslim who personally met the Prophet (s) and ranges in an hierarchical system of 13 categories, the most important of which are: the first four Caliphs; the six persons to whom the Prophet (s) promised Paradise; the Muhajirin and the Ansars. The Companions played a very important role in the development of the religious system. On their witnessing of the sayings and acts of the Prophet (s), the principal foundation of Islam was built.

Shafi'i. One of the four Sunni schools of law, founded by Imam al-Shafii (d. 820). Preeminent in Southeast Asia, Egypt, Syria and the Hijaz.

Shaikh. (lit., "old man") Chief of a tribe; any religious leader; in particular, an independent sufi "master" in a position to guide disciples in his sufi way.

Shariah. (lit., "the way") The moral and legal code of Islam. The two main sources of it are the Qur'an and the Sunnah.

Shirk. Idolatry, polytheism. This is a heinous sin that is condemned in the Qur'an. The Arabic word means literally "sharing": man is forbidden to share his worship of God with that of any other creatures, and to ascribe partners to God as sharers of His Divinity. Polytheism is the one sin which the Qur'an tells us cannot and will not be forgiven. This is because it denies God's very existence.

Sunnah. (lit., "path") This is the term used for the customs, actions and sayings of the Prophet, later documented and collected into an enormous body of material which constitutes a model upon which Muslims pattern their lives.

Sunni. (lit.;, from ahl al-sunna, "people of the Sunna") This is the large, majority group in Islam. Sometimes described as "orthodox." Sunnis consider themselves traditionalists whose self-definition grew out of their emphasis on the Qur'an and the Hadith in the development of their four Schools of Law (the Hanafi, the Hanbali, the Maliki and the Shafii). Sunnis recognize the first four caliphs as legitimate rulers and successors to the Prophet.

Sufi. The term used for those who have chosen the path of mystical understanding and devotion to God. Sufism is the dimension of Islamic spirituality.

Shura. Consultation, a process whereby rulers, scholars and others develop a means of consulting with each other on important decisions.

Surah. A chapter of the Qur'an.

Sutra. A symbolic barrier put in front a person offering prayer so that others can pass.

Tafsir. Exegesis, interpretation, commentary, especially relating to the Qur'an. Classical Qur'anic tafsir concentrated on such matters as grammar, identification or provision of proper names, textual ambiguities, provision of more information on central characters, lexicography, philology, etc., all with the intention of clarifying the Qur'anic words themselves.

Takbir. The expression "Allahu Akbar" meaning "Allah is the Greatest." In other words, takbir means magnifying the greatness of God.

Glossary

Takbir at-Tahrima. The utterances of takbir at the opening of prayers is so named. The words tahrim or ihram mean prohibition. This particular name is given to this takbir because with this utterance, attention to everything other than prayer is prohibited.

Taqdir. Predestination. The Qur'ān contains verses which may be interpreted in favor of both free will and predestination.

Taqwa. The fundamental Muslim quality of "awe" before God, piety, duty, devoted avoidance of evil.

Tasbih. Glorifying God with subhanallah (for explanation, see under "Symbolism" in the section "Manners . . .").

Tasmiyah see **Basmala**

Taurat. The title given in the Qur'ān (3:3), and Islamic works in general, for the Books of Moses.

Tawbah. Repentance. The Arabic verb taba, said of a man, indicates "to repent"; when it is said of God, it means "to forgive." Polytheism (shirk) is the only sin which will not be forgiven. Otherwise, those who turn to God in repentance will be forgiven.

Tawhid. Unity of God (absolute monotheism), absolute sovereignty over the universe.

'Ulama. One who knows, a learned man. Title given to the scholars of Muslim theology and canon law. There are several recognized categories of ulama: (1) faqih, an expert in jurisprudence; (2) mufti, a legal expert, sometimes but not always acting in an official capacity, whose rendered opinion (fatwa) is not legally binding but carries considerable authority; (3) Quadi, Judge appointed by a political leader whose opinions are binding. the term mujtahid is often used for such scholars among the Shia.

Wahabi. A movement of religious reform in Islam, created by Muhammad ibn Abdul Wahhabi in the middle of the seventeenth century. It is essentially based on the teachings of Imam Ahmad ibn Hanbal and a famous Hanbali scholar, Ahmad ibn Taymiyah, who both stood for literal adherence to Qur'an and Sunnah as the sole valid source of religious and moral law. It aimed at the return to the original, pure faith and the restoration of the simplicity and austerity in public and private life in conformance with the example set by the Prophet (s) and the first caliphs. Wahhabis proscribes the cult of saints and the veneration of their tombs or any other shrines.

Actually there is no Wahabism or Wahabi in existence. Nowhere in the world Muslims call them as Wahabi although they call them as Hanafi, Maliki, Hanbali or Shafi'i. It is the British colonial masters who pubicised and emphasised it to such an extent that there were even Wahabi trials in British India. The flag of anti-wahabi propaganda is now being carried on by the Jewish and Christian orientalists and missionaries. Actually Abdul Wahab's mission was to eradicate shirk in any from (see discussion in the text) bid'a from the Muslim society and bring back pristine form of Islam as practiced during the time of the Prophet (s) and his Sahabis.

Ummah (lit., "people") This term occurs many times in the Qur'an to refer to people of a religious community, such as the "umma of Ibrahim." The word has come to represent the concept of the Muslim community as a whole.

BIBLIOGRAPHY

Primary Sources

(For other references and abbreviations see pp. xv-xvi.)

Abdalati, Hammudah
  Islam in Focus. Indianapolis: American Trust Publications, 1975. 200 pp.

`Abd-al-Baqi, M. Fuad
  Al-Mu'jam al-Mufarhas li-Aftaz al-Qur'ān al-Karim bi hāshiyah al-Mushaf al-Sharîf. (Complete text in Arabic) Beirut: Dar al-Ma`arifah, 1994. 950 pp.

Ahmad, Anis
  Prayers of the Holy Prophet. Trans. by M. Abdul Hamid Siddiq. 3rd. ed.. New Delhi: Kitab Bhavan, 1992. 63 pp.

Armstrong, Karen
  A History of God: the 4,000-Year Quest of Judaism, Christianity and Islam. New York: Ballantine, 1993. 460 pp.

Ali, Muhammad
  The Religion of Islam: A Comrehensive Discussion of the Sources, Principles and Practices of Islam. Columbus, Ohio: Ahmadiya Anjuman Ishaat, 1990. 617 pp.

Ashraf, Sh. Muhammad
Salat, or Islamic Prayer Book (illustrated). Lahore: Sh. Muhammad Ashraf, 1971. 49 pp.

Badawi, Jamal A
Selected Prayers: A Collection of Dua from the Quran and Sunnah. Indianapolis: Islamic Teaching Center, 1979. 77 pp.

Bassiouni, M. Cherif
Introduction to Islam. Chicago: Rand McNally, 1988. 72 pp.

Dhakariya, Muhammad
The Virtues of Salat: An English translation of Fadail-i-Namaz (a book in Urdu). Lyallpur: Malik Brothers, 1973. 111 pp.

Encyclopedia of Islam. New ed. Leiden: E. J. Brill, 1965-1998. v. 1- 10..

Encyclopedia of Religion. New York: Macmillan, 1987. 16 vols.

Fakir, Abu Bakr
Manual of Prayer and Fasting (including relevant devotions). Cape, South Africa: Al Jaamia Institute of Islamic Studies, 1978. 535 pp.

Farid, Abdul Hamid
Prayers of Muhammad: the Messenger of God; with an epitome of the teachings of Islam. Lahore: Sh. Muhammad Ashraf, 1969. 263 pp.

Al-Faruqi, Ismail R. & Al-Faruqi, Lois Lamyaa
The Cultural Atlas of Islam. New York: Macmillan, c. 1986. 512 pp.

Bibliography

al-Ghazzali, Abu Hamid bin Muhammad bin Muhammad
Book of the Ihya on the Worship. Trans. by Rev. Edwin Elliot Calverley. Westport, Conn: Hyperion Press.

Al-Ghazzali, Abu Hamid bin Muhammad bin Muhammad
Worship in Islam; being a translation, with commentary and introduction of al-Ghazzali's book of the Ihya on the worship. By the Rev. Edwin Elliot Calverley. Westport, Conn.: Hyperion Press, 1981.
242 pp.

Haider, Syed Iftikhar
Al-salat in Qur'an (As-salat fil Qur'an). Lahore: Institute of Islamic Culture, 1991. 267 pp.

Haneef, Susanne
What Everyone Should Know About Islam and Muslims. Chicago: Kazi Publications, 1979. 202 pp.

Haykal, Muhammad Husayn
The Life of Muhammad. ; translated from the 8th ed. by Islmail Ragi A.al –Faruqi. Indianapolis: .North American Trust Publications, c1976. 639 pp.

Ibn al-Naqib, Ahmad ibn Lu`lu' (d. 1368)
Reliance of the Traveller: The Classic Manual of Islamic Sacred Law 'Umdat al-salik (in Arabic with facing English text, commentary, and appendices edited and translated by Nuh Ha Mim Keller. – rev. ed. Evanston, Ill. Sunna Books, 1994. 1232 pp.

Ibn Qayyim al-Jawziyyah, Muhammad ibn Abi Bakr
Patience and Gratitude.; an abridged translation of *Uddat as-Sabirin wa dhakhirat ash-Shakirin* ; translated by Nasiruddin al-Khattab. London: Ta-Ha Publishers, 1997. 75 pp.

Imran, Muhammad
Salat-ul-Tahajjud. Lahore: Kazi Publications, 1984. 165 pp.

Jeffery, Arthur
Islam; edited by Arthur Jeffery. New York: Liberal Arts Press, 1958. 252 pp.

Jeffery, Arthur
Reader on Islam:. passages from standard Arabic writings illustrative of the beliefs and practices of Muslims ; compiled and edited by Arthur Jeffery.Gravenhage: Mouton & Co., 1962. 678 pp.

Kazi, Mazhar U.
All About Salat; compiled by Mazhar U[ddin] Kazi. New York: Message Publications, 1993. 70 pp.

Mawdudi, Abul A'la
Let Us be Muslims.; edited and translated by Khurram Murad. Leicester, U.K: The Islamic Foundation, 1982. 311 pp.

Nadwi, S. Abdul Hasan Ali
The Musalman.; translated by Muhiuddin Ahmad. Lucknow: Academy of Islamic Research & Publications, 1972.

Oxford Encyclopedia of the Modern Islamic World. John L. Esposito, Editor-in-Chief. New York: Oxford University Press, 1995. 4 vols.

Bibliography

Padwick, Constance E
Muslim Devotions: a Study of Prayer Manuals in Common Use. London: S.P.C.K., 1961. 313 pp.

Qur'ān. *The Holy Quran*: English Translation of the Meanings and Commentary. Revised and edited by The Presidency of Islamic Researches, IFTA, Call and Guidance. Madinah: Saudi Arabia: King Fahd Holy Quran Printing Complex, 1411 A. H. 2082 pp.

Qur'ān. *Interpretation of the meanings of the Noble Quran in the English language*: a summarized version of at-Tabari, al-Qurtubi, and Ibn Kathir with comments from Sahib al-Bukhari, summarized in one volume by Muhammad Taqi-ud-Din al-Hilali and Muhammad Muhsin Khan. 4th rev. and enl. ed. Riyadh, Saudi Arabia: Maktaba Dar-Us-Salam, 1994. 1098 pp.

Qur'ān. *The Meaning of the Glorious Qur'an*: Text and Explanatory Translation, by Muhammad M. Pickthall. Makkah: Muslim World League, 1977. 768 pp.

Qur'ān. *The Message of The Quran*; translated and explained by Muhammad Asad. Gibraltar: Dar Al- Andalus, 1984. 998 pp.

Saqib, M. A. Karim
A Guide to Prayer in Islam; edited by M. A. Karim Saqib. 2nd ed. London: Ta- Ha, 1986. 78 pp.

Al-Sawwaf, Shaikh Muhammad Mahmud
The Muslim Book of Prayer.; translated into English by Mujahid Muhamnmad Al-Sawwaf. Makkah al-Mukarramah: Mujahid Muhamnmad Al-Sawwaf, 1977. 70 pp.

Shad, Abdul Rahman
The Prescribed Islamic Prayer: Salat ; compiled by Abdul Rahman Shad ; revised by Abdul Hameed Siddiqi. Lahore: Qazi Publications, 1979. 118 pp.

Thanvi, Ashraf Ali
Heavenly Ornaments; being English Translation of Ashraf Ali Thanvi's Bahisti Zewar. Lahore: Sh. Muhammad Ashraf, 1981. 483 pp.

Umm Muhammad
Realities of Faith. Jeddah; Abdul Qasim Publishing House, 1994. 89 pp.

Zeno, Muhammad bin Jamil
The Pillars of Islam and Iman: And What Every Muslim Must Know About His Religion. Trans. of Arkan al-Islam wal-Iman. Riyad: Dar-us-Salam Publications, 1996. 264 pp.

Zepp, Ira G
A Muslim Primer: Beginner's Guide to Islam. Westminster, Md.: Wakefield Editions, 1992. 292 pp

al-Zujuri, M.
Hisne Hasin (Bengali) Trans. by Abdul Hai. Dhaka: Muhammadi Library, n. d. 448 pp.

INDEX OF THE QUR'ANIC VERSES

Sûrahs: Verses	Pages
1: Sûrah al- Fātihah	
1: 1	10
1: 1-7	306
2: Sûrah al- Baqarah	
2: 2	15
2: 4	3
2: 25	222
2: 28	8
2: 29	226
2: 30	68
2: 31	372
2: 43	54, 185, 186
2: 74	71
2: 82	221
2: 83	54, 221, 243
2: 86	258, 278
2: 92	223
2: 110	54, 185
2: 112	4
2: 115	8, 102
2: 127	285
2: 128	320
2: 131	86
2: 132	263
2: 136	16, 372
2: 152	183
2: 155	240
2: 156	240
2: 157	240
2: 163	11, 64
2: 164	8
2: 168	226
2: 172	241
2: 173	230, 231
2: 177	54, 110, 185, 223, 238, 248, 250
2: 183	189
2: 185	16, 155, 189
2: 186	133, 190
2: 187	193
2: 188	190, 233
2: 190	76
2: 195	54
2: 196	205, 250
2: 201	319
2: 215	54
2: 216	77
2: 222	11, 241
2: 224	258
2: 228	268
2: 229	268, 269
2: 230	268
2: 231	268
2: 232	268
2: 233	268

Sûrahs: Verses	Pages	Sûrahs: Verses	Pages
2: 239	54	3: 156	8
2: 255	8, 177, 305, 335	3: 157	78
		3: 158	78
2: 256	85	3: 159	11, 173
2: 263	243	3: 172	78
2: 271	188	3: 185	275
2: 275	54, 218	3: 190	8, 23
2: 276	54	3: 191	182, 323
2: 277	222	3: 193	323
2: 278	54	3: 194	324
2: 284	8		
2: 285	54, 320		
2: 286	321		

4: Sûrah al-Nisã'

Verse	Page
4: 1	265

3: Sûrah Ali 'Imrãn

Verse	Page
3: 3	395
3: 7	219
3: 16	322
3: 17	87, 240
3: 19	3, 86
3: 26	307
3: 27	308
3: 29	8
3: 31	11
3: 64	68
3: 76	11
3: 92	187
3: 97	197, 251
3: 102	265
3: 104	215, 216
3: 114	222
3: 115	222
3: 130	54
3: 144	32
3: 145	276
3: 146	11
3: 151	70

Verse	Page
4: 3	266
4: 9	243
4: 17	173
4: 18	173
4: 26	8, 233
4: 27	233
4: 28	233
4: 29	233
4: 34	8
4:35	268
4: 36	245
4: 37	245
4: 38	245
4: 40	11
4: 43	105, 110
4: 48	68
4: 58	233, 249
4: 59	42, 53
4: 74	278
4: 76	54
4: 77	54
4: 82	20
4: 101	155
4: 103	54
4: 118	359

Index of the Qur'anic Verses

Sûrahs: Verses	Pages
4: 119	359
4: 125	250
4: 129	267
4: 135	247
4: 136	54
4: 142	95
4: 145	252
4: 150	54
4: 151	54
4: 162	185
4: 164	372
4: 217	163

5: Sûrah al-Mã'idah

5: 2	xv
5: 3	32, 86, 87, 227
5: 4	227, 231
5: 6	103, 108, 241
5: 8	247
5: 13	12, 71
5: 15	15, 16
5: 16	16
5: 32	85
5: 42	12
5: 44	73
5: 54	10
5: 55	185
5: 72	70
5: 87	225, 227
5: 89	248
5: 90	253
5: 91	253
5: 95	195

6: Sûrah al-An'ãm

6: 3	8
6: 12	175
6: 13	8
6: 19	11
6: 54	250, 277
6: 70	277
6: 84	372
6: 95	8
6: 103	8
6: 151	232
6: 152	232
6: 153	291
6: 162	35

7: Sûrah al-A'rãf

7: 8	277
7: 9	277
7: 23	322
7: 29	276
7: 31	234
7: 32	227
7: 33	227
7: 35	224
7: 55	133
7: 65	372
7: 73	372
7: 85	67, 372
7: 143	324
7: 151	11
7: 156	175
7: 167	11
7: 180	363
7: 205	181

8: Sûrah al-Anfãl

8: 1	53
8: 2	61
8: 20	53
8: 24	53
8: 40	339

Sûrahs: Verses	Pages	Sûrahs: Verses	Pages
9: Sûrah al-Tawbah		14: 24	53
		14: 40	324
9: 20	78	14: 41	324
9: 34	186		
9: 40	27, 28	**15: Sûrah al-Hijr**	
9: 60	188		
9: 67	251	15: 20	10
9: 68	251	15: 23	8
9: 103	186, 188	15: 27	295
9: 108	241		
9: 112	357	**16: Sûrah al-Nahl**	
9: 119	237, 247		
9: 128	25	16: 18	23
		16: 22	11
10: Sûrah Yûnus		16: 23	8
		16: 64	42
10: 3	277	16: 72	264
10: 6	8	16: 89	23
10: 31	66	16: 90	245
		16: 91	245
11: Sûrah Hûd		16: 107	278
		16: 116	226
11: 1	23, 218	16: 125	78
11: 107	281		
11: 108	281	**17: Sûrah al-Isrā'**	
13: Sûrah al-Ra'd		17: 1	288, 289, 294
		17: 9	20
13: 11	217	17: 12	299
13: 14	70	17: 24	325
13: 28	71	17: 32	233, 254
13: 35	61, 279	17: 51	281
		17: 79	164
14: Sûrah Ibrahîm		17: 89	21
		17: 99	281
14: 3	278	17: 106	17
14: 7	241, 257		
14: 21	281		

Index of the Qur'anic Verses

Sûrahs: Verses	Pages
18: Sûrah al-Kahf	
18: 23	258
18: 24	258
18: 27	15, 22
18: 28	69, 239
18: 110	222
19: Sûrah Maryam	
19:56	372
20: Sûrah Tā Hā	
20: 4	8
20: 5	8
20: 6	8
20: 14	11, 94
20: 55	148
20: 82	174
20: 114	325
20: 132	94
21: Sûrah al-Anbiyā	
21: 4	8, 10
21: 26	10
21: 47	11, 277
21: 85	372
21: 87	339
22: Sûrah al-Hajj	
22: 31	68
22: 78	75, 86, 339

Sûrahs: Verses	Pages
23: Sûrah al-Mu'minûn	
23: 1	96, 132, 354
23: 2	132, 354
23: 3	354, 355
23: 4	354, 355
23: 5	354, 355
23: 6	354, 355
23: 7	354, 356
23: 8	354, 356
23: 9	96, 354, 356
23: 10	96, 354, 356
23: 11	96, 354, 357
23: 51	218, 229, 246
23: 91	11
23: 92	11
23: 94	325
23: 100	276
23: 101	277
23: 118	326
24: Sûrah al-Nûr	
24: 21	176, 361
24: 32	264
24: 33	266
24: 35	7, 122
25: Sûrah al-Furqān	
25: 12	280
25: 27	87
25: 32	17
25: 43	69
25: 44	69
25: 63	347
25: 64	347, 348
25: 65	347, 348

Sûrahs: Verses	Pages	Sûrahs: Verses	Pages
25: 66	347, 348	30: 31	94
25: 67	347, 348	30: 58	21
25: 68	347, 349		
25: 69	347, 349		

31: Sûrah Luqmãn

25: 70	176, 347, 349	31: 13	68
25: 71	347, 349	31: 14	243
25: 72	347, 349-350	31: 18	253
25: 73	347, 350	31: 34	276
25: 74	347, 350		
25: 75	347, 350		
25: 76	347, 350		

32: Sûrah al-Sajdah

32: 11	275
32: 17	279

26: Sûrah al-Shu'arã

26: 83	326
26: 227	181

33: Sûrah al-Ahzãb

27: Sûrah al-Naml

27: 60	12	33: 21	33, 42
27: 61	13	33: 35	81, 87, 247, 358
27: 62	13	33: 41	180
27: 63	13	33: 56	332
		33: 70	265
		33: 71	266

28: Sûrah al-Qasas

28: 77	250

34: Sûrah Saba

34: 22	69

29: Sûrah al-'Ankabût

35: Sûrah Fãtir

29: 8	243		
29: 43	21, 23, 219	35: 1	54
29: 45	94, 96	35: 6	360

30: Sûrah al-Rûm

36: Sûrah Yã-Sîn

30: 21	264, 268	36: 37	8
30: 22	68	36: 38	8

Index of the Qur'anic Verses

Sûrahs: Verses	Pages
36: 39	8
36: 40	8, 23
36: 60	360

37: Sûrah al-Saffāt

37: 1-5	11
37: 96	65

38: Sûrah al-Sād

38: 29	20
38: 65	11
38: 66	11
38: 67	11
38: 68	11

39: Sûrah al-Zumar

39: 3	252
39: 23	20, 219
39: 41	15, 20
39: 44	277
39: 53	10, 176
39: 62	65

40: Sûrah al-Ghāfir

40: 28	252
40: 60	22, 319
40: 78	372

41: Sûrah Fussilat

41: 33	246
41: 44	24

42: Sûrah al-Shûrā

42: 4	13
42: 5	13
42: 11	8, 66
42: 38	173
42: 40	249
42: 41	249
42: 42	249
42: 43	249

43: Sûrah al-Zukhruf

43: 13	336
43: 84	10
43: 85	10

44: Sûrah al-Dukhān

44: 3	163
44: 6	8

45: Sûrah al-Jāthiyah

45: 13	68
45: 18	39

46: Sûrah al-Ahqāf

46: 15	243, 326

47: Sûrah Muhammad

47: 4	78
47: 8	73
47: 19	57
47: 24	20, 24.

Understanding Islam and its Practices

Sûrahs: Verses   Pages

47: 33   54

48: Sûrah al-Fath

48: 29   57

49: Sûrah al-Hujurât

49: 11   216, 253
49: 12   216, 235, 252
49: 13   217, 242, 244
49: 14   60

50: Sûrah al-Qâf

50: 15   281

51: Sûrah al-Dhâriyât

51: 20   23
51: 21   23
51: 56   91, 278, 345

52: Sûrah al-Tûr

52: 28   133

53: Sûrah al-Najm

53: 18   293
53: 39   217
53: 40   217
53: 41   217

54: Sûrah al-Qamr

53: 32   23

Sûrahs: Verses   Pages

55: Sûrah al-Rahmãn

55: 2   20
55: 3   20
55: 4   20
55: 28   20

57: Sûrah al-Hadîd

57: 3   8

59: Sûrah al-Hashr

59: 10   154, 327
59: 22   12, 305, 308
59: 23   12, 305, 309
59: 24   12, 305, 309

62: Sûrah al-Jumu‘ah

62: 9   140
62: 10   142, 144

63: Sûrah al-Munâfiqûn

63: 9   181

64: Sûrah al-Taghâbun

64: 4   8
64: 14   249

65: Sûrah al-Talâq

65: 1   268
65: 2   268
65: 3   61

Index of the Qur'anic Verses

Sûrahs: Verses   Pages

68: Sûrah al-Munâfiqûn

64: 4   33

69: Sûrah al-Hâqqah

69: 18   277

70: Sûrah al-Ma'ârij

70: 19   351
70: 20   351
70: 21   351
70: 22   351
70: 23   351
70: 24   186, 352
70: 25   352
70: 26   352
70: 27   352
70: 28   352
70: 29   353
70: 30   353
70: 31   353
70: 32   353
70: 33   353
70: 34   96, 351, 354
70: 35   96, 351, 354

71: Sûrah al-Nûh

71: 28   327

73: Sûrah al-Muzzaammil

73: 4   22

Sûrahs: Verses   Pages

73: 6   166

76: Sûrah al-Insân

76: 25-26   181
76: 26   181

78: Sûrah al-Naba'

78: 21   280

83: Sûrah al-Mutaffifîn

83: 1   218
83: 2   218
83: 3   218

87: Sûrah al-A'lâ

87: 15   94
87: 16   278

91: Sûrah al-Shams

91: 9   21

92: Sûrah al-Lyl

92: 13   8
92: 18   185, 186

94: Sûrah al-Sharh

94: 4   33

Sûrahs: Verses	Pages
95: Sûrah al-Tîn	
95: 8	8
96: Sûrah al-'Alaq	
96: 1	26
96: 2	26
96: 3	26
96: 4	26
96: 5	26
97: Sûrah al-Qadr	
97: 1	163, 310
97: 2	163, 310
97: 3	163, 310
97: 4	163, 310
97: 5	163, 310
98: Sûrah al-Bayyinah	
98: 5	188
103: Sûrah al-'Asr	
103: 1	239, 311
103: 2	239, 247, 311
103: 3	239, 247, 311
107: Sûrah al-Mâ'ûn	
107: 1	224
107: 2	224
107: 3	224
107: 4	224
107: 5	224
107: 6	224
107: 7	224
108: Sûrah al-Kawthar	
108: 1	312

Sûrahs: Verses	Pages
108: 2	94, 312
108: 3	312
109: Sûrah al-Kafirûn	
109: 1	313
109: 2	313
109: 3	313
109: 4	313
109: 5	313
109: 6	313
110: Sûrah al-Nasr	
110: 3	328
112: Sûrah al-Ikhlâs	
112: 1	10, 63, 314
112: 2	10, 63, 314
112: 3	10, 63, 314
112: 4	10, 63, 314
113: Sûrah al-Falaq	
113: 1	316
113: 2	316
113: 3	316
113: 4	316
113: 5	316
114: Sûrah al-Nâs	
114: 1	317
114: 2	317
114: 3	317
114: 4	317
114: 5	317
114: 6	317

GENERAL INDEX

A

Aaron see Harun
Abbreviations xiv, xxiii
'Abd-Allah 91
'Abdul Wahab, Muhammad ibn 48, 396
'Abdullah bin 'Abbas 142
'Abdullah bin 'Umar 142
Ablution 102, 105
Ablution, Dry 108-109
Ablution, how to perform 103-105
Ablution, nullification of 105
Ablution, special consideration of 106-108
Abraham see Ibrahim
Abu Bakr 26, 27, 32, 382
Abu Dawud xxiii, 43, 373
Abu Hanifah 9, 45, 46, 47, 49, 373
Abu Hurairah 143, 374
Abu Talib 26
Abyssinia 26, 27
Acceptance of prayer 132-133
Adab 383
Adam 371
Adhan 111-113
Adhan and Iqamah 111-115, 126
Adhan, conditions when should not be responded 113-114
Adhan, response to 113
After prayer supplication 176-178
After sunrise prayer 166-167
Ahadith xxiii

Ahkam 383
Ahl al-Bayt 383
Ahl al-Kitab 383
Akhirah 278
Al-Amin 25
Al-Azhar University 225
Al-Biruni 300
Al-Fatihah xvi, 127
Al-Ghazzali 19, 131, 144
'Alim see 'Ulama
Al-Isra 291
Allah xxiii, 7-13, 50
Allah, Supreme Being 13
Allah's love 11
Alms tax (obligatory) 185-188, 209, 210, 211, 218, 221
Al-Qardawi, Yusuf 225
Al-Razi, Fakhr al-Din 131
Al-Shaybani, Muhammad 47, 49
'Amal 53
Amnesty to Makkans 30
Analogy 50
Annual Congregation see Hajj
Ansar 383
Aqiqa 263, 384
Arafat 201-202, 384
Arkan al-Hajj 207
Arkan al-Salat 127
Arkan al-'Umrah 207
Arrogance 253
Ashura 300, 384
Asma' al-Husna 8, 363-370
'Asr Prayer 98, 100, 134, 136
Assalamu 'alaikum 117, 127, 258

Atonement see Tawbah
Attahiyat 124
Attributing partners to Allah 63, 67-71
Avecena see Ibn Sina
Awliyah 384
Ayat / Ayah 385
Ayat al-Kursi 176-177, 385
Ayyub 371
Azrail 275

B

Back biting 252
Badr, battle of 29
Baihaqi, Ahmad bin al-Husain 375
Basic elements of Salat 127
Basmala 255, 385
Bath 102
Bayt al-Mamur 286
Bayt-Allah 285
Belief 5, 7, 8
Belief in Allah 54
Belief in Angels 54
Belief in Divine Decree 54, 56
Belief in Qadr 54, 56
Belief in revealed Books 54, 55
Belief in the Day of Judgment 54, 56
Benevolence and generosity 250-251
Bid'ah 385
Al-Birr 223-224
Birth 263-264
Bismillah 255, 385
Black stone of Kaaba 385
Books of prayer xv-xvi
AL-Bukhari xxiii, 190, 43, 375-376
Burial ceremony 270

C

Calendar, Islamic 299-301
Caliphate 84
Call to Prayer 111-115
Charity tax (compulsory) 185-188
Chastity 266
Childhood 263-264
Christianity xvi, 3
Christians 26
Chronology 381-382
Circumcision 386
Cleanliness 241-242
Code of conduct 5
Compassion 250-251
Concentration in Prayer 131-132
Congratulatory greeting 257-258
Congregational prayer 129-131
Consensus 40
Covenant of Yathrib 28

D

Dar al-Islam 386
David see Dawud
Daw'a 386
Dawud 371
Day of Judgement 275-281
Death 278
Death of the Prophet (s) 32
Deceit and lying 252
Details of prayer 117-133
Dhikr 93-94, 386
Dhul Hazza 301
Dhul Qa'ada 301
Dhul-kiffl 371
Dhuhr prayer 98, 100, 134, 136
Din 386
Din (Religion) 39
Disbelief 63, 71-73
Disbelief, Major 72

General Index

Disbelief, Major 72
Disbelief, Minor 72-73
Disbelievers see Kafir
Divine blessings 21-22
Divorce 267-269
Dogmas xv
Drink 231
Drinking 253
Du`a 93-94, 319-330, 335-341, 386
Du`a and dhikr 93-94, 180-184
Dunya 278
Durud 260, 330-334, 387

E

Eid 144-148
Eid al-Adhha 203, 297
Eid al-Adha prayer 144, 145
Eid al-Fitr 297
Eid al-Fitr prayer 144, 145
Eid prayers 144-148
Eid Salat prerequisites 145
Eidgah 145
Elias 371
Enoch 371
Ezekiel see Dhul-kiffl
Ezra see Uzair

F

Faith 5, 8, 10
Faith in Allah 54
Faith in Angels 54
Faith in Messengers 54
Faith in Qadr 56
Faith in revealed Books 54, 55
Fajr prayer 98, 100, 134, 136
Fakir, Abu Bakr 47
Family 216-217
Family life 265

Fard 40, 387
Fard Salat 98, 117, 136
Farewell pilgrimage 30-32
Farewell sermon 30-32, 202
Fasting 189-195, 209, 210, 211,
Fasting in Muharram 195
Fasting in Sa`ban 195
Fasting in Sawwal 195
Fasting, compensatory 192
Fasting:, expiratory 195
Fasting of elderly persons 192
Fasting of feeding women 192
Fasting of pregnant women 192
Fasting, restriction on voluntary 195
Fasting: what breaks 193
Fasting :what does not breaks 193
Fasting: when prohibited 193
Fasting :who may not 192
Fatwa 387
Fazlur Rahman 223
Feasts and festivals 291-297
Fidayah 195
Fiqh xxvi, 41, 50, 51, 387
Fitnah 387
Five pillars of Islam 209-211
Food and drink 231
Food, permitted see Halal
Food, prohibited see Haram
Food, prohibited 232
Forbidden times of prayer 101
Forgiveness 249-250
Friday prayer 140-142
Friday prayer, conditions for 141-142
Friday sermon 142-143
Friday, virtue of 140
Fundamentals of `Umrah 207
Fundamentals of Hajj 207
Funeral prayer 148-153
Funeral service 271

G

Gabriel see Jibril
Gambling 253
General Institute of Islamic Culture 225
General nawafil salat 169-176
Generosity 250-251
Al-Ghazzali, Abu Hamid 376
Ghusl 102, 242
Gift of Allah 23
God xxi
God see Allah
Greater Jihad 76-77
Gregorian calendar 300

H

Hadith 41, 43-45, 50, 51, 387
Hadith al-Qudsi 44, 387
Hadith, subject matter of 44
Hadrat 387
Hajar 198, 200
Hajj 40, 85, 91, 197-205, 209
Hajj and 'Umrah 197-208
Hajj rituals 207
Hajj, fundamentals of 207
Halal 40, 92, 235, 388
Halal and Haram 225-235
Halal at-Tayyibah 231
Halal, principles of 226, 227-231
Hanafi school 45-46, 47, 49, 388
Hanbal, Ahmad bin 47-48, 49, 375
Hanbali school 45, 47-48, 49, 388
Haram 40, 92, 225, 226, 388
Haram al-Sharif 388
Haram, principles of 226, 231
Harun 371
Hashr 388
Hell 275, 280

Highlights of prayer 142-144
Hijab 388
Hijrah 27-28, 204, 388
Hijrah calendar 299-301
Hijrah year 299
Hira, cave of 26
Homosexuality 254
Honesty 248-249
Hud 371
Huffaz 16
Husain ibn Ali, Imam 300
Hypocrisy 251-252

I

'Ibadah xv, 5, 91-184, 205, 389
'Ibadat 389
Iblis 389
Ibn Hajar al-Asqalani 43
Ibn Majah 43, 377
Ibn Qayyim al-Jauziyah 47
Ibn Sina on prayer 345
Ibn Taymiyah 47, 377
Ibrahim (Prophet) 16, 198, 199, 285, 371
Idris 371
Iftar 191
Ihram 199, 201, 204
Ihram obligations 208
Ijma 40, 41, 50, 389
Ijtihad 40, 41, 50, 51
Ilias 371
Imam 121, 193, 389
Iman 5, 8, 10, 53-61
Iman al-Mufassal 58-59
Iman al-Mujmal 58
Immoral characteristics 251
Inna li-llah 259
Inquiry 50
Intention of ablution 103
Intention of prayer 116

General Index

Intercession 277-278
Invocation after Salat 178
Iqamah 114-115, 143, 263
Iqbal, Muhammad 82
Isa see Jesus
Isaac 16, 371
Isha prayer 98, 100, 134, 136
Ishaq 371
Islam 3-6
Islam as a way of life 221, 215-219
Islam, a definition 82
Islam, an American religion xvi,
Islam, Five pillars of 209211
Islam, meaning 3-4, 81-88
Islam, practical 53
Islam, theoretical 53
Islamic calendar 299-301
Islamic festivals 291-297
Islamic law 39-51
Islamic schools of law 45-49
Ismail (Prophet) 198, 199, 251, 371
Isnad 50, 51
Istithna 258
Italicize xxii
Itidal 116, 117
Itikaf 193, 390

J

Jackob 16, 371
Jama'ah prayer 129-130
Jami' Tirmidhi 43
Janajah prayer 148-149
Jannah 279
Jazak-Allah 259
Jesus 16, 26, 372
Jews 28
Jibril 15, 26, 110
Jihad 75-79

Jihad al-Akbar 76-77
Jihad al-Assghar 77-79
Jihad, lesser 77-79
Jihad, greater 76-77
Jinn 91
Job see Ayyub
John see Yahya
Joseph 371
Judaism xvi, 3
Julus 117
Jumada al-Akhir 301
Jumada al-Awwal 301
Jumu'ah prayer 134, 140-142

K

Kaaba 30, 199, 200, 206, 295, 115
Kaffarah 195, 390
Kafir 390
Kalimah Shahadah 56, 58, 270
Kalimah Tayyibah 53, 56
Karbala, battle of 300
Keeping promise 248-249
Khadijah 26
Khutba 142, 390
Kindness and compassion 250-251
Koran see Qur'an
Kufr 71-73
Kufr al-Akbar 72
Kufr al-Asghar 72

L

Last Prophet see Muhammad (s)
Last wish 269
Latecomer in congregation (Jama'ah) 130-131
Law, Islamic see Shariah
Lawful see Halal
Laylat al-Isra 291, 293-294

Laylat al-Miraj 291, 293-294, 390
Laylat al-Nisf Sa'ban 295
Laylat al-Qadr 190, 296, 390
League of Nations 28
Lesser Jihad 77-78
Life after death 275-281
Life, concept of 269-270
Lord's prayer xvi, 343
Lot see Lut
Lut 371
Lying 252

M

Madhhab 41, 45-49, 119, 391
Madinah 28, 30, 35, 287
Madrasah 84, 391
Maghrib prayer 98, 100, 134
Making up for missed salat 157-159
Makkah 25, 35, 198, 199, 203, 286-287
Makkah, conquest of 29
Makruh 40
Malik (Allah) 9
Malik, Imam 43, 44, 45, 46, 47, 49, 378
Maliki school 45, 46, 47, 49, 391
Man xxii
Mandub 40
Mankind 91
Manners 237-261
Marriage 264-266
Marwah see Safa wa Marwah
Masjid 391
Masjid al-Aqsa 288-289, 384
Masjid al-Haram 295
Masjid al-Nababi 286
Mawlana 391
Mawlid al-Nabi 36, 291, 292-293
Mi'raj 291

Millat see Din
Mina 200
Minbar 142
Mindset for prayer 110-111
Miqat 198
Mishkat xxvi
Mohammedan / Mohammedanism : misnomer 86-87
Monotheism 16
Morals 237-261
Moses 16, 26, 371
Muadhdhin 113
Muamalat 39
Mubah 40
Mughals 84
Muhajirun 391
Muhammad (s) 25-37, 86, 110, 371, 381-382
Muhammad (s) among the 100 33
Muharram 300
Muharram, fasting in 300
Mujaddid 391
Mujtahid 50
Mukabbir 392
Musa see Moses
Musalla 145
Muslim (Imam) 378
Muslim brotherhood 82-83
Muslim images 81-88
Muslim life cycle 263-271
Muslim, Imam 43
Muslim, Sahih xvi
Muslims 60, 81-88
Mustahab 40
Muttaqi 392
Muwatta xxv, 43, 46
Muzdalifa 202

General Index

N

Na`at 36, 392
Nafl see Nawafil
Naqsabandi 392
Nasai 43, 379
Nation of Islam 392
Nawafil Salat 98, 117, 159-160
Nawawi 379
New converts xvi
Night vigil prayer 99, 164-166
Ninety-nine names see Asma al-husna
Niyyah of prayer 116, 118, 126
Niyyah of Wudu 103
Noah 371
Non-Muslims xvi
Noon prayers see Dhuhr prayer
Nuh 371
Nullification of Ablution 105
Nullification of Wudu 105

O

Obligations during Ihram 208
Obligatory prayer 98
Obscenity 254
Oneness of God see Tawhid

P

Pagan 28
Paradise 221, 275, 279
Parents 242-243
Patience 237-238
Performance of prayer 135
Permitted and forbidden 225-235
Physical purity 109-110
Pilgrimage see also Hajj 197-208, 209, 210, 211
Pilgrimage, farewell 30-32
Pilgrimage, little 205-206
Polygamy 266-267
Polytheism 67-71
Polytheism, invisible 71
Polytheism, major 70
Polytheism, minor 70
Prayer : reasons of 96
Prayer : significance of 96-97
Prayer 91-184, 209, 210, 211, 221
Prayer: acceptance of 132-133
Prayer asking for Rain 99, 168-169
Prayer at Night of Ramadan 99, 160-164
Prayer behind Imam 121-124
Prayer books xv-xvi
Prayer for Repentance and Seeking Forgiveness 173-176
Prayer for Saluation for the Mosque 169
Prayer for the Guidance 171-173
Prayer in the Night of Power 99, 163
Prayer of Divine Glorification, 99 170-171
Prayer of Early morning 100
Prayer of Evening 100
Prayer of Noon 100
Prayer of Post ablution 99
Prayer of Repentance 99
Prayer of Salutation for Mosque 99
Prayer of Solar and Lunar Eclipse 99, 167-168
Prayer of Sunset 100
Prayer see also Salat
Prayer: concentration in 131-132
Prayer: conditions for the validity 126
Prayer: congregational 129-131
Prayer: details of 117-133

Prayer: direction, facing Kaaba 102
Prayer: forbidden times 101
Prayer: forms and parts of 115-135
Prayer: invalidation 127-128
Prayer: kinds of 97-99
Prayer: meaning of 94
Prayer: Obligatory 98
Prayer: Sunnah 98, 117
Prayer: Supererogatory 98
Private judgment 50
Profession, condemned 232-235
Promise, keeping of 248-249
Prophets of Allah 371
Prostration of forgetfulness 128-129
Purification 102-111
Purification of heart 109
Purification, Physical 109-110

Q

Qada 392
Qada Salat 156-157, 159
Qadar, night of 163
Qiblah 102, 111, 115, 126, 392
Qiyam 116, 119, 127
Qiyas 40. 50
Qunut 137-139
Qur'an 15-24, 50, 83, 85, 88
Qur'an a gift of Allah 23
Qur'an an unconventional book 17
Qur'an and Bible 20
Qur'an commentary 219
Qur'an memorization 16
Qur'an revelation 15
Qur'an subject matter 19
Qur'an translation 17, 21
Qur'an, a literary masterpiece 18-19
Qur'an, allegories in 17
Qur'an, devine blessing 21-22
Qur'an, division of 16
Qur'an, parables in 17
Qur'an, purifies souls 19-20
Qur'an, reading and recitation 20
Qur'anic description of pious Muslims 347-358
Qur'anic laws 42-43
Quraish 25, 26, 27, 29

R

Rab 9, 392
Rabi al-Akhir 301
Rabi al-Awwal 300
Rabubiyat 9-10, 65
Raddil kufr 59
Rahim 9
Rahm 9
Rahman 9
Rajab 301
Rakha in salat 134
Ramadan 189, 190, 193-194
Rami al-jumar 203
Ray 50
Reasoning, analytical 40
Reciting behind Imam 121-124
Religion 39
Resurrection 278
Revelation 6
Ridicule 253
Righteousness 221-224
Rituals 5
Rituals of Hajj 207
Riyadh al-Salihin xxiii
Rubay 36
Ruku` 116

General Index

S

Sabr 237-241
Sadaqat al-Fitr 392
Safa and Marwa 200
Sahaba 392-393
Sahih Bukhari 43
Sajdah 123, 127
Sajdah sahw 128-129
Sajdah tilawat 342
Salah see Salat
Salat 91-184, 209, 210, 217
Salat : Nawafil 98, 159-176
Salat : reasons of 96
Salat : significance of 96-97
Salat `ala al-Nabi 117
Salat ad-Dakhlil Masjid 99, 142, 169
Salat al-`Asr 98, 100, 134, 136
Salat al-`Isha 98, 100, 134, 136
Salat al-Dhuhr 98, 100, 134
Salat al-Duha 99, 166-167
Salat al-Fajr 98, 100, 136
Salat al-`Isha 100, 136
Salat al-Ishraq 99, 166-167
Salat al-Istikhara 171-173
Salat al-Istikharah 99
Salat al-Istisqa 99, 168-169
Salat al-Jama`ah 129-131
Salat al-Kasuf 99, 167-168
Salat al-Maghrib 98, 100, 134, 136
Salat al-Qasar 154-155
Salat al-Witr 136-139
Salat at-Tahajjud 99, 164-166
Salat at-Tahyat al-Wudu 99, 142, 169
Salat at-Tarawih 99, 160-162
Salat at-Tasbih 99, 170-171
Salat at-Tawbah 99, 173-176
Salat behind Imam 121
Salat Lailat al-Qadr 99, 163

Salat, du`a, dhikr relationship 93-94
Salat: acceptance of 132-133
Salat: conditions for the validity 126
Salat: definition 91-93
Salat: Details of 117-133
Salat: Fard 98
Salat: Forbidden times 101
Salat: Forms and parts of 115-135
Salat: General discussion 91-94
Salat: invalidation 127-128
Salat: Kinds of 97-99
Salat: Kinds, times, value 94-102
Salat: meaning of 94
Salat: Obligations 101
Salat: Prerequisites 101-102
Salat: Sunnah 98, 117
Salat: Times of 100
Salih (Prophet) 371
Salih / Salihin 221-224
Salla ala Nabi 260
Salution see Taslim
Satan 359-361
Sawm 91, 92, 209, 210
Sayi 200
Sha`ban 301
Shafi` school of law 45, 49, 393
Shafi`, Imam 45, 46-47, 49, 379-380
Shahadah 56-58, 63, 91, 209, 217, 260-261
Shaikh 393
Shariah 39-51, 83, 393
Shariah process 50
Shariati, Ali 199
Shawwal 309
Shirk 67-71, 393
Shirk al-Akbar 70
Shirk al-Asghar 70-71
Shirk al-Khafi 71

Short Surahs or passages 305-318
Shuaib 371
Shura 394
Shaytan 359-361
Siwak 241
Solomon see Sulaiman
Special nawafil salat 99, 160-169
Sufi 26, 394
Sujud 117, 123
Sulaiman 371
Sunan Abu Dawud 43
Sunnah 42-45, 50, 51, 83, 88, 393
Sunnah Ghair Mu'akkadah salat 160
Sunnah Mu'akkadah salat 159, 160
Sunnah Salat 98, 159-160
Sunni 394
Supplication for the dead 154
Sutra 394
Symbolic expressions 254-261

T

Tafsir 394
Tahajjud prayer 223
Tahara 241-242
Tahmid 256, 341
Taif 26-27
Takbir 116, 255-256, 394
Takbir at-Tahrima 119, 120, 127
Takbir al-Tashriq 146
Takbir in Eid prayer 145-146
Takbir in Janajah 149
Talaq see Divorce
Talbiyah 202, 204, 207
Tamjid 259
Taqwa 217, 223-224, 395
Tarawih prayer 160, 191
Tasbih 257, 341, 395
Tashahhud 117, 124, 125

Tashriq days 146
Taslim 117, 127, 258
Tasmiyah 255, 395
Taurat 395
Tawaf 199
Tawaf al-ifadah 207
Tawbah 395
Tawhid 10, 56, 63-73, 395
Tawhid al-'Ibadah 65, 67
Tawhid al-Asma 65, 66
Tawhid al-Rububiyah 65-66
Tawhid al-Sifat 65, 66
Tayammum 108-109
Thana 119-120
Throne verse 176-177
Tirmidhi 43, 380
Trade, condemned 232-235
Tradition 5-6, 39-51
Transactions 39
Transliteration xxv
Trinity 3
Trustworthiness 249
Truthfulness 247-248
Tuma'nina 116
Twilight years 269

U

'Ubudiyah 91
'Ulama 84, 395
Um al-Qura see Makkah
'Umar bin Abdul Aziz 43
'Umar, Khalifah 300
Umm al-Kitab 15
Ummah 28, 47, 205
'Umrah 198, 205-206
'Umrah, fundamentals of 207
Unbelievers see Kafir
United Nations 28
Unity of God 63-73
Uzair 372

General Index

V

Validity of Salat, Condition of 126
Verse of the Throne 176-178
Visiting graves 153-154

W

Wahabi 396
Wajib 40
Wajib Salat 136
Walid, Khalifah 43
Waliullah, Shah 19
Waraqa 26
Way of life 5-6
Western critics 87
Wiping over the shocks 106-108
Witr prayer 136-139
Woman xxii
Worship see 'Ibadah
Wudu 102, 241, 242
Wudu, how to perform 103-105
Wudu, nullification of 105
Wudu, special consideration of 106-108
Wuquf 201, 207

Y

Yahya 371
Yaqub 371
Yasa (al-Yasa) 371
Yathrib 27, 28
Yunus 371
Yusuf 371

Z

Zacharias see Zakariyya
Zakah 185-188, 91, 92 209, 210, 218, 221
 Zakah distribution 188
Zakah system 187-188
Zakariyya 372
Zamzam 200, 206
Zayid 26

Qur'anic calligraphy
in Kufi script, fourfold,
quadrangular, it reads:
A. Huwa Allah (He is God)

ERRATA IN ARABIC TEXTS

1) p.58
   - (Arabic text) 1st line. The last three words should read: *Muhammadan (Nunation) 'abduhu wa rusuluhu.* (The dammah should be over *ra*, not shaddah.)
   - (Arabic text: middle of page) The 5th word should be: *biasmaihi.*
   - (Arabic text: bottom of page) In the 1st line, the last word should read: *sharrihi.* (The shaddah should be over *ra*, not Fatha).

2) p.59
   - (Arabic text) bottom para, 1st line prior to last word should have *Maddah* over *la.*
   - In the last line, the first word should be ommitted.

3) p.104
   - (Arabic text): 1st dua, 1st line, prior to last word, *Muhammadan (Nunation).*
   - (Arabic text): 2nd dua, last word, *muta tahhirin*, shaddah over *ha.*

4) p.114
   - (Arabic text): 1st dua, 1st line, between last two words, a small *nun* in between is missing; no shaddah over the last letter ta, and it should read: *Muhmmadanil wasilata.*
   - (Arabic text) 1st letter on next line *kasra* (jer) under *Dad.*
   - (tranbsliteration) 2nd line, 2nd word should be: *Muhammadanil.*

5) p.120
   - (Arabic text) 1st dua, 1st line, 4th word, *kasra (jabar)* over *nun*, the word is *bayna*;
   - 2nd line, 2nd word *shadda* over *Qaf*, the word is *naqqini* and again *shadda* over *Qaf* on the 6th word, *yunaq-qath*;
   - The next word is *abyadu*, the letter is *ya*, not ba.
   - (Translit.) 3rd line, 4th word, *thawbul*, no 't' after 'tha'.

6) p.124:
- (Translit.) 1st line, 6th word should be: *Wat Tayyibatu*, (there is no "h" after the "y").

7) p.137
- (Arabic text) 3rd line, 5th word, it is *man* (not min).
- (Translit.) 3rd line, 7th word should be: *yuqda* (not yaqdi).
- The last line should read *man* (not min).

8) p.138
- (Arabic text) 2nd line, the 5th word should be: *Nakhla'u* (there is a sukoon on the Kha).
- (Translit.) 4th line, 1st word should be: *yafjuruk* (There is a dhamma on the *ra)*.

9) p.150
- (Translit.) 1st word should be: *Allahumaghfir*.

10) p.174
- (Arabic text) In the 1st line after 3rd word, omit *waw* after Rabbi;
- In the 2nd line, the 2nd word should be *Masta'tu* (there is a dhamma on the Taa, not fatha).
- The 8th word should be: *Sana'tu* (It is not a *meem*, but a *saad* and there is a dhamma there, not fatha).
- (Translit.) after 4th word, omit 'wa'
- In the 2nd line, the 5th word is *ahdika*;
- In the 3rd line, the fifth word is *'Sanatu'*.

11) p.175
- (Arabic text) 1st word in the 2nd line should be; *minni*.
- (Arabic text): In the 2nd line the word should be *Amadi* (There is no sukoon on the meem, it is a fatha).

12) p.191
- (Translit.) 1st dua, 5th word, should be: *rizqika*.

13) p.316
- (Translit.) 4th line, should be: *fil-uqad* (not waqad).

14) p.320
- (Translit.) 2nd sentence, 2nd word should be: *Muslimatal.*
- The words *"wa arina"* are two separate words.

15) p.320
- (Translit.) The last line, 4th word should read: *Unzila* (No Jeem);
- The last word is *mu'minuna* (there is an i needed).

16) p.321
- (Translit.) The 1st word should be: *Kullun*;
- The 5th word: *Malaa Ika tihi* (should be separate words)
- The 2nd sentence, 2nd word should be: *bayna* (not bayina).

17) p.321
- (Translit.) 4th para, 4th word should be: *nafsan illa wus'aha*;
- In the next line the 4th word, *Tua Khizna Aw Akhta'na*, should be separate words.

18) p.327
- (Arabic Text) The last word should be: *tabara* (not abara).

19) p.335
- (Arabic Text) 1st dua, should be *Amutu* (in English and Arabic).

20) p.336
- (Translit.) In the last dua, 1st sentence, the word prior to last should be: *lahu*.

21) p.337
- (Translit.) In the 4th line the last words run togeather. They should read: *"min wagthai is safari."*
- (English text) 2nd to last paragraph. The 1st line should read: … *"given on page 17,"* (not 7).

22) p.339
- (Translit.) 1st line, 3rd word should read: *attaammaati*.

23) p.340
- (Translit.) 2nd sentence. The 5th word should be: "ya" and not baa and and hence should read: *"ya ar hamar raahimeen."*

24) p.340
- (Arabic Text) 2nd dua, 1st line. The 7th word should be: *yar ji us*, (kasra under the Jeem, not a fatha).

Other Errata

1) *p. xiii: Item on p. 290 should be:* Dome of the Rock

2) *p. 290 Illustration description should read:* Dome of the Rock, (Jerusalem) This majestic Dome is centered over the Rock from which the Prophet ascended to heaven. Adjacent is Masjid Al-Aqsa, which the Qur'an refers to as his prayer site

3) *Back cover: The description of the cover design should read:* Cover: Three holy places of the Islamic faith; Kaaba in Makkah, Prophet's Mosque, in Madinah and Dome of the Rock in Jerusalem.